Norway: A History from
the Vikings to Our Own Times

Rolf Danielsen
Ståle Dyrvik
Tore Grønlie
Knut Helle
Edgar Hovland

Norway: A History from the Vikings to Our Own Times

Translated by Michael Drake

Scandinavian University Press (Universitetsforlaget AS)
P.O. Box 2959 Tøyen, N-0608 Oslo, Norway
Distributed world-wide excluding Norway by
Fax +47 22 57 53 53

Stockholm office
SCUP, Scandinavian University Press
P.O. Box 3255, S-103 65 Stockholm, Sweden
Fax +46 8 20 99 82

Copenhagen office
Scandinavian University Press AS
P.O. Box 54, DK-1002 København K, Denmark
Faz +45 33 32 05 70

Boston office
Scandinavian University Press North America
875 Massachusetts Ave., Ste. 84, Cambridge MA 02139, USA
Fax +1 617 354 68 75

© Scandinavian University Press (Universitetsforlaget AS), Oslo 1995
Reprinted 1998

ISBN 82-00-21803-1

All rights reserved. No part of this publication may be reproduced, stored in a retrieval system, or transmitted, in any form or by any means, electronic, mechanical, photocopying, recording, or otherwise, without the prior permission of Scandinavian University Press. Enquiries should be sent to the Rights Department, Scandinavian University Press, Oslo, at the address above.

Translated by Michael Drake
Cover design: Anne Vines
Typeset in Times 10/12,5 by Universitetsforlaget AS
Printed by Tangen Grafiske Senter A/S, Drammen, Norway

Preface

Norway: A History from the Vikings to Our Own Times is the first single-volume academic history of Norway. It was originally published in Norwegian as a textbook for students attending a distance learning course in Norwegian history, organized by the Department of History, University of Bergen, in co-operation with the Norwegian Broadcasting Corporation (NRK), the history departments of Norway's three other universities, and seven regional colleges.

The book has been translated into English to give both foreign university undergraduates and a broader international public a modern overview of Norwegian history.

The authors are grateful to Professor Michael Drake, Open University, UK, for the translation, to the University of Bergen for financial support, and to our colleagues Professor William Hubbard and Senior Lecturer Jan Oldervoll for assistance in preparing the English edition. We extend our warmest thanks to all of our colleagues in Norwegian historical research. We have freely drawn upon their work and their ideas from seminal discussions without being able, in a publication of this type, to acknowledge their individual contributions. Last but not least, we wants to express our graditude to Betty Atkinson and Deirdre Collins Kolle for making the text machine-readable.

The authors
Department of History,
University of Bergen, August 1995

Contents

PART I Down to 1536
Knut Helle

1	**The country and the people**	3
	The human impact on the natural environment during historic time	3
	The original environment	5
	Held together by the sea	10
2	**'Land of the Norsemen'**	13
	People in Norway before Ottar	15
	Early social organization	17
	The road to Europe	20
	The unification of Norway begins	23
	Territorial consolidation	25
	The Church, the aristocracy and national unification	27
	The king and the wider society	30
3	**Population, settlement and the economy up to around 1350**	33
	Population size and population growth	34
	The growth in the number and density of settlements	37
	The causes and effects of population growth	40
	Agriculture in the Middle Ages	41
	Agricultural settlements and production units	43
	Trade and crafts	45
4	**Society in the high Middle Ages**	50
	The renting of land and social status	51
	The development and extent of the tenancy system	54

	Urban society	56
	The social position of women in the high Middle Ages	58
	Aristocracy and clergy	62
	A comparatively weak aristocracy	65
5	**A society regulated by the monarchy and the Church**	**67**
	The monarchy and the Church under the Sverre family	68
	Increased political activity abroad	70
	Government administration in the high Middle Ages	73
	The ecclesiastical administration	77
	The roles of monarch and Church in society	78
	The income of Crown and Church and local self-management	84
	A dawning sense of Norwegian community	87
6	**The great crisis**	**89**
	The contraction of settlement and the loss of population	90
	The causes of the crisis and its economic effects	92
	The Hanseatic hegemony	96
	The effects of the crisis on the aristocracy and the clergy	98
	Social conditions in town and country	100
	The political and cultural results of the crisis	102
7	**The political system of the late Middle Ages**	**104**
	The *len* system	105
	Self-management in town and country	109
	The political position of the Church in the late Middle Ages	111
	The council of the realm	112
	Towards a stronger monarchy	115

PART II 1536–1814
Ståle Dyrvik

8	**Union with Denmark**	**123**
	Two opposing viewpoints and an attempted synthesis	123
	Norway as a part of Europe's periphery	125
	Must the periphery bear the heaviest burden?	127
	The structure of the presentation	129
	Norway gets new frontiers	129

9	**Demographic and social patterns**	131
	Was this pattern of population growth an advantage or not?	132
	A closer look at the period of stagnation	134
	The crofter (*husmann*) system arrives	136
	What was the purpose of the crofter system?	137
	Social and cultural differences in the towns	139
	Demographic differences between the social groups	140
	The social contact area	142
10	**The economy**	144
	The holding and the croft	145
	What did Norwegian agriculture produce?	145
	Self-sufficiency and a barter economy?	147
	Fish from sea to market	148
	The development of the most important fisheries	149
	The water-powered gate saw opens up a new Norwegian resource	152
	Regulating the timber industry	152
	The metal industries	154
	Shipping: a great Norwegian industry	155
	Was Norwegian society richer?	156
11	**Income and power**	158
	The ownership of land down to 1660	158
	The Norwegian peasant becomes a freeholder	160
	Ownership and control in the fisheries	163
	The timber industry: from peasant hands to those of the urban elites	164
	The capital requirements of mining and shipping	165
	The elite and the working masses	166
	Did the merchants exploit or provide a safety net for the peasantry?	169
12	**The state and its subjects**	172
	The constitutional position	173
	Resources and administration	174
	The beginnings of administrative reform	175
	The end of aristocratic rule?	177
	Where did power lie?	179

The *embetsstand*	180
The bourgeoisie: monopoly and competition	181
The peasants as taxpayers	183
Political and social benefits of the peasantry	185
A society in equilibrium?	186

13 Denmark and Norway — 188
The Danish language in church and school	189
A veneer of elite culture?	190
Taxes and transfers	191
Economic policy	194
Norway – a kingdom or a collection of administrative areas?	196
Norwegian self-awareness	197
Were Norwegians dissatisfied with the union?	198

14 The union collapses — 201
Relations with Sweden	201
A neutrality that did not last	203
Living through the crisis years	204
The Peace of Kiel and the Norwegian rebellion	206
Independence – but in a union with Sweden	208
The constitution	209
The two main actors	211
Who was right in 1814?	213

PART III 1814–1945
Rolf Danielsen and Edgar Hovland

15 The consolidation of the new state (R.D.) — 217
Defence of the constitution	219
Under the guidance of the *embetsmenn*	222
The national identity	224
The king and his council	225
The shift in power	228

16 Recovery and growth: the Norwegian economy, 1815–75 (E.H.) — 230
Population growth and population movement	230

Agriculture: the basic industry grows	232
Forestry and the timber trade	233
The fisheries and the export of fish products	235
The shipping saga	239
The first wave of industrialization	241
Modernization and liberalization	243
Economic growth and the standard of living	247
Occupational diversity and social change	251

17 The *embetsmenn* state: golden age, decline and fall (R.D.) — 255

Modernization	257
Local self-government	260
The constitutional conflict	261
The new power consciousness	264
On to 1884	267

18 Modern Norway takes shape, 1875–1920 (E.H.) — 271

Lines of development	271
A market-led agriculture	275
Fishing and the fish-processing industry	277
Forestry and the wood products industry	280
The process of industrialization	282
From sail to steam	284
Commerce, banking and communications	287
The pattern of employment changes	288
The self-employed and the wage earners	290
State intervention	292
A more modern society	294

19 The political sphere, 1884–1918 (R.D.) — 297

Changes in the party political system	299
The union conflict	302
The period of conflict, 1885–1905	304
Why did the union collapse?	307
The Liberals' last heroic age	309
Seeking the middle ground	312

20 The inter-war years — 314

Crises yes, but growth too	314

The wartime economy and the post-war boom	316
Crisis and convalescence	319
The parity crisis and the international boom	321
The need for income and the growth of output	324
The Great Depression	325
Out of the crisis	326
The regulation of the market and competition	328
Patterns of development	331

21 Crisis and war: from discord to unity (R.D.) — 334
A revolution of the masses?	335
A Labour Party majority?	339
A crisis agreement and a relaxation of tension	341
Norway's war	345
From a neutral to an ally	348
Nazification and resistance	350
Break and continuity	352

PART IV The years since 1945
Tore Grønlie

22 Reconstruction, radical change or continuity? — 357
The devastation of war and the problems of reconstruction	357
Post-war history viewed as 'reconstruction'	360
The decade of economic optimism	361
Contemporary history: a case of radical change or continuity?	362

23 A quarter of a century of growth — 364
Population and work	364
From scarcity to affluence	366
Industrialization and the service society	368
Urbanization	372
The primary industries: a technological revolution	373
The reasons for growth	375
Crisis, war and growth	379
A two-phased picture of growth	381

24 The welfare society — 383
Increased public involvement	383

Policies for welfare and economic growth	385
The equalization of incomes	386
Housing	386
Education	390
Social benefits	393
Equality and the regions	395
Local authority welfare and the leveller state	401
Welfare society – change or continuity?	403

25 A state in search of co-operation and consensus — 405
Labour Party dominance and non-socialist divisions	407
A 'one-party state'?	410
The King's Bay crisis and a non-socialist government	411
The campaign for a planned economy	413
From detailed regulation to liberalization	415
Running the economy in the 1950s and 1960s	418
'Organized capitalism' – 'the corporate state' – 'the segmented state'	422
Post-war politics and management – a new system?	426

26 Norway – a hesitant internationalist — 428
Bridge building, cold war – and NATO	429
NATO – continuity or change?	431
A cautious ally	432
The left-wing opposition	433
Norway and the Third World	434
From the Marshall Plan to EFTA	436
The fight over membership of the European Community	439

27 The post-war years in perspective — 443
The 'post-war years' – from 1935 to 1972?	443
The 1970s and the 1980s: economic downturn and uncertainty	445
The welfare society: expansion or contraction?	447
Political destabilization	448
The welfare society and state management in crisis?	449
The 'post-war era' and its historians	452

Norwegian governments after 1873	454
Chronology	456
Select bibliography	472
Glossary of Norwegian terms	476
Subject index	483

Part I
Down to 1536

Knut Helle

1
The country and the people

Our story begins, to all intents and purposes, around the year 800, with the dawn of the Viking Age. Nature had by then all but completed her task, so that the country appeared much as we know it today. It is true that certain things have changed since then. For instance, parts of the land mass have continued to rise – very slowly – above the sea and climatic changes have occurred. Thus it appears likely that from the end of the twelfth century the climate became gradually colder and wetter, a deterioration that culminated in the 'little ice age' of the seventeenth and eighteenth centuries. Since then the climate has taken a turn for the better. But such changes are, in any case, of little importance compared with the totality of natural conditions existing around the year 800.

The changes brought about by human activity in this period are, however, something else altogether. With their technology and organizational skills people reacted to nature's offerings and transformed them. Even if Norway belongs to those countries of Europe where natural conditions have been least affected by human activities, the changes have nevertheless been considerable.

The human impact on the natural environment during historic time

During the many centuries of the pre-industrial period, the human impact on the natural environment proceeded slowly and the end results were slight. Forests gradually gave way to fields, but the areas that were tilled never amounted to more than a tiny fraction of the total land mass; little more than 2–3 per cent even in very recent times. Grazing and the gathering of fodder affected the vegetation of certain areas and contributed, among other things, to the heather-decked

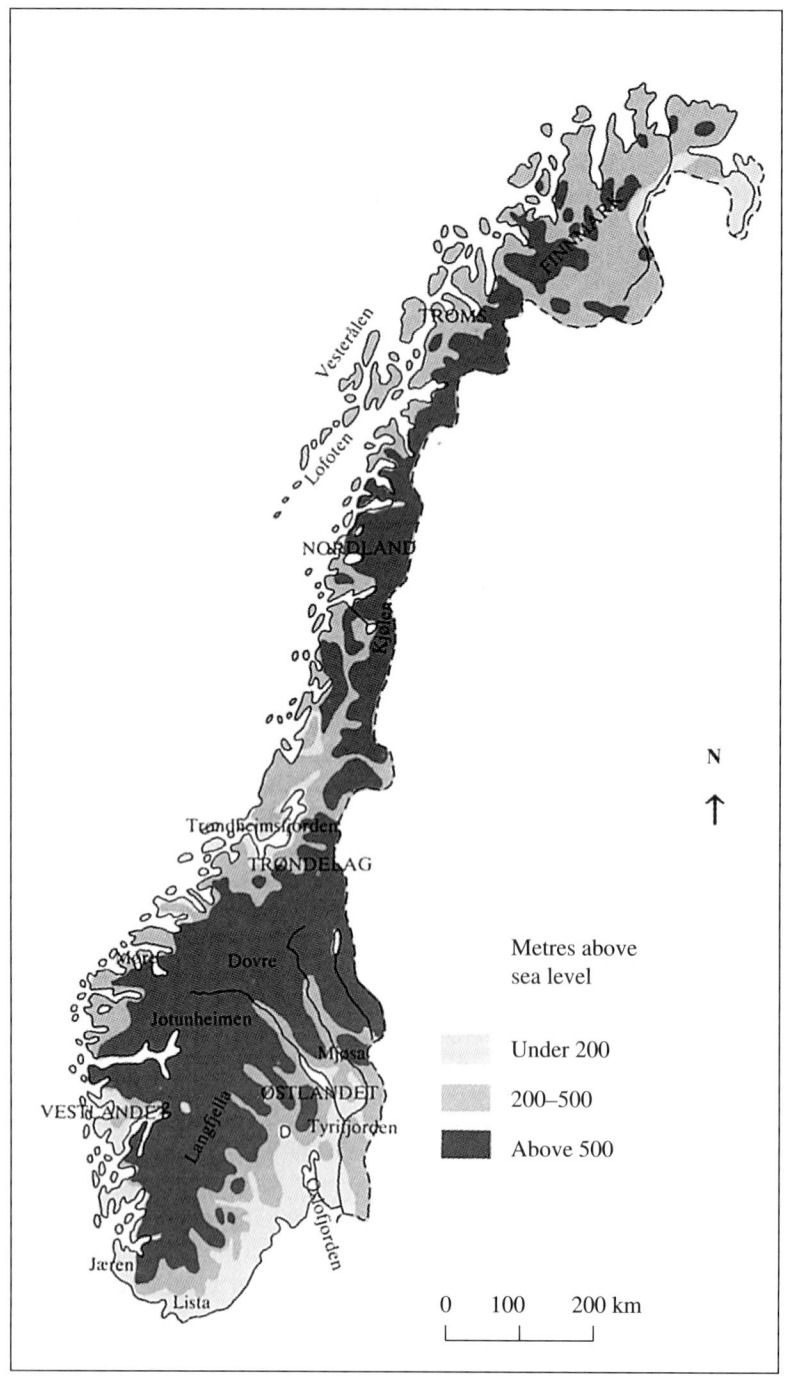

moorlands along the southern and western coasts as far north as Vesterålen. But none of these activities had much impact on the enormous areas of forest and mountain that predominated. There were but a few small towns and they too had little impact on the landscape outside the small areas that they occupied.

Hunting and trapping affected stocks of certain animals. The land fit for agriculture was exploited intensively during periods of population pressure. The export of timber did eventually make itself felt in certain areas, especially in the southwest of the country. Mining in the seventeenth and eighteenth centuries used up local supplies of wood and the more easily accessible deposits of silver and copper. For all that, the natural resources of the country were neither heavily exploited nor terminally exhausted during the pre-industrial period, even if people lived much more directly off the land than they do today.

With the rise in population and the increased tempo of technological and social change that occurred from the middle of the nineteenth century, man's impact on the natural environment was of quite a different order. In recent decades that impact has increased dramatically: the main features of this development being industrialization, urbanization, the mechanization of agriculture and forestry, the building of roads and the damming of lakes and rivers. The consumption of natural resources from both sea and land has become a serious problem. These resources are also threatened by environmental pollution, an international problem that cannot be solved by domestic initiatives alone. For the first time in history, it would appear that human activities are in the process of disturbing the natural climatic conditions of the globe.

If we are to conjure up a picture of Norway's physical geography at the outset of historical time, we must try to ignore the environmental changes man has been responsible for since then.

The original environment

Norway contains most of the extensive chain of mountains that forms the backbone of the Scandinavian peninsula. In the south of the country the Langfjella (The 'Long Mountains') separate Østlandet (eastern Norway) from Vestlandet (western Norway). The Jotunheimen area, with peaks rising 6,000 feet and more above sea level, marks their northern limit. From here the Dovre mountains continue eastwards and divide Østlandet in the south from Trøndelag in the north. Further north still, this mountainous spine dominates the landscape, reaching even to the coasts of Nordland and Troms. Here too are to be found the highest points of the Kjølen ('the Keel') – the mountainous terrain that forms the border between Norway and Sweden. South of the Dovre the Kjølen gradually loses itself in lower ranges of forest-covered hills, which occupy adjacent areas of Østlandet and Sweden. The mountainous backbone of Scandinavia runs on through northern Troms near its eastern boundary with Finnmark, from which it sends a lower ridge eastwards, south of the innermost reaches of the great Finnmark fjords.

Taken together, this mountainous spine stretches across 13 degrees of latitude and is almost as long as the country itself. Pivot Norway on an axis at its most southerly point, and its most northerly point would touch Rome. Thus Norway is the most mountainous country in Scandinavia, with particularly dramatic changes of height where the fjords of the west and north cut deep into the mountains. Furthermore, the mountainous terrain has a decisive influence on the country's climate.

The Norwegian climate is harsh for those used to conditions further south in Europe, but, taking into account its global position, it is remarkably benign. The country lies across the course of the westerly airstream of the North Atlantic. The wind drives the Gulf Stream and brings both warm air and warm water to the west and northwestern coasts. This gives Vestlandet and the northern Norwegian coastal areas a damp oceanic climate with mild winters and comparatively warm summers. The sharply rising terrain to the east squeezes the water out of the winds from the sea and gives the highest rainfall to areas a little inland from the west coast: as much as 120–160 inches a year in the central parts of Vestlandet. The mountainous backbone of Scandinavia forms a barrier against the prevailing westerly winds, so that the climate to the east is drier, with warmer summers and colder winters. Østlandet is the part of Norway that benefits most from this effect; here too the Dovre mountains offer protection from northerly winds. The extensive high moors of Finnmark are similarly protected from westerly and northerly winds by the northernmost spur of the Scandinavian mountain ridge. Nevertheless, one will not find a typical continental climate anywhere in Norway: the country is spared extremes of cold and drought. This favourable balance between precipitation and temperature produces a richer vegetation than one would otherwise expect in a latitude so far north.

The major features of Norway's topography and climate outlined here characterized the natural environment at the start of the Viking Age. But if the climate was favourable, considered in relation to the latitude, the soil was meagre. The glaciers of the last ice age had more or less scraped the mountains bare of soil over most of the country. And the thousands of years that had passed since the ice melted had not been enough to form much in the way of friable soil, not least because the country has few rocks that crumble easily. Conditions for a more abundant vegetation occurred mostly where ice and water had piled up adequate amounts of loose soil.

Such conditions were to be found, above all, in areas covered by the sea during the period when the ice had melted and before the land had begun to rise from under the weight of ice. The ice had been at its thickest and heaviest the further inland one went, so the subsequent rise was much the greater: from some 50–100 feet on the coasts to over 600 feet in Trøndelag and Østlandet. But before the land rose, the sea had laid down fine deposits of sand and clay. The greatest areas of comparatively flat land with such soils stretch along both sides of the Oslofjord and inland towards the great lakes of Østlandet. Today we find a quarter of Norway's cultivated land here. The other large area with the same soils lies in Trøndelag, south and east of the Trondheimsfjord. Apart from these areas, marine deposits gave opportunities for growth in smaller pockets along the coasts and fjords over the whole country.

The great glaciers wrenched loose the materials that the sea subsequently sorted and deposited. Under these glaciers the shifting ice left coarser matter, such as the two long terminal moraines on either side of the Oslofjord. Less well sorted morainal deposits were to be found on the surface above the shore line, wherever they were not covered by finer deposits laid down during, or after, the ice retreated. These finer deposits came from rivers and lakes previously dammed up by the ice and are now most commonly found in a crescent-shaped area of Østlandet above the coastal plain. In a stretch of land from Mjøsa, Norway's largest lake, southwest to lake Tyrifjord, the morainal deposits were especially fertile. This was because the underlying rocks consisted of softer slate, chalk and sandstone from the Cambrian–Silurian period. The lowland areas of Jæren and Lista along the southwest

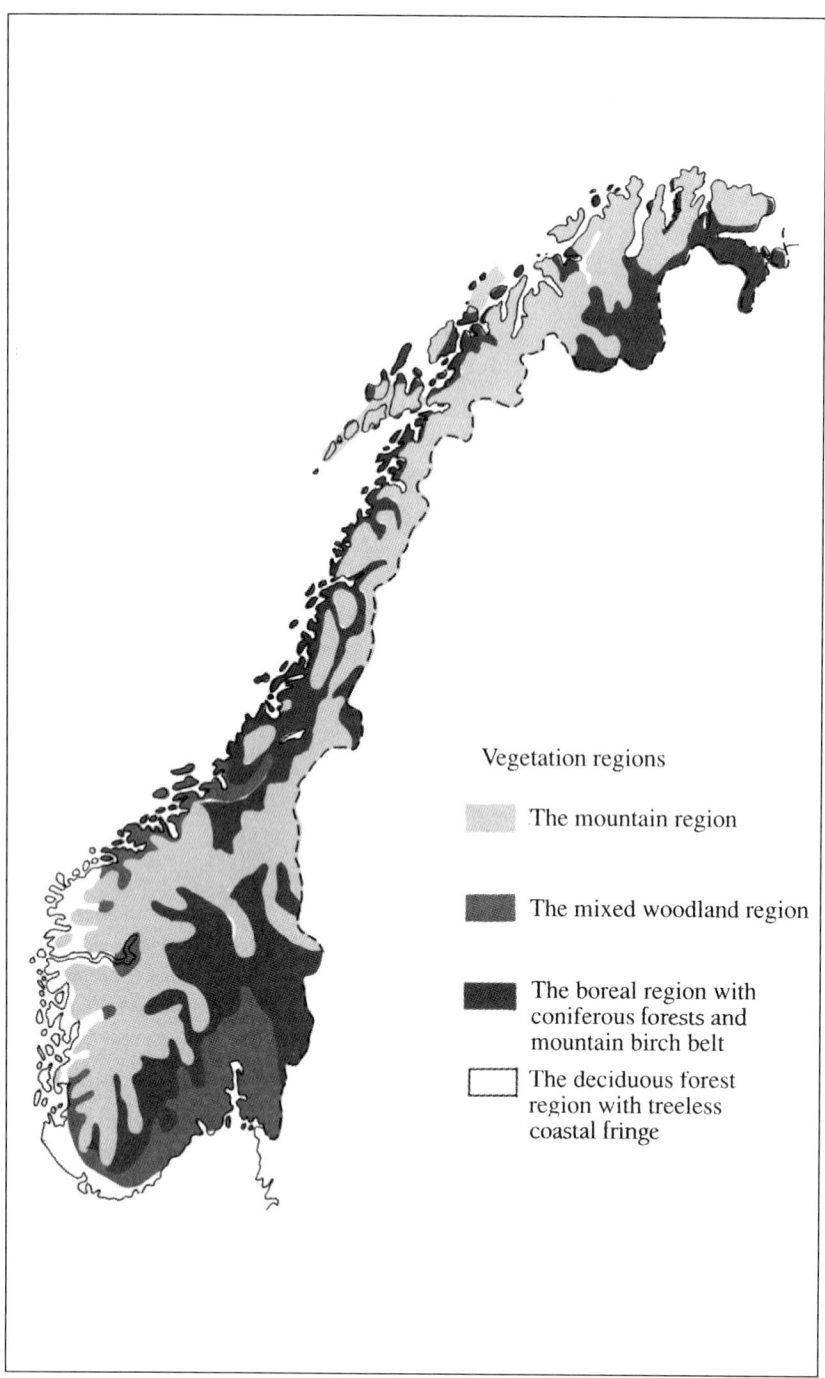

coast were also almost entirely covered by morainal deposits. Smaller or more limited stretches of good morainal soil were to be found too alongside the fjords and in the valleys to the west and north of the country. Locally favourable growing conditions occurred also in patches of weathered soils and wherever finer material had been deposited by rivers and ice-dammed lakes.

Soil and climate determined the nature of the vegetation. The landscape was heavily forested. Oak and other warmth-loving deciduous trees grew along the south coast. Deciduous forests continued northwards along the west coast, though mixed with increasing amounts of hardier types as well as pine. The further inland and the further north one went, the more mixed the woods became, with conifers predominating. Mixed woodland stretched around the Oslofjord and deep into the inner reaches of the country. Such woods were to be found too at the head of the Vestland fjords, along the coast of Nordmøre and in the lowland areas around the Trondheimsfjord. Of the warmth-loving varieties only oak reached the most northerly of the mixed woodland districts.

In the uplands and further north, purely coniferous forests of pine and spruce took over. Pine arrived soon after the end of the last ice age. It formed forests far out along the west coast and as far north as the head of the Finnmark fjords. The more recently arrived and more demanding spruce was not to be found in Vestlandet during the Viking Age. However it did extend to the coast of north Trøndelag and formed forests somewhat further north into Nordland. On the better soils of inner Østlandet and in Trøndelag, spruce tended to displace pine. As one climbed or moved towards the far north, the coniferous forests grew gradually more sparse. Mountain birch took over more and more, often forming a belt high up close to the bare rock. Heather and grass held out a little longer, before only moss and lichen were left to cover the naked crags. More than half the country was covered by exposed rock and forests of mountain birch. Besides this there were vast areas of swampland, perhaps around 7 per cent of the total land area, whilst lakes and tarns made up close to 5 per cent.

Decisive for the people who were to live off this land was the fact that so little of it was suitable for actual cultivation, which inevitably affected the Norwegian economy. It did, however, offer good grazing both above and below the tree line as well as plants suited to winter feed. The human diet could be supplemented by wild berries, nuts, edible plants, sea birds' eggs and mussels. But next to farming it was above all fishing, hunting and trapping that supported human life on the eve of historic time. The sea was so rich in fish that it was impossible to empty it, given the equipment of the pre-industrial era. In addition, the seal, whale, walrus and sea bird meant much to the coastal populations. Inland, the rivers and lakes offered good opportunities for fishing, whilst animal and bird life drew hunters to both the mountains and the forests. Forestry and the extraction of iron from the boglands were also early methods of exploiting the land.

For all that, it was the cultivated land that produced most of the food, so that in pre-industrial times permanent settlement was predominantly tied to such land. However, where there were good conditions for raising animals or catching fish for domestic consumption or for other life-supporting activities, people settled in areas that were less satisfactory from a purely agricultural point of view. The result was a settlement pattern that left most of the country unpopulated, as it does to this day. The population was concentrated above all in the less densely forested coastal areas and around the fjords, as well as in the low-lying districts of Østlandet and Trøndelag. The cultivated soils of these latter districts, together with Jæren, amounted to between 15 and 25 per cent of their total area in recent times. With the passage of time this settlement pattern has been reinforced by the fact that urbanization and industrialization have occurred primarily in the coastal areas and the lowlands of Østlandet. Natural lines of communication have also had a decisive influence on where people came to settle, both in earlier times and recently.

Held together by the sea

There were many natural obstacles in the way of those who attempted to travel widely in Norway. A mountainous terrain together with dense forests in many places made the going tough for travellers overland – especially those with a heavy load – and necessitated many a detour. Travel by sea proved much easier from an early period. From certainly no later than the Migration Period (AD 400–600), the use of iron had made it possible to build larger seaworthy vessels. From then onwards people could journey around the entire coast, on a regular basis, not only in the lee of the hundreds of thousands of islands and skerries that

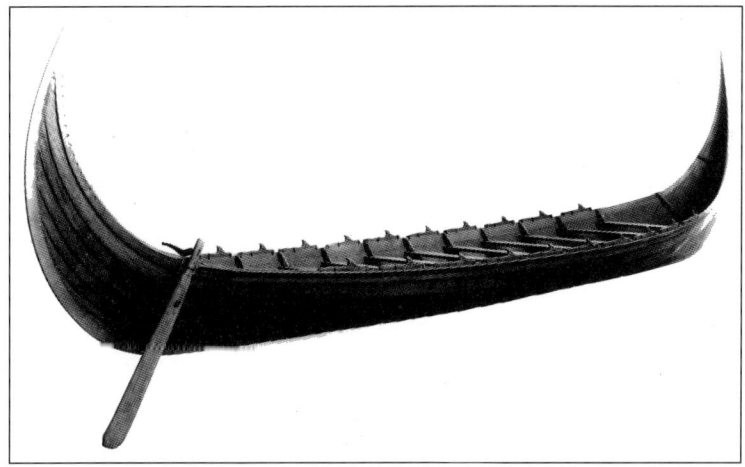

Model of an 18 m. long ship which one assumes was destroyed sometime in the seventh or eighth century and buried in a bog by the sea on the farm of Kvalsund in Herøy (Sunnmøre). This elegant, seaworthy vessel was rowed with 10 pairs of oars, and must have been able to raise a sail, though there is no sign of the heel of a mast. The Kvalsund boat shows that already before the Viking Age boats were being built in Norway which made it possible to travel safely along the entire coast and across the sea to other countries.

protected much of the coast, but also across the exposed stretches of sea where there was no such protection.

It was also possible to reach deep into the country by rowing and sailing up the fjords and then by following the rivers and valleys through the forests and up towards the mountains. Other navigable water courses were also used, especially the great lakes. Travel in the winter was more manageable on the frozen lakes, rivers and bogs. But apart from this, the volume and tempo of travel increased in the lighter summer half-year, both by sea and across the mountains, where the treeless moors and passes permitted communication between inhabited areas. In the dark winter months whole districts and many individual communities were pretty well cut off from each other.

Since Viking times, relations with the outside world have been governed by the sea. It provided a way out, for to the east access to Sweden was blocked by forests and mountains. But to the south, west and north the country was surrounded by sea so that once people had learned how to make seaworthy craft it was much easier to travel abroad. Access to Norway too was easiest by sea from the more populous Danish territories to the south, whilst Sweden and Norway have up to our own times lain, as it were, with their backs to each other. Contact with Denmark and the northern parts of the continent, and through the Kattegat and Øresund with the lands around the Baltic, has been decisive for Norway's overseas relations up to our own times.

To the north and east along the shores of Finnmark and the Kola peninsula to the White Sea, the possibilities for fishing and hunting proved tempting. Here, conditions were ripe for both trade and conflict with Sami, Finnish and Russian peoples. Norwegian interest in the Nordkalotten (literally, the 'northern skullcap' or the whole northern part of the Scandinavian peninsula including Kola and the White Sea), and later in the northern Arctic region generally, can be traced back to the seafaring activities of the Viking Age.

But above all, Norway's overseas interests in the Viking Age were focused on the islands across the Norwegian and North seas. Shetland was no more than one or two days' sail from the west coast of Norway, and from here southwards to the Orkneys and the rest of the British Isles a landfall was never far away. From Shetland one could sail past the Faroe Islands to Iceland and Greenland. It was along these westerly routes that most Norwegians sailed abroad during the Viking Age, and via the British Isles the country received in return major cultural impulses from Europe. Here too we find the origins of the Atlantic orientation that later was to influence Norway far more than Sweden or Denmark.

By around the year AD 800, the stage was set for the social and cultural development that Norway was to follow for many hundreds of years. Now the people who occupied the country were about to step onto that stage.

2
'Land of the Norsemen'

At some time during the last two or three decades of the ninth century, Ottar (Ohthere), the north Norwegian chieftain, visited King Alfred in England. He told him of his homeland and of his travels. The king had the account written up in Old English.

Ottar said that he lived 'northernmost of all Norsemen' – it is now generally thought to have been somewhere in the Malangen district of south-Troms. From there he had sailed southwards past the *Norðmanna land* (land of the Norsemen) to the port of Skiringssal in southern Vestfold. Ottar also called the land of the Norsemen *Norðweg*, 'the north way' or 'the north region'. It is from this name that we get our Norway (*Noreg, Norge*). And it is to Ottar that we owe the first known account of Norway and the Norwegians.

Ottar describes Norway as a long and narrow country. To the north was the territory of the Finns or Sami, later to be called Finnmark, whilst to the south Ottar had *Denamearc* (Denmark) on his port side when he sailed from Skiringssal to the port of Hedeby at the base of Jutland. This suggests that at that time Denmark included the present-day west coast of Sweden north towards Svinesund and perhaps even further. East of Norway, Ottar was able to tell of the land of the Swedes, *Sweoland*, and north of that, *Cwena land*, the land of the west Finnish *kvener* round the Gulf of Bothnia. North and east of his own home, Ottar knew of no permanent settlements before one came to the land of the Finnish-speaking *bjarmeets* (*bjarmer*) by the White Sea. In Finnmark and on the Kola peninsula, nomadic Sami hunters and fishermen roamed. They also made use of the mountainous plateaux of the interior a long way to the south of Finnmark.

It is in this way that Norway and the Norwegians step onto the historical stage, against a Nordic backdrop; a distinct people with their own territory stretching from southern Troms to the Oslofjord, or Viken as it was then called.

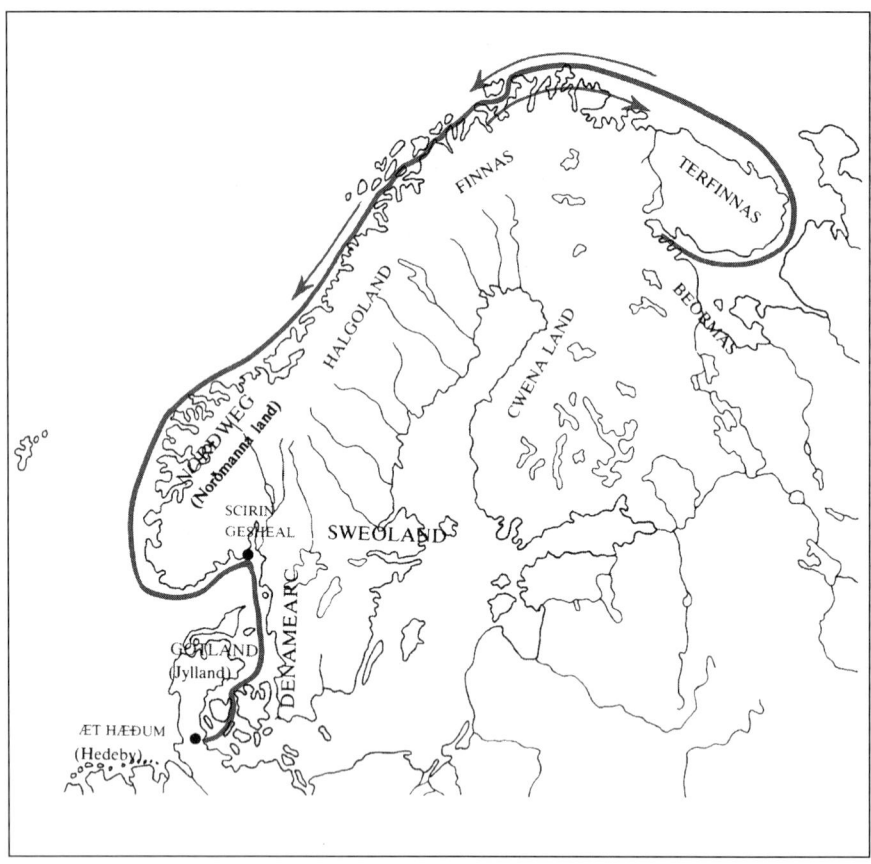

Ottar said that he was one of the leading men in his home territory, Hålogaland (the old name for that part of Norway north of Trøndelag), even though his farm was modest by English standards. He had 'no more than' 10 cows, 20 sheep and 20 pigs, and a small amount of arable land which he ploughed with horses. His wealth came from hunting, fishing, whaling and from taxing the Finns or Sami. He once ventured out to see how far north his country stretched and to get walrus teeth and skins. He sailed for 15 days round Finnmark and the Kola peninsula to the land of the bjarmeet in the western bay of the White Sea. He took over a month to sail to Skiringssal in the south, even with a good wind, as he anchored at night. From there he took 5 days to reach Hedeby.

People in Norway before Ottar

People had lived in Norway long before Ottar. Eleven to twelve thousand years ago, when the ice retreated after the last ice age, hunters and fishermen began to settle along the Norwegian coast. About 4000 BC they moved in greater or smaller groups over most of the country. At this time people also began to cultivate the soil, but only in the far south. Animal husbandry soon reached the coasts of the west and north, but it took longer before arable farming became established there. The latter supported more people on the same area than did the former, and tied them more closely to a particular territory. The emergence of real property in the form of animals and, especially, cultivated soil distinguished these people from the pure hunters. Settlements became denser, more permanent and, after a while, more hierarchically organized.

By the end of the Later Stone Age, around 1500 BC, agriculture had long been the principal occupation in southern Norway, more important for most people than either fishing or hunting. In the north, on the other hand, hunting and fishing continued to be the primary activities. But as agriculture reached the coastal districts up as far as southern Troms a cultural division developed between these districts and the purely hunting and fishing areas of the far north. By Ottar's day, the Norsemen and the Sami formed two distinct cultures in north Norway and it is conceivable, though it cannot be proved, that the pure hunting and fishing culture had been represented by the Sami from the end of the Stone Age.

How long Norsemen had lived in the rest of Norway is unknown, and what do we mean by 'Norse' or 'Norwegian'? One precondition of an ethnic community is that there should be a common language. Runic inscriptions indicate that from about AD 200 there was a common Nordic language, which later developed into the present-day Nordic national languages. This basic Nordic 'tongue' was probably to be found, at the latest, around the beginning of the Christian era. In Ottar's time there were dialects in Norway that were different from those further east and south in Scandinavia and this may have been the case much earlier.

Norsemen in Ottar's time were also bound together by a common religion. Evidence of religious cults in Norwegian place names reveals that Norsemen had worshipped the same deities for several hundred

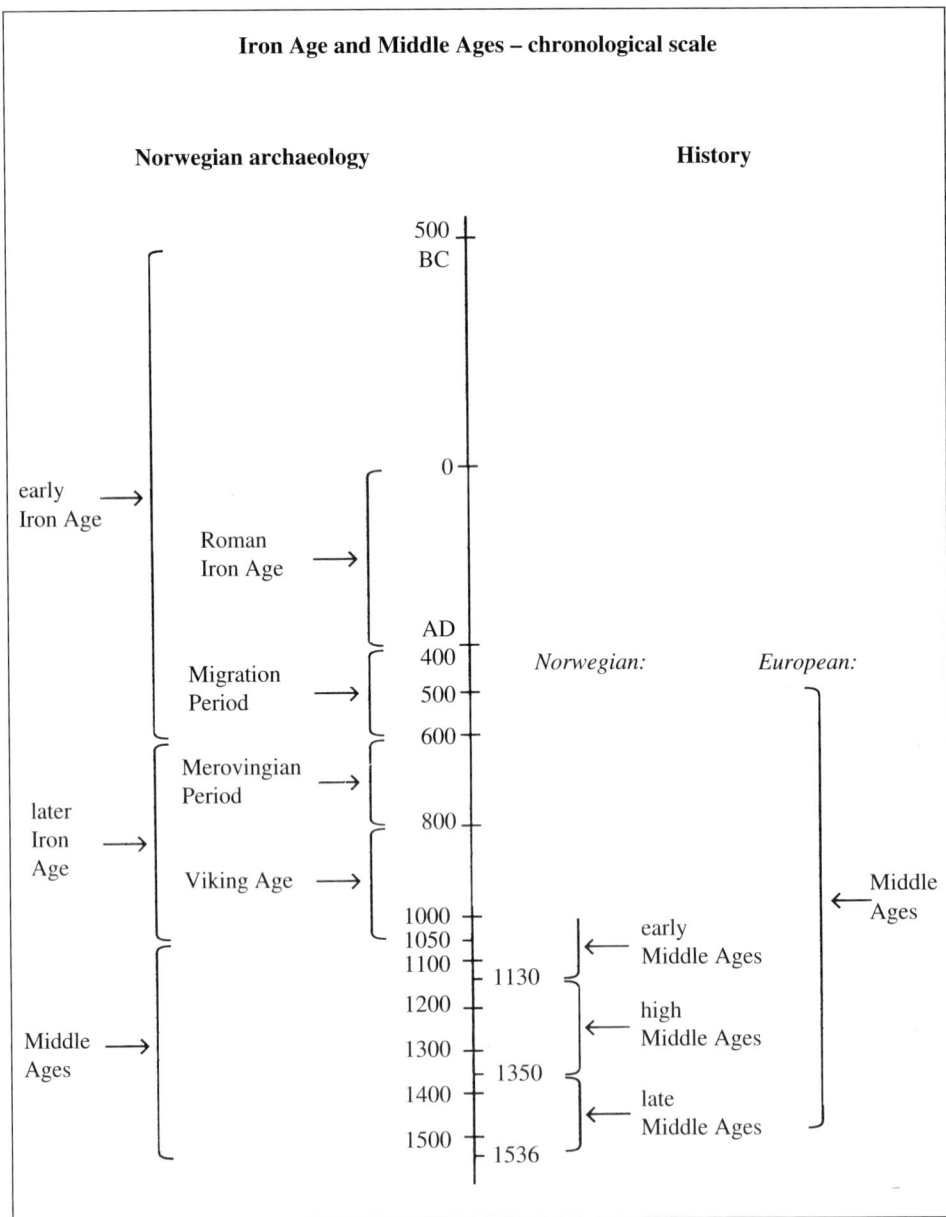

The scales indicate the different eras into which the period ca. 500 BC to 1536 AD has been divided; up to and including the Viking Age (to 1050) by Norwegian archaeologists and in the following period by Norwegian historians.

years. Building ships in wood – a technique stemming from the Iron Age – had long made it possible to make regular journeys along the entire Norwegian coast. It is very possible that it was this coastal route that gave the country its name: 'north way' or Norway. In any case, together with inland routes (see Chapter 1), it tied the country together. Trade along these routes occurred from an early date, smoothing out the differences between the economies of different parts of the country and helping to forge links overseas. Social and cultural ties were made alongside the economic.

It was in these ways that we can reckon on Norway having become Norwegian by Ôttar's time. Language and religion are, however, unlikely to have distinguished Norwegians sharply from other Scandinavian speakers. But mountainous plateaus and dense forests lay between the Norwegians and the Swedes to the east and it was perhaps the lie of the land, seen from the perspective of the Danes in the south, that caused the names Norway and Norsemen to come into being. This suggests that, in the eyes of their neighbours too, Norsemen were somewhat different. And though they were a long way from constituting a fully-fledged society, they perhaps had something of an ethnic and cultural identity.

Early social organization

The basic unit of settlement in Ottar's time was the farm or *gard*. It had permanent buildings for people and animals, usually close together within a fenced or otherwise defined area of cultivated land. The area outside this, whilst providing grazing, wood and other resources, was less well defined. The farm had its own name, such names going back at least to the early Roman Iron Age (ca. AD 0–400).

Probably quite a lot of people lived in many of the agricultural dwelling places that at that time and in the next centuries had names we have come to recognize as farm names. A common view is that these were the settlements of patriarchal grand families. Such a kin group was not only a social and economic entity, it was also held together through a cult of ancestor worship. Kin, too, were an essential ingredient in what there was of a wider social organization.

We cannot prove all this and we shall see later (Chapter 3) that, given that the average life expectancy at the time was low, there was not

This farm at Hanaland, Time in Rogaland, was settled in the Migration Period (ca. 400–600 AD) and continued under occupation down to and throughout the high Middle Ages. From the aerial photograph we clearly see the farmyard with the sites of long houses dating from the Migration Period. From this, a long, narrow, walled lane led to the outfield, so protecting it from animals. New houses that were not so long as the earlier ones were built in the Middle Ages on the farmyard, one of them inside an earlier long house. It also appears that the lane was extended and widened, with the stone walls enclosing a larger area of infield.

much chance of creating vertically extended families containing two or more generations of adults. The labour requirements for the rather extensive farming of the large areas occupied by the early agricultural dwelling places could therefore only with difficulty be met from purely kin-based units. One must then reckon on a goodly number of subordinate farmworkers and, as a result, a less egalitarian social structure than the thesis of the extended-family farms would suggest. A number of these farmworkers could have been thralls or slaves; certain old farm names that incorporate references to slaves indicate this.

The earliest Norwegian legal texts, the provincial laws, which give a picture of conditions in the twelfth century, show a society in which kinship was inherited both through the male and female line. And there is nothing to indicate that the situation was any different during the earlier Iron Age. Such a bilateral system where people were reckoned to belong to both the father's and the mother's line did not favour well-defined and organized kin-based entities. Nevertheless kin could play an important social role. Kin gave security and protection for the individual and bound individuals and families together into a larger grouping. Such a grouping's right to economic resources was to some extent stronger than that of the individual or the family, as witnessed by the later *odel* right (*odelsrett*) (Chapter 4), as well as being of decisive importance in other legal, political and religious spheres. But this does not mean that the society of the Iron Age (which lasted to around 1050) was a kin-based one, though this is often said. For if that were the case, the bonds of kinship would need to be so strong as to dominate other social arrangements, and it is doubtful if this was so.

Place names and archaeological evidence suggest that settlements *(bygder)* containing several kin groups living on their farms could form social units, with a common organization for religious, judicial and defensive purposes. And it also appears that such an organization was to some extent developed for larger areas. In the latter case one obviously needed more than kinship bonds to hold people together.

Around the year AD 550 the Gothic chronicler Jordanes mentioned several peoples in Scandinavia. Behind his distorted latinized names we can, so far as Norway is concerned, plausibly identify *ranrikinger, romerikinger, grener, egder, ryger,* and *horder*. It is of some importance that the first two groups were attached to their own domains (or *riker*). Besides Ranrike (the domain of the *rener,* the present-day Bohuslän) and Romerike (the domain of the *raumer),* several such 'folklands' are indicated by extant territorial names: Hedmark, Hadeland, Ringerike, Grenland (land of the *grener*), Telemark, Rogaland (land of the *ryger*), Hordaland (land of the *horder*), Jemtland and Hålogaland. The linking of a folk name with a territory suggests, at least in some cases, a more organized community. For instance, both place names and archaeological finds provide circumstantial evidence of a common religious and defensive organization for Romerike in prehistoric times.

In parts of the country, especially in the settlements of eastern Norway and the interior of Trøndelag, it has been postulated that a regional organization arose primarily from the need for association amongst a number of farmers, of more or less equal standing, living on their ancestral farms. But there is much to suggest that such organizations were universally dependent on a more clearly defined leadership and had a more markedly aristocratic character. The question turns rather on what we can call *chieftainships* headed by men who were both political and religious leaders and who tied their people to them by bonds of personal allegiance.

It is very likely that the chieftainships were constantly in dispute over territory and resources and could quickly change both their rulers and power bases. Geographically, the conditions for such social arrangements were present along the entire Norwegian coast, with natural centres in good agricultural areas and where great waterways and fjords met the coastal shipping route. From such a central area, a chief would seek to control the coast on both sides as well as the interior along the banks of the great waterways, as far as the mountains. By the great rivers of Østlandet with their many tributaries, where the distance from the coast to the mountains was considerable, and where great lakes and extensive agricultural areas were to be found far into the interior, there was room for several regionally based societies along one and the same waterway. In Vestlandet, conditions were right for groupings around the great fjord systems, but the rough terrain also favoured smaller social units. In central Norway the Trondheimsfjord linked many rich agricultural districts. In the far north of the country, hunting and fishing played an especially important role. At the same time there were particular opportunities for north Norwegian chieftains to exercise their power by exploiting the Sami, or simply by trading with them. Ottar was an example of such a magnate.

In all probability the natural conditions for regional social organizations had been exploited in order to build up a number of greater or lesser chieftainships in Norway at the beginning of historic time. Several of the old 'folklands' could have been linked in this way. The inbuilt tendency for the chieftainships to expand at the cost of rivals was the starting point for the development of ever more extensive social units.

The road to Europe

It is during the Viking Age (ca. 800–1050) that we begin to get a clearer picture of the power of the chieftains. Several factors contribute to explain Nordic expansion overseas at this time. The Vikings followed the old trade routes, lured by the riches they knew were to be found along them. Plunder was often the motive, but there was also more peaceful trade, as in Ottar's case. Political unrest at home may have contributed to Viking expansionism, as believed by the Icelandic historians of the twelfth and thirteenth centuries, but a significant increase in population and the resulting pressure on resources were probably more decisive factors. Such conditions must have stoked up the desire for adventure and the need to escape, thus providing an explanation for the fact that many settled as farmers in several areas.

It is difficult to explain the Viking expeditions except within the context of an aristocratic society. One would expect that chiefs and leaders were needed to organize the ships, equipment and manpower required for the voyages. As far as one can tell, many of those who travelled with the chieftains stood in a dependent, patron–client relationship to them at home as well. Gradually, as the Viking expeditions increased they produced their own warrior chiefs. The foremost among them were able to found kingdoms both at home and abroad. Viking wealth acquired by warfare and trade was an effective means of winning support and building up power and prestige within a social system where the exchange of gifts was one means of binding people to each other.

The first Viking expeditions we are aware of consisted of sporadic attacks on the British Isles in search of plunder during the closing decades of the eighth century. The migration of Norsemen to the Shetlands and the Orkneys probably began, at the latest, at about the same time and led, in the course of the Viking Age, to the complete Norse domination of these island societies. Further north, the Faroes and Iceland were colonized partly from Norway and partly from the outlying Norse territories to the south. Iceland got Norse settlements towards the end of the ninth century and from there migrants reached Greenland around a century later. They sailed further to North America (*Vinland*) but without settling permanently there.

The marauding expeditions directed at the British Isles were followed, in the course of the ninth century, by Norse settlements on the northern tip of Scotland, the Hebrides and the Isle of Man and in Ireland. After a time Norse kingdoms were established with their centres in Dublin and the Isle of Man. From early in the tenth century Norse migrants from Ireland settled in the northwest of England. From there they reached Northumberland and Yorkshire, where kings of Norse

'Saga Siglar', a replica of a vessel dating from the first part of the eleventh century and excavated from the Roskilde fjord in 1962. Because it was constructed mostly of pine, it is assumed to have been Norwegian in origin. The vessel was 16.3 m. long and 4.5 m.. wide and built for sailing rather than rowing. It shows that, even in the Viking period, specialist merchant or cargo ships were being constructed alongside the narrower war ships with their lower freeboards. The latter were rowed by a large crew when unable to move forward fast enough under sail. With vessels like the 'Saga Siglar', it was possible to sail across the Norwegian Sea to Iceland and Greenland and onwards to North America. Indeed the 'Saga Siglar' sailed round the world in 1984–86.

lineage ruled for a time from York. The Viking expansion in the east of England, continental western Europe and further into the Mediterranean was, however, primarily carried out by people from Danish areas, whilst the thrust across the Baltic and along the Russian rivers to the Black Sea and the Caspian was mostly the work of people from Swedish areas.

The Scandinavians had a lasting impact on the districts in which they settled in large numbers and organized a number of kingdoms and earldoms. At the same time, it was during the Viking Age that Scandinavia was opened to Europe in earnest. Christian influences began to trickle in and led eventually to what amounted to a cultural revolution. It was also of importance that the Scandinavians abroad became aware of more sophisticated forms of political organization under a princely leadership. Amongst other things they discovered too the role that urban centres could play in this context.

The unification of Norway begins

The last two or three decades of the ninth century were to witness not only Ottar's journey and the beginnings of Norse settlement in Iceland. At some time in the course of this period there also occurred the celebrated battle of Hafrsfjord in Rogaland. Contemporary skaldic

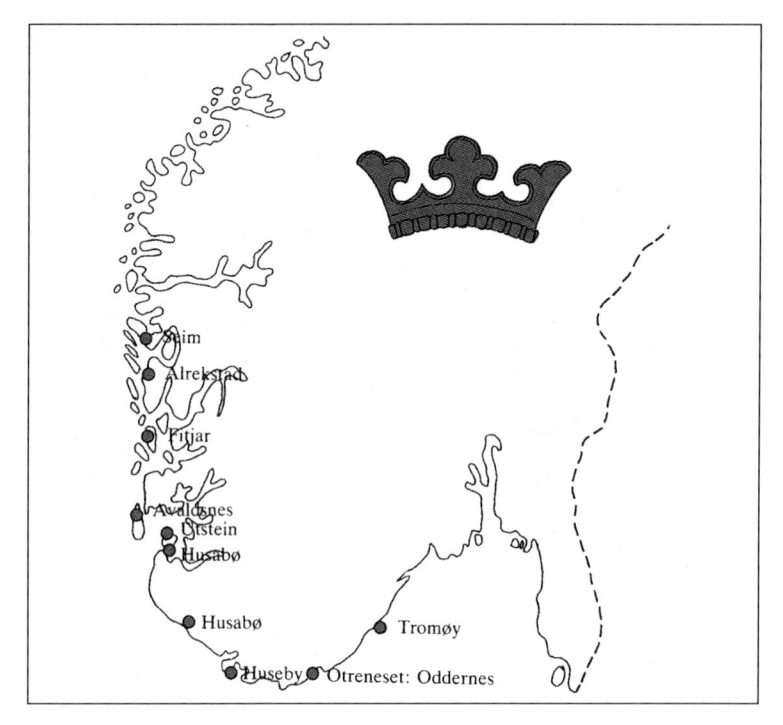

The royal estates of Harald Fairhair and his more immediate successors in southwestern Norway. Before towns came into existence it was in such places along the coast that the kings and their retainers stayed. King Haakon I (Adalsteinsfostre) was at Fitjar when he was attacked by the sons of King Eirik Bloodaxe. He died of his wounds on his way to Alrekstad, the forerunner of Bergen, and was buried in a barrow at Seim in Nordhordland.

poetry relates that King Harald Halvdansson (later nicknamed 'Fairhair') won a victory here that, according to the context of the verses, gave him control of Rogaland and possibly also Agder. Icelandic and Norwegian saga writers and chroniclers from the twelfth century onwards reckon him to have been the first king to rule over the whole of Norway. And in his collection of kings' sagas, 'Heimskringla' (which dates from around 1230), Snorri Sturluson believed that Harold had systematically conquered one chieftainship after another until that final victory at Hafrsfjord.

Snorri's story of the unification of Norway is obviously a later construction. Yet there were probably reasons why Harald made a more lasting impression on historical accounts than previous Norwegian warrior chiefs. It would appear that the heart of his kingdom and that of his more immediate successors lay in the southwest of the country, and, from there, north, to include Hordaland. Here, along the coastal shipping lane, there were important royal estates which were used as major stopovers by the king and his *hird* or body of retainers. They travelled from farm to farm taking goods in kind, that is to say, living off the produce of their landed property as well as from contributions from the local population. This was the only way of effectively exercising royal power before a more permanent local administration was developed.

There is little reason to doubt that Harald's power was exercised on occasion in other parts of the country as well. But it is, and will continue to be, uncertain how strongly he made his presence felt there. The traditional view that he was descended from kings of Opplandene (the inner upland parts of Østlandet) and Vestfold and began his conquests in Østlandet is uncertain and disputed. In the context of the period's communications, instruments of power and level of political organization, it is difficult to believe that he could exercise permanent, direct control over much more than his own heartland. To the extent that he ruled over other parts of the country, it would seem that he did so through petty independent chieftains.

Today it is reasonable to see Harald Fairhair as a ruler who took an important early step towards the medieval unification of Norway. He initiated a process that many others would follow.

We can see the unification of Norway as part of a broader picture. It occurred in parallel with what was happening in Europe generally and what was to produce a system of small and middle-sized states based on territorial unification under a royal or princely power. So, for instance, in Scandinavia the unification of Denmark and of Sweden took place at roughly the same time as that of Norway.

Developments in Scandinavia had broad implications for the rest of Europe. Provoked by Viking invasions, many areas were forced to consolidate power in order to resist. In turn, the Scandinavians learned useful lessons in political organization from those abroad they hoped to subjugate. Furthermore, these expeditions produced wealth and greater military know-how, which the Viking chieftains used to their advantage upon returning home. Some of the early Norwegian kings built their power on the basis of their experience as Vikings.

The three Scandinavian kingdoms were, then, organized under the influence of similar circumstances. During the struggle for political leadership, the warring parties within each of them often sought support in the neighbouring kingdoms. They also competed to some extent over the same territory. During the Viking Age the Danish warrior kings were the strongest. They had territorial ambitions on both Norwegian and Swedish land and had an impact on political development there.

Territorial consolidation

The actual consolidation of Norwegian territory was a politico-military process that took more than three hundred years to complete. Roughly speaking it fell into two main phases. The first phase began in earnest with Harald Fairhair and lasted to the middle of the eleventh century. Throughout most of this period a kingdom with its roots in the west Norwegian coastal districts sought to win control over other parts of the country, with shifting, but never permanent, success. King Olaf Haraldsson (St Olaf after his death) was apparently the first who managed to make his power felt over most of the country at one and the same time, in the years 1015–28. But his rule was merely an interval in a period when Danish kings had authority over greater or smaller parts of Norway, principally Viken (the Oslofjord area), the territory closest to them.

It was not until the dissolution of the Danes' North Sea empire, on the death of King Knut in 1035, that it was possible for the Norwegian royal power to maintain permanent control over the bulk of Norwe-

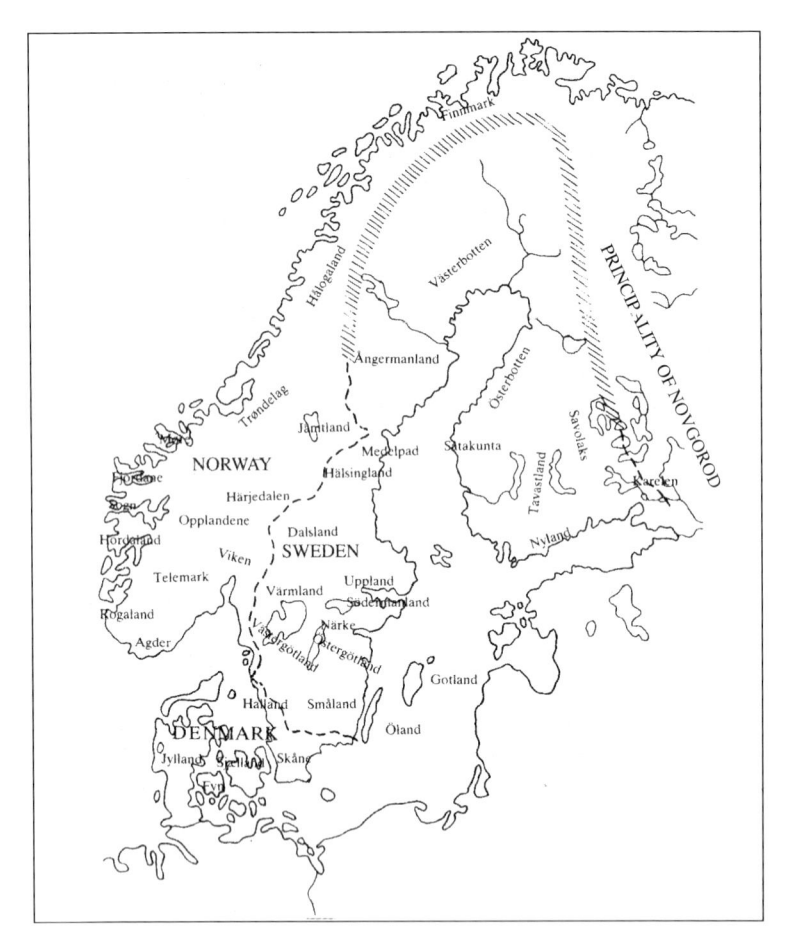

National boundaries and major provinces in Scandinava at the end of the high Middle Ages.

gian territory. For a time in the eleventh century, under King Magnus Olafsson and King Harald Sigurdsson Hardråde ('the Hard-ruler'), Norway was on the offensive against its neighbours. Norwegian territory was secured to the south through Ranrike, as far as the Göta River, while Harald Hardråde managed to complete his half-brother Olaf Haraldsson's plan to take control of the whole kingdom, including the rich agricultural districts of Trøndelag and in Opplandene.

There now followed a period of relative political stability and peace. But there were times when two or more kings, each with a power base in a different part of the country, ruled at one and the same time – clear evidence that political unity was far from being realized. After the death of King Sigurd Jorsalfar, 'the Crusader', in 1130, the ambition of his son Magnus to be sole ruler contributed to the outbreak of disputes over the throne. These were to occupy the following hundred years and have subsequently been called the 'civil wars'.

The civil wars made up the second and last phase of the unification process. They ended with victory and exclusive control over the whole country for the Sverre family's 'Birchleg' kingdom. This had its first effective foothold in Trøndelag. Sverre's victory over Magnus Erlingsson brought control of Vestlandet in the 1180s. The later years of Sverre's rule and those just after his death in 1202 were marked by conflict between the Birchlegs and the 'Croziers', primarily over Østlandet. Here the Birchlegs finally managed to win control under Haakon Haakonsson in the 1220s. This marked the end of the conflict over the territorial unification of Norway under one king.

All that now remained was the Norse colonisation north and east along the coast of Finnmark. This took place in the high and late Middle Ages. From Sverre's time Jemtland also lay under the Norwegian crown. But ecclesiastically the population there belonged to Sweden and was never wholly incorporated into Norwegian society. To the south the kingdom stretched to the mouth of the Göta River, which was where the three medieval Scandinavian kingdoms met.

The Church, the aristocracy and national unification

The earliest national monarchy was a product of conquest. The realms the first kings managed to control were held together by little more than the kings' personal and often short-lived power. What authority they had revolved around the control of subordinate groups of people rather than of actual territory. And power was built to a considerable degree on the personal presence and manipulative skills of the king himself. He got support through gifts and favours and by punishing enemies and disturbers of the peace. There was still no impersonal administrative apparatus that could maintain the unity of the kingdom on the death of a warrior king.

Why territorial unification took so long was because of the time-consuming process of building up a social and political organization and an associated ideology that could bind the kingdom together and that was, to a certain extent, independent of the king's person. This organizational process of unification did not seriously begin before the middle of the twelfth century (Chapter 5). Some important steps were nevertheless taken in the first phase of unification.

An important aspect of the development of a kingdom that embraced the entire country was the relationship between the royal power and the *secular aristocracy*. In the skaldic verses and in the sagas, conflict between kings and chieftains is an underlying theme. Nevertheless, a Norwegian aristocracy with local and regional influence was a necessary precondition for the unification of the kingdom. If Harald Fairhair and his immediate successors were to rule outside their core areas, they were forced to ally themselves with chieftains and leaders who had a power base they themselves lacked. By binding such men to himself through a relationship of mutual dependence, a king could get them to exercise official power on his behalf and provide military support in exchange for a share of royal income as well as royal patronage. But such an administrative arrangement has always been a two-edged sword: the chieftains cooperated with the king only so long as it served their own interests.

There are indications that Olaf Haraldsson had a more thought out programme for controlling the old regional chieftain-aristocracy. One means was to appoint effective royal servants or *ármenn* – we would call them 'stewards' – on the king's estates up and down the country and to give them official duties besides running the estates themselves. Another method was to win the support of prominent freemen who could act as a counterweight to the power of the chieftain-aristocracy. By, at the latest, Olaf's time, the monarchy sought to strengthen its ties with both chieftains and other leading men by making them *lendmenn* ('landed men'), i.e. men who in return for fealty and service were provided with an income in royal land, in addition to their own. Olaf Haraldsson did not manage to tame the chieftain-aristocracy during his lifetime. Nor did he manage, in the long term, to hold his own against King Cnut's Anglo-Danish power in his alliance with those Norwegian chieftains who had seen their influence reduced by Olaf. But his son Magnus and half-brother Harald Sigurdsson killed or drove from the country the most wilful of the old chieftains. The end of the first phase in the conflict over territorial unification came when some of the chieftains had been thus destroyed and the rest of them tied to the king as *lendmenn*.

Royal relations with the *Church* and the *clergy* were more unambiguously positive during this first period than were those with the secular aristocracy. The contact with Europe during the Viking Age soon led to Christian influences reaching the Norwegian coastal areas. But it was kings like Haakon Adalsteinsfostre (the foster son of King Athelstan of Wessex), Olaf Tryggvason and Olaf Haraldsson who got Christianity established among the larger part of the population to the exclusion of other beliefs and who introduced the first elements of a church organization.

The missionary church was under the leadership of the king. The king built the first churches and settled property on them. An early and substantial core of the later extensive ecclesiastical estates came as donations from the king. The missionary bishops were members of the king's *hird* or retinue and the bishops continued to be appointed by the king when they, from the reign of Olaf Kyrre ('the Quiet') (1066–93), began to take up permanent residence – in Nidaros (the usual ecclesiastical name for Trondheim) and Bergen and perhaps somewhat later in Oslo.

The missionary kings had been converted to Christianity whilst overseas and learned there of a pattern of cooperation between the monarchy and the church that they naturally wished to transfer to Norway. This was clearly not just for religious reasons. The introduction of a new religion could serve to break down the old pagan organization of society, wherever it stood against the king. This was the case in Trøndelag and in Opplandene (south-central Norway). Here it appears that the unification of the country, together with the acceptance of Christianity, led in the twelfth century to the confiscation of the estates belonging to heathen peasant leaders and to the transfer of a good deal of their property to the church.

Everywhere the conversion to Christianity could be made a component of the reorganization of local societies and their incorporation into the monarchy. Gradually the country was covered by local churches, which increasingly came under the control of the bishops. As a result, an ecclesiastical apparatus was created that was to form the first mechanism for holding together a country-wide social system. Through this apparatus a uniform religious doctrine was promulgated with basic features that stuck in the minds of most people. Rules too were adopted for the observance of Christianity, which created a common pattern of behaviour.

As the protector of the Church and its head, the king acquired both power and an exalted position in society. From amongst the clergy he found people who were especially suited to act as his counsellors and helpers. They could read and write, had close contact with other countries and were familiar with the more advanced organization of society there. In a wider sense the clergy pleaded the king's cause before the people. Christian teaching allowed itself, without difficulty, to be harnessed in support of the more permanent secular arrangement of society that the monarchy stood for.

The king and the wider society

Even if the aristocracy and the clergy played the main roles in organizing a more unified kingdom, Norway was, and continued to be throughout the Middle Ages, a peasant society. No significant official authority could be created without being rooted in the public opinion of this society. The peasantry's need for a minimum level of peace and tranquillity, of legal and political stability, was an essential feature of the politico-administrative development. This need was met by the king in his capacity as upholder of the law and as military leader. In these ways he took on social functions that produced the conditions required for a more lasting support of the monarchy as an institution.

Contemporary skaldic poetry praises early kings such as Harald Fairhair, Haakon Adalsteinsfostre and Olaf Haraldsson as stern prosecutors of thieves and men of violence; the latter two are mentioned also as creators and upholders of the law. Upholding the law gave, after a time, an income in the form of receipts from fines and confiscations, and led to the building up of a legal and administrative apparatus that also became a power base.

As military leader, the king entered into agreements with the peasants in different parts of the country for permanent economic and military assistance during times of crisis. It was in this way that the *leidang* or naval levy was formed, a conscripted force under the leadership of the king and for which the peasants provided ships and crews, food and weapons. It was probably in Haakon Adalsteinsfostre's reign, around the middle of the tenth century, that this force was organized in Vestlandet and very likely also in Trøndelag. Later it spread, along with the monarchy, to other coastal areas.

A central feature of the relationship between the king and the peasantry was the popular assembly or *ting* (Old Norse *þing*). General assemblies of all freemen (*allting*) must have met throughout the country in pre-historic times, for dealing with judicial and, to some extent, also political matters of common concern. Later in the Middle Ages such assemblies continued as local bodies in both town and country. Some of them acquired a special role as assemblies for the acclamation of kings. Here the pretender was 'taken' or adjudged to be king in a legal ceremony at which pledges were exchanged between him and the peasants. This approval was felt to be necessary by all aspirants to the throne and all sought it.

During the first phase of territorial unification the *lagting* appear in the sources. These assemblies were different from the *allting* in that they covered larger areas and occupied a more elevated position. In contrast to the *allting*, they were representative assemblies where specially appointed men met on behalf of the local peasant communities. The old provincial law codes reflect, in their extant form, the legal situation of the twelfth century, though several provisions go further back in time. Here the *lagting* were the highest judicial assemblies in the country and the only ones that could ratify laws. The two oldest, the west Norwegian *Gulating* and the *Frostating* in Trøndelag, are, in the legal texts, strongly influenced by the monarchy's interests and ability to organize. We first learn of the two other early *lagting,* the *Eidsivating* and the *Borgarting* in Østlandet, from the national law code of King Magnus Lagabøte (the law-mender), the so-called *Landslov* of 1274.

The monarchy's contribution to the organization of the *lagting* is easy to understand. Through them, the inhabitants of large areas of the country could be legally associated with important government initiatives. It was in this way that Christianity and the central elements of church organization were adopted in Norwegian rural districts and the naval levy established. As the highest courts of law, the *lagting* promoted law and order according to legal regulations that presupposed the royal enforcement of justice and brought the king an income from legal fines and confiscations. The *lagting* have been assumed to date back to pre-historic times, but none of them can be clearly shown to have existed before the reign of Harald Fairhair. And it is clearly very possible that it was actually the monarchy that set them up, at least in this advanced form, as representative institutions for larger regions of the country.

The organizational development of the monarchy demanded more permanent and secure administrative and military bases than those provided by the old estates along the coastal shipping route. It is in this light that we must assess the monarchy's contribution to the establishment of the oldest Norwegian *towns*. The king and his representatives could dwell both more securely and more comfortably in the towns than round about in the countryside and could, from there, exercise control over surrounding districts. Added to which the monarchy was interested in promoting and exploiting the specialized economic activities that have always distinguished towns from their hinterlands. These activities in the Middle Ages were mainly confined to trade and crafts.

The first Norwegian towns came into being, at the expense of a wider network of seasonal local and regional centres, during the first phase of the conflict that led to the unification of the country. At this time the kings had many sound strategic reasons for building up bases at just those places where, according to the sagas, they promoted the development of towns from around the year AD 1000 onwards: namely, in Trondheim, Borg (Sarpsborg) and Oslo. Later, Konghelle, by the northern mouth of the Göta River, became a royal harbour and the kingdom's southern outpost. When Bergen was promoted as a town in Olaf Kyrre's reign it was probably because the monarchy wanted to establish an ecclesiastical and administrative centre for its old core region of Vestlandet. In AD 1135 the Anglo-Norman chronicler Ordericus Vitalis mentions the five centres given above, plus Tønsberg, as towns (*civitates*) along the Norwegian coast. They were obviously all an indication of a certain degree of royal and ecclesiastical centralization.

3
Population, settlement and the economy up to around 1350

In Europe, medieval populations were struck by two major crises, each involving immense losses and each caused by plague. From AD 540 and into the seventh century large areas were racked by epidemics of plague. The second crisis came with the Black Death, which struck most of Europe in the years 1347–51 and was followed by renewed outbreaks of plague in the immediately succeeding decades. Between these two catastrophies it would seem that the population grew steadily throughout Europe. Population growth was especially strong in the period 1050–1300 along with the growth of agricultural and urban settlement and an increasing output from agriculture and other economic activities.

Norway and, indeed, Scandinavia as a whole fit into this general picture of development. Archaeological detection of abandoned farms in Rogaland and Agder suggest a fall in population and a reduction in the number of settlements towards the end of the Migration Period, at about the time the first demographic crisis hit the southern parts of Europe. The Viking Age, on the other hand, was characterized by the growth of population, settlements and output in Norway. This development continued into the early Christian Middle Ages and further through the high Middle Ages, which in Norway can be set around the years 1130–1350. From the middle of the fourteenth century Norway too was struck by the second great demographic crisis of medieval Europe (Chapter 6).

Decisive for the development of a closer sense of community in Norway was the growth in population, settlement and production from the Viking Age to the high Middle Ages. A precondition for this sense of community was the shorter distance between settlements so that people came closer together in their daily lives.

Population size and population growth

It is not possible to calculate the size of Norway's population with any degree of accuracy before around the year 1665 when we get counts of male persons above the age of 12. At that time the total population was about 440,000 (Chapter 9). All estimates of population size for earlier periods must be considered very approximate and uncertain. The method that seems to serve us best is to count the farms and holdings we can identify through names and other information from contemporary and later sources. The possibilities are there for a reasonably reliable estimate of the number of *named farms (navnegarder,* i.e. farms with their own names*)* existing in the years around 1300. At this time it is reckoned that the medieval settlement had reached its greatest extent, just before the demographic crisis of the late Middle Ages.

It is, however, doubtful whether one can extrapolate from the number of farms to the number of people. There are two reasons for this. First, it is impossible to measure the extent to which the named farms were divided into *holdings* without names of their own in extant sources, i.e. the actual units of production occupied by individual households, during the course of the Middle Ages. Second, we do not know the average number of people living on each holding. The counts from around 1665 would suggest that the figure at that time oscillated around 6. This is the figure that has normally also been used to estimate the medieval population. However, in other parts of Europe a figure of 4–5 inhabitants, or even fewer, has been reckoned for the average pre-industrial household and the same number has been suggested also for Norway. Obviously it makes a lot of difference to one's estimate of the total population if one's household total varies by 1–2.

The latest estimate of the maximum number of named farms in Norway during the high Middle Ages lies around 36,500. Estimates of the number of holdings come out at between 60,000 and 75,000. Working on the basis of 6 persons per holding and allowing for the number of people in towns and the number in the countryside not living on farms and holdings, the leading historians in the field have estimated the total population to have been between 400,000 and 500,000. Given the uncertainty of our average population per holding and making yet another estimate, this time of the population living in the areas later added to Sweden (Båhuslen, Jemtland and Herjedalen), we arrive at a figure for the population of mainland Norway, around the year 1300, of somewhere between 300,000 and 550,000 persons. In between lies an average of about 425,000, corresponding to the number of 400,000 which has so far been the most widely accepted estimate of the high medieval population of present-day Norway, without the areas later ceded to Sweden.

A rough estimate of the population of Denmark, including the areas that are now Swedish (Skania, Halland and Blekinge), for the second half of the thirteenth century would lie around 1 million. A figure of 600,000-750,000 is one we come up with for Sweden in the second half of the sixteenth century. Allowing for the fall of population in the late Middle Ages, it is likely that Sweden had a population at least this size in the high Middle Ages. The totals for Denmark and Sweden are even less certain than those for Norway. Yet in terms of population and output Norway's two neighbours undoubtedly commanded greater resources. Moreover, Denmark was both more easily controlled geographically and more densely populated. This helps explain the Danish dominance of Scandinavia in the Viking Age as well as Norway's weak position in the Nordic unions of the late Middle Ages.

There can be no doubt that the population grew from the Viking Age down to the end of the high Middle Ages. It is, indeed, difficult to explain the Viking expansion overseas without a growth in population. However, the clearest indication of this growth is the increasing extension of agrarian settlement from the tenth to the mid-fourteenth centuries. Thousands of new farms were cleared, and whole districts were settled outside the older, agricultural heartlands.

Looking at the country as a whole, this development emerges at its clearest in a number of large classes of farm names that can be dated using linguistic and other criteria. Especially noticeable are the 3,000–4,000 names ending in *rud/rød* (clearing), which reflect the last phase in the expansion of settlement that took place from the eleventh to the mid-fourteenth centuries. For the most part these were small, less valuable holdings on the margins of the old-established agricultural settlements. Many of them were deserted in the late Middle Ages and some of the names disappeared. In total there may have been some 5000 of these *rud* (clearance) farms before the mid-fourteenth century.

Rud-names are less common west of Telemark and in Trøndelag. It is usually reckoned that this indicates less clearing here than in the forested Østlandet, principally because there was less land left to be

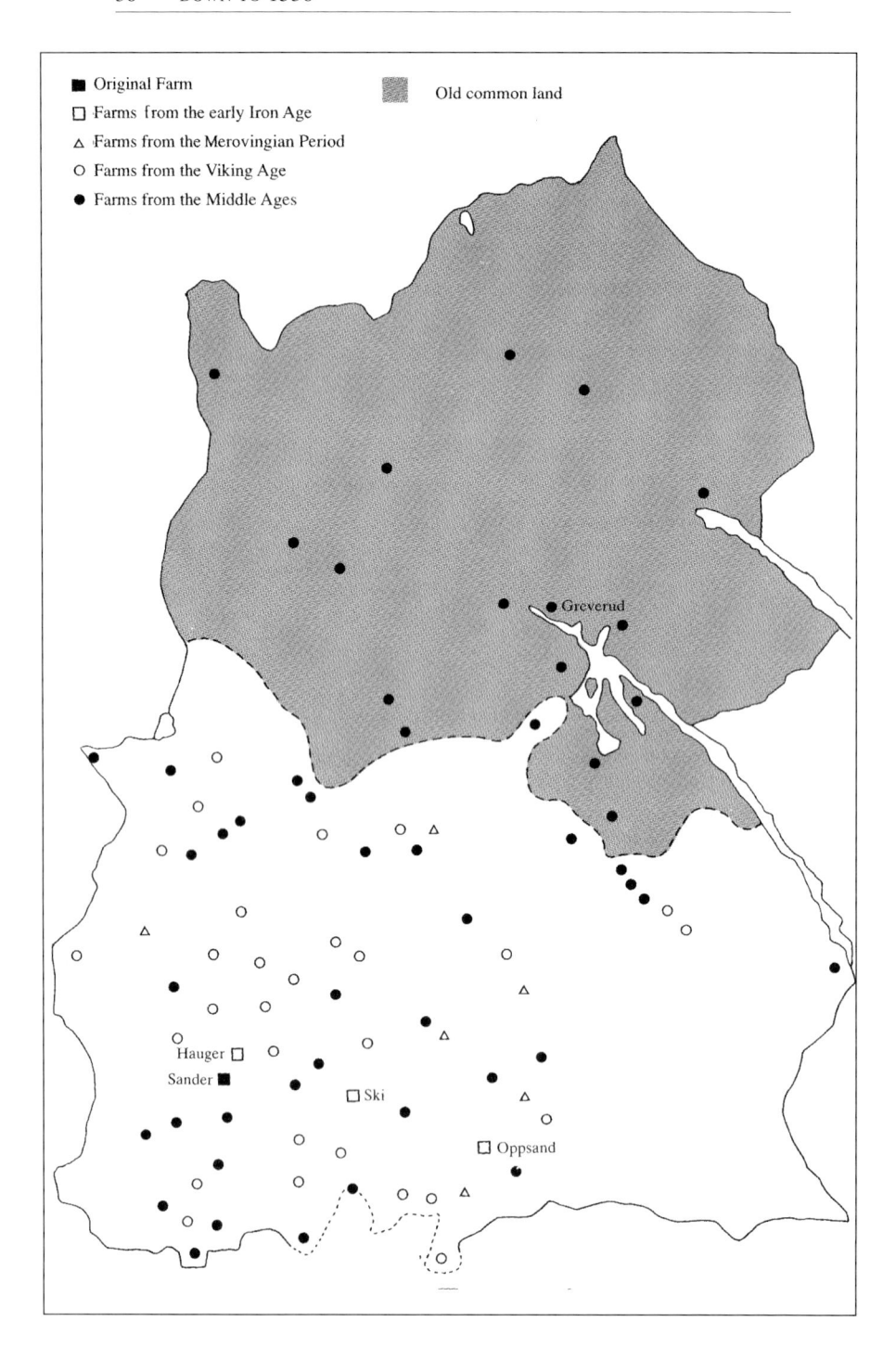

■ Original Farm
□ Farms from the early Iron Age
△ Farms from the Merovingian Period
○ Farms from the Viking Age
● Farms from the Middle Ages

Old common land

cleared. Resources of land in Vestlandet were already comparatively modest in the Viking Age. This has been used to explain why the bulk of Viking expeditions left from coastal areas in the west.

In the early fourteenth century, older farms all over the country had been divided into several holdings. Probably this had occurred as early as the Viking Age but the tempo increased in later centuries. The process of division went especially far in Vestlandet. By contrast, in Østlandet, fewer farms were divided and, those that were, not to the same extent as in the west. Trøndelag clearly occupied a position midway between Østlandet and Vestlandet when it came to both clearing new farms and dividing old ones. To sum up: the clearing and the subdivision of the land is evidence that there was strong population growth in Norway from the Viking Age to the high Middle Ages. It is not possible, however, to put reliable figures on this growth at any stage within this period.

The growth in the number and density of settlements

Through clearing and subdivision, agricultural settlement spread across a greater part of the country: into the forests, along the valleys, up the hillsides and ever further north. The movement was, in the main, one that went towards the periphery and away from the districts

← *The map shows the expansion of settlement from the early Iron Age to the high Middle Ages, inclusive, in Ski parish in Follo, Akershus, based on location, extent and names of the farms. The farm name Sander – 'the sands' or 'the sanded region' – is possibly an indication of the original settlement on the Ski moraine during the first centuries after Christ. From this, other holdings were gradually established. There followed new farms with their own names. The expansion gathered pace in the Merovingian and Viking Ages, with 36 new farms being added to the already existing four. A further 40 or so were added in the Middle Ages (ca. 1050–1350 AD). During this period, farms spread into the earlier area of common woodland to the north, with the clearing of at least 20 farms. At the same time the older farms were divided into several holdings which were not given their own names. Agricultural settlement extended further in this period than at any time since – an experience shared by other areas.*

that can be considered central in terms of the then current lines of communication and political organization. At the same time the movement was towards land less suited to agriculture (see Chapter 1). Clearing and subdividing led to many small holdings, so that the average size of holdings in Norway as a whole diminished.

The growth of settlement and population, as we have already indicated, varied from region to region. Østlandet, which had the greatest reserves of land, clearly bore the brunt of the changes. That settlement became denser on the coast from Romsdal northwards was in all likelihood brought about as much by fishing, whaling, sealing, etc. as by agriculture.

Around 1200, the border between Finnmark ('Sami country', i.e. the land of the Sami, the indigenous people) and the area of the settled Norwegian population went through the fjord of Malangen in southern Troms. This was also the northern limit of grain cultivation. Thus it was the *agricultural* population that stretched unbroken as far north as Malangen. This does not mean, therefore, that there were not Norwegians settled further north, albeit more thinly, and with fishing, hunting and a little animal husbandry as their means of livelihood. Archaeological finds from the Viking Age indicate this to have been the case. And Norwegian settlement along the coast from northern Troms to Finnmark expanded towards the end of the high Middle Ages.

The Sami continued to occupy the fjords and the interior of Finnmark. As earlier, they were nomads who exploited the available resources seasonally: hunting wild reindeer in the interior during the autumn, settling in the inner parts of the fjords for the winter, and fishing and hunting seals etc. out along the coast during the spring and summer. It is not until later that we find Sami permanently settled on the coast or herding tame reindeer in the mountains.

The earliest Norwegian towns appeared in the eleventh century (Chapter 2). They grew in the twelfth and thirteenth centuries and new ones appeared. Written sources from the twelfth century speak of the episcopal residences of Stavanger and Hamar as towns, together with the commercial centres of Veøy in Romsdal and Kaupanger in Sogn. It appears likely that both Borgund in Sunnmøre and Vågan in Lofoten also had the status of small market towns at this time. Skien, situated at the mouth of the Telemark river system, is first mentioned in the thirteenth century, and, in the same century, the port of Marstrand in Båhuslen was built. The latter had town status in the late Middle Ages.

Places in Norway described as towns in medieval sources.

It is reasonable to suppose that the origins of most of these towns lay far back in time. For Borgund and Skien this has been proved archaeologically.

Urban development in this period was confined to a comparatively small number of places. This appears clearly when one compares the situation with that in neighbouring kingdoms. During the Middle Ages, Sweden (together with Finland) witnessed the growth of around 40 towns. By the end of the Middle Ages Denmark (including the areas now in southern Sweden) contained 100 or so towns. Norway, on the other hand, had but 16.

As a rough estimate, scarcely more than 20,000 people lived in Norwegian towns at the end of the high Middle Ages. Only Bergen had more than 5,000 inhabitants, possibly as many as 7,000. This would have been a medium-sized town by the standards of contemporary Europe, though for a time it could have been the biggest in Scandinavia. Trondheim, Oslo and Tønsberg probably counted their inhabitants in the low thousands, whilst the rest of the Norwegian towns had scarcely more than a few hundred permanent residents.

But if the Norwegian towns were few in number and, generally speaking, small, they were nonetheless an indication of the general growth of population and settlement. This was, not least, because the towns had a pretty constant excess of deaths over births. They were therefore dependent on in-migration to maintain and increase their numbers.

The causes and effects of population growth

We are in the dark as to the causes of the growth in population and the expansion of settlement from the Viking Age to the high Middle Ages. From what we know of the contemporary European situation and the situation in Norway in later years, there can be little doubt that the average life expectancy at birth was very low. Examinations of skeletal material from a number of Scandinavian graveyards suggest it lay well under 30 years. It was kept low above all by high infant mortality and deaths amongst young people. Even those who lived to adulthood did not become especially old. People over 60 were probably quite rare.

When, in spite of this, the population rose, it must have been because a high death rate was more than matched by an even higher birth rate. Women must, for the most part, have begun to produce children on reaching the fertile age. Early and frequent births seem to have been the main cause of a lower expectation of life amongst women at this time.

Population growth would not have been possible without a growth in food production. It is possible that the two grew for a time at an approximately equal rate. But, during the course of the thirteenth and in the early part of the fourteenth centuries, living conditions undoubtedly worsened for many. Agricultural settlement reached a geographical extent that has never subsequently been exceeded. Sources from the high Middle Age, especially the legal texts, indicate that the agricultural resources that could be exploited with the technology of the day were exploited to a great extent. It is hardly likely that in such a large and thinly populated country as Norway the finite resources set a fixed ceiling on the number of people who could support themselves and that this ceiling was reached. Nor do contemporary sources give a clear impression of population pressure and distress. Nevertheless, the comparatively heavy exploitation of the available land area could have led to the ending of population growth, even a decline, towards the end of the high Middle Ages. There are clearer signs of such a development elsewhere in Europe from the second half of the thirteenth century (Chapter 6).

Agriculture in the Middle Ages

The overwhelming majority of Norwegians in the Middle Ages supported themselves directly by agriculture, together with some secondary employment. To a great extent, the rest of society did so indirectly. The clergy, the secular aristocracy and others in the royal and ecclesiastical administrative apparatus drew their main economic support from land rents and other payments from the agricultural population.

We have seen that natural conditions allowed only a very small part of the total area of Norway to be cultivated (Chapter 1) – far less than today because the draining of bogs and waterlogged soils had not taken place. It was, however, arable farming that, in energy terms, supplied most of the food. But, given that most of the area was suitable only for foraging and various gathering, hunting and extractive activities, farming of the cultivatable land was closely linked to an extensive exploitation of the outlying areas, above all for animal husbandry. Arable farming provided fodder for the livestock, which, in return, provided draught animals and manure.

The balance between arable and animal husbandry varied from district to district. Naturally, the latter was at its most important, relative to the former, in the coast and fjord districts in the west and north of the country as well as in the mountain communities. Cattle, sheep and goats predominated, though many horses were kept and pigs, hens and geese were also to be found. From the thirteenth century there is evidence that Norwegian animal husbandry produced a certain surplus for export in the form of butter, wool, homespun cloth and the skins of sheep and goats.

Indispensable for a combined farming and hunter–gatherer system were the rights and privileges individual farms had to exploit the forests, to hunt, to trap and to fish. For domestic consumption, fish was an especially important supplement to the diet of the peasant families living on the comparatively scarce soils of the north and west coasts – so much so that in these areas they are commonly called fisher–farmers. This is an even more appropriate term in view of the seasonally based commercial fishing that developed during the high Middle Ages. This has continued down to the present day. In some favourably situated districts timber became an article for sale in the high Middle Ages. It was used for buildings and other construction work in the towns and in the production of boats and ships. From the thirteenth century a certain amount was exported across the North Sea. Another important secondary activity was the production of iron in areas where this could be extracted from the bogs.

Not surprisingly, arable farming was most important on the more extensive cultivable soils of Østlandet and Trøndelag, as well as in special areas such as Jæren and the slate-rich soils of the islands of Ryfylke. But the land was cultivated wherever it was possible to do so, even as far north as southern Troms. Given the techniques of the day it was above all the light, self-draining soils that were cultivated: hills, slopes, patches of flat land with easily penetrable soils. Lower and heavier land was left for hay meadows and pasture.

The open country of Østlandet and Trøndelag had scarcely enough animals to provide adequate amounts of manure for the fields. The *Frostating* law code required that tenant farmers in the rural districts of Trøndelag keep a minimum number of animals relative to the amount of seed sown, in order to ensure that there was enough manure and to prevent the exhaustion of the soil. Every year a quarter of the arable area was to be left fallow and the animals were to be let on to it so it would be manured. Also, if necessary, manure accumulated during the winter (when the animals had to be housed) was to be spread. These resolutions were repeated in Magnus Lagabøte's *Landslov* of 1274, probably with an eye to Østlandet as well as Trøndelag. There is, however, no mention of manuring in the *Gulating* law code with regard to Vestlandet. Here, it would appear that the number of animals relative to the amount of arable land was such that an adequate amount of manure was usually produced each year. In the rest of Europe it was common to leave the land fallow every second or third year (the two or three field rotation system). That Norway should continue to sow every year, or leave the land fallow only every fourth year, meant a relatively heavy use of the small area of cultivable land. Some scholars have argued that, by the end of the high Middle Ages, the soil was on the point of exhaustion in several areas.

Grain was overwhelmingly the dominant crop. Barley and oats were the most important grains, sown separately or together. There is a debate as to just how much of each was sown, though oats was favoured where the climate was relatively cold and wet. A small amount of wheat and rye was sown, especially in the south and east of the country. In the better arable areas, corn growing gave a fairly regular surplus, which provided the means of trade with other parts of the country. But the export of Norwegian grain was unusual. In fact, quite the contrary, increasing amounts of wheat and rye were imported during the high Middle Ages.

The expansion of settlement brought more land into cultivation. At the same time the growth of population presumably led to an increased labour input and, therefore, greater output per acre. It is also possible that minor changes in methods of cultivation, such as a greater supply of manure as well as more extensive utilization of the best types of tools and seed, had the same effect. We must, in any case, believe that agricultural production grew. But, as mentioned above, after a while this increase was probably more than outweighed by an increasing population.

In recent years attempts have been made to calculate the calorific value of Norwegian agricultural production during the high Middle Ages and set this in relation to the total population. The lively discussion surrounding the various estimates has added much to our knowledge of medieval agriculture. But the estimates so far are based on such uncertain assumptions, and have such wide margins of error that they do not yet provide us with a reasonable basis for a precise assessment of living conditions in the high Middle Ages.

Agricultural settlements and production units

As mentioned earlier, agricultural production was based on the farm (*gard*) and the holding (*bruk*). The latter were usually independent settlement and production units, irrespective of whether they were 'named farms' or had come into existence through the subdivision of such farms. The buildings on a farm that was divided into several holdings could be located together on the same site. And, especially in the heavily subdivided coastal districts from Agder northwards, clusters or rows of buildings were to be found that, externally at least, looked like small hamlets. The impression was strengthened by the development of a plot (strip) system, by which each holding controlled several distinct small patches of land within the common infield. Generally, however, the villages in the other Scandinavian countries, as well as in the rest of Europe, were larger and adopted stricter, more regular strip systems on the arable land. Besides, during the Middle Ages, the European village developed into an official communal entity and normally a religious one too, with its own church and priest.

If one looks at the settlement and production units of Scandinavia as a whole, one is struck by an important geographical division. In the north and west, i.e. Iceland, Norway and the peripheral areas of Sweden, settlement is seen to be tied overwhelmingly to separate farms and holdings. In the best agricultural districts of the south and east, on the other hand, village settlement with a comparatively well-developed system of cultivation in common was usual. Topographic conditions were decisive in this for we find villages where it was possible to cultivate larger, contiguous areas of land, and isolated farms where cultivable land was more dispersed, especially in forest and mountain areas. A similar division between districts with villages and those with isolated farms can also be found further south in Europe.

It was possible to create larger and more compact concentrations of landed property (estates in fact) in the Danish and Swedish village districts than it was where farms were isolated. At the centre would lie the manor farm, which would be run by the owner or his agent, with the help of a large labour force. Under the manor would be rented farms operated by the tenants on their own account and paying rent to the owner of the estate.

Such a pattern could be found in some places in Norway too, but the estates were uniformally smaller than in Sweden or Denmark. Especially in the coastal districts in the west of Norway, one could find tenanted farms so close to the manor farm that one is reminded of the more compact estates in other parts of Europe. But in most cases, topography and a settlement pattern based on separate farms and holdings gave Norwegian estates a far-flung and scattered character. They consisted of tenanted farms and holdings, or even parts of holdings, spread over considerable areas and often lacking a distinct centre in the form of a larger property run on the owner's account. Furthermore, the properties of the different estate owners were jumbled together with land belonging to peasant proprietors lying between them.

Society in districts with separate homesteads that lacked large, compact properties in the hands of one owner tended to be less aristocratic than society in the regions dominated by villages. It could be said that this tendency has characterized the social structure of the Nordic countries down to our own time.

Trade and crafts

The exchange of goods developed so rapidly in the Europe of the twelfth and thirteenth centuries (geographically, organizationally and quantitatively) that the term 'commercial revolution' has been used to describe what happened. Trade became more market-oriented and more professional. Whilst previously trade had been dominated by comparatively expensive luxury and prestige items, it now provided, in line with the general growth in population, an increasing element of everyday commodities. These were carried over long distances for use by a wider range of consumers. This applied particularly to northern Europe, where the east–west axis between the Baltic and the North Sea was the most important one in the long-distance trade of the time. Denmark lay on this axis, and there were branches to Norway, Sweden and Finland.

Norway's contribution to the new general commodity trade of the high Middle Ages consisted primarily of fish products, especially dried fish or 'stockfish'. Fish for drying was caught along the entire north and west coast of Norway, but the bulk of it consisted of cod from the winter fisheries of Lofoten and Vesterålen in the north. The seasonal fishing here was carried out on a larger scale from, at the latest, the beginning of the twelfth century.

England was apparently the most important market for Norwegian stockfish towards the end of the high Middle Ages. Customs accounts from ports in eastern England in the first decade of the fourteenth century indicate that at least 1,500 tons of stockfish went there each year. At the same time, dried fish was carried to continental North Sea ports and then up the Rhine and other German rivers. It also went to Lübeck and other ports in the Baltic. Altogether some 3,000 tons or more of

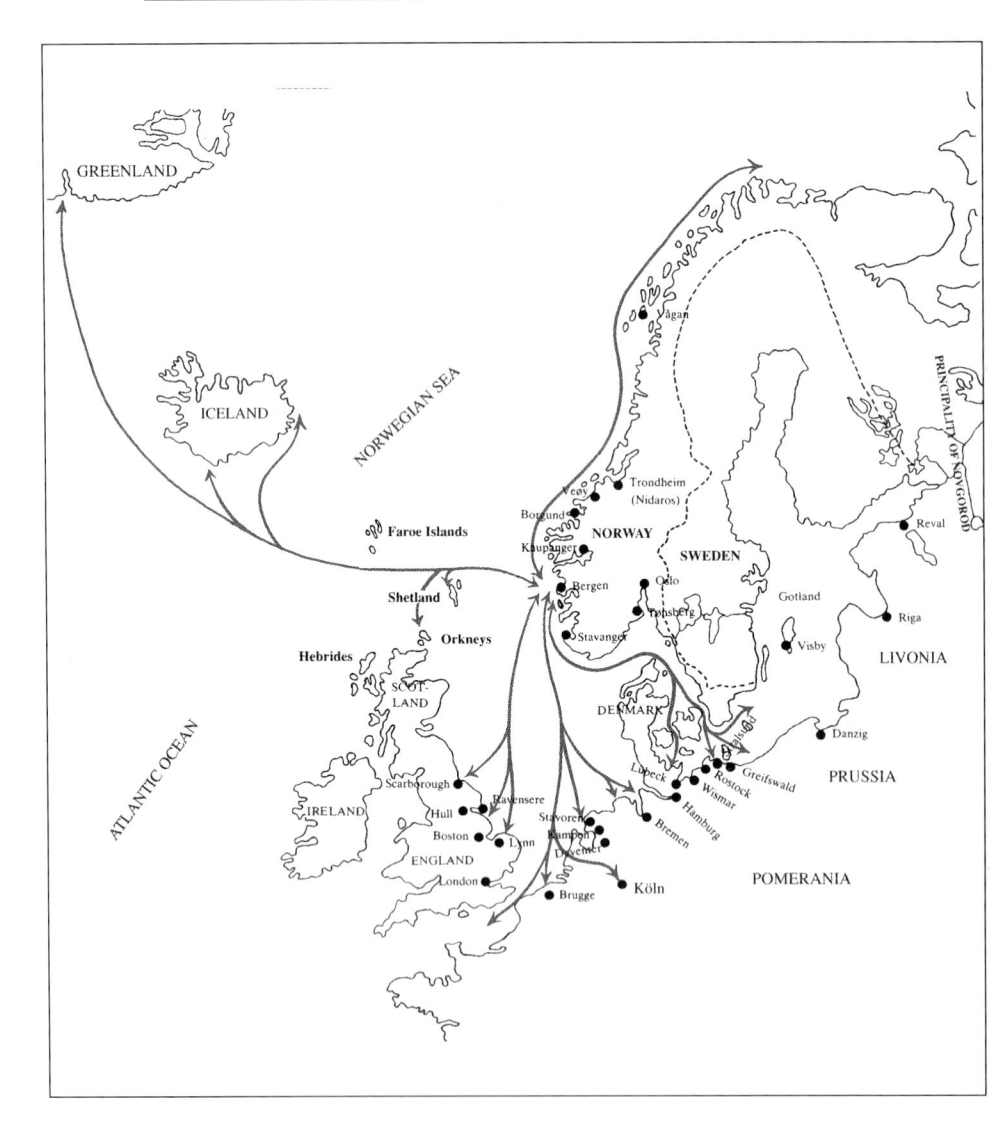

Trade routes to and from Bergen in the early fourteenth century. The map shows the town's strategic situation between the Norse producing areas and the European market. Bergen's site was an important cause of her becoming Scandinavia's first international trading centre and Norway's largest and most important medieval town. It served as a staple, i.e. loading, warehousing and sales centre, for the exchange of goods between Norway north of the Dovre mountains, the colonial areas in the seas to the west, and Europe.

stockfish may have been sent to foreign ports, which represented at least half of the very considerable exports of the mid-seventeenth century. Given that dried fish fetched comparatively high prices in medieval Europe, this export must have meant much for the coastal economies of west and north Norway at that time.

There is little doubt that, in value terms, stockfish accounted for the overwhelming bulk of Norwegian exports towards the end of the high Middle Ages. After stockfish, other fish products, namely cod liver oil and dried herring, were of the greatest importance. Cod liver oil was essentially a by-product of the dried fish industry. Herring was caught along much of the Norwegian coast, though Båhuslen, to which large fish shoals came from the thirteenth century onwards, was by far the most important area. Also from the thirteenth century we find timber exported from Norway.

As mentioned earlier, some products of Norwegian animal husbandry were exported. There was, too, great a demand for products of the chase – whether from the sea or land (furs, walrus ivory, etc). These received very high prices though the quantities involved were small. Such products came not only from Norway proper, but also from the Norse island communities to the west.

The oldest Norwegian towns were probably established, for the most part, as royal and ecclesiastical centres. Prior to this, however, they had, at least some of them, in all likelihood been through a proto-urban phase as seasonally based trading points. As more developed urban centres they attracted additional commercial functions. Trade fuelled their further expansion. From the end of the thirteenth century royal policy was directed at giving the towns a monopolistic position with regard to local and, especially, foreign trade. They were to function as centres of exchange for goods that producers and merchants brought there, as well as for goods made in the town. Consequently, in 1299 peddling in the countryside was forbidden. From 1294 German, and probably also other foreign merchants, were obliged to sail with their wares to the towns and to sell them there. Goods intended for the northern coastal districts had to be landed at Bergen and from the beginning of the fourteenth century the same applied to the Norse colonies in the seas to the west.

These regulations formalized the position Bergen had more or less attained already as the dominant outlet for the export of dried fish and other products from north and west Norway and from the colonies in the western seas. It was trade that made the town of Bergen supreme in the Norway of the day. It became the centre of a network of smaller towns and markets to the west and north, including seasonal trading points in Iceland. For the development of such places and for that of other Norwegian towns, the commercial revolution of the high Middle Ages was of decisive importance.

As commercial centres, the towns stimulated the production of more specialized items in the country districts – items that could be exchanged for goods for which there was a demand. This applied especially to the districts that Bergen traded with, i.e. the areas to the west of Langfjella and north of Dovre, as well as the colonies to the west. Foreign goods, especially grain, were imported through Bergen, which contributed to the specialization. For, as the terms of trade between dried fish and grain favoured the former, it paid the populations of the coastal areas that could obtain grain via Bergen to lay greater emphasis on fishing, in continued combination with animal husbandry, than on arable farming, a situation that existed from the high Middle Ages onwards. Those rural areas that could deliver timber and animal products to the towns (for export or for the use of the towns themselves) also experienced a certain amount of specialization.

The towns attracted craftsmen right from the start. As time passed they became more specialized as a result of opportunities offered by an urban milieu. In Bergen, Magnus Lagbøte's urban law code of 1276, the so-called *Bylov*, together with later sources, mentions 30 or so different crafts. Written sources show that other towns also had a wide variety of crafts, and archaeological finds give concrete evidence of their activities.

To be a creative force in urban growth, craftsmen had to produce not only for the permanent residents of the town, but also for those who were passing through and for markets outside the towns. We do not have the sources to tell us the extent to which the products of urban craftsmen were a realistic alternative to those produced in the largely self-sufficient rural districts. But there is little doubt that the multifarious crafts in Bergen did find a market amongst Norwegians and foreigners visiting the town, and that their products were exchanged, to some extent, for goods brought to the town from the whole of west and north Norway and the western islands. It is also reasonable to suppose that, although the craftsmen in other towns produced mostly for their residents, they too had a number of customers in the neighbouring rural districts.

As a factor in urban growth, however, crafts fell far short of the contribution made by trade. Nor did they have the same stimulating effect on increased specialization in the rural areas.

4
Society in the high Middle Ages

Norway reached its zenith as a peasant society during the high Middle Ages. Land was the most important means of production, and rights over land were crucial determinants of economic and social status.

Given this it is understandable that the so-called *odel* right *(odelsrett)* was a central feature of the legal texts that have been preserved. The essential element in this right was the title of kin, in a legally determined order, to have first refusal on the sale of land on which the *odel* right applied. Land sold to non-kin without having been offered the legal heirs could be redeemed according to specific rules. Thus the *odel* right indicates the importance of family and kin in the old peasant society (see Chapter 2).

There is some indication that the term *odel* (Old Norse *óðal*) originally stood for landed property in general, at a time when land was, for the most part, passed by inheritance to members of the family. *Odel* right, in its strict sense, may have originated as a defence of the inheritance rights of the family at a time when the transfer of land by other means became more common, e.g. as gifts, by buying and selling, through confiscation by the Crown or the Church. According to the *Gulating* law, land first attracted the right of *odel* after it had been in a family's ownership for six generations. The *Frostating* law and the *Landslov* of 1274 reduced this to four generations or, in the case of the latter, 60 years.

The *odel* right undoubtedly satisfied the traditional interests of the peasantry. At the same time the conditions attached to it were so strict that a good deal of landed property of necessity fell outside it and so could be transferred more freely. Nor, in practice, does it appear that the right was used to any great extent to handicap important buyers.

The renting of land and social status

The legal texts devote a great deal of attention to the *renting of land*. Tenants had the right to use the land they rented on condition they fulfilled two main obligations towards the landowner: the payment of land rent or *landskyld* and the duty of *åbud*, i.e. maintaining the property they leased. The *landskyld* was an annual payment that was fixed according to the utility value of the land. Current estimates indicate that the level of rents was about one-sixth of the average gross output of the holding. The *landskyld* was usually paid in kind from the output of the holding, most commonly in grain and butter.

In that the *landskyld* was fixed in relation to output, it was a convenient measure of the value of agricultural land. The joint ownership of a holding could be arranged by giving other owners rather than the farmer himself the right to *landskyld* according to the size of their shares. Thus part-ownership became a characteristic feature of the Norwegian tenant system, both in the high Middle Ages and later. A farmer could then be a pure tenant under one or more owners, or he could own his holding completely. He could also own a part of the holding and rent one or several other parts of it. In all these cases he could receive *landskyld* from the ownership of parts of holdings worked and leased by other farmers. This kind of ownership pattern came about for the average farmer, not least through the rules of inheritance and the transfer of landed property as a consequence of marriage settlements, as well as by way of donations to the church and the payment of arrears of taxes and fines, etc.

During the latter part of the thirteenth century the renting of land had become so common that the *Landslov* fixed the *leidang* tax to the crown (see Chapter 5) according to the size of the *landskyld*. This involved valuing all the land in the country, including that cultivated by its owners. In this way each holding got a fixed *landskyld* assessment.

Åbud, the second main obligation of tenants towards landowners, consisted of duties associated with living on (Old Norse *búa á*) a holding and cultivating it. The sources from the high Middle Ages mention specifically the maintenance of the buildings, but a tenant was also obliged to keep the soil in good condition and to avoid over-exploiting the resources outside the cultivated area, principally timber.

From the end of the thirteenth century an increasing number of docu-

The *Gulating* law code	The *Frostating* law code	The Christian law sections of the *Eidsivating* and *Borgarting* law codes	The *Landslov* 1274
King Earl *Lendmann, stallare* (marshal)	King Archbishop Bishop, earl Abbot, abbess *Lendmann*	 *Lendmann*	King Archbishop, duke Bishop, earl Abbot, abbess, other prelates Baron, *stallare* (marshal), *merkesmann* (standard bearer)
Hauld *Bonde*	*Hauld* *Årbåren mann* *Rekstegn*	*Hauld*	*Hauld* *Bonde*
Freed slave of higher class Freed slave of lower class Slave (thrall)	Freed slave of higher class Freed slave of lower class Slave (thrall)	Freed slave of higher class Set free Slave (thrall)	Not mentioned

Socio-legal hierarchy of 'right' according to the medieval law codes.

ments concerning landed property have been preserved. In these there appear, mainly on Church land, some cases of tenants receiving leases for their own lifetime, with their heirs occasionally having the right to continue to hold the land. At the same time one finds time-based leases, most commonly for periods of three years. But such agreements, it would seem, were normally renewed so that a tenant had in practice a life interest in the property and enjoyed a relatively large measure of security of tenure.

The Norwegian tenant was, in the latter part of the high Middle Ages, a legally free individual. He was in no way personally beholden to the landowner. This distinguished him from the peasantry in much of the rest of Europe – the so-called *serfs* and *villeins*. Their lack of freedom consisted principally in that they were tied to the soil, had to perform labour services on land (the *demesne*) that was cultivated on the landowner's own account, and were subject to his private manorial jurisdiction. Like the Norwegian tenants, those in Sweden and Denmark were also legally free during the high Middle Ages. However, on the larger estates of the neighbouring kingdoms there was a tendency to move towards the normal European position as regards labour services and the judicial rights of the landowners.

Descent, together with rights over land, constituted the twin pillars of social status in peasant society. This status found expression in law as a man's 'right', broadly speaking the sum of his individual rights. Most notably, the laws categorized members of the peasant society according to their rights to compensation if their personal rights were violated.

The *hauld* (Old Norse *hauldr*) had the very highest status in the peasant society of the high Middle Ages. In the extant fragments of the twelfth-century provincial law codes from eastern Norway, the term *hauld* was apparently still used in its original sense to refer to a freeman or peasant in general. But in the west and north the term had by then come to be used in a stricter sense: to denote a peasant who owned his land by *odel* right, as distinct from other freemen. At the time of the *Landslov* (1274), the term *hauld* had acquired this meaning all over the country and referred to an upper, but probably not very numerous, group of *odelsbønder*.

According to the provincial law codes, the lowest layer of peasant society consisted of bondmen and bondwomen together with their descendants. Actually, the thralls or slaves were a freeman's personal property almost in the same sense as his cattle. More extensive personal rights came only when they were 'freed'.

The law codes of Magnus Lagabøte from the 1270s show no sign of bondmen or women, or of freed slaves, as socio-legal categories. There is much to suggest that the unfree, as a category, were beginning to disappear in the twelfth century and that by the next century they were little in evidence. There is much debate, however, as to how extensive the condition was in earlier times. The fact, however, that thralls figure so prominently in the provincial law codes suggest that they cannot have been insignificant. We have already noted (Chapter 2) that during the Iron Age, and for that matter earlier, agriculture was probably carried on with the help of bondmen and women.

In the twelfth century, in the west and north of Norway, there was a special category of freemen who did not have *odel* status. They were principally tenants and freeholders and maintained a position in society between the freed slave and the *hauld*. The *Gulating* law calls such people, simply, *bønder*. Bonde (Old Norse *bóndi, búandi*), of which *bønder* is the plural), is the universal Scandinavian term for peasant – the word literally means a man who lives permanently in one place. In the *Gulating* law, however, the term carried the stricter socio-legal meaning of a free peasant *under* the status of *hauld*. In the *Landslov* of 1274 the distinction between *hauld* and *bonde* applied to the whole country. Accordingly there is evidence too that by that time the tenant system was general, even in Østlandet.

The development and extent of the tenancy system

Around 1300 most peasants were tenants, in whole or in part, renting their land from clerical or secular landowners. At this time, the distribution of land in terms of *landskyld* value has been roughly estimated as follows: about 7 per cent for the Crown, about 20 per cent for the secular aristocracy, about 40 per cent for the Church, and the remaining 33 per cent or so for freeholding peasants and town burgesses. The implication of this was that a considerable part of what agricultural surplus there was went to the Crown, the Church and the secular aristocracy.

Generally speaking we find that the tenancy system as a foundation for landed estates was most widespread in the best and most centrally placed agricultural districts: around Oslo; on both sides of the Oslofjord; old settlements in Opplandene; the coastal strip from Jæren northwards; most of Trøndelag; and parts of north Norway. Settlement was at its densest here, and the output of the farms at its highest. Conditions were also favourable for creating, and effectively controlling, more compact groups of tenant farms. It was for these reasons that the Crown, ecclesiastical institutions and the aristocracy found land in these areas so attractive. The system of landed estates was especially dominant in the rural districts lying closest to the important towns.

The opposite situation was to be found in remoter districts such as Telemark, Agder, the eastern valleys up towards Langfjella, the forest districts in the southeast of Norway, along the Swedish border, and certain fjord and mountain areas of Vestlandet. Here the yield of the farms was everywhere lower than in the typical landed estate areas.

One of the basic problems of research into medieval Norway is how this pattern of landownership came about. The tenancy system existed as far back as it is possible to go with the help of written records, but before 1300 or thereabouts it is impossible to measure just how widespread it was, relative to the freeholder system. There have been two main schools of thought on this issue. An older one suggests that the tenancy system was well developed and probably embraced the majority of the country's farmers long before the high Middle Ages. A more recent view suggests that the shift from freeholder to tenant status took place, for the majority of farmers, only in the last two or three centuries before 1300.

There is little evidence to support either hypothesis. Perhaps the truth lies somewhere in between. An early form of the tenancy system, characterized by the creation of subordinate and dependent holdings, may have developed with the growth of population and agricultural settlements from the seventh century onward – perhaps earlier. There are indications that from the Viking Age, at the latest, collections of dependent holdings were to be found in the coastal districts of western Norway around the seats of landed proprietors. Later the system of tenant farmers spread more widely. What was said earlier about the development of the meaning of the term *hauld* can be taken as supporting the notion that initially the renting of land was more common in the west and north of the country than in Østlandet. The colonisation of new land led to more and more tenants under public or private landowners. The larger landowners could in a time of rising population and high land rents find it more profitable to rent out their lands than to farm them on their own account. This, together with the clearing of land, could be the main reason for the disappearance of the unfree. Economically it paid to put freed slaves on rental land rather than to work it with the help of slaves. The tenant system expanded only partly at the expense of the freeholder farmers. Thus it is important to note that the amazing growth of land owned by the Church – from none at all at the beginning of the missionary period – was to a very considerable extent the result of donations from kings and chieftains and not from freeholders.

This picture of the growth of the tenantry raises doubts about the time-honoured view that the starting point of Norwegian social history was a society of freeholding peasants all with holdings of more or less equal size. A question mark has already been put against this opinion in the course of our discussion of Iron Age society (Chapter 2).

It is usually reckoned that the growth of the tenant system contributed to falling living standards and social degradation for the majority of the country's peasants. The matter is hardly so simple. The freed slaves who were put onto rented land clearly advanced socially. Those who, towards the end of the high Middle Ages, wanted to work the best land in the country were obliged to do so, for the most part, as tenants of the large landowners in the best agricultural areas. The better-off tenants could, to some extent, become really large farmers, who themselves owned other land for rent. Some tenant farmers undoubtedly produced a greater surplus than many freeholders on smaller and poorer holdings. The economic and social differences in the peasant society of the time probably, then, owed as much to the size and quality of the holding as to whether one enjoyed the status of freeholder or tenant. Besides, the widespread system of part-ownership blurred the distinction between freeholders and tenants.

Urban society

Urban society was different from peasant society. The towns had central place functions in relation to their hinterlands in the form of: royal and ecclesiastical administrative activity; economic specialization in regard to trade, crafts and services; as well as religious and other cultural activities. These activities were the province of groups of specialists and it was these specialists who gave urban society its distinctive character.

As royal and ecclesiastical centres, the towns were home to a considerable number of royal officials, other members of the royal *hird* and churchmen. The top stratum of the other townsmen were the so-called *husfaste menn* (men "firmly" attached to houses), who were defined in Magnus Lagabøte's *Bylov* of 1276 as people who owned or rented, for at least six months, at least one quarter of an urban tenement or *gard*. Only such men bore the full obligations and enjoyed the full rights associated with the management of the town. Through their control of property and land they were in an especially favourable position to take part in long-distance trade and to act as commercial middlemen.

Craftsmen and small retailers formed the core of a *middle group* in urban society. Attempts at establishing trade guilds of artisans and others in Bergen were hampered by a royal ban of 1293/94 and it seems that the European guild organization was never firmly rooted amongst Norwegian urban craft workers during the Middle Ages.

In order to function, the town required a large group of *workers* and *servants*. The records in Bergen speak of porters and female house servants. It is also clear that the towns had a poverty problem towards the end of the high Middle Ages. In order to remedy it, the towns organized, as had the rural districts, a system of support for paupers: the poor were to be moved round from house to house. Hospitals for the poor were also founded from the second part of the thirteenth century onwards. These were run by the Church, partly in cooperation with the Crown.

Foreigners in great numbers came to the long-distance trade centre of Bergen no later than the end of the twelfth century. Amongst these foreigners, English and Germans predominated. Such foreign 'guests' also began to appear annually during the sailing season in the coastal towns to the south of Bergen. From the end of the 1250s, Hanseatic and probably also other foreign merchants began to settle permanently in Bergen as 'winter-sitters'. German and other foreign craftsmen followed. Foreigners also began to settle in other Norwegian coastal towns, especially in Oslo and Tønsberg.

Originally foreigners had the same legal position in Norwegian towns as the native-born. From 1278 special guest rights for visiting Germans were developed, which freed them from certain official obligations, whereas permanent foreign residents were never officially freed from such obligations in medieval times. Gradually the monarchy tried to limit the economic activities of foreigners in the towns. In Bergen, from the end of the thirteenth century, the Germans combined in order to protect and extend their rights and began in that way to cut themselves off from the rest of the urban society. Foreigners were far fewer in number in other Norwegian towns and, therefore, easier to assimilate.

'Town air makes free', it was said in the Europe of the twelfth century. By settling permanently in a town, people from the rural districts could rid themselves of their unfree status. Because slavery had virtually disappeared from Norway in the course of the twelfth century and the rest of the peasantry were legally free, Norwegian towns could not have the same liberating impact. Nevertheless, the town law for Trondheim in the twelfth century states that all should have equal rights in the town, namely those enjoyed by the *hauld* group. This shows that urban society in Norway also worked towards equality before the law.

The social position of women in the high Middle Ages

About half the population in town and country during the high Middle Ages, as in later years, were women. Also there were large numbers of children, but Norwegian sources tell us little about them and little research has been done into their conditions.

Women most frequently appear in the sources when, through either inheritance or marriage, they attained an economic and social position of significance. For medieval women, access to property came primarily via family connections.

According to the Norwegian provincial laws, a daughter had the right to inherit from her father only if she had neither brothers nor grandfather. That sons inherited before daughters was an ancient feature of Germanic law. The *Landslov* (1274) gave inheritance rights to both sons and daughters, though the former were to get twice the amount of the latter; this later came to be called the 'brother's share'. More distant female relatives of the deceased were also placed after the males with the same kinship position.

If we look at the rules regarding marriage, we find less of a difference between the provincial law codes and the later *Landslov*. Marriage was the foundation of a child's right to inherit, in that children born within marriage took precedence over those born outside it. If a woman came from a family of means, then she got a dowry. The husband-to-be was obliged to pledge a more or less corresponding sum in return. Under the provincial laws, the dowry gave a daughter a share in her father's assets. The size of the dowry then determined whether her later half-share (relative to her brothers) in whatever her father left was to her advantage, since her dowry under the *Landslov* was to be reckoned as part of her share of the inheritance.

The legal texts of the high Middle Ages still reflected the fact that, previously, marriage had been very much an agreement between two extended families or lineages. The economic interests of the lineage were protected via a special financial settlement, according to which a woman's share of a family's assets consisted of her dowry and any

Woman and child in the kitchen area of a house on the Wharf (Bryggen) in Bergen during the high Middle Ages. This reconstruction is to be found in the Bryggen Museum. It is based on clues left by women and children and discovered by archaeologists after a fire in 1955 had destroyed a part of the Wharf. The kitchens were the women's domain in the complex of buildings lining the Wharf in the high Middle Ages. Here they prepared food and produced textiles whilst the children played around them.

other personal inheritance, whilst a man's share was to consist of what he possessed after whatever he had given to match his wife's dowry had been taken into account. The sum pledged by the husband occupied an intermediate position. It was returned to the husband if he outlived his wife, but served as a widow's pension if she outlived him. When a marriage partner died, his or her personal estate was inherited by the children of the marriage. Where there were no children, it returned to the deceased's family. It was, in other words, the extended families of both lineages and not the surviving marriage partners that inherited from the deceased.

The Church went some way towards accepting that marriage was an agreement between two families, though, according to its teaching, marriage was primarily a covenant between two individuals. Down through the high Middle Ages, marriage in Norway, as in other European countries, came more and more under the influence of the Church. It became a sacrament, monogamous and virtually unbreakable. Legal access to divorce, which had been possible earlier, was ended during the second half of the twelfth century. From the thirteenth century the Church refused to recognize betrothal as an acceptable entrée into marriage. Not until the banns had been read in church and the nuptials celebrated was the marriage legitimate, and only then did any children get full rights of inheritance. In addition, married couples could have their marriage consecrated in church, but this was not obligatory in Norway until after the Lutheran reformation.

Once she had come of age, an unmarried woman could control her own property, but according to law the married woman handed over control to her husband, who also was to represent her in any legal disputes that might occur over it. Only as a widow did she become more independent as regards economic agreements and legal disputes. In reality, of course, a married woman could have considerable influence on the economic side of her marriage simply through her personal qualities.

The joint handling of the marital economy was strengthened as the Middle Ages wore on through increased access to joint ownership or *félag* in property matters. According to the *Landslov*, the husband could demand that all his wife owned should be held in common. On the death of one or other marriage partner, his or her estate should be shared between the surviving partner and the deceased's heirs, so that the former got a share of what the couple had produced jointly. *Félag*, in other words, broke away from the principle that married couples could not inherit from each other. This is one of several examples indicating that the individual and the immediate family were liberated, to some extent, from the control of the lineage or extended family during the high Middle Ages. The changes brought about by the Church as regards marriage worked in the same direction, though they also led to a woman being more closely tied to, and placed under, her husband than had been the case previously.

In peasant society a woman played an important and independent role alongside her husband in their joint economic activities. Traditionally a line was drawn at the doorstep. Everything inside was woman's work; everything outside – in the fields and meadows, in the woods, together with the hunting and fishing – was a man's. Of course, a woman too must step outside at harvest time, and for haymaking and the gathering of fodder for the animals. And women's particular responsibility for the dairy took them to areas of grazing and the shielings often associated with them. It was, nevertheless, indoors that they had their domain: food preparation, washing, spinning and weaving, and the care of children. The married woman was responsible for the management of the home. In larger households she would have other women with her and could leave the heavy work to the servant girls (in earlier times, to the female slaves). But in the Middle Ages there were many smallholdings where servants were conspicuous by their absence and husband and wife had to carry the burden themselves in a state of mutual dependence. In the coastal fisher–farmer districts, the wife would often be the farmer while the husband was taking part in the seasonal fishing.

Inheritance and marital law was the same in town and country. But whereas married women in the countryside could make only very limited economic arrangements on their own account, the *Bylov* of 1276 gave all women in the towns the right to make their own agreements. One finds several examples of women house owners in the towns. Within the middle layer of urban society there is mention in the sources of specifically female occupations such as bath attendants, baking women, beer sellers and small traders generally. That the *Bylov* gave urban women greater economic independence was probably not least in recognition of the economic role played by women in the middle and upper strata of urban society. Married women in the countryside took their share of agricultural work but did not get the same legal recognition.

Lower down the social scale, the existence of a guild of domestic female servants in Bergen (forbidden in 1293/94) indicates both the desire and the ability of the town's servant women to organize themselves. Urban society also led to organized prostitution. This seems to have been especially widespread in Bergen because of the massive influx of strangers during the shipping season. It increased during the late Middle Ages through the development of celibacy-bound communities of male Germans (wives were not allowed) at the Hanseatic settlement or *Kontor* and among the craftsmen.

Aristocracy and clergy

A secular aristocracy distinguished itself more clearly from the rest of the population in the course of the Middle Ages. From the eleventh century the king's *hird* developed into more than just an ordinary retinue that combined the tasks of household and personal bodyguard with those of the core of the king's military force. The *hird* came, to an increasing extent, to include magnates and freemen who resided throughout the country. Gradually these people took on duties and came to share in an organizational structure that embraced all the leading men. As a consequence of this process, *hird* membership became the criterion of secular aristocratic status.

The *lendmenn* (Chapter 2) formed the top layer of this aristocracy. Under them ranged the lords-in-waiting or *skutilsveiner* (together with the *lendmenn,* the officers of the *hird),* ordinary 'hirdmen', constables or 'guests' and 'candlebearers' (equivalent to page boys at foreign courts).

The liegemen of the *hird* enjoyed the king's special protection and got economic recompense for the special fealty and service they accorded him. The top men were paid with royal land and/or administrative posts. In 1277, or shortly before, the liegemen were exempted, together with three (for lower ranks two) of their men, from the *leidang* tax, as well as other obligations associated with the naval levy. Owing to a change in the *leidang* tax, land rather than individuals was taxed. Thus a practice developed whereby the liegemen ceased to pay tax on land belonging to their main residence. As a result of this tax exemption, the liegemen stood out as a privileged class. But the distinction between them and the rest of society was not a sharp one. The *hird* was continually being recruited from both peasant and urban society. The king could also promote efficient and reliable men from outside the leading families to the highest positions and the most important posts.

The external aristocratic character of the *hird* increased from the end of the high Middle Ages, with coats of arms on shields and the acquisition of seals and foreign titles. It was King Magnus Lagabøte who decided that the *lendmenn* should henceforth be called *barons*, as their counterparts in England were then titled, and his lords-in-waiting *knights*. Both were granted the right to use the title of *herre* (corresponding to Lord and Sir). From the time of Haakon 5, the Latin title *armiger* (man-at-arms) and its Nordic equivalent were used for the ordinary hirdman. The title of *lendmann* or baron went out of use when, in 1308, the king gave up creating new ones. In the following decades, 'guests' and 'candlebearers' disappeared. The result was that the aristocracy proper came to consist of knights and men-at-arms, as in Europe generally. From the mid-thirteenth century, and under European influence, a distinctive court culture was consciously fostered. Thus the old martial virtues were augmented by courtly manners and elegant appearance. This helped attach the aristocracy to the service of the crown.

The similarities between the Norwegian *hird* aristocracy and the European feudal nobility went beyond mere appearances. The liegemen were in reality vassals of the king. They owed him their allegiance and service, both military and administrative, in return for his protection and economic rewards that corresponded in principle to the feudal fief: the income from royal land and/or a share of other royal revenues. But such incomes were modest by European standards and did not carry with them regal rights, such as the private administration of justice. Elsewhere in Europe such rights went some way to turning an aristocratic estate into a state within the state. The bonds of personal dependence, which penetrated European feudal society to its lower levels, applied in Norway only to its top echelons, i.e. in the relationship between the king and his liegemen. Feudal tendencies in the Norwegian society of the high Middle Ages were, therefore, limited, viewed from a traditional west European standpoint.

In the early 1300s the Norwegian *hird* aristocracy comprised hardly more than 300 men of the status of hirdman or man-at-arms and above. The number of *lendmenn* or barons of the highest rank was rarely more than 15 in total in the thirteenth century, and had been reduced to around 10 in 1308. The private means of this aristocracy were not great enough for its numbers to exercise power in society independently of the Crown, as was, to some extent, the case in the neighbouring kingdoms and particularly in Denmark. As noted earlier, the Norwegian aristocracy received tax relief only on their main residence, whilst the Danish and Swedish received it on their tenanted land and, because there the tax burden was heavier, the relief was that much greater. The Norwegian aristocracy were, then, very dependent on the comparatively modest income received from royal service. Both because of that and because their land was widely spread, the leading aristocrats were keen to build up a comparatively strong national administration. This goes a long way towards explaining why relations between the Crown and the secular aristocracy in Norway, after the civil wars ended, were remarkably harmonious, seen from a European perspective.

Far more numerous than the aristocracy was that other privileged group at the top of medieval society: the clergy. Numbering well over 2,000 towards the end of the high Middle Ages, the clergy were more clearly different from the rest of the population than were the aristocracy, partly because of their spiritual duties and partly because of deliberate efforts on the part of the Church to separate them from the rest of society. Their separation was enhanced by the separate ecclesiastical jurisdiction enjoyed by the clergy and celibacy (both of these developed gradually in the course of the high Middle Ages), the tonsure (shaved crown), and special attire. From the second half of the twelfth century, at the latest, the clergy were freed from military and economic *leidang* obligations. Later, tax exemption was also extended to non-clerical retainers of the archbishop and, in 1277, the entire episcopacy's retainers were freed from taxes in line with the royal liegemen, amounting to 100 for the archbishop and 40 each for the rest of the bishops.

Although the clergy as a whole set themselves off from society, there were, nevertheless, considerable differences of status and income amongst them. At the top we find a comparatively small number of prelates: the archbishop, bishops, abbots, abbesses, deans of the royal chapel, canons of the cathedrals and the royal chapel. These numbered no more than 100 or so persons, but the culture and the learned tradition of the Church had, on the other hand, formed them into a more or less homogeneous elite. The vast majority of the clergy were less well educated and enjoyed a far more modest economic and social position. Here too there were considerable internal differences.

A comparatively weak aristocracy

The ecclesiastical and lay aristocracy may have reached around 3,000 in total by the early 1300s, less than 1 per cent of the estimated population (Chapter 3). Of these but a tiny minority stood out as having a distinct aristocratic status: a good 100 prelates and perhaps three times that number of royal liegemen with the rank of hirdman or man-at-arms or above. Amongst this second category we can reckon on an upper crust drawn from no more than 10–15 families. Together with a corresponding number of prelates and leading officials of the royal central administration, with the bishops at the top, they formed the absolute peak of society, essentially on account of their office. In other words, the clerical and lay elite formed, in numerical terms, a very modest group.

It is true that this group did command a considerable amount of the country's economic resources. These resources were, however, limited in a country so short of good land as Norway. The ecclesiastical and lay aristocracy did not, therefore, have the economic resources to control society to make up for their small numbers.

Compared with the situation in the neighbouring kingdoms and in Europe generally, Norwegian society in the high Middle Ages was not particularly aristocratic in nature. The Norwegian historian Ernst Sars once put forward the hypothesis that social conditions in Norway under the monarchs of the Sverre family were more 'democratic' than in the neighbouring kingdoms and that no proper aristocracy existed. There is a kernel of truth in this. The clergy and the *hird* set themselves above the population generally in terms of status and economic resources. But the boundary between these groups and the rest of society was, as noted already, not fixed and the top aristocratic layer amongst them was not powerful enough either to dominate society at home or to make its presence felt abroad to the same extent as in many other countries.

This means that, although Norwegian society was more strictly controlled by Church and Crown in the course of the high Middle Ages

(Chapter 5), it was much less under aristocratic influence than was usual in contemporary Europe. And Sars was probably right to suggest that this has affected the further development of Norwegian society down to our own times.

5
A society regulated by the monarchy and the Church

In 1152 or 1153, Cardinal Nicolaus Brekespear came to Norway as papal legate to establish a separate archiepiscopal see in Nidaros. Originally the Norwegian Church had come under the Archbishop of Hamburg–Bremen and then, since 1102–3, under the Danish Archbishop of Lund. Now it was to be the centre of a new province of the Church with 11 bishoprics: 5 in Norway (Nidaros, Bergen, Oslo, Stavanger, Hamar) and 6 in the Norse islands in the seas to the west (Greenland, Skálholt and Hólar in Iceland, the Faeroes, the Orkneys together with Shetland, and the Isle of Man together with the Hebrides). The new arrangement had its origins in a papal policy aimed at bringing the smaller provinces on the periphery of Europe into a more directly subordinate relationship with Rome.

Some 10 years later, in 1163 or 1164, Scandinavia's first royal coronation took place in Bergen. Through this the Church gave divine sanction to Magnus Erlingsson's (1161–84) royal position, the primary duty of which was to uphold the law as a just ruler (*rex iustus*). This Augustinian–Gregorian ideology, turning kingship into a divine office, has left its mark on official documents of Magnus' reign.

The first two national assemblies in Norwegian history were called in order to set the seal on the great events of 1152/53 and 1163/64. Both appear to have been made up of bishops, royal liegemen and representatives of the peasantry, and both gave their approval to ecclesiastical reforms and legal enactments covering the kingdom as a whole. The laws were sent to the various *lagting* with advice as to their final enactment. A law determining the right of succession, which in all probability came out of the meeting of 1163/64, laid down that a national assembly should choose the king. Peasant representatives were to make the formal decision, with the bishops as influential advisers.

The principle of one king for the whole of Norway was established by this law of succession. The intention behind it was to end the conflicts surrounding the throne by removing the legal foundation for joint rulership and rival claims to the throne, which had led to civil war. The eldest legitimate son of a deceased king should have the first right to the Crown, and after him, other legitimate sons, subject to their being qualified in accordance with the ecclesiastical *rex iustus* ideology.

Through this royal–ecclesiastical cooperation a society organised nationally by the monarchy and the Church came one step nearer. The Church took the initiative with the new archbishopric at the head of a country-wide system of dioceses and local congregations. The monarchy followed, under the ideological and organizational influence of the Church.

Thus the Norwegian Church took the first decisive step away from its heavy dependence on the monarchy and the peasantry, towards a position marked out by the Gregorian papacy. The goal was to free the Church from secular influence and place it under the leadership of the papacy. The monarchy in 1152/53, and later under Magnus Erlingsson, made concessions in three areas that were seen to be especially important. First, the Church should have the decisive say in the election of bishops and the appointment of priests. Second, it should have financial control of the churches and of their property. Third, it should have jurisdiction over its own personnel and in matters of particular concern to the Church. It was, however, only with time and after some conflict that the Church gained ground more permanently in these three areas.

The monarchy and the Church under the Sverre family

The civil wars ended with victory for the Sverre family. Sverre Sigurdsson had to win his kingdom from the alliance between Magnus Erlingsson and the Church. This stopped neither him nor his successors from further developing the national organization of the monarchy that had started to take shape during his predecessor's reign. However, under their royal authority there was no room for such a politically independent Church as had existed in the days of Magnus Erlingsson.

Ideologically this emerged when the Sverre family tied their monarchy directly to the grace of God, without admitting the Church to a

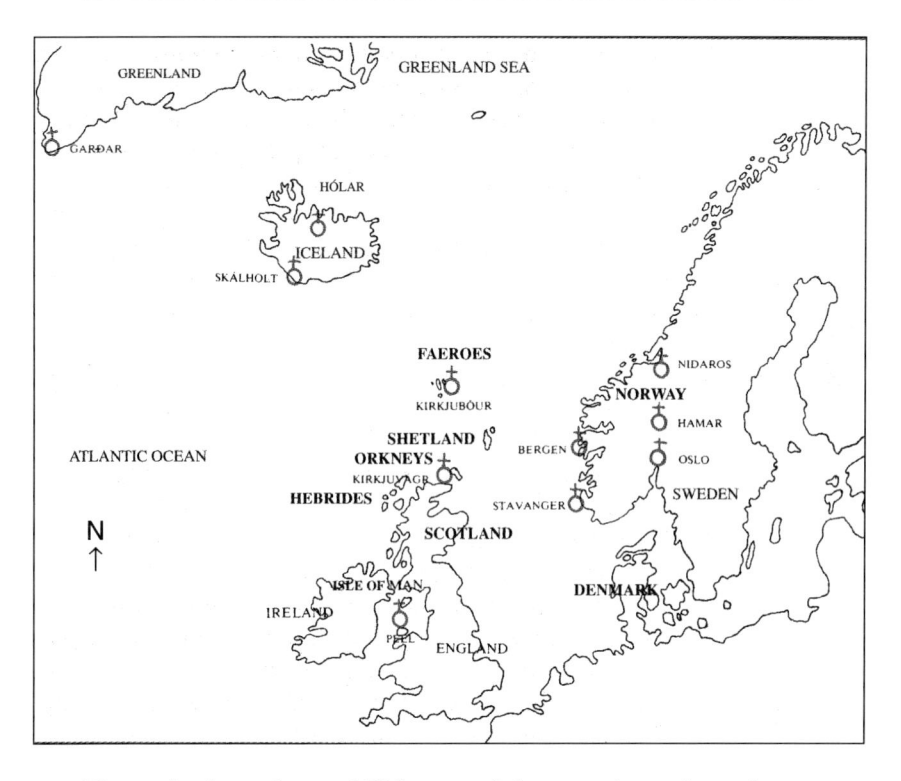

The archepiscopal see of Nidaros and the ten other episcopal sees that were incorporated into the Norwegian church province in 1152/53.

decisive intermediate position. Here the king's right of inheritance played a central role. From 1260 new laws governing the succession to the throne recognized a virtually automatic right of inheritance, with the king being 'chosen by God' and not by man. In *The King's Mirror* (a Norwegian work dating from the 1250s and setting out current political ideology), the king appears as God's true representative on earth, not expressly responsible to any human authority; nor is he in Magnus Lagabøte's great national law texts and the royal decrees of later times, which have been coloured by *The King's Mirror*.

King Sverre refused to accept significant features of the Church's reforms from 1152/53 and the other benefits the Church had secured during Magnus Erlingsson's reign. He tried to return to the previous situation and demanded that the Church place itself under royal leadership. This led the Church to give its political and military support to his opponents. Sverre was excommunicated and his kingdom threatened with a papal interdict (the cessation of services provided by the Church). This, the most bitter conflict between the monarchy and the Church in medieval Norway, was not settled until after Sverre's death in 1202.

Sverre's grandson, the illegitimate Haakon Haakonsson (1217–63), was not the ideal candidate for the throne from the ecclesiastical point of view. But the Church's leaders were realistic enough to support him when, after a time, it became clear that through him peace and a united kingdom were most likely to be realized. Early in Haakon's reign most of the country's leading lay figures were organised into one royal *hird*. With that the civil wars faded away in the 1220s. At last the country was permanently united under the monarchy of the Sverre family.

This monarchy took the political lead in its relations with the Church. At the same time it gradually acknowledged a considerable degree of ecclesiastical autonomy. Haakon's son and successor, Magnus Lagabøte (1263–80), in the Tønsberg Concordat of 1277 made greater legal and economic concessions to the Church than it had ever received previously. Its freedom in relation to secular society was expressly recognized as regards most of the matters in dispute.

After Magnus' death the baronial government that ruled on behalf of the young Eirik Magnusson (1280–99) refused to respect completely all the rights obtained by the Church. This led to a bitter, albeit brief, conflict at the beginning of the 1280s. By the time that the relations between the monarchy and the Church had gradually returned to normal, the Church was able to enjoy a comparatively high degree of autonomy over its internal affairs, even if there was continued conflict over the legal limits of this autonomy throughout the rest of the high Middle Ages.

Increased political activity abroad

With the ending of the civil wars the now consolidated kingdom had both more energy and more resources to devote to foreign policy. Continuing a tradition going back to the Viking Age (Chapters 1–2) this policy was partly oriented towards the west. It was strengthened through the establishment of the separate Norwegian Church province in 1152/53 and through the especially important trading links with the British Isles.

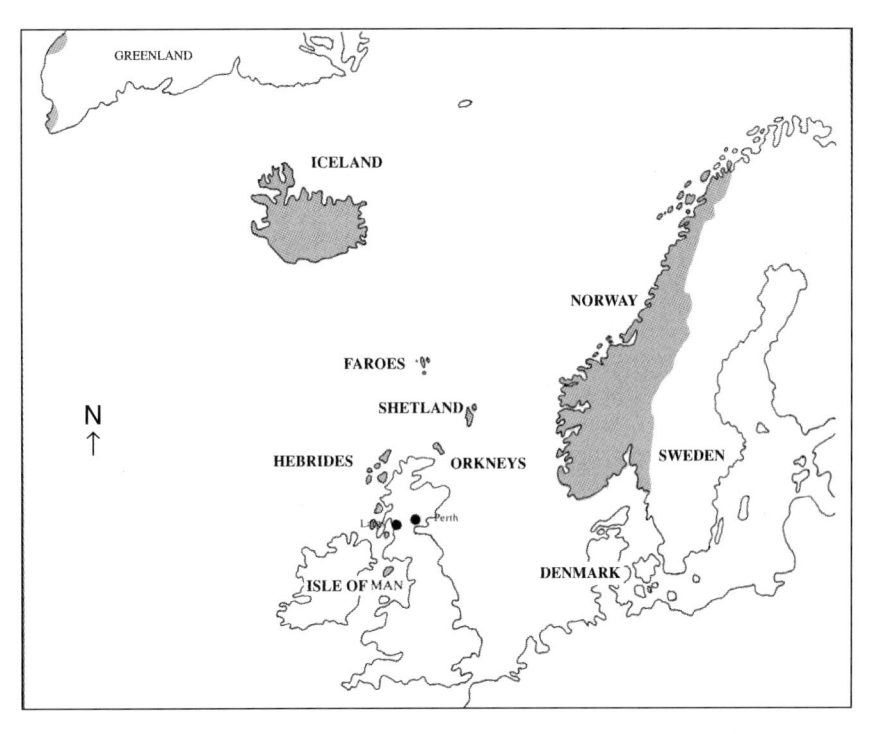

In the high Middle Ages, Norway's territorial power peaked in 1265, the year before the Hebrides and the Isle of Man were ceded to Scotland at the Peace of Perth.

The westward orientation reached its peak in the thirteenth century in the so-called 'Norwegian dominion'. In the early 1260s the Greenlanders and Icelanders placed themselves under the Norwegian Crown. Further south, the islands stretching from the Faeroes to the Hebrides and the Isle of Man had periodically paid tribute to the Norwegian king from the Viking Age onwards but, with the inconclusive Scottish campaign that ended Haakon Haakonsson's reign in 1263, the Hebrides and Man were in 1266 ceded to the Scottish king. However, further north, Norwegian rule continued over the Orkneys, Shetland and the Faeroes. In 1468/69 the Orkneys and Shetland were pledged to the king of Scotland, but the remaining 'tributary lands' in the seas to the west formally belonged to the kingdom of Norway for the rest of the Middle Ages.

In the course of the second half of the twelfth century merchants from the German Hanseatic towns became responsible for the major part of Norway's growing overseas trade. At the same time the organizational links between the regional groups of German towns increased. Of particular importance for Norwegian trade was the so-called league of Wendish towns headed by Lübeck, the core group in the increasing cooperation between Hanseatic towns.

After the Norwegian authorities had in 1282 sought, for the first time, to limit the Germans' economic activities in Bergen, the Wendish League responded with a blockade of German trade with Norway in 1284–85. The Hanseatic rights to trade under the same conditions as Norwegians were restored, but only in Bergen and the towns to the south of it. In 1294 a comprehensive royal charter laid down what the Germans were to regard as their basic rights throughout the rest of the Middle Ages: free trade and legal security in the towns mentioned, together with exemption from certain public duties for visiting German 'guests' in the sailing season (see Chapter 3).

These concessions were partly withdrawn during the reign of Haakon 5 Magnusson (1299–1319). An economic policy limiting the Hanseatic privileges was now pursued more consistently. Retail trade in Norwegian towns was to be reserved for Norwegians and restrictions were imposed on the foreigners' middleman and overseas trade too; for one thing customs dues were placed on their exports. This national trade policy continued for a couple of decades into Magnus Eriksson's reign (1319–55). At times it led to strained relations between the king and the Hanseatic towns and between Norwegians and Germans in Bergen. It did not, however, prevent the Hanseatic merchants from strengthening their grip on Norway's foreign trade.

From the middle of the thirteenth century, relations with the German ports became tied up with a more active inter-Scandinavian policy. This drew Norwegian overseas interests to the south and east at the expense of the traditional westerly orientation.

In Denmark, internal conflict weakened royal power after the death of Valdemar 2 in 1241. Economically and strategically the districts along the Kattegat and Øresund became of greater importance, because of the herring fisheries off Båhuslen, the international Skania fair and the increase in shipping between the North Sea and the Baltic. From the 1250s the Norwegian government tried to turn this situation to its advantage. It opened up contacts with Danish circles opposed to the ruling line of the family of Valdemar 2 and did not flinch from taking military action against Danish territory. It appears that the immediate aim was to annex Danish Halland, though the more distant Skania may also have been an attractive prospect.

This active Scandinavian policy continued down to the first half of the reign of Haakon 5, with a break under the peace-loving Magnus Lagabøte. As part of an attempt at creating an alliance between Norway and Sweden against Denmark, Haakon 5 betrothed Ingebjørg, his only legitimate daughter, to Erik, the Swedish duke and king's son.

Haakon's Scandinavian plans failed. He was out-manœuvred by Duke Erik, who broke with his brother, King Birger, and on his own account took control of the areas around the point at which the three Scandinavian kingdoms met, near the mouth of the Göta River. Erik was imprisoned by his brother and died in captivity in 1317, but his son by Ingebjørg – Magnus – was next in line for the throne of Norway.

In the course of the reign of Haakon 5 it became clear that the economic and military resources of Norway were not sufficient to enforce the intentions of the government's Scandinavian policy. The Norwegian *leidang*, or naval levy, which had been used against Halland in the 1250s and which was still able to operate comparatively freely in Danish territorial waters during the first half of the 1290s, was unable, after the turn of the century, to do much in a warfare that was based more and more upon strong castles and professional military personnel. In the long run, Norway, short of good land and sparsely populated, was no match for its more resource-rich neighbours.

This would explain the dawning isolationism that is noticeable in Norwegian government circles towards the end of Haakon 5's reign. The king and his advisers clearly felt the need to withdraw from a game in which they were being outplayed by stronger Scandinavian allies and opponents. But it was too late. Purely dynastic circumstances led Norway into a personal union with Sweden after Haakon's death in 1319: Magnus Eriksson inherited the Norwegian throne and was elected to that of Sweden. This was the beginning of the Scandinavian unions of the late Middle Ages (Chapter 7).

Government administration in the high Middle Ages

Before the onset of the Scandinavian unions the organizational aspects of Norway's unification had reached their medieval limits. A royal

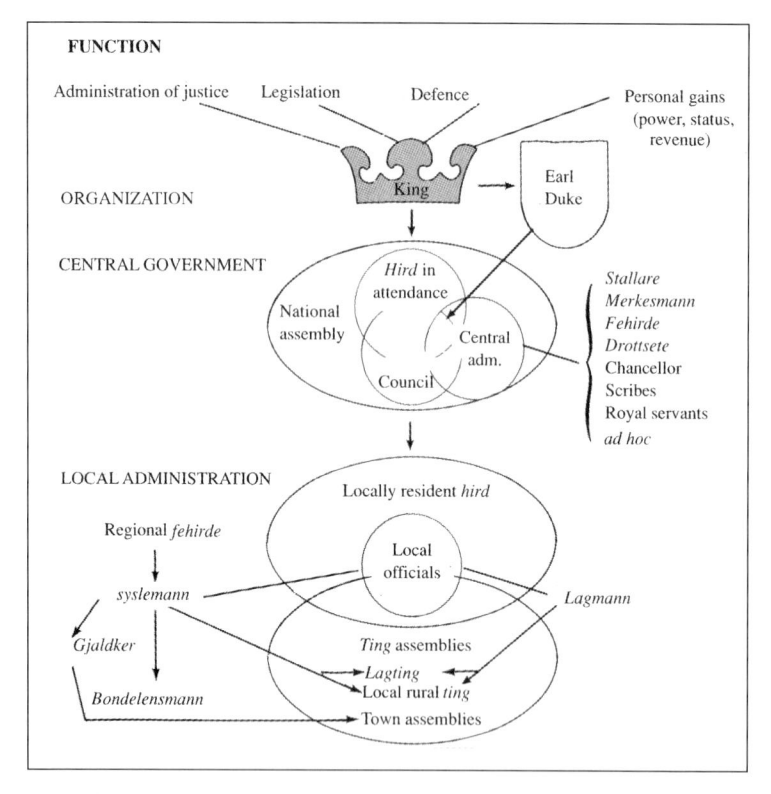

```
FUNCTION
  Administration of justice   Legislation    Defence            Personal gains
                                                                (power, status,
                                                                 revenue)
                                                   Earl
  ORGANIZATION            King                     Duke

  CENTRAL GOVERNMENT         Hird in
                             attendance             Stallare
                   National                         Merkesmann
                   assembly              Central    Fehirde
                                         adm.       Drottsete
                             Council                Chancellor
                                                    Scribes
                                                    Royal servants
                                                    ad hoc

  LOCAL ADMINISTRATION    Locally resident hird

  Regional fehirde
                             Local
     syslemann              officials              Lagmann

  Gjaldker                 Ting assemblies
                           Lagting
  Bondelensmann            Local rural ting
                           Town assemblies
```

A model of the royal government apparatus which held the kingdom together at the beginning of the fourteenth century. At the top are the functions carried out under this system of government in the interest of both society as a whole and the functionaries themselves.

administration was developed that, for the first time, made Norway into what we may call a *state*. This word was still not in use, but 'the Norwegian King's Realm', which appears in the *Landslov* (1274) and subsequent legislation, expresses much of the same thing: one people, one territory and an independent political organization covering the country as a whole. The Norwegian development was clearly influenced by the political systems of monarchies that had taken shape elsewhere in Europe in the period from about 1150 to 1300 and it paralleled a corresponding process in the realms of Norway's neighbours. At the same time, the Church, through its national organization and country-wide functions, helped to advance a closer Norwegian commonality.

By the early 1300s the royal apparatus of government consisted of a local and a regional organization that covered the entire country more or less systematically. Some 50 or so royal officials or *syslemenn* (comparable to the English sheriffs) represented the king locally in fiscal, judicial and military matters within fixed administrative districts. The country was divided into 10 districts, each with its own lawman *(lagmann)* who represented the king as a judge. He administered the law courts of his district, which, in most cases, would have its own annual *lagting* (Chapter 2). A regional treasurer *(fehirde)* resided in the royal estate in the four main towns of Bergen, Trondheim, Oslo and Tønsberg. He was to receive the king's revenue for the areas he was responsible for and make payments on his behalf. The king also had his own urban administrator in the four towns – the *gjaldker* – who had in part the same functions as the local *syslemann,* yet was subordinate to him.

The *central administration of government* lay in the king's hands and those of his inner circle. The attendant part of the *hird* contained in embryo the country's first central administration; here the leading officers (the marshal or *stallare*, the standard bearer or *merkesmann*, the treasurer or *fehirde*, and the grand seneschal or *drottsete*) were also entrusted with functions of state. From the middle of the thirteenth century, the chancellor emerges as the most important of the central administrators. He was responsible for issuing royal letters and documents, and keeping accounts and records. He led a small staff of royal clerks.

The use of writing facilitated regular contact with the different levels of the national administration and gave the central government a means of controlling distant areas. This reduced the necessity for the king to be present personally in the different parts of the country. The *Landslov* established the principle that more important economic transactions should be attested in writing, and in the fourteenth century the use of writing gained ground in private matters.

The organization of the royal *hird* helped to bind together the local and central administrations. The royal officials were the king's liegemen and all other members of the *hird*, wherever they happened to be, were obliged to support the officials in their activities.

The *national assemblies* which were called together from 1152/53 onwards, were at their most frequent during the reigns of Haakon Haakonsson and Magnus Lagabøte. It was clearly the intention that such assemblies should, to the greatest extent possible, take over the local and regional assemblies' role of sanctioning laws, their involvement in the succession to the throne, as well as other national political matters. The summoning of representatives of the peasantry to a number of important national assemblies can be seen as a move in the direction of a national *ting*. The nature of its work also gave the Church an interest in such mixed lay and clerical assemblies, functioning as national synods.

The Norwegian national assemblies were in line with the larger political assemblies convoked in the neighbouring kingdoms, the *danehoff* in Denmark and the *herredager* and corresponding assemblies of prelates and magnates in Sweden. Elsewhere in Europe the parallel was with the royal assemblies, corresponding assemblies of prelates and magnates that were originally feudal councils and came increasingly to be called 'parliaments', a term occurring also in Denmark and Norway. In the late Middle Ages these developed on the continent into assemblies of estates, and in England into a unique institution, the English parliament.

Such a development did not take place in Norway. National assemblies were difficult to handle in such a far-flung and topographically fractured country as Norway, and in Eirik and Haakon 5 Magnussons' time it appeared that both the monarchy and the Church could, for the most part, manage without them. In their place the royal council, later the 'council of the realm' (*riksråd*), was brought in as the advisory and consenting body at the national level. This was a more restricted body of royal officials, magnates and bishops than were the national assemblies. Similar developments in Denmark and Sweden in the course of the fourteenth century ensured that an aristocratic national *riksråd* became the sole true central decision-making body at the king's side (Chapter 7).

With the spread of the government's administrative apparatus over the whole country, it became possible to rule it from a small number of urban centres. In the thirteenth century, Bergen clearly became the most important of the country's royal residences. Most of the national assemblies met in Bergen and here one got the first indication of a Norwegian central administration attached to the royal castle. The town deserves, therefore, to be called the country's first real capital. From the reign of Haakon 5, Oslo became a politico-administrative centre of equal status with Bergen, for that part of the country south of the Dovre mountains and east of the Langfjella, whilst Bergen retained its position for the rest of the country together with the colonies to the west.

The rest of the kingdom's towns became seats of local and regional administration and thus gained far greater importance than their modest number and populations would in themselves indicate. The administrative central place function of the towns was strengthened considerably by the fact that they provided the same service for the Church administration.

The ecclesiastical administration

From the point of view of the Church, a nationwide royal administrative apparatus was a necessary condition for peace and order in society. The Church gave its tacit support to the establishment of this apparatus in the years after the civil wars, comparatively unaffected by the clashes that sometimes occurred. All the time the Church supplied the royal administration with competent aides. With the exception of the short-lived conflict at the beginning of the 1280s, the bishops acted as counsellors and political guarantors for the king. Competent clergy of lower rank carried out missions for the king as well as administrative tasks.

Only a small part of the Church's personnel and income was, however, put at the disposal of the Crown in this way. Overwhelmingly, the Church used its own resources for it own purposes. For this reason it is understandable why monarchs from Haakon Haakonsson onwards deliberately built up their own body of clergy in association with specially created royal chapels.

The foundation of Church organization was the parish. Gradually the whole country was fitted into a parochial system that, to a large extent, has survived down to our own times. This provided a much tighter network and a more pervasive local organization than was at the disposal of the monarchy. Ecclesiastical administration in the various bishoprics was brought together under the bishop and the cathedral chapter, the latter consisting of the leading members of the cathedral's clergy who acted as the bishop's advisers. The cathedral chapter had secured, in accordance with the universal practice of the Church, the decisive role in the election of a bishop, though this did not prevent the continued exercise of influence by the Crown. At the top of a nationwide hierarchy of bishops sat the archbishop. From 1280, a purely clerical provincial council took on the synodical role of the national assemblies.

Religious houses appeared in Norway from the beginning of the twelfth century. The first wave consisted of monasteries and nunneries of the Benedictine order and its reformed wing, the Cluniacs. In the 1140s the Cistercians arrived from England. The Augustinian canons led the field in the foundation of religious houses in the second half of the twelfth century, and from about 1240 the mendicant orders – Dominicans and Franciscans – established themselves in the Norwegian towns.

In the first half of the fourteenth century around 30 religious houses were to be found in Norway – few and generally small as compared with those in the more southerly Europe. But they played an important role in the development of the Church in Norway, serving as educational centres and points of contact with European church life. The earlier religious houses had been built in close cooperation with the bishops for whom they played a supportive role. However there soon developed a more tense situation between the secular clergy, on the one hand, and the outward-looking and independent mendicant orders on the other. Since it was the aim of the latter to propagate the gospel amongst the people, they came to poach on the preserves of the secular clergy as regards both the cure of souls and the income derived from it.

The Church generally tried to appear as a united body. But in reality it consisted of a series of different organizations and units, each with their own special interests and frequently shifting areas of authority. This helps us understand the tendency for internal divisions to appear within the Norwegian Church from the end of the thirteenth century, not only between the bishops and the mendicant orders, but also between individual bishops and their chapters and between the secular clergy and those attached to the royal chapel, which the monarchy sought to organize into a body as independent as possible of ecclesiastical authority.

The roles of monarch and Church in society

The conflicts within the Church towards the end of the high Middle Ages are one of several indications that the desire for power, status and income was a motivating force in the development of public administration. Nevertheless, neither a monarchical nor a clerical national organization could come into being unless, at the same time, the monarchy and the Church took on important social roles and in that way acquired a more positive hold on public opinion.

The basic need for peace and order throughout the country was best secured by the monarchy. From this sprang the medieval monarch's two principal roles in society: as the upholder of law in the widest possible sense and as military leader. As military leader, the king, in the *Landslov* of 1274, entered into a contract with the peasantry for reciprocal duties and services.

As upholder of the law, the king, in legislation from the second half of the thirteenth century, claimed to be both the source of laws and the highest judge in the land. And it is clear that with the aid of his administration he went a long way towards putting these claims into practice. The result was national legislation in the king's name, with national assemblies, the royal council and the various *lagting* in an advisory and ratifying capacity. With the *Landslov* Norway got a common code of laws for the whole country earlier than most other countries in Europe. As judge, the king was 'above the law', with the rights and duties of clarifying and supplementing it in individual instances. Nevertheless in practice he usually entrusted the final decision on individual cases to law commissioners. At lower levels the judicial activity both in and outside the *ting* was in the hands of lawmen and *syslemenn*.

At the same time the monarchy was behind the development of an official penal system. This replaced an earlier system to which society had taken a comparatively neutral stance, leaving the injured parties to seek redress. With the new system, breaking the law was subject to official punishment in the form of fines or outlawry with the confiscation of property. Under the influence of Roman law and universal canon law, such punishments were increasingly based on the principle of individual guilt, thus replacing the collective responsibility of the family, remnants of which were still to be found in the earlier provincial laws. This led, among other things, to the legal abolition from the second half of the thirteenth century of blood vengeance and the collective obligation and right of kin to pay and receive private compensation in consequence of homicide. Here we see more clearly than in any other area how the hold of kin on its individual members was being loosened.

Nidaros cathedral seen from the north-east in 1930. The archbishop's church is the most impressive example of ecclesiastical and royal building in Norway from the high Middle Ages. It shows how receptive Norwegians were to European culture. The oldest parts of the church today are the transepts, which were begun in the Romanesque (Anglo-Norman) style in the first half of the twelfth century and completed in a Romanesque-Gothic transitional style by Archbishop Øystein after he took over the see in 1161. Whilst Øystein was in exile in England in the years 1180–83, he learned more about the Gothic style. On his return he began to build the richly decorated Gothic octagon over the grave of St Olav, seen here to the left. His successors completed this in the course of the thirteenth century, together with most of the rest of the church, under the influence of the further-developed Gothic style. Later the cathedral suffered from several fires which led, in the course of restoration, to modifications being made to the original fabric. The view shown here does, however, indicate much of the original.

Parallel with the development of official punishment came its antithesis, the royal prerogative of mercy. The king could, for a price, give outlaws the right to reside freely in the country. Through its local officials, the monarchy in the high Middle Ages took upon itself more and more responsibility for bringing charges for breaches of the law, for policing and for implementing judgments. Upholding the law strengthened the king's power and prestige in society and contributed, more than anything else, to ensuring the obedience of his subjects.

As well as the monarchy, the *Church* exercised its own independent authority in the public domain, in such a way that it appeared almost as a state within a state during the high Middle Ages. A distinctive Norwegian Church law was framed. It appeared in the secular law codes under separate sections of Christian regulations, i.e. rules as to how Christianity should be observed and practised and how relations between Church and society should be regulated. Church law was also made through decisions taken in synodical assemblies, as well as in pastoral letters from the bishops. At the same time, universal canon law was applied to Norway via papal letters and the resolutions of ecclesiastical General Councils. The Church did not manage to make itself independent of the monarchy and the *lagting* when it came to legislation pertaining to the Christian sections of the secular law codes. It did, however, take the initiative in such legislation and produced within the framework of internal Church law additional rules that had a considerable impact on society.

In the Tønsberg Concordat of 1277, the judicial authority of the Church was recognized for all cases brought against the clergy (*privilegium fori*) as well as in a series of 'spiritual' matters affecting Christianity and regulated in the Christian sections of the secular law codes. Partly these were infringements of the Church's commandments and teaching, and partly matters affecting the Church's financial and legal position. The limits of this jurisdiction were disputed throughout the rest of the high Middle Ages, but this did not prevent the creation of a separate system for administering the law, under the leadership of the bishops. Thus ecclesiastical courts got to bring prosecutions, to judge them and to mete out temporal punishments, in addition to demanding the expiation of sin through the purely ecclesiastical system of penance, with its starting point in the confessional.

The source of the Church's public authority was its religious role: to implement Christianity as the sole prescribed religion and to administer

Haakon's Hall in the royal palace in Bergen was probably the largest and most impressive of the secular buildings of Norway during the high Middle Ages. It was built by King Haakon Haakonsson in the years 1247–61, probably along the lines of Gothic stone buildings in contemporary England. The hall was literally a monument, serving not only the monarchy's everyday and ceremonial needs, but also as a witness to the high status of the Crown. Here the culture of the court, under European influences, could develop better than anywhere else in the country.

its rules. The Norwegian Church did succeed, to a very considerable degree, in bringing into effect the external forms of a European and Catholic Christianity during the high Middle Ages. One sign that the Church's activities also established deeper roots can be seen in the large number of gifts or so-called 'soul donations' it received for the saying of prayers and the holding of masses for the deceased, in order to ease and shorten their stay in purgatory on the road to salvation. A considerable amount of the Church's landed property came to it in this way.

Through the parish system, the Christian message reached people throughout the whole country. And with its sacraments the Church marked each of life's stages from birth to death. Its calendar of festivals and religious services divided each year and each day and night into fixed intervals. With its religiously based norms of behaviour, the Church penetrated deeply into everyday life. The religious ideology was in this and other ways transformed into generally accepted conceptions and attitudes, to common *mentalités*.

Closely linked with its religious purpose were the social tasks that the Church took upon itself, above all the care of the poor, the sick and the old. This was done with the help of the poor's share of the tithe (a quarter of which was put at the disposal of the peasants); alms and hospitals for the poor and the sick; healing and nursing; and by offering bed and board in religious institutions for those who could afford it.

The church also played an important cultural role. Its teaching was the only form of popular education, through learning the Creed, the Lord's Prayer and the Hail Mary by heart. Virtually all formal education in medieval Norway took place in ecclesiastical institutions such as the cathedral and monastic schools. It was also primarily the clergy who sought higher education in Europe, at the universities that appeared there from the second half of the twelfth century. The Church was first and foremost interested in educating the clergy, but what it did in this field also benefited the royal house, the lay aristocracy and the royal administration.

It was the Church and the Crown that created the milieux for contemporary art and intellectual life and funded the activities there. The writing used in legislation and other documents formed the basis for the development of the 'Old Norwegian' literary language. This had features that were clearly distinct from Danish and Swedish (East Nordic) and, together with the almost identical Old Icelandic, made up an 'Old Norse' or West Nordic language form. So far as literary activity was concerned, the milieux surrounding the archbishop's seat in Nidaros and the royal court in Bergen were especially important. Both encouraged the writing of history in the form of kings' sagas and chronicles. In this the Icelanders played the main role by virtue of their story-telling traditions and their exceptional literary ability. Nidaros was also a centre for religious writings.

In the thirteenth century the court circle in Bergen took the literary lead through an extensive series of translations of heroic–romantic works, as well as through its historical writings. This was one element in a conscious attempt to introduce the chivalrous culture of European courts. The circle around the monarchy was also fertile soil for the development of a political literature. *The King's Mirror* was the most notable work in this genre.

In the high Middle Ages building styles were set by the monarchy and the Church in the shape of impressive stone buildings: royal castles and palaces, bishops' palaces, churches and religious houses.

Architecture such as this not only served a practical purpose; it also symbolized the dominant position in society of the monarchy and the Church. Pictorial art in the high Middle Ages, in both sculpture and painting, was primarily tied to places of worship and to their furnishings. For a population that, for the most part, could not read, the religious message conveyed by the clergy was brought to life by this church art, and helped to establish it in the collective consciousness.

Together the monarchy and the Church were responsible for an impressive cultural flowering in the high Middle Ages. This owed much to European influences, especially in religious writings, in court literature and in Romanesque and, later, Gothic architecture and pictorial art. This fusion of foreign and domestic traditions fuelled the conditions for independent creative activity of a high order.

The income of Crown and Church and local self-management

A necessary condition for the development of both the monarchy and the Church was an economic structure stable enough to provide the conditions for regular contributions from the agricultural population. Through the system of tenant farming both the monarchy and the Church had, by the end of the high Middle Ages, a regular income from their landed estates. The estates of the Church were now very extensive, but those of the crown were modest (Chapter 4), not least because so much of what had been acquired during the unification of the country had been passed on to ecclesiastical institutions.

Fines and confiscations received through upholding the law were an important source of income for the Church and the Crown, especially so for the latter. Both bodies also levied taxes. The contemporary state tax was the *leidang*, supplemented by the so-called '*vissøyre*' ('fixed due') from the inland districts of eastern Norway. The *leidang* had come into existence as a tax through the conversion of the population's military obligations into an annual payment during peace time. This was eventually legally incorporated into the *Landslov*. The tax income of the Church in the form of the tithe was considerably larger. The tithe originally was mainly levied on corn growing. It was made legally binding for most of the country in Magnus Erlingsson's time. In 1277 the attempt was made to extend it to all economic activities, though in practice the Church never quite managed this. A number of smaller sources of income supplemented the main ones given here.

There is no doubt that the income of the Church at the end of the high Middle Ages was much greater than that of the Crown. A direct expression of this was the very much larger number of clerics as compared with the liegemen of the Crown, a point made earlier (Chapter 4). It is equally clear that the income of the Norwegian monarchy was very small in comparison with that enjoyed by the rulers of the neighbouring kingdoms and elsewhere in Europe.

The question therefore arises: how was it possible for the Norwegian king and his helpers to administer the kingdom as effectively as they apparently did towards the end of the high Middle Ages? Here a decisive factor was that the population not only provided the king with goods and money, it also made a contribution, in the form of unpaid services, that was very considerable. The fact was that the monarchy entrusted a great deal of public activity in society to what we may call *local self-management*, in both town and country. Here was the foundation of a tradition that subsequently was to become a characteristic feature of Norwegian public administration.

Even if there was a clear transfer of authority from the local and regional *ting* to the king and the central authorities, the system of such assemblies was not only maintained but also expanded under royal control. In Magnus Lagabøte's reign the largest towns were given their own *lagting* as were, in later decades, most of the 10 districts, each of which had its own lawman. In the localities, the settlement and town assemblies were the focus of public life.

Both in and outside the *ting*, a local elite of 'good' or 'judicious' men was systematically drawn into the local public administration. An important intermediary between the royal administration and rural community life was the *bondelensmann* or bailiff, drawn from the ranks of the peasantry, who, from the end of the thirteenth century, acted as the aide of the *syslemann*. In the more densely populated and specialized urban communities, town councillors (*rådmenn*) appeared from the second half of the thirteenth century. They carried out judicial and administrative functions under the leadership of the local royal officials. The wider grouping of *husfaste menn* (Chapter 4) also played an important role.

In upholding the law Magnus Lagabøte's legislation laid considerable tasks on local society. Especially noticeable is the frequent use of panels of 'good' men, usually containing 6 or 12 members. Continuing an older tradition of peasant society, such panels were appointed as arbitrators and appraisers to help settle local disputes. They were to clarify actual legal rights and conditions by taking evidence; assess damages resulting from a breach of the law; and fix the compensation due to the injured party. Whereas previously they had been a private organ of justice, they were now also attached to the *ting*. Here, amongst other things, they were to work as assessors with the lawman to pronounce sentence in serious criminal cases. But their main task continued to be that of providing the basis for judicial settlements. Besides this, 'good' men, in both town and country, served as compurgators (so as to 'cleanse' or convict a defendant in cases where no other way of clarifying the facts of a case was possible); as valuers; as providers of bail; and as witnesses to economic transactions.

Magnus Lagabøte's legal codes also placed a considerable number of official duties on self-governing local bodies, quite apart from upholding the law. In the rural districts these included: the maintenance of the military *leidang* system; the provision of transport for public officials; the maintenance of roads; the transport of messages; and the support of the poor. In the towns the fire service and the drawing-up of ships for repairs were notable collective responsibilities. The house-owning heads of urban households acted, in a number of situations, as the long arm of authority. The Church added to the number of communal duties by demanding participation in the building and maintenance of the parish churches and by appointing churchwardens to exercise financial control of them.

The increasing amount of documentary evidence from the end of the thirteenth century confirms that local self-management in both town and country functioned to a large extent as the law intended it should. This shows that the monarchy of the high Middle Ages had an authority that was based on more than the interests of the aristocracy and the support of the Church. It could also rely on the participation of the local population in public affairs.

It is true that disagreements did occur between the monarchy and the local populations – partly because of the Crown's demands for financial and military assistance and partly because the king's servants took the law into their own hands to promote their own interests. Legislation towards the end of the high Middle Ages shows, however, that the central government was concerned to prevent such and other exploitation of the king's subjects and that it attached importance to maintaining the legal basis and the support the monarchy had obtained within peasant society. The level of *leidang* taxation was lower than in the neighbouring kingdoms. This was linked with the fact that the *leidang* duty in times of war still involved a military role, whereas in Europe generally the mustering of the general population had, for the most part, been replaced by the use of more professional military personnel. Generally speaking, therefore, the Norwegian peasantry kept more of their political influence than their counterparts in most other contemporary European countries.

A dawning sense of Norwegian community

We have noted earlier that neither the ecclesiastical nor the secular aristocracy in Norway was strong enough to exercise power in society independently of the Crown. If we also take into account peasant and urban society, we detect the outline of a situation in which none of the main groups in society was strong enough to dominate the others or to go against the interests of the monarchy. On the contrary, all were to some extent dependent on the king, and this gave him and his ruling circle greater manœuvrability than their power base and income, in itself, would suggest.

One must not, however, confuse the state in the high Middle Ages with the state today, in terms of the latter's importance for and control of society. Individuals in the high Middle Ages were left to themselves, their local milieu and private interests to an extent that is hardly imaginable today. People in town and country were both much less controlled and much less protected by the activities of the state authorities. They did not sense their constant presence. For that, the royal administration was too modest and the social tasks it took upon itself too limited.

The Church had a much greater impact on an individual's life than did the monarchy. This was reflected in its income and the size of its organization. Throughout the entire country, this organization sought to present the same message and to carry out the same Christian practices. Christianity, as administered by the Church, was undoubtedly the strongest social cement in the more cohesive Norwegian society that took shape in the high Middle Ages.

When it came to asserting the character of this society in relation to others, the role of the monarchy would still seem to be more important than the more internationally oriented role played by the Church. With ecclesiastical support there developed a specifically Norwegian political ideology, in which 'Norway's eternal King' (*rex perpetuus Norvegiæ*), St Olav, played the role of the great, mythical legislator, the epitome of Norwegian law and justice. And in the policies pursued by the monarchy in times of tension and conflict with foreign interests, we find a fertile soil for a Norwegian self-assertion that here and there shines through in the kings' sagas.

When, towards the end of the high Middle Ages, the 'land of the Norsemen' had become 'the Norwegian King's Realm' it was a reflection of the fact that the development of a Norwegian sense of community had progressed considerably relative to the loose ethno-cultural society we dimly perceived in the early Viking Age, in the days of Ottar.

6
The great crisis

In the years 1347–51 most of Europe was struck by the catastrophic plague that was later known as the Black Death. In our presentation of Norwegian history it marks the divide between the high and late Middle Ages.

The plague reached Bergen from England in the summer of 1349. Possibly it reached Østlandet from abroad too. In any case it spread throughout the entire country. It ravaged Denmark and most of Sweden too, but Finland and Iceland were spared on this occasion. New outbreaks occurred in Norway during each subsequent decade of the fourteenth century and more occasionally in later years. This pattern was repeated over most of western and northern Europe.

Plague is endemic amongst wild rodents in certain areas, and usually spreads to, and amongst, humans through the bite of the rat flea. The normal plague is of the bubonic type, which leads to the swelling of the lymphatic glands in the armpits, groin and neck. Without medical treatment, as was the case in the Middle Ages, bubonic plague could have killed 80–90 per cent of those infected. The infection can enter the bloodstream, leading both to blood poisoning (septicemic plague) and pneumonic plague, both of which are even deadlier than the bubonic plague itself.

The outbreaks of plague that appeared repeatedly after the Black Death itself brought further falls in the population. Growth was restricted still more because it appears that both women and children were struck particularly hard. Other epidemics, famines, war and natural catastrophes all worked in the same direction. Recent research suggests that the population of Europe as a whole could well have fallen by 50 per cent in the second half of the fourteenth century, and that the population continued to decline, albeit slowly, down to the middle of the fifteenth century. Only then are there widespread signs of a new upturn.

The contraction of settlement and the loss of population

In Norway, as in most other countries, we can estimate the extent of the population loss only indirectly, through its more or less measurable effects. The clearest evidence is the desertion of thousands of farms and holdings. According to tax registers of around 1520, half to two-thirds of all the named farms of the high Middle Ages lay deserted at that time. Possibly two-thirds of the holdings existing in the high Middle Ages remained unoccupied. These abandoned farms and holdings were not without economic significance. Many were exploited by neighbouring farms or from the towns they surrounded, especially for hay and pasture. Nevertheless they are evidence of an enormous demographic crisis.

The plague spared neither built-up nor sparsely populated areas, but in the long term people congregated in those areas offering the best economic opportunities. Thus, the plague years reversed the expansion of settlement that had taken place from the Viking Age to the high Middle Ages (Chapter 3). Depopulation affected particularly the newly colonized areas in the forests and hills and on the margins of older agricultural districts, as well as in the inner fjords and the more remote valleys and mountains. On the whole it was the districts with poor opportunities for agriculture and little prospect of alternative means of subsistence that were hardest hit. The populations of good agricultural areas held up better. Because of the possibilities offered by fishing, the coastal areas from Vestlandet northwards coped better than did the inland agricultural settlements of the same region.

For those who survived more land was available. This tenants' market brought about a dramatic fall in land rents. Although there were major local variations, it is reckoned that for the country as a whole the rental income from the farms and holdings that continued to be occupied fell to around one-quarter of its pre-1350 level. If we include the deserted holdings, for which little or nothing was paid, it would appear that landowners on average got only one-fifth of their earlier rental income. Land prices fell, though not as strongly as rents, so that returns on capital invested in rented land were less. Church receipts from the tithe on corn fell markedly, on average to perhaps around one-third of their level before 1350. This reflected a heavy fall in output.

Agricultural historians, basing their estimates on the abandonment of holdings and the other crisis phenomena, believe that the fall of popu-

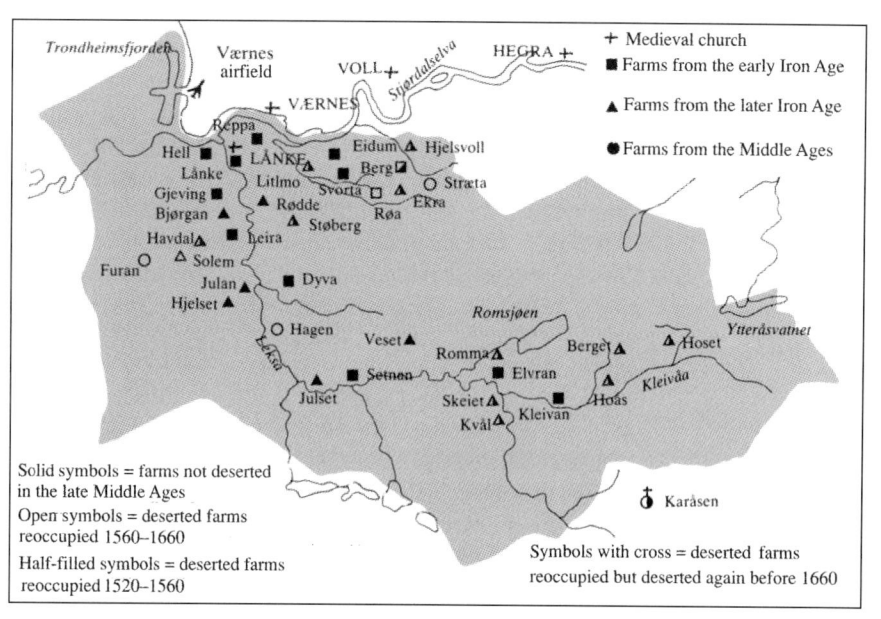

The map shows farms in Lånke, Sør-Trøndelag, abondoned in the late Middle Ages. Nineteen of the thirty-six farms were abandoned. People withdrew to the best farms, which invariably were the oldest. Only two of the thirteen farms dating from the early Iron Age were abandoned, whilst a majority of those from the later Iron Age and all that had been cleared during the Christian Middle Ages were deserted. This was typical of the contraction of settlement across the country; broadly speaking, this reversed the expansion that had taken place from the Viking Age to the high Middle Ages.

lation amounted to between one-half and two-thirds of the maximum reached in the high Middle Ages. One cannot, however, automatically conclude from the extent of such phenomena a corresponding reduction in population. In that it was the most marginal units that were abandoned permanently, the total number of deserted farms and holdings is not a direct measure of the population loss, whilst the fall in the land rents was clearly conditioned by the state of the market. Nevertheless it is clear that the population fall in late medieval Norway was catastrophic and lasting. Not until the second half of the fifteenth century do we detect the first tentative signs of a new growth in agricultural settlement. And not until well into the sixteenth century are the signs of growth clear across the country as a whole.

The desertion of holdings was also widespread elsewhere in northern Europe during the late Middle Ages. Nevertheless, it does appear to have been quite insignificant in Finland, where agricultural settlement in general expanded strongly; and it was comparatively slight too in the better agricultural districts of Denmark and Sweden. In the poorer parts of these countries and in Iceland more holdings were abandoned, but nowhere to the extent, according to current estimates, experienced in Norway. The same conclusion applies to Germany and England. On this basis, it has therefore generally been reckoned that the demographic crisis in Norway was particularly widespread and long-lived, though why this was the case has not been satisfactorily explained.

Recent European research emphasizes the extent of the population decline and its duration in other countries too, such that it is difficult to point to anything peculiar about the situation in Norway. Possibly the sharp reduction in settlements owes more to the settlement pattern in Norway than to the loss of population. Because settlement was tied to separate farms and holdings, their abandonment was both more extensive and more conspicuous than in areas dominated by villages, since villages usually continued in existence in spite of population loss. In addition, a greater number of landless or near-landless labourers were to be found further south in Europe and to some extent too in Denmark and Sweden. They could disappear without leaving a trace on the actual agricultural settlement pattern. To the extent that they survived and settled on available land, they limited the number of abandoned settlements.

The causes of the crisis and its economic effects

There have been widespread discussions in Scandinavia and elsewhere in Europe about the causes of the crisis of the late Middle Ages. There can be no doubt that the plague epidemics were a major cause of the loss of population. On the other hand, there is evidence of crisis before the middle of the fourteenth century in several parts of Europe. From the second half of the thirteenth century one sees signs of stagnation and population decline. Generally this has been explained in Malthusian terms – the growth of population exceeding resources, with the consequent over-exploitation of agricultural land. At the same time, more specific explanations are noted such as harvest failure, natural catastrophes and war. Price developments and market conditions have been used to account for earlier signs of economic crisis (e.g. the fall in Danish land prices).

All this raises the question as to how far the crisis in late medieval Norway had its origins in factors that were already beginning to make themselves felt in the high Middle Ages. Comment on abandoned land from the second half of the thirteenth century and a few examples of falls in land rents before 1350 can be interpreted as early signs of crisis. Nor can we ignore the possibility that in Norway too the population reached such a high level relative to agricultural resources that it stagnated and began to decline before 1350 (Chapter 3). To explain both this and the extent and duration of the later crisis, scholars have pointed to indications of a somewhat cooler and damper climate and the particular risks of soil exhaustion in marginal agricultural areas such as Norway. To pursue this further one could well imagine that a poor dietary situation towards the end of the high Middle Ages reduced the population's resistance to the effects of crop failures and epidemics.

Nevertheless, recordable indications of crisis in Norway before 1350 are few and weak. The major shake-up of Norwegian society no doubt came later, with the Black Death and the subsequent outbreaks of plague. As to the possible causes of this shock to the medieval social system, there is much that remains to be established scientifically.

Plague epidemics were a dreadful agony for those who experienced them and left a permanent mark on the collective consciousness. If we examine the *long-term effects* of the population loss, however, the picture is less distressing.

Economically we are dealing with a mass crisis. It led to an enormous reduction in both productive capacity and material demand. For the great majority of survivors, however the effects were undoubtedly favourable. Readier access to land must have led to increased output per head. When, in addition, one was paying but a fraction of the old rent for tenanted land, conditions generally in the peasant society of late medieval Norway must have been easier.

Financially the crisis struck primarily those in receipt of rents and taxes, i.e. the landowning aristocracy, the Church and the monarchy. The situation of the upper levels of society was made more difficult too, because the value of their incomes in kind (agricultural products) fell in relation to the prices of manufactured goods and wages.

The loss of population contributed to two noticeable developments in Norway's economy. The first was an increased emphasis on animal husbandry relative to corn growing. Because of the greater amount of pasture and meadow-land that was now available, animal husbandry became more productive relative to the input of labour. Prices of butter and other animal products also held up better than those of corn during the general price fall of the late Middle Ages. People had the means to eat more animal products, by contrast with the carbohydrate- and starch-rich diet that had been the dominant one towards the end of the high Middle Ages.

The second tendency was for fishing to become a relatively more important industry. As noted already, settlements on the coasts of the west and north survived well. In the far north of Norway a tendency that was already noticeable in the high Middle Ages (Chapter 3) continued: namely, people relied more and more on livestock and inshore fishing for their own food requirements, whilst at the same time, through their participation in the great seasonal fisheries, producing dried fish, which they could exchange for grain and other products. Throughout the late Middle Ages fish provided the conditions for permanent settlement in villages on the west and northern coasts right up to Vadsø.

Tax lists from around 1520 not only indicate a relatively high population in the coastal areas of the west and north, they also show that people there were wealthier than in the best agricultural districts of the interior. The explanation appears to lie in the excellent opportunities for the sale of dried fish via Bergen at a price that compared favourably with that for grain and other imported goods. It is true that the output of dried fish fell considerably because of the population loss and had not reached the level of the early fourteenth century until well into the sixteenth. On the other hand, prices rose strongly in the middle of the fourteenth century and remained at a very high level into the 1400s. One indication of this profitable Bergen connection can be seen in the expensive art imported from Germany and the Netherlands that now began to appear in north Norwegian churches.

The economic effects of the crisis of the late Middle Ages on the towns of Norway is still but little understood. Because they were collection centres for royal and ecclesiastical revenues and places of resi-

The fishing station of Grip in Nordmøre had 48 taxpayers in 1520. It is one of many illustrations of the fact that, in the late Middle Ages, it was fishing that provided the foundation for permanent settlement along the outer coasts of western and northern Norway.

dence for private landowners, the towns were inevitably hit by the fall in agricultural rents, taxes and other official sources of income. This must have had an especially strong impact where the central place functions of the Church dominated urban life, as in Trondheim, Stavanger and Hamar. Reduced supplies from the rural areas probably meant that the population of other towns too remained at a lower level than before 1350.

On the other hand, the marketing of goods came to play a greater role in the economy of late medieval Norway. One indication of this was the greater use of coins. Thus the conditions were right for the stabilization, and even growth, of towns whose economic rationale lay in the exchange of goods. Besides fish, timber became a major export item. It attracted Dutchmen and Scots to the Norwegian coasts, contributed to the maintenance of town life in the east (Skien, Tønsberg, Oslo) and brought about a certain concentration of settlement in early loading ports along the Oslofjord (forerunners of the later *ladesteder*, Chapter 12), where timber duties were paid from the end of the fourteenth century. The water-driven saw appeared during the closing decades of the fifteenth century in the far southeast of the country, helping, in 1498, to give urban status to Oddevall (Uddevalla) in Båhuslen.

Bergen retained its position as the export channel for fish and other products from northern Norway and the colonies in the seas to the west, even if the trade with Iceland dried up after 1400 as Englishmen, followed by German merchants from the North Sea ports, began to fetch their fish from there directly. Also the trade between Bergen and the towns of eastern England lost much of its previous importance to the benefit of continental fish markets. The built-up area of Bergen grew in the late Middle Ages, at the same time as it became in parts more densely populated, for the population clearly grew rapidly again after its fall in the second half of the fourteenth century.

The Hanseatic hegemony

It appears that the Hanseatics took the opportunity to fill the vacuum that appeared when the Black Death and later plagues carried off a good proportion of the Norwegians previously active in the Bergen trade. Rising prices for dried fish from around the middle of the fourteenth century undoubtedly stimulated interest in this trade and help to explain why a more organised Hanseatic trading station or *Kontor* (Office) was finally established in Bergen around 1360. Probably decisive too was the fact that a comprehensive Hanseatic League (formed by the Hansa towns) had come into existence in the 1350s and wanted to keep a firmer hand on its people in Bergen. The *Kontor* rapidly took over the warehouses on The Wharf (*Bryggen*), where around 1,000 Germans took up permanent residence. At the same time, German guilds came to dominate several branches of the town's crafts.

In the course of the late Middle Ages the Hansa set up smaller 'factories', or trading stations, in Oslo and Tønsberg. For them Rostock was the leading 'mother city', while Lübeck was in charge of the *Kon-*

The Wharf (Bryggen) *on the oldest preserved illustration of Bergen, the Scholeus print from around 1580. Tilt-cranes for loading and unloading can be seen along the edge of the quay. After the Hanseatic* Kontor *had finally been established in Bergen around 1360, the Germans gradually took over all the warehouses and other buildings on the Wharf. There they organized their lives on a semi-extra-territorial basis.*

tor in Bergen. From the outset the main competitive edge the Hanseatic merchants had over their Norwegian counterparts was their professionalism, their geographically extensive trading organization and their greater capital base. These gave them advantages both as purchasers of Norwegian goods and as suppliers of sought-after imports. The mounting strength of their position in the late Middle Ages was due not least to the increasing amount of credit they advanced Norwegian suppliers (including equipment and other goods) in order to secure regular supplies of articles for export. Through this they worked their way into the town's middleman trading (i.e. the buying of goods with a view to re-sale) at the same time as they strengthened their already dominant position in the overseas trade.

Of especial significance was the credit system created by the *Kontor* in Bergen. The peasant fishermen and others from the north (so-called 'north-farers') who brought fish products to the town were the main recipients of credit. More independent Bergen townsmen who previously had bought fish in the north and transported it to Bergen came to play a modest role during the late Middle Ages, at the same time as the *Kontor* took the lead in the Bergen middleman trading. The Hanseatic merchants also sought to work their way into the retail trade in Bergen and other Norwegian towns. But here most of the activity continued in Norwegian hands, benefiting, as they did, from the protectionist trade policies of the authorities.

Both at the *Kontor* in Bergen and at the 'factories' in eastern Norway, the Germans had a tendency to withdraw from the rest of society. They usurped control of their own internal affairs under their own aldermen according to statutes sanctioned by the Hanseatic League's highest organ, the *Hansetag* or diet. It was, however, only in Bergen that they lived close together and organized themselves extra-territorially, to the extent that marriage to Norwegian women was prohibited. Here too they managed to some degree to avoid using Norwegian courts in cases of serious crime and in disputes between Hanseatic merchants and Norwegians. And it was only in Bergen that they were numerous enough openly to defy the Norwegian authorities sometimes and to introduce tough economic sanctions against their competitors, partly backed up with acts of violence.

Norwegian historians have tended to take a negative view of the economic role of the Hanseatic merchants; they exploited the fishermen of northern Norway, and hampered the development of an independent Norwegian urban middle class. That the latter was the case, especially in Bergen, can hardly be denied. On the other hand, the Hanseatic merchants did enlarge the Norwegian economy by expanding the European markets for stockfish and other products from Norway and its dependencies. Clearly this had a positive effect on the coastal economies of north and west Norway and on the development of Bergen and other towns, even if a large part of the trade surplus was drawn out of the country.

The effects of the crisis on the aristocracy and the clergy

An important social effect of the demographic crisis was that the secular *aristocracy* was weakened. The organization of the *hird* went into decline under Magnus Eriksson and Haakon 6 Magnusson (1355–80).

The ownership of landed estates was an essential condition for of the aristocratic way of life. With the sharp fall in the income from landed tenants in the late Middle Ages went the means of support for many of the king's liegemen. They were compelled to live off land they themselves cultivated and could no longer devote themselves to the royal service. Conversely, fewer liegemen were able to base their finances on a share of the king's income, since that fell too. The result was that many in the *hird* who belonged to the lower echelons of the aristocracy sank into the ranks of the peasantry. This is the most likely reason why the aristocracy's share of the country's landed property fell from approximately 20 per cent before 1350 to about 13 per cent around 1500.

The formal aristocracy of the late Middle Ages consisted of an upper set of knights and a lower set of men-at-arms. Any significant recruitment was no longer economically viable, especially as the demands of an elegant life-style rose through an increasing contact with the aristocracy of the neighbouring kingdoms. For an hereditary peerage, the upper strata of the *hird* were already so depleted by the end of the high Middle Ages that they would have had difficulty in reproducing themselves. The loss of population in the late Middle Ages made this impossible. Against this background it is understandable that the tendency towards endogamy and the amalgamation of estates increased. By the early 1400s the old Norwegian baronial families were wholly extinct on the male side. Lower-ranking families could still provide recruits for the peerage, but they were, in spite of the import of male marriage partners from the neighbouring kingdoms, too few to prevent further shrinkage. Around 1500 there was only a handful of high-ranking aristocratic families left and they disappeared almost entirely in the course of the next 30 years. It was not without foundation that Christian 2, in his accession charter *(håndfestning)* in 1513, was able to declare that the Norwegian aristocracy was all but extinct.

There was, in the late Middle Ages, below the aristocracy and above the peasantry, a grey area, socially speaking, that has been little researched. It encompassed a large group of families that had not given up their aristocratic ambitions. They revealed themselves by, amongst other things, having a coat of arms on their seals. Men of such families could strengthen their finances and set themselves apart by occupying the posts of lawmen or tax-exempted town councillors. They could get themselves into high ecclesiastical office, occupy administrative positions under aristocratic lord lieutenants (*lensherrer*), and take service as tax-exempted retainers of bishops or noble lords. Originally only the *lendmenn* had the right to have armed retainers, but during the 1300s it became usual for the aristocracy in general to employ such men. Under Haakon 6, such retainers were accepted and employed for military purposes by the crown.

As a result of the reduction in the Church's income, the number of Norwegian *clergy* was permanently reduced. At the local level one priest would often serve several churches. Higher up there was a tendency to amalgamate the incomes from several ecclesiastical posts in order to provide the finance for a smaller number. The religious houses, whose finances were almost entirely based on income from land, were especially hard hit by the fall in rents. In order to maintain their extensive range of religious observances and to take care of their other duties, the convents and monasteries required a minimum number of monks and nuns. A fall in the amount of income needed for this led internally to demoralization and decay and externally to a loss of prestige. Thus, even before the Lutheran Reformation several religious houses had ceased to function.

Nevertheless, as Church personnel were so numerous before and as its organization was so finely meshed, it could reduce its establishment in relation to the fall in population without losing its influence in society. Quite the contrary, it seems as though the influence of the Church increased during the late Middle Ages. One indication of this is that its share of landed property increased to almost half of the national total in terms of value, not least because of new gifts for the saying of masses for the deceased.

Social conditions in town and country

In the better-off peasant society of the late Middle Ages, we meet a self-confident elite that had its own seals and took upon itself a wide range of local public duties. This elite had received an influx of impoverished aristocratic families and it merged into the grey area, socially speaking, between the peasantry and the nobility. It was often men from such families who took the lead locally in opposing financial impositions from the centre during the late Middle Ages. At the same time, self-respect amongst the peasantry was nourished by the fact that economic circumstances improved for the majority over the country as a whole.

That the income from rents fell more in Norway than in neighbouring countries could be linked with the fact that the Norwegian peasantry were in a stronger position vis-à-vis their landlords. This meant that the market mechanism operated more freely in a period when there was a shortage of tenants. In the neighbouring kingdoms, a stronger landowning aristocracy was able to force its tenants to pay higher dues. On the Sjælland group of islands in Denmark, even serfdom was introduced in the late Middle Ages with labour dues for tenants. Thus Denmark found itself on the edge of that area of eastern Europe where peasant freedoms were lost through the manorial lords' exercise of power.

The outbreaks of plague in the second half of the 1300s hit the urban populations hard. We have seen that, in Bergen, the Hanseatic merchants and German craftsmen established themselves in the vacuum created by the loss of population. Nevertheless, there was still a place for Norwegian traders and artisans, even if most of the former no longer took part in foreign trade and had only a modest middleman role. In Oslo and Tønsberg there was more room for native business people alongside the Hanseatics, including foreign and middlemen trade.

During the late Middle Ages the elite of *husfaste* men in the towns was replaced by a class of burgesses, distinguished by their being independent traders and master artisans. Since this group also came to include craftsmen and retailers previously belonging to the middle ranks of urban society, it formed a broader grouping than that of the *husfaste* men. One result of this development was a social structure more clearly divided into two parts: a bourgeoisie and a proletariat.

After a time, the acquisition of burgess status became a condition for conducting business on one's own account in the towns. This was possibly in part linked with the need to limit the activities of the Hanseatics in the towns of eastern Norway. Formal citizenship is first recorded in Tønsberg and Oslo in the first half of the fourteenth century. It is known to have existed in other towns in the fifteenth century. In Tønsberg and Oslo a number of Hanseatic merchants found it advantageous to leave the organization and take Norwegian citizenship, while the Hanseatic *Kontor* in Bergen forbad its people to do so in that town.

The native bourgeoisie were provided with capital and expertise from increasing numbers of foreign immigrants: Germans, Dutch,

Scots (Orkney islanders amongst them) and – towards the end of the late Middle Ages – quite a number of Danes. This bourgeoisie benefited from the fact that the Crown from the 1440s ceased to forbid trading activities in the rural districts. Increasingly the merchants acquired the right to buy and sell in the districts round the towns, partly within a more closely defined circumference. The Hanseatic merchants were not allowed into these districts. They had instead to concentrate on defending their already established position in the towns against competition from native citizens and other foreigners, as well as against the policies of the authorities relating to trading concessions. The eastern Norwegian towns saw the Hanseatics on the defensive sooner than did Bergen.

It was usual for leading burgesses to have one foot in the town and one foot in the rural districts. Members of the rural elite took part in the economic life of the towns and the urban bourgeoisie in their turn invested in land, not least land in the neighbourhood of the towns, which they farmed on their own account. This gave a greater return than renting it out for a low figure, and led, together with a similar form of management on the part of the urban ecclesiastical institutions, to clusters of permanently abandoned holdings around the towns. The elites of town and country came to have close ties, and marriages took place between them and the lower aristocracy. The urban councillors' families in the towns enjoyed, in this context, a marked transitional status.

The political and cultural results of the crisis

The most important *political* result of the demographic crisis was the weakening of royal administration. Besides the great fall in land rents, it would appear that regular tax income was halved. Attempts at raising extra taxes failed to compensate for this, and such initiatives were, in any case, thwarted by the opposition and tendency to revolt on the part of a more self-confident peasantry. The income from fines and confiscations fell with the decline in population. Also the customs dues that the Crown, in Haakon 5's reign, had levied on exports by foreigners were given up after Hanseatic pressure in 1343.

Even before the crisis, administrative personnel had been scarce in relation to the formidable tasks of ruling such a large and topographically fractured country as Norway. Now the income base of the monarchy was clearly more than halved. The crisis of the late Middle Ages also further reduced Norway's economic and military strength *vis-à-vis* its neighbours, which had a growing desire to exert influence in Norway. With the decline of the Norwegian nobility, the military and political leadership weakened too. Consequently it became difficult, if not impossible, to maintain an effective central administration in Norway. Against a background such as this the union with Denmark after 1380 (see Chapter 7) may seem a natural development.

Conditions were now right for the Church to strengthen its position as an independent public authority and to increase its influence over the secular power. At the same time, the weakening of the royal administration opened the way for a decentralization of the political and legal system, with greater independence for local authorities in town and country (Chapter 7).

The crisis of the late Middle Ages also had a *cultural* side. The fall in royal and ecclesiastical incomes reduced the possibilities the two powers had of sustaining a cultural milieu. The monarchy's desire to do so disappeared completely when it left the country.

The literary activity that had developed in royal and ecclesiastical circles in the high Middle Ages died out in the late Middle Ages. No longer was high-quality domestic church art produced in Norway. The bulk and the best of such art was imported in the late Middle Ages from the continental Hanseatic areas. At the same time, building work by Crown and Church more or less came to an end and several of the architectural monuments from the high Middle Ages fell into decay.

Influenced not least by the use of writing in the king's central administration, the Old Norse written language had come close to fostering a common Norwegian literary form. During the late Middle Ages, Norwegian dialects developed further towards a more modern spoken language but without the milieu required to create a parallel written form. The 'middle-Norwegian' written language (ca. 1350–1550) was characterized by an increasing mixture of Swedish, Danish and Low German and gradually had to give way to pure Danish. By around 1500 the Old Norse written language was no longer understood by most people.

In such circumstances what there was of a Norwegian literary tradition lived on only within the oral tradition of the peasant society, in popular ballads and folk verse, fairy stories and legends.

7
The political system of the late Middle Ages

High politics in the Scandinavia of the late Middle Ages was controlled by the privileged: the aristocracy, the clergy and, of course, the Crown. It was, then, of critical importance for Norway's position in the Nordic unions that its aristocracy, especially its upper echelons, were few in number, weak at the outset and shrank still further in the course of the period.

In the more fertile soils of Norway's neighbours lay the conditions for a much more numerous body of aristocrats and clergy. On the whole the leading members of both groups were individually better off than their Norwegian counterparts. Only exceptionally did Norwegian landowners have estates that could be compared with those of leading magnates in Denmark and Sweden. The aristocracy's major privilege – freedom from royal taxation – was far more important in the neighbouring kingdoms than in Norway, because there it also included the aristocrat's tenant farmers. The owners of large estates also acquired greater control of their tenants than was the case in Norway (Chapter 6). As, in addition, each of the aristocratic and clerical estates was generally more compact than in Norway, the conditions existed for a greater political independence and power on the part of their owners – as a group. Noble lords and bishops could, in the neighbouring kingdoms, have their own castles, whilst this was unknown in Norway with one exception – the one erected by the country's last archbishop on Steinviksholm in the Trondheimsfjord in the 1520s.

Castles came to play a key role in the late Middle Ages. Until cannon balls and gunpowder began to be of practical importance at the close of the Middle Ages, well-built and garrisoned castles were practically unassailable by military means. From them it was possible to dominate the surrounding districts. Aristocratic horsemen and their retainers played the leading role in warfare pursued on an open terrain, though gradually more and more professional foot soldiers took over. In Norway the aristocracy's retainers were more important militarily from the 1300s onwards than the conscripted *leidang*.

The *len* system

In order to live in a manner consistent with their station in the difficult economic situation of the late Middle Ages, the Scandinavian nobility were dependent, to a greater extent than before, on supplementing their private incomes with a share of the Crown's. This share was obtained by the secular aristocracy, and to some extent by the ecclesiastical aristocracy too, via the system of *len* (fiefs). This involved the exercise of royal authority in a fixed district, in return for a share of the king's income obtained from it. In Norway, the *syslemenn* of the high Middle Ages represented the Crown in districts that were *len* in this sense of the word and, to some extent, went under that name. In the late Middle Ages there were changes in the size of the *len*, and new conditions of service helped lay the foundation for their becoming more independent centres of power.

The operational heart of this system was the royal palace or castle, whose captain was the most important *lensmann* or lord lieutenant, in command of a permanent garrison and exercising direct official authority over the immediately surrounding area, the castle *len (slottslen)*. It might also be the captain's task to collect royal revenue from a wider area which historians have called the chief *len (hovedlen)*. It was divided up into smaller *len (smålen)* in addition to the castle *len*, each of which was under its own lord lieutenant. In Norway, the administrative areas of the *syslemenn* continued to a great extent to serve as local *len*. The lord lieutenant took over the role of the *syslemann* as the king's representative and continued sometimes to carry that title until it went out of use in the first half of the fifteenth century.

In Norway, castle *len* were formed around the fortified royal palaces in Bergen, Trondheim and Tønsberg (Tønsberghus), while from the reign of Haakon 5 the earlier royal palace in Oslo was replaced by the castle of Akershus. The royal palace in Bergen was, after its restoration around 1520, called Bergenhus. In the far southeast of the country, Haakon 5 built the castle of Båhus. Because of its military strength and its strategic position at the point where the three Scandinavian

Akershus, painted by S.S. Bruun in 1741. Haakon 5 constructed the first castle on the Aker promontory. Historical references to it date back to 1299; it withstood its first attack in 1308. During the late Middle Ages the monarchy's leading representative in Norway was the lord lieutenant at Akershus. The captains of the two other castles in eastern Norway, Båhus and Tønsberghus, only controlled the castlen in the immediately surrounding area, whereas Akershus was the centre of a chief len *which came to comprise the bulk of Østlandet.*

kingdoms met, Båhus was an especially important castle in the late Middle Ages. The Båhuslen (Bohuslän) that still exists (now in Sweden) lay under this castle. Vardøyhus in the extreme north controlled Finnmark. It formed its own *len*, though it came under the chief *len* of Bergen.

After the mid-1300s the royal representatives in Bergen, Trondheim, Oslo and Tønsberg combined the functions of regional treasurer (*fehirde*) and *syslemann*. Whilst here the administrative districts of the *syslemenn* (which comprised the town and a greater or lesser part of the surrounding area) became castle *len*, the larger regions for which the treasurers were responsible were the beginnings of the chief *len*. Over the long term it was, however, only the royal palaces of Bergen and Akershus that became centres for larger chief *len*. The Bergen *len* originally consisted of Vestlandet up to and including Sunnmøre, northern Norway and the tributary lands in the seas to the west. Later the regional treasuryship of Trondheim was put under Bergen. This

Bergenhus on the Scholeus print from around 1580 showing Haakon's Hall and the Rosenkrantz Tower. The latter was constructed in the 1560s with the medieval stone keep of King Magnus Lagabøte as its core. Whilst Akershus was the military and secular administrative centre of Østlandet in the late Middle Ages, Bergenhus served a similar function for western and northern Norway, together with the tributary territories in the seas to the west.

probably took place when the archbishop took over as lord lieutenant for most of Trøndelag in 1475. The bulk of the area south of the Dovre mountains was placed under the chief *len* of Akershus. Here the lord lieutenant became the leading representative of the Crown in Norway during the period of union with Denmark.

Royal revenues from the *len* fell into the same categories as in the high Middle Ages. The so-called 'certain income' was principally made up of regular taxes (the *leidang* and the *vissøyre*) and the rents from the royal estates. The 'uncertain income' varied from year to year and consisted of revenues from the courts, customs dues, salvage from shipwrecks, etc. A separate category consisted of the 'extraordinary taxes' that were demanded in the late Middle Ages to strengthen the royal finances. From the end of the fourteenth century the 'expeditionary' *leidang (utfareleidang)*, originally the financial and military contribution made to the conscripted naval force in wartime, was sometimes demanded as an extraordinary tax. In the militarily exposed and heavily pressed Båhuslen this was made permanent, probably from the beginning of the fifteenth century. A tax to pay for food for the king and his retinue as they travelled round the country (*gjengjerd*) also stems from this period. Extraordinary taxation rose sharply in the years around 1520 because of King Christian 2's war against Sweden. These taxes were now, for the most part, demanded in money, which made its transfer to Copenhagen that much easier. The chief lieutenants of Akershus and Bergenhus were put in charge of collecting these taxes. This led to the castle *len* being extended at the same time as their control of their chief *len* was strengthened.

In the high Middle Ages the *len* of the *syslemenn* were *len of audit*, their incumbents having to account for all the king's revenue and expenditure and pay in what remained after taking their share or salary. This system continued in the late Middle Ages. Not least were the castle *len* held as *len* of audit.

At the same time the general economic and financial situation led to *len* being allocated in a way less favourable to the Crown. They could be held as *len of service*, so that the lord lieutenant collected for himself most, or all of the royal revenues in return for providing the king with politico-administrative and military services. This was usual in the small *len*. Here, too, was to be found *len of fee*, for which the lord lieutenant paid a fixed amount of the revenues to the Crown and kept the remainder. Gradually also *mortgage len* were given to the Crown's creditors. Here the royal revenues served as interest or instalment payments until the loan was repaid. To counter these unfavourable terms, the king created special '*pantry len*' for the support of the queen and himself, i.e. all the income went straight into their private accounts.

The nobility and the leaders of the Church in Scandinavia claimed the sole right to hold castles and *len* from the king and, for the most part, succeeded in making good this claim in practice. The nobility fought in their own interest against royal attempts to introduce foreigners into the *len* (Danes in Sweden and Norway, and Germans in all three kingdoms) other than those married to native noblewomen.

The late medieval *len* administration had a decentralizing effect. The Scandinavian kingdoms tended to break up into castle *len* and there was a tendency to privatize the local administrations under the lord lieutenants. In Norway, the gap between the king and his subjects increased even more because after 1380 the Dano-Norwegian kings resided in Denmark. On the other hand, the captains of castles were able, over the long term, to create quite a strong administrative apparatus in Norway, especially at Akershus and Båhus.

Some of the lord lieutenants lived a long way from their *len* and in any case needed local deputies. The major one of these in Norway was the local official called *fogd* (pl. *fogder*). He operated within the old administrative districts of the *syslemann* and partly also within smaller districts. He was the private servant of the lord lieutenant, paid by him, and replaced the *syslemann* in official contacts with the general public. The main job of the *fogd* was to collect taxes, fines and other forms of *len* revenues. Usually he had no local connections and through his financial role often came into conflict with the peasantry. This was particularly likely to happen when the *fogd* was a foreigner.

The *bondelensmenn* (Chapter 5), in contrast to the *fogder*, were recruited from the peasantry and occupied a middle position between the population and the authorities. They appear in the documentary sources not only as assistants to the lord lieutenants and *fogder* in collecting revenue and administering the law, but also as representatives of the local communities.

The royal lawmen still acted in a judicial and administrative capacity. This was the one part of the high medieval royal administration that changed the least, even though the urban lawmen in Bergen and Trondheim disappeared after the middle of the fourteenth century.

Self-management in town and country

The late medieval Scandinavian peasantry insisted on their rights in the face of all new financial demands. They would not contribute more than they were obliged to according to ancient custom. In Norway, the peasants stood by 'St Olaf's law' (i.e. the *Landslov*) and insisted on their right to ratify all new payments to the authorities. Under the leadership of an active elite the peasantry displayed a stubborn resistance to new taxes and dues, and, on occasion, engaged in open conflict – especially in the years 1424–38 and 1496–1507 and during the levying of the extraordinary taxes in the years around 1520; both then and at other times some *fogder* were killed. The European-wide peasant uprisings of the late Middle Ages had, in other words, parallels in Norway as they did elsewhere in Scandinavia.

The local communal apparatus that had been developed on the initiative of the Crown and Church during the high Middle Ages (Chapter 5) continued its activities in the late Middle Ages, though with a greater degree of independence than earlier. The local assembly *(ting)* strengthened its position as the focus of official activities in the rural districts. Here depositions were taken, judgments made and other legal matters dealt with. Private transactions were entered into and made official. The local assembly also had a political role. It was the place where the authorities negotiated with the peasantry and where the peasantry presented their grievances.

Writing was now used more by the peasantry. Panels of 'good men' were more frequently employed for settling local disputes, both at and even more outside the local assemblies. In passing formal judgments they worked together with the lawman, but they also had a *de facto* judicial function on their own account. Increasingly the leading men of the localities were authorized by the lawmen to act as assessors, so-called *lagrettemen*. From the early 1400s it was such men who took charge of the local population's official duties, as *de facto* judges, assessors and appraisers in different contexts. They handled and attested financial transactions, so making them entirely legal. They were also usually churchwardens.

Thus rural Norway took care of much official life itself in the late Middle Ages. It was further removed from the central powers than it had been in the high Middle Ages. Gradually, however, the chief lord lieutenant and his servants moved in, especially with the growing tax demands towards the end of the Middle Ages. The peasantry still needed the king and his servants for upholding the law. But the level of royal power they required for support was less than the power desired by the monarchy and the aristocracy at the top. Therefore the peasants were against paying for a more extensive governmental apparatus. This was to be an ongoing theme in Norwegian history.

The military significance of the peasants was reduced during the late Middle Ages and this contributed to the increased distance between them and the central powers. The conscripted *leidang* played only a minor role after the reign of Haakon 5. The peasants still had a duty to help defend the country, and down to around 1500 they were occasionally mobilized, locally and regionally, for waging war on behalf of the Crown and the nobility. But for the most part it was professional soldiers who determined the outcome of military engagements in this period, eventually using firearms that the peasants themselves were unable to acquire.

Because the towns were the seats of local and regional administration, they felt the presence of the authorities more than did the rural districts. Nevertheless it is probably the case that the urban bourgeoisie of the late Middle Ages played a more independent role in official life than had the *husfaste* men of the high Middle Ages.

The lay assessors or *lagrettemenn* occupied the leading positions in the official life of the towns as well. They were recruited from the ranks of the burgesses. However, the leading men in charge of civic activities were the town councellors. In the late Middle Ages they controlled to an increasing extent the town bailiff *(byfogd)*, the earlier *gjaldker*. The town council now also became established in important towns other than Bergen and developed, under the leadership of the lawman, towards being a permanent bench of magistrates, in keeping with the intentions of Magnus Lagabøte's *Bylov*. That the councils, in the course of the late Middle Ages, acquired one or two mayors as chairmen implied a greater independence. They appeared first in Oslo and Tønsberg in the years around 1440. We do not, however, come across them in Bergen, Trondheim and some other towns until after the Lutheran Reformation.

The political position of the Church in the late Middle Ages

As we have noted already, the Norwegian Church was less hard hit than the monarchy in the late Middle Ages (Chapter 6). When, after the mid-1300s, it sought to assert its rights according to the Concordat of 1277, it met much less opposition than earlier. The Church in Norway, as in the neighbouring kingdoms, was obliged to submit to the late medieval papacy's claim to fill vacant bishoprics, by so-called 'provision', and to increased taxation. But the Dano-Norwegian Crown's collaboration with the papacy in order to put its own candidates into Danish bishoprics affected Norway only slightly. One exception was the Oslo bishopric, where foreigners in the confidence of the Crown were a common occurrence. In the same way it gradually became more usual for foreigners to captain the castle of Akershus.

The archbishop and some of the bishops also held *len* from the

Crown. They strengthened their position too through the tax-exempted secular retainers they had positioned around the rural areas. This was especially so in the case of the archbishop. Archbishops like Aslak Bolt (1430–50) and Olav Engelbrektsson (1523–37) had the finances to start great building programmes, against the general run of things in the late Middle Ages, and they also controlled considerable military forces.

In 1458, Christian 1 (1450–81) ratified the Concordat of 1277 in exchange for the council of the realm's acceptance of his son Hans (1483–1513) as designated heir to the throne. In the immediately succeeding decades the Church was left free to conduct its own internal affairs. For the most part the bishoprics and the other important ecclesiastical positions were filled by Norwegians, usually from the minor aristocracy and the upper ranks of the peasant and urban societies. But from the time of Duke Christian (later Christian 2) as Norwegian viceroy (1506–13) the Norwegian Church was exposed to a serious threat. For it came under pressure from a monarchy that was increasingly sympathetic to Lutheranism and that wanted to cut back the economic and political rights and privileges of the Church.

The council of the realm

The privileged elite's political institution in Scandinavia during the late Middle Ages was the council of the realm (*riksråd, consilium regni*). At the accession of new rulers in all three Scandinavian countries in 1319–20, this council emerged as a more independent body than the royal council it superseded (Chapter 5). It operated on behalf of the kingdom – in Norway and Sweden as the regency council for Magnus Eriksson; in Denmark clearly as the effective force behind the election of Christoffer 2.

The Scandinavian councils sought a nationally representative role, which, as time passed, came to overshadow their position as royal counsellors, which they had inherited from the royal councils. The trend towards a broader representation of the different estates or classes was for a long time weak and fortuitous in Scandinavia. Only in Sweden did such a representative function become more firmly established through the development of general estates from the second half of the fifteenth century.

The council of the realm consisted of members of the high nobility as well as leading churchmen, with the archbishop and the bishops as more or less self-appointed advisers. It was quite large, the Norwegian council frequently having 20–30 members. Towards the middle of the fifteenth century the number rose to between 30 and 40, the result of a strong recruitment drive, partly from amongst the minor aristocracy. During the subsequent contraction of the Norwegian nobility, the number of lay members declined, apparently not exceeding 10 after 1500.

The Norwegian council never had a permanent formal chairman. Haakon 5's plan had been that the chancellor should occupy a leading position in the council, but he was soon pushed to one side and, during the late Middle Ages, was reduced to drawing up and issuing standard legal documents. The union kings usually tried to avoid appointing chancellors or other national officials who were in a position to lead a more independent council. It is true that when the Crown was vacant or the king under age, and sometimes also in the king's absence, a grand seneschal (*drottsete*) could, following the Swedish pattern, occupy the leading position in the council. From the middle of the fifteenth century such a situation came to a definite end. The archbishop in due course now emerged as the head of the council, going some way towards being its *de facto* chairman.

To the extent that the council served as a representative body for the aristocracy, tension between it and the monarchy could arise. Seen as a whole, the politics of the late Middle Ages appears as a tug-of-war between two political agendas. On the one hand, we have the monarchy seeking to maintain its power as free from restrictions as possible; on the other hand, the aristocracy seeking to use the council of the realm to set limits to royal power, following a programme of constitutionalism. Both took their inspiration and shape from monarchical and constitutional movements in contemporary Europe, partly in royal and princely circles, partly from the relationship between the papacy and the conciliar movement.

According to the constitutional programme, the king should rule in accordance with the laws of each individual kingdom. The council of the realm should participate in all important governmental decisions: legislation, the granting of privileges and *len*, financial matters, foreign and trade policy, etc. The unions of Scandinavian kingdoms should, from this viewpoint, be largely personal unions, with each kingdom having considerable powers of self-government through its council. Offices in the council and the holding of castles and *len* should be reserved for the higher nobility, whilst the Church in each kingdom should for the most part govern itself. The aristocratic members of the Norwegian council for a time in the fourteenth century continued the policy of isolationism that had made itself felt in relations with the other Scandinavian kingdoms during the last part of Haakon 5's reign (Chapter 5). But it later moved closer to the aspirations of its counterparts in Denmark and Sweden for a union based on constitutional grounds.

Support from society generally for the programme of the councils was neither wholehearted nor widespread. Quite the opposite: there was dissatisfaction among the peasants and the bourgeoisie with the aristocratic rule. When it came to clashes, the aristocracy sought to channel the dissatisfaction against those foreigners who held positions as lord lieutenants or *fogder,* as well as against the monarchy. This happened in the 1430s with the Engelbrekt Revolt in Sweden and the subsequent revolt in Norway under the nobleman Amund Sigurdsson. But the aristocratic members of the councils could also deal harshly with rebellious tendencies when that proved feasible, as when Erik Puke, the Swedish peasant leader and Engelbrekt's collaborator, was executed in 1436 and when Halvard Gråtopp's revolt in eastern Norway was put down in 1438.

The programme of constitutionalism did not have as much support in Norway as in the neighbouring kingdoms. This was partly because of the weaker position of the aristocracy in Norway and partly because of its tradition of service to the Crown. It was also weakened by the Danish union kings, who appointed foreign favourites who had married into noble families, and thus obtained Norwegian citizenship, to hold castles and other important lord lieutenancies. It was also easier for them to grant Norwegian castles and important *len* to men outside the council than was the case in Denmark and Sweden. Nevertheless, the Norwegian council did from time to time try to realize the programme of constitutionalism, especially at the accession of a new king or during periods when the throne was vacant. Then the council of the realm stepped forward as the sole bearer of governmental power.

The Norwegian council had moreover its own agenda, part of which was the national trade policy relating to the Hansa. This first became a serious issue under Haakon 5 (Chapter 5). The monarchy inclined in the same direction as the council on this, but it was, from time to time, so dependent on reaching an understanding with the Hansa that it confirmed its old privileges. From the reign of King Hans onwards, however, the monarchy did show a greater determination to restrict the economic freedom of action enjoyed by the Hanseatic merchants in Norway.

The Norwegian council also tried to retain the old colonies in the seas to the west and the country's economic links with them. After King Christian 1 pledged Orkney and Shetland to the Scottish king in 1468/69, the council tried several times to force the Crown to enter into meaningful negotiations to recover the islands. It also tried to counteract the direct trade carried on with Iceland by Englishmen and North Sea Germans in the fifteenth century, as well as to keep Iceland and the Faeroes as Norwegian *len* under the chief lord lieutenancy of Bergen. But neither policy had a successful outcome.

Towards a stronger monarchy

One should not exaggerate the effects of the antagonism between the monarchy's desire for independence and the constitutional aspirations of the council. A united aristocratic front was prevented by the need of individual nobles to keep in with the king, whilst separate personal interests continued to play an important part in top-level politics. Nevertheless, there is something to be said for seeing political developments in Scandinavia during the late Middle Ages in the context of relations between the two 'ideal types' of programme discussed above.

It was in the course of the fourteenth century that the councils of all three countries emerged as significant forces *vis-à-vis* the monarchy. The Swedish council took the initiative on several occasions during the accession to the throne of new rulers, and as a body that imposed limits on the power of kings and regents. It meant much in this connection that both Denmark and Sweden were elective monarchies and that the councils there came to serve as the actual electoral bodies.

In Norway, Duchess Ingebjørg, after 1319, pushed aside the council in its role as regent for her son, King Magnus Eriksson, but the council, following the Swedish precedent, expelled her from the government in 1323. In 1343 the council came to an agreement with Magnus to make his younger son, Haakon, king of Norway. With that, the decision was made to end the personal union between the crowns of Norway and Sweden. From 1355, Håkon 6, now of age, drew the Norwegian council into the government. But his marriage with Margareta, the daughter of the Danish king, Valdemar Atterdag, was, in the long run, to change the situation completely. Their son, Olaf, was elected king of Denmark and later inherited the crown of Norway from his father in 1380. Thus Norway was drawn into the union with Denmark that was to last until 1814.

Margareta was in reality the regent for her son and showed her strength when he died in 1387. In the course of 1387–88 she was chosen regent by the councils of all three Scandinavian kingdoms. The Norwegian council decided that the line of succession should stem from her, and in 1389 acclaimed Erik of Pomerania, the son of her sister's daughter, as king of Norway. Officially Norway continued to be a hereditary monarchy; but in 1343 and again in 1388–89 the council dealt with the right of inheritance in such a way that in reality it began to assume the electoral role the councils enjoyed in the neighbouring countries.

From 1389, Margareta controlled all three Scandinavian kingdoms. The union of the three kingdoms under her and Erik of Pomerania (1389–1439) is usually called the Kalmar Union, after the meeting in Kalmar in 1397 of the Scandinavian councils and greater nobles. At this Erik was crowned king of all three kingdoms. The councils had played an active, indeed decisive, role in all three countries during the establishment of a joint regency under Margareta, but from now on they were pushed aside by a distinct pro-monarchical policy. In Norway, Margareta ruled for the most part through a few favourites. Erik of Pomerania pursued her monarchical policy in such a controversial manner that he brought about the Engelbrekt Revolt against him in Sweden and was dismissed by the councils of Sweden and Denmark. In his place they elected Christopher of Bavaria, the son of Erik's sister, to the Crown in 1439. The Norwegian council hesitantly followed the example of its neighbours and in 1442 accepted, on behalf of the people and the kingdom, Christopher as king of Norway. Even on this occasion the right of inheritance was not formally abolished. But in reality an election of a king by the council had taken place. This marked the end, for the time being, of the pro-monarchical policy that had characterised the Kalmar Union.

During the years 1439–50 the constitutional ideal of a personal union of kingdoms governed by the councils became more of a reality in Scandinavia than in any other period, though it was to be shortlived. In Norway, the council, under the leadership of the grand seneschal Sigurd Jonsson, enjoyed the essentials of power in the years 1439–42. It kept its influence too after the accession of Christopher in 1442. Two permanent departments of the council now took on a clearer form – the continuation of a tradition stemming from the days of Haakon 5 – one in Bergen, for the area west of the Langfjella and north of the Dovre mountains, and one in Oslo for the rest of the country. The council involved itself especially in trade policy and law enforcement. Also, for the first time the members of the council received a general authority from the king to administer his justice by sitting on the court at the highest level.

After King Christopher died without issue in 1448, Sweden and Denmark each went their own way. Karl Knutsson was elected to the Swedish throne and Count Christian of Oldenburg to the Danish. Factions supporting both were formed inside and outside the Norwegian council. In order to secure support, both sides drew up accession charters or *håndfestninger*, documents making far-reaching promises based on the spirit of council constitutionalism. This was the first time this had happened in Norwegian history.

It was to be Christian 1 who was victorious in the conflict over the Norwegian crown. On his way back from his coronation in Trondheim in 1450, he stopped in Bergen. Here the councils of Norway and Denmark drew up an agreement for a permanent union between two equal kingdoms. Norway was now definitely made an electoral monarchy, with the council as the electoral body.

For what remained of the Middle Ages, 1450–1536, the power of the monarchy was again in the ascendant throughout Scandinavia, as it was in several other European countries. In Denmark, the Oldenburgs sat on the throne for the whole of this time. Christian 1, his son Hans and his grandson Christian 2 (1513–24) all tried to bring Sweden back into the union of three kingdoms but without permanent success. After Christian 2's brutal massacre of bishops, noble members of the council and citizens in Stockholm in 1520, Sweden unequivocally slipped out of the hands of the Oldenburgs. Gustaf Vasa now began to build up the strong Swedish monarchy that was to set its stamp on Scandinavian history in the following centuries.

For the Norwegian council, the period 1450–1536 witnessed a

downward, if uneven, trend. It was still able to play a part during an interregnum, and, to some extent, got its demands accepted through the promises made in the *håndfestninger* issued before a king was elected. But under reigning monarchs it was not able to win acceptance of the underlying assumption of these charters, namely that the council should share in all important governmental undertakings. Only in the administration of justice did it play a more or less permanent role. As the Duke of Norway and viceroy, the later-to-be Christian 2 pushed aside the council completely. He made fewer concessions than his predecessors had done in the *håndfestning* prepared before his coronation in 1513, and continued to exclude the council of the realm during his reign. In particular he weakened it by making use of foreign and minor nobility, together with men of bourgeois descent, as holders of Norwegian castles and *len*, at the same time as he directed a crushing blow against the Norwegian bishops.

When Christian 2 was banished from his kingdoms in 1523, the Norwegian council could again bring its influence to bear to some degree. This was brought about by a favourable political situation and by the efforts of individual activists on the council such as the Danish nobleman Vincens Lunge (married into the leading Norwegian noble family of the time) and Archbishop Olaf Engelbrektsson. But increasing antagonism within the council, especially between the archbishop and Lord Vincens, provided the right conditions for a monarchical reaction during the reign of Frederik 1 (1524–33) and prevented the council from exploiting the new interregnum in 1533–36. A factor here was that Vincens leaned in the same Lutheran direction as Frederik 1 and Christian 3 (1536–59), whereas Archbishop Olaf's primary goal was to defend the Catholic Church.

When Archbishop Olaf carried out a coup d'état in January 1536 and permitted the execution of Lord Vincens, the Norwegian council fell apart completely. After his flight from the country the following year, the council died without being formally dissolved. From the Crown's point of view, the archbishop's attempt to take Norway out of the union made it expedient to bring the country more completely under Danish control. This is the background to the so-called 'Norway Article' in the Danish *håndfestning* drawn up before the coronation of Christian 3 in 1536. Here it was stated that Norway should no longer be an independent kingdom, but should be a part of the kingdom of Denmark, in the same way as Jylland, Fyn and Sjælland and that it should remain under the Danish crown for ever more. After this, Christian 3 formally ruled Norway as a Danish king without any Norwegian national body at his side.

Norway was, however, geographically too large and distant and the traditions from the high Middle Ages too strong for the country to be ruled as a purely Danish province. A Norwegian sense of community could in the late Middle Ages draw new strength from many factors, amongst them the fear of the aristocracy and leading churchmen of losing their positions to foreigners, as well as the peasantry's opposition to having foreign lord lieutenants and *fogder*. Together, the facts of geopolitics, tradition and the Norwegian sense of identity were sufficient to ensure that Norway continued to be treated as something other than a Danish province.

Part II
1536–1814
Ståle Dyrvik

8
Union with Denmark

When the Danish king and the Danish nobility decided in 1536 to get rid of the Norwegian national council, they destroyed Norway's instrument of national sovereignty. Norway was to be completely integrated into Denmark – becoming but a Danish province. This was then no idle threat. The land was to be sacrificed for the benefit of the Danish ruling class. The Reformation gave the new rulers powerful ideological and cultural weapons. One could now expect that Norway would be swallowed up by its stronger neighbour to the south – both politically and culturally. Historically this union turned the clock back to the Battle of Hafrsfjord: the kingdom was being dissolved, and offered, moreover, to foreigners.

Less than 300 years later, in 1814, the union between Norway and Denmark ended. What had it been like? The population had increased sixfold; economically the country was richer and much more developed; and it had got back its own ruling classes. Admittedly it had taken over the written language of Denmark, and the spoken language of Norway too was much influenced by Danish. But there was an awareness of Norway's distinctiveness that was at least as strong in 1814 as it had been in 1536. Thus the break itself in 1814 was surprising. The close union with Denmark was replaced by independence under the Swedish crown – a personal union with Sweden, no more. An authoritarian absolutism gave way to what was, for its time, an advanced democracy. Yet this sudden transition occurred without friction, without social conflict, without institutional disturbance.

Two opposing viewpoints and an attempted synthesis

In Norwegian historiography there has been a clear tendency to see the union with Denmark in the light of the events of 1814.

Although Denmark-Norway was one of the minor European powers, it took part in European overseas expansion. Denmark secured the islands of St Thomas, St John and St Croix in the West Indies as well as trading posts in Ghana and India. This picture (from the Trade and Naval Museum at Kronborg) shows a Danish merchant ship sailing into Canton, the only port in China open to European ships.

For some historians, 1814 was the natural culmination of a long process of internal development leading to political and national independence. For others, 1814 was the result of the involvement of foreign powers in a Danish-Norwegian union that was still both close and strong. The exploration of these perspectives has sharpened the arguments of both sides and no doubt stimulated the historical interest of the general public in the whole period of the union. But perhaps the contrast between the moralizing and the judgemental, on the one side, and cool, clear objectivity, on the other, has created confusion. And perhaps the narrow focus on relations between Denmark and its dependency has led to too little awareness of Norway in its European and global context during this period. Here we shall examine the opinions of the different sides and attempt to bring them closer together.

(1) That the union with Denmark developed in a completely different direction than anyone would have expected in 1536 can hardly be denied. Norway was not swallowed up by Denmark, but rather enjoyed 300 hundred years of growth that, when that unique moment

of opportunity presented itself in 1814, put it in a position to stand on its own feet again.

(2) That the main trend of development was positive must not blind us to the fact that the union with Denmark had its drawbacks. Population growth, economic expansion and political progress were characteristic of European development generally in this period. One must, therefore, ask oneself: is it conceivable that the developments in Norway would have been even more positive without the Danish connection? Should one, instead of praising Danish moderation, ask if perhaps Norway was in a better position to defend itself against subjugation and exploitation than appeared to be the case in 1536? Was the way to national rehabilitation possible only through an intense and mounting struggle against a menacing and aggressive union partner?

Norway as a part of Europe's periphery

The course of Norwegian development perhaps emerges more clearly when it is seen within a wider geographical perspective. Obviously in other countries of Europe the years 1500–1800 were not called the Danish period or 'the time of union'. Rather one talks of the 'early modern period'. The overall trend was for both population growth and economic growth – the latter somewhat faster than the former – which prepared the way for the great leap forward during the industrial revolution of the eighteenth and nineteenth centuries. This economic growth seems to be associated with a greater regional and international division of labour; better communications; increased trade; and urbanization. Some see this as a long-term development with its roots in the Middle Ages. It becomes clearly visible in our period as the great breakthrough around 1800 approached. What was new in the period 1500–1800 was the gradual development of closer ties with other parts of the world that followed the great discoveries around 1500. It was the Europeans who got the lion's share of the economic benefits of these new contacts, as evidenced by their positive trade balances and a considerable import of, among other things, precious metals. The flow of silver made trade easier and led to inflation-driven growth.

But it was only certain countries in Europe that had these contacts with other parts of the world. Over time the locus of these shifted from

Denmark-Norway was at war with Sweden for much of the seventeenth century. Norwegian forces advanced deep into Swedish territory during the Gyldenløve War, 1675–79. The picture shows the Viceroy, Ulrik Frederik Gyldenløve, during the capture of the town of Marstrand and the fortress of Karlsten in Bohuslän. (Woven tapestry from the Rosenborg Palace, Copenhagen.)

the Mediterranean to Spain and Portugal, then further north to France and the Netherlands and finally to England. It was in England that the next major economic development began: the industrial revolution. From its European bridgehead the effects of these global contacts spread further. For Norway the stimulus came via an increased demand for, above all, timber, fish and metals. In exchange, Norway took not only corn and cash, but also a wide variety of more finished goods. In this one sees a feature that was much clearer in the relationship between Europe as a whole and the other parts of the world: the heartland built up the production of ever more advanced goods while the periphery stagnated as a supplier of raw materials. Apparently, one finds in Europe a corresponding periphery, of which Norway was a part.

Must the periphery bear the heaviest burden?

The period 1500–1800 is characterised by an irrepressible rivalry between the European states. Much of this was the outcome of an economic development that varied in tempo. A part of the rivalry took the form of protectionism and very considerable state support for new economic initiatives. Never before had the state involved itself in economic activities to the extent it did during this mercantilist period. This is a matter of great interest for developments in Norway. For through its economic policies the Danish government could discriminate to a very considerable extent against its Norwegian dependency.

The rivalry between the European states was most apparent in the wars that raged, almost continuously, in one part of the world or another. The use of large armies and more expensive weaponry demanded great expenditure. The state had to find ways of mobilizing far more of the economic resources of its subjects. The fiscal state had arrived. Norway was now vulnerable if the Danish government chose to favour the centre at the expense of the periphery.

Thus Norway, as a part of Europe, shared in the progress that this area of the world experienced in the years 1500–1800. But economically Norway also belonged to the European periphery whose ties with the leading countries was as a producer of raw materials. Furthermore, it should be emphasized that, in a period when the state was putting ever-increasing burdens on its subjects, and was also pursuing an active economic policy, it was especially unfortunate for Norway that the seat of government was placed outside the country's borders. To repeat: a development that in absolute terms was positive could turn out to be negative when compared with that experienced by the mother country, Denmark, or by the other leading states of Europe.

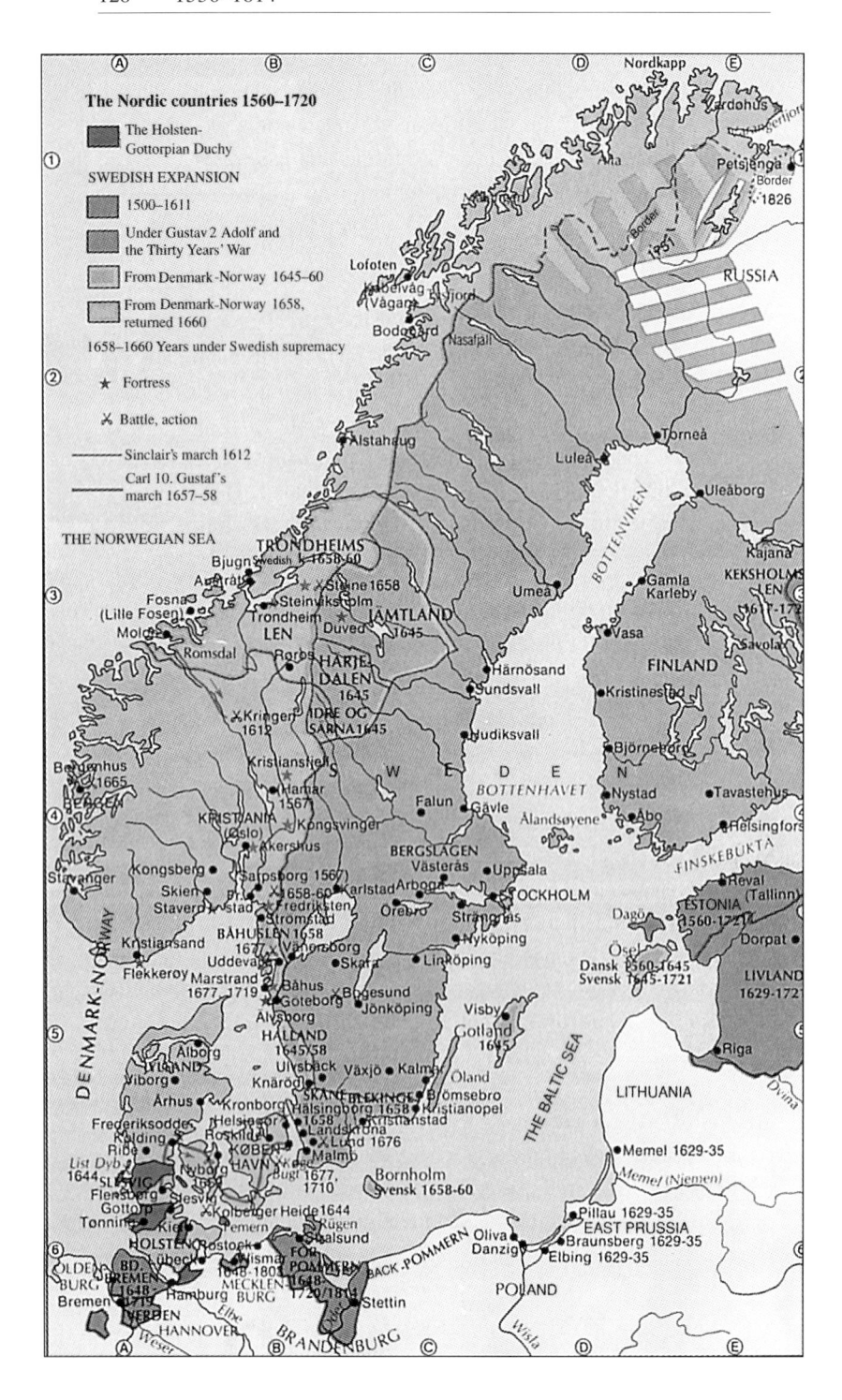

The Nordic countries 1560–1720

- The Holsten-Gottorpian Duchy

SWEDISH EXPANSION
- 1500–1611
- Under Gustav 2 Adolf and the Thirty Years' War
- From Denmark-Norway 1645–60
- From Denmark-Norway 1658, returned 1660
- 1658–1660 Years under Swedish supremacy

★ Fortress

⚔ Battle, action

——— Sinclair's march 1612
═══ Carl 10. Gustaf's march 1657–58

The structure of the presentation

We have now presented some of the key questions. The following account of Norway's history in the period of union, 1536–1814, starts with the basic elements of society: population and the economic structure (Chapters 9 and 10). We then turn the spotlight in Chapter 11 on the distribution of resources, on social groups and on the social structure. Chapters 12 and 13 deal, respectively, with the relationship between the Danish government and its Norwegian subjects and the relationship between the Danish mother country and its Norwegian dependency. Here will be found our final thoughts on the internal development of Norway down to 1814. Part II concludes with a chapter on the dramatic events of 1814 itself that led to the dissolution of the union, in the most remarkable year of Norwegian history.

Norway gets new frontiers

Before writing about Norway during the period of union with Denmark, it is perhaps appropriate that we look briefly at its frontiers. For it was at this time that the country took on its present territorial form. The wars with Sweden down to the beginning of the seventeenth century did not lead to any border changes. But after the war of 1643-45 (the Hannibal Affair), Norway was forced to surrender to Sweden the large, thinly populated areas of Jemtland and Herjedalen. Båhuslen was lost in the first traumatic Charles Gustaf War (1657-58) and Norway was split in two when Sweden also took Trondheims len, which was made up of Trøndelag, Nordmørc and Romsdal. At the final peace settlement in 1660 Trondheims len was returned. Subsequent wars did not lead to any loss of territory.

After 1720 there was a period of peace that made it possible to settle the frontier with Sweden in an amicable fashion. During the years 1742-51, the borders were painstakingly walked, marked and recorded. This procedure had its greatest impact in north Norway. The treaty of 1751 fixed the borders in the area occupied by the Sami, which had the effect of dividing them between the two Nordic states. It is true that the Sami nomads were to be allowed to move freely backwards and forwards across the frontier, but the treaty took for granted that they were now subjects of either the Danish or the Swedish Crown. To round off this account it should be noted that the final section of the frontier with Russia was fixed in 1826.

Economic contacts between Norway and its earlier dependencies in the seas to the west (Iceland, the Faeroes and Greenland) improved during the sixteenth and seventeenth centuries, but suffered a blow in the early 1700s when the so-called trade monopolies were centralized in Copenhagen. When the Danish Crown gave up Norway as a result of the Treaty of Kiel in 1814, it held onto the Faeroes, Iceland and Greenland. Compared with its medieval might, it was, then, a territorially smaller Norway that came out of the union with Denmark.

But how did Norwegian society look within these borders?

9
Demographic and social patterns

From around 1520 we find that tax lists have been preserved for considerable areas of the country. The taxpayers were listed by name, so that for the first time in Norwegian history it is possible to make a rough estimate of the size of the population. The evidence shows that in the rural districts there were about 24,000 taxpayers, all peasant farmers. If we reckon 6 people for each taxpayer and add to this 12,000 town dwellers, we arrive at a population of 150,000, within today's frontiers. The population of the high Middle Ages is reckoned to have been between 300,000 and 550,000. Even if this includes the present-day Swedish areas, it is immediately apparent that there had been a major decline.

The first actual census was taken in 1769, though one must wait until 1801 for a completely trustworthy picture of the Norwegian population. In the latter year there were at least 880,000 people in the country. This was six times as many as in 1520 and, roughly speaking, double the maximum reached in the high Middle Ages.

We have too a certain amount of demographic data for the period between the tax lists of 1520 or thereabouts and the censuses of 1769 and 1801. The most important are the muster rolls from the 1660s. On the basis of these it is estimated that the population in 1665 was 440,000. Thus the population had increased threefold from 1520 to 1665 and was to double again between 1665 and 1801. The average annual rate of growth was somewhat over 0.7 per cent in the period 1520–1665 and 0.5 per cent from 1665 to 1801.

Probably all areas of the country grew at about the same rate down to 1665. After that, although population growth continued steadily in Østlandet, in the rest of the country, from Agder to north Norway, it fell away markedly. Thus a great area of coastal Norway stagnated when seen against a still vital inland Norway. The pattern is reminis-

Population 1520–1801

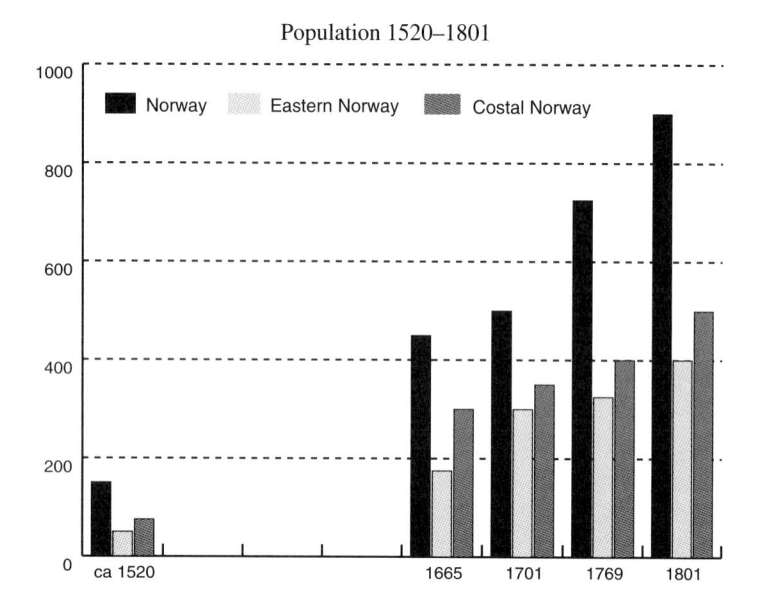

cent of the final years of the high Middle Ages. Some smaller districts such as parts of Sunnmøre and the interior of Agder experienced no growth of population whatsoever. This puzzling division of the country lasted for about 100 years, down to the middle of the eighteenth century. After that the population grew at about the same pace again throughout the entire country. But the results of this interlude remained: in 1665 some 35 per cent of Norwegians lived in Østlandet, by 1801 this percentage had risen to 45.

Was this pattern of population growth an advantage or not?

Behind the growth in population lay, of course, the interplay of births, deaths and migration. Little is known about these events until a new source appears in the second half of the seventeenth century, namely the parish registers. In the course of the eighteenth century, we get such registers for most of the country's parishes. Then, from 1735, we have a national return of the annual totals of baptisms, burials and marriages. The parish registers allow us to make a very detailed analysis of population conditions, especially if we use the material to re-create families through a technique known as nominal record linkage.

Marriage was universal. Just about all who could did get married. Divorce was rare but, when a spouse died, re-marriage occurred quickly, even at the higher ages. Within marriage, births took place at short intervals and right to the end of a woman's reproductive period. There is no sign of birth control. Nevertheless the average number of children per family was no higher than four to five. This was brought about by the late age at marriage: for men the average age was 27-29 years and for women a year or two younger. One would have expected that the long period of early adulthood lived outside marriage would have produced many illegitimate births, but such was not the case. Around 1750, illegitimate births amounted to only 2–3 per cent of all births. But from this point in time the percentage began to rise, reaching a peak, for the pre-industrial period, of just under 10 per cent in the middle of the nineteenth century.

In this period it is the death rate that shows the greatest difference from today's conditions. The first thing that strikes one is the extreme volatility in the number of deaths. Whilst, on average, 25–30 per 1,000 of the population died each year (as against 10 today), one can find, in a number of parishes, 100 or perhaps 200 deaths per 1,000 of the population. That is to say, some 10–20 per cent of the population was struck down in the course of a single year. Looked at over a larger area such an impact was averaged out. Nevertheless, in certain years, such as 1743 and 1773, one finds death rates of respectively 52 and 48 per 1,000 for the country as a whole. Such peaks go under the name of demographic crises. A closer analysis of the figures reveals the extent of the crisis, for the deaths were actually confined to a very short period, usually less than three months.

There can be little doubt that the main reasons for these crises were epidemics, food shortages or a combination of the two. Contemporary records give us little help as to which of these took the greatest toll. We know less, in fact, about disease than about harvest failure and shortages of food. For, in all the great crises that struck large areas of the country or the country as a whole, both epidemics and shortage of food were present. Sickness is always present in the minor crises. On the other hand, harvest failure often does not lead to higher mortality. It has been difficult to discover whether or not there is a social pattern to mortality, but there is little evidence that the risk of death was greater amongst the poor than amongst the well off. All this suggests that the crises were produced by infectious diseases but that the outcome of the diseases could be reinforced by malnutrition. The most common of the epidemic diseases in the eighteenth century were dysentery, typhoid fever, typhus and smallpox. This last usually affected children and young people. Plague had disappeared from the country by the middle of the seventeenth century.

Towards the end of the eighteenth century, the expectation of life at birth was probably around 35-40 years. This was high by contemporary European standards and was clearly over the medieval level, which it is thought lay under 30 years. Nevertheless it was still less than half today's average. The reason for the comparatively low life expectancy was the high death rate amongst children and the young. Less than half of all who were born reached adulthood and as many as 25 per cent died in their first year. This frighteningly high level of infant mortality had a far greater impact on the average expectation of life than did the demographic crises.

Around 1815 the pattern of mortality in Norway changed dramatically. The crude death rate fell from 20–25 per 1,000 of the population to under 20. Most striking was the complete disappearance of demographic crises. Yet at least equally important was the fact that infant mortality fell sharply at roughly the same time. There has been a great debate as to the reasons for this surprising fall in mortality, which we will come back to in Chapter 16.

Our picture of migration is rather sketchy. The country as a whole had net out-migration. A considerable number must have gone to Denmark for, among other reasons, military service in the navy. A considerable migration from the most southerly part of the country to Holland also occurred. Migration from overseas to the Norwegian towns was not enough to match this, nor were the waves of Finnish settlers to the forest areas of Østlandet and the far north of Norway.

A closer look at the period of stagnation

Can any of the recent discoveries in the population history of eighteenth-century Norway be used to cast light on the stagnation of coastal Norway during the years 1650–1750? Since this began at about the same time as the population returned to its level of the high Middle Ages, was one factor the shortage of land for new settlement? The contrast between the coast and the interior also leads to speculation about changes in the fortunes of secondary employment – a failure of the fisheries or an expansion of forestry. The comparatively high tax levels from 1625 to 1720 may also have checked economic growth in marginal areas of the country.

To the extent that one can really speak of such an economic problem (the details of which we shall return to in a later chapter), one thing is certain: it was not caused by more demographic crises or higher average mortality in the coastal areas than in the interior. Too little is known about migration.

Attention has, however, been focused increasingly on the restrictive marriage pattern. A slightly higher average age at marriage in coastal Norway would be enough to reduce slow growth to no growth at all. If the condition of establishing a family was that the head had to have a means of livelihood sufficient to support a wife and children, for example a farm, the age of marriage and, through that, the growth of population would be tied to the number of opportunities for employment. Economic stagnation would then lead to a reduction in population growth, without any dramatic crises. If one looks overseas one finds that in the period 1650–1750 there was a tendency towards demographic stagnation over great areas of western Europe. And it is believed that the reason for this was just this close tie between family formation and a fixed number of occupations suitable for its support. This should serve as a warning against looking for especially local explanations of the stagnation in coastal Norway. Looked at in a European context, what really requires an explanation is the growth of population in Østlandet during this period.

The new growth in coastal Norway around the middle of the eighteenth century is also a cause for speculation. If it appears that neither agriculture nor fishing experienced better times in the second half of the eighteenth century, then it is necessary to look again for a demographic explanation. People strove to keep the level of population down, but because to do so they had placed so much weight on the age of marriage and did not employ birth control, the balance could be destroyed by an otherwise welcome fall in mortality. In this connection it is interesting that, though the onset of the fall in mortality for the country as a whole can so clearly be dated to 1815, it actually began quietly in Sørlandet (coastal counties of south Norway) and Vestlandet several decades earlier.

The crofter *(husmann)* system arrives

The demographic stagnation, which lasted 100 years in coastal Norway, raises significant questions about the social consequences of population growth. Here we confine our attention to the 90 per cent of the population who belonged to the peasant society. The population counts from around 1665 included occupational data, which lead us to believe that society at that time was still socially homogeneous. The vast majority of family breadwinners were *peasant farmers (gardbrukere)*. But we find too a group of *crofters (husmenn)*. Earlier in the seventeenth century this latter title had been used for a tax class within the peasantry. There, and in the muster roll of 1701, many of the crofters were old, suggesting that they were retired peasant farmers. But some were young and this alerts us to something new. In the course of the eighteenth century this new type of crofter grew rapidly in number. By the census of 1801 the picture is clear. Counting just heads of households there were, broadly speaking, 55,000 crofters as against 77,000 peasant farmers; i.e. around 30 per cent of the total membership of the agricultural community belonged to this rapidly expanding proletariat. In other words, it would appear that the population growth of the last half of the period of union with Denmark had resulted in more people being forced down into an underclass.

A crofter is a person who rents a piece of land from a farmer – land that was not separately registered for tax purposes. If the piece is big enough to work agriculturally, one speaks of a crofter's holding and of a crofter with land. If one is merely talking about a piece just big enough for a house, one uses the expression crofter without land. Crofters who lived by the sea were usually called 'shore sitters'. As noted above, a crofter's holding was not separately registered for tax but formed, for fiscal purposes, part of the farm to which it belonged. Crofters, then, paid no land tax. On the other hand, they had to pay rent and provide help in other ways to the farmer from whom they rented the cottage or holding. In many cases they entered into written contracts, from which we can get a good idea of their living conditions. The rent for the holding could be fixed in money terms or in so many days' work, or a combination of the two. The work itself could be unspecified or set down as particular tasks. In addition a crofter could be obliged to work when required, i.e. go to the farmer and work for him, in return for wages, whenever there was a need. The agreements between a peasant farmer and a crofter could be for a crofter's life, for a year, or until he was given notice.

What was the purpose of the crofter system?

Most crofters had land, but it goes without saying that this would not amount to much relative to the farm of which it formed a part. The available sources on output suggest that the average crofter owned a couple of cows and 5–10 sheep or goats and produced 8–16 bushels of grain. Horses were exceptional. One thing is therefore clear: the output of a holding was almost always too small to support a crofter's family. One needed alternative sources of income. But here our records desert us. Undoubtedly one important means of livelihood was to work for short periods for neighbouring farmers, especially during harvest time. In forested areas, cutting timber, transporting it to a river or lake and then floating it downstream also provided employment. Similar paid work, but no doubt not so widespread, was to be found in mines, at the fisheries and in shipping. Some crofters were in business on their own account as craftsmen or petty traders, or perhaps as working partners on a fishing boat or as owners of other seagoing vessels.

Our understanding of the crofter system must then take account of activities outside the agricultural activity on the holding. It is, therefore, a pity that even as late as the nineteenth century we know so little about how crofters made ends meet. Simon Skappel's first attempt at analysing and interpreting the crofter system took as its starting point the amount of work required of a crofter by his landlord, either in the form of rent for the holding or as normal wage labour. On this basis it is possible to talk of worker–crofters in the rich farming districts of Østlandet and Trøndelag. Here the need for labour explains the growth of the crofter system. Where the farmers were less interested in using the labour of their crofters and would rather see them looking after themselves through one or other source of outside income, the expression 'leasehold crofters' was used. Such crofters were to be found in the rest of the country. Skappel's distinction is of interest, though it is now clear that, since both types are represented in all areas, it is too crude.

Of course it is not difficult to see population growth as the essential cause of the expansion of the crofter system. Such an explanation

A croft called Vatnhusteigen belonging to the farm of Bråtveit at Suldal in Ryfylke. The buildings seem small and in poor condition, thus giving the appearance of poverty. But this is an old croft that had been deserted. When crofters found secondary employment, they managed all right.

accords well with the situation in the country as a whole; for in 1801 it was in Østlandet that there were the greatest number of crofters per farmer. But if one looks at smaller areas, such as an individual parish, the waters muddy, as there appear to be too many exceptions to the general rule. Another way of approaching the question is to try to establish what attraction different economic structures had for crofters. Are they distributed according to the demand for labour in agriculture, as indicated by the size of farms, or are their numbers related to the growth of such important secondary sources of income as forestry and fishing? Again we find marked exceptions to the expected pattern of the greatest growth where the greatest employment opportunities were to be found.

Until better data and analytical tools are available it is difficult to draw any conclusions about the Norwegian crofter system other than to say that it was a very complex social institution. For it represents not just one, but many ways of economic adjustment. In one place it could be a means of supporting an unemployed and impoverished excess population. In another, it was an effective system for recruiting and disciplining a cheap and stable labour force for the farmer. In yet another, it was perhaps indicative of a division of labour, of specialization, of economic development. But above all one should perhaps see all three functions in a constantly shifting mix.

Social and cultural differences in the towns

Because of the archival situation, our knowledge of the population and social structure of the towns is more uneven than for the countryside. The growth of the urban population was faster than that of the rural population, without this leading to much of a shift in the balance between them. Roughly 6–8 per cent of Norwegians lived in towns at the beginning of the sixteenth century; the figure had risen to 10 per cent by 1801. This does not take into account the growth of built-up areas that gradually formed outside the judicial boundaries of the towns. As in the rural districts, so in the towns we find a clear social division, with burgesses on the one hand and workers on the other, rather than peasant farmers and crofters. The burgesses had control of the actual business of the towns, namely trade, handicraft and shipping. Many of them were joined together in guilds, which regulated recruitment to the trades. The towns also had a certain amount of internal self-government in which each burgess participated. The burgesses too decided amongst themselves who they would admit to their ranks. All these were mechanisms that drew a sharp formal line through the urban population. There were, however, clear divisions amongst the burgesses. The merchants formed an elite, whilst a large proportion of the craftsmen were in modest circumstances akin to those of the better-off workers. It is not possible to say how many there were of each group before the middle of the seventeenth century, and even then our figures are very approximate. The situation also varied from town to town. But speaking generally the burgesses probably made up somewhat under half of the urban population. The trend down toward 1800 was for the proportion to diminish gradually at the same time as the division between the top and bottom of urban society increased. This corresponds well with the situation in the countryside, though the proletariat there grew from a much smaller base. Common to town and country was the clear, in part legally based, two-part social division; the more rapid growth of the lower of these; and the development of greater inequality within each of the two groups.

Throughout the whole period a considerable number of foreigners joined the ranks of the burgesses. Almost half of all who were legally admitted to the status of burgess in Bergen during the seventeenth century were foreigners and half of these again were German. The Hanseatic League gradually lost its grip on the town's foreign trade and the Hansa Office came formally into Norwegian hands in the 1750s. However, the foreign presence amongst the burgesses continued to be strong. In Østlandet the trickle of people from Denmark and Slesvig-Holstein was important and, since they were citizens of the same country, they were, during the seventeenth century, able to combine trade with public office. On the whole these long-distance migrants were resourceful individuals. This led to a sharpening of the social division within the Norwegian towns: the upper class acquired a strong foreign element, while the underclass remained overwhelmingly Norwegian.

Demographic differences between the social groups

The age at marriage of men seems to have been pretty much the same right across the social spectrum, but that of women varied widely. The

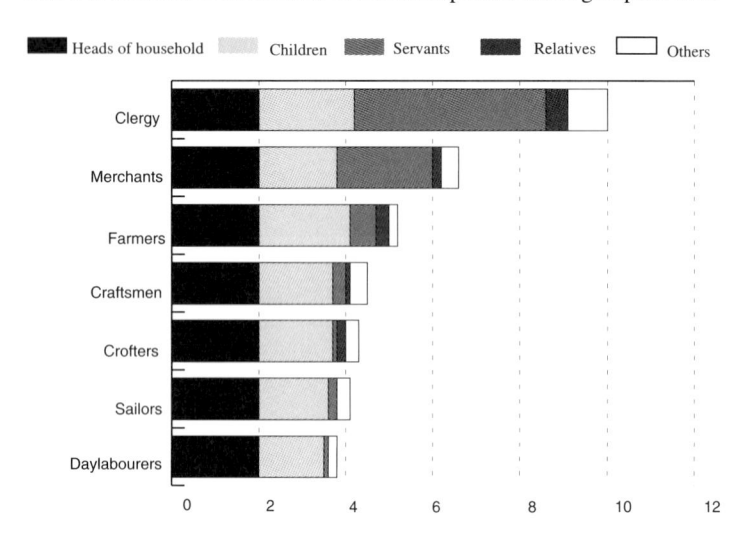

Size and structure of households of certain important social groups in 1802

A sloop from Hardanger photographed by Knud Knudsen in 1872. Wooden vessels of this size were the workhorses of the Norwegian transportation system before trains and cars. They could be sailed along the entire Norwegian coast, even in the dark and bad weather of winter.

higher the social group to which a woman belonged, the earlier she married. Amongst the upper middle class, the average age at marriage for women could be round about 20 years, whereas amongst crofters and labourers it was nearer 30. In the former case the wives were much younger than their husbands, while in the latter they were often older. The amount of time married women spent in the childbearing age group varied, therefore, according to the age at which they married. In general then, women at the top of the social scale had far more children than those at the bottom – quite the reverse of what both contemporaries and subsequent generations believed. The difference was increased a little because lower-class mothers practised lengthy breastfeeding, which increased the gap between births. When it comes to the mortality experience of different social groups, our understanding is still limited. But it would appear that the risks of death varied little. This gives further support to the point raised earlier under our discussion of demographic crises; namely, that starvation and material needs had no great impact on mortality.

A demographic feature that deserves a separate treatment is the structure of the household. In 1801 the average Norwegian household had 5.4 members. But behind this figure lay great social variations, with a household size of 3–4 amongst crofters and workers generally and up to 7–10 amongst the larger farmers, prosperous townspeople and top public officials. Some of this difference stems from what has already been said about the age at marriage and the level of fertility. The main reason, however, was the number of servants. The growth of the lower classes and the increased social polarization prepared the ground for a massive net transfer of labour between the classes. In practice this took place within the context of the service function. During the long period that stretched from entry into the labour market down to entry into marriage, the young formed a vast and cheap source of labour that was moved from the poorer to the better-off households. But as a time in service was also regarded as a kind of apprenticeship, it was usual for peasant farm households too to exchange their older children as servants.

There were 105,000 servants in Norway in 1801, enough to provide every farmer and burgess household with one servant each. Those who would go looking for exploitation in this society should not ignore the under-aged and badly paid youngsters hidden in the households of the well-to-do.

The social contact area

Norway's topographic and cultural landscape ranked its population in a hierarchy of distinctive local societies. Compared with the European continent, the low density of population and the great distances between settlements are what catch the eye (Chapter 1). However, a very large proportion of the population lived by the sea and here boats and small vessels were, for the period, a rapid means of communication. Great quantities of goods could also be transported by sea without difficulty, although winter, with its bad weather and darkness, put something of a damper on movement, especially in the far north. Communications were more difficult in the interior of the country, particularly in Østlandet and the mountain areas. The network of roads suitable for wheeled transport was small. But when winter came and the rivers and lakes froze over, an excellent surface was provided for transport by horse and sleigh. All in all, communications in Norway were easier than in most places in Europe. This is an important point for our later discussion of output and trade.

In spite of the great increase in population in the century after the crisis of the late Middle Ages, there emerged no settlements in Norway of the type found in the rural areas of the rest of Europe. Only in certain areas of Vestlandet do we see collections of dwellings that resemble a nucleated village. The foundation stone of the Norwegian settlement pattern was, as in the Middle Ages (Chapter 3), the *gard*, understood here to mean a farm (often divided into a number of holdings) with its own name and later its own number in the land register. By the end of the period of union with Denmark there were around 40,000 such farms in Norway. The actual units of agricultural production were the holdings, which made up the farms, and, in turn, as enclaves within them, the new crofts. In drawing comparisons between the Norwegian *gard* and the continental village, it is immediately apparent that the great difference is one of size: around 1800, the average Norwegian *gard* consisted of only two holdings and one croft. In the next chapter we shall examine the physical appearance of the Norwegian farm, but before we do so it is worth noting that not only was it a small unit, socially speaking, but also it was characterized by a much looser sense of community than the continental village.

If, on the other hand, we define the local community more widely, as the parish, the result is quite different. The average population of the Norwegian parish in 1801 was around 2,500–3,000, which is several times larger than that found in Denmark and further south. None of the Norwegian towns was large by European standards: the largest was Bergen, which, in 1801, had 18,000 inhabitants, followed by Christiania with 9,200, Trondheim with 8,800 and Kongsberg with 6,800. On the other hand, we do not find in Norway that mass of small market towns that is so characteristic of the situation on the continent. At the local level, however, Norwegians had a greater circle of contacts. Taken together with the ever-wider interaction brought about through travel or seasonal migration in connection with trade, transport, shipping and fishing, the impression is sharpened that Norway was unusually mobile and unusually open, both internally and externally.

10
The economy

As in the Middle Ages, agriculture was the main source of employment in the years 1500–1800. Even at the end of the period some 80–85 per cent of the population had access to land and at least 75 per cent drew their main income from it.

The easiest way to understand the structure of agriculture is to start with the farm. The typical farm embraced land 'from *fjord* to *fjell*'. Surrounding the farmhouses and yard lay the infield. This was made up of arable and of hay meadows. Outside the rich agricultural areas of Østlandet and Trøndelag, the arable was under constant cultivation. Soil exhaustion was prevented, to some extent at least, by heavy manuring and improvements of one sort or another. The meadow land was as nature made it, with, at most, a little manure added. In areas where the land was rotated between arable and hay meadow, no grass seed was sown when the land was left fallow. The infields were used for pasture in early spring and late autumn. Everything that lay outside the boundaries of the infield was given the name 'outfield'. Usually there was plenty of forest here, which supplied firewood and timber; and in some areas wood for sale. Much of the summer grazing took place in the outfields, commonly in association with the mountain huts (*sæter*). In some areas several such huts and associated pastures were to be found, with the animals being moved in stages up the mountain side. In the autumn the procedure was reversed. Much of the winter fodder was gathered in the outfield areas and close by the mountain huts. Leaves, bark and small twigs were also gathered from the woods. Slash and burn techniques were usual in Østlandet in order to produce patches of land on which corn could be grown. All this bears the hallmarks of a foraging economy.

The holding and the croft

On farms with several holdings, the arable and meadow land in the infield areas was usually clearly divided between the different occupiers. Since one of the objects of this was to give each occupier an equal share of the different kinds of soil, each holding had its pieces of land mixed in with those of the others. Not until the 1800s was there a move to consolidate the pieces by reapportioning them. Very often a valuable resource such as woodland was also divided amongst the different occupiers and fenced off. Land in the outfield, used for grazing and haymaking, was held in common to be used as one wished, by the different occupiers, within the boundaries of the farm. Rights to hunt and to fish in lakes and rivers were also usually held in common. Sometimes the right to exploit the outfields and fells was held in common by neighbouring farms or groups of farms. When such rights were widely held one used the term 'rights of common'. However, an increasing population and pressure on resources often led to conflicts, with the result that vague rights were replaced by an unambiguous fixing of boundaries. Ownership in common was on the decline long before the enclosure movement began, with the result that the latter consisted, for the most part, of a reorganization of already well-defined holdings.

The new crofts were usually to be found inside the boundaries of a particular holding and only rarely in the areas held in common. The normal site was a less valuable piece of land in the infield, or in grazing or haymaking areas in the nearby outfield, a fact evidenced by croft names such as Traet (fenced-in area) or Hagen (enclosed pasture). A croft cleared close to the existing infield could later be given up and incorporated into the farm. In many districts the crofter system was used systematically for clearing land in just such a way. But on the whole the new croft distribution pattern was one that was dispersed on the periphery of the farm.

What did Norwegian agriculture produce?

The two distinguishing features of Norwegian agriculture were that, within a European context, it was carried on close to the climatic limits of cultivation and that, on the whole, it gave the same amount of weight to arable and animal husbandry. These features were but little changed since the Middle Ages (Chapter 3). Areas devoted solely to grain were hardly to be found. On the other hand, grain cultivation was carried on in the mountain districts and as far north as mid-Troms, even though there one must reckon on the harvest failing on occasion. This balance between arable and livestock meant the fields were well manured. The productivity of the arable was high by European standards, especially given that widespread soil exhaustion was avoided, as was fallowing. An exception was provided by the oat-producing areas of Østlandet. Putting one's eggs in two baskets, as it were, can also be seen as an attempt to reduce the effects of climatic variations.

The first agricultural statistics covering almost the entire country come from the seventeenth century. A register giving the value of the output of all Norwegian farms (not holdings) was drawn up for tax purposes. Within this, an estimate was given of what the farm normally sowed and harvested and the number of animals that were overwintered. A new register was created in the 1720s, but not used. The valuation carried out in 1802 in connection with the so-called 'land tax' can be compared with the other two, though it has not been completely preserved. More formal counts of animals were made for the 'war tax' of 1657 and again in 1808. In 1809 an assessment was made of the amount of seed sown each year. Some doubts as to the accuracy of these counts must be raised as they were all linked, directly or indirectly, to the payments of tax. Agricultural statistics were collected as part of the population censuses from 1835 onwards but they too were unreliable in the beginning.

A certain amount of qualitative information can be relied on. As in the Middle Ages, the usual grains were oats and barley or a mixture of the two (*blandkorn*). Oats dominated in central Østlandet, *blandkorn* in the coastal areas and Trøndelag, and barley in the interior in the south and the whole of north Norway. Potatoes were first planted in Norwegian soil around the middle of the eighteenth century, but one must wait until after 1800 to see their use widespread. Countless numbers of local breeds of animals were to be found. On the whole the animals were much smaller than today. This had the advantage that they were able to live on short rations during the winter, yet come quickly into production on the rich summer pastures.

Self-sufficiency and a barter economy?

It is more difficult to estimate output, although it is recognized that the figures in the registers are too small. This can be seen at the micro level, to some extent, if one compares the totals of animals and seed sown given in the registers with those in the inventories prepared after a farmer's death. Such inventories are to be found in the greatest number around the 1723 registration. The comparison here suggests that figures for seed sown and numbers of horses and cattle are broadly similar in the two sources, whilst the number of sheep and goats given in the register must be increased by as much as 50 per cent. Were the Norwegian people self-sufficient in food? To answer this it is necessary to pose another question: what were the yields of arable and animal husbandry? As noted earlier, the registers give the amount of corn harvested, but was this before or after the following year's seed corn had been taken out? Uncertainty surrounding animal output is even greater, for one must extrapolate slaughter weights and milk production backwards from the nineteenth century.

By 1720, despite these many qualifications, one reckons that agriculture produced a little over 2,000 calories per inhabitant per day, i.e. 500 calories less than the amount regarded as adequate. Even discounting the contribution of hunting and fishing, the shortfall is serious. However, once imported grain is taken into account, the figures look better. In the early eighteenth century, overseas imports amounted to 500,000 hectolitres (hl), or 1 hl (3 bushels) per head. With imports of this magnitude added to the home production of milk, meat, corn and fish, the average Norwegian was well fed. It is interesting to note that, of the total calorific intake, well over 60 per cent came from grain, 30 per cent from milk and milk products, while fish and occasionally meat played a much smaller role than is usually assumed. Norwegians were a nation of porridge eaters.

It is reasonable to assume that throughout the whole period 1500–1800 (and down to today, for that matter) Norway was self-sufficient in food, reckoned in calories. But long before our period we find a trading system that involved the exchange of Norwegian fish calories for foreign corn calories. Trade was so extensive that the use of such concepts as self-sufficiency and a barter economy is questionable.

Did this trade in food products increase over time? It is interesting to see that if one compares agricultural output per farmer in, for example, the 1660s, 1723 and 1855 one finds no decline; in fact quite the opposite. It is true that a crofter class had grown up whose food production was clearly lower. Despite this, Norway had not become more dependent on imported grain in the course of the 300 years down to 1800. Norwegian agriculture had kept pace with a rising population remarkably well. The growth of population and the division of the land into ever more holdings and crofts had been compensated for by the colonization of new land and more intensive working. In spite of the great expansion in productive capacity, there is no sign of a resource ceiling being reached, such as might have occurred in the Middle Ages.

But what of the situation locally? It is easy to see that there were considerable and enduring divisions in agricultural output between the different parts of the country. Corn growing was at its most extensive in mid- and southeast Østlandet and in inner Trøndelag; and at its least extensive in Agder and above all north Norway. Livestock holdings were greatest in inner Østlandet and in northern parts of Vestlandet, and smallest in Agder and north Norway. For both products, output per head differed by a factor of one to two. The differences were even greater when the same areas came high or low with regard to both arable farming and animal husbandry. That the crofter system was less widespread in the weaker areas reduced the gap, though it remained palpably great.

Despite these variations, agriculture itself provides the main reason for the astounding rise in Norway's population in the period of union with Denmark – to a level far above its medieval peak. The development of three other industries (fishing, lumbering and mining) came as a surplus and contributed significantly to the increase in prosperity of the country. It remains to be seen if these other activities served to wipe out the great regional differences that show themselves in agricultural output.

Fish from sea to market

The fish in the seas off the Norwegian coast is a wonderful resource. It is, however, a difficult one to exploit. There are several reasons for this. First, the greatest prize – the cod and herring fisheries – last only two to three months a year, when the fish spawn. Second, although the fish come into the coast in order to spawn, when they come and to which part of the coast could vary, the herring is particularly unstable. Third, the catch must be preserved, otherwise it would be unfit for human consumption within a few days. Finally, it is difficult to think of a diet in which fish, in calorific terms, is the only or even the most important element. A Norwegian fishing population could never, therefore, be self-sufficient; it must exchange fish for other foodstuffs. It needed, in other words, a market and a trading system to serve it.

It is, then, within this context that the development of the Norwegian fishing industry in the years 1500-1800 must be seen as a series of adjustments.

It has already been shown in Chapter 3 how marketing channels for Norwegian fish were opened in the Middle Ages to a huge and apparently insatiable market on the continent. At the beginning of our period, the Hanseatic traders in Bergen were the most important link with this market. They also took charge of the return trade, of which corn was the most important item. These trading arrangements changed substantially down to 1800. The Hanseatic traders gave way to a native group, and Bergen's special position became less evident as other towns took over more of the fish export business. The markets shifted – the Baltic and especially the Mediterranean becoming more important, Germany and the Netherlands less so. This meant a broadening of the market. At the same time, new ways of exploiting the fish resources were found and a wider range of products came on offer.

Marketing, in other words, was not the limiting factor for the industry.

The development of the most important fisheries

Fishing, in late winter, for the cod coming to spawn took place mainly off the coasts of Lofoten and Møre. The Lofoten fisheries went into decline from the 1620s and after a brief upsurge in the middle of the century continued to decline to a low point in the decades around 1700. An undoubted period of growth began in the 1740s, which reached its peak just after 1800. Møre, too, experienced a crisis at the end of the seventeenth century. Then catches increased to a peak around 1750. This was followed by fluctuating fortunes and an almost empty sea in the years 1790 to 1820.

In the seventeenth century the most important herring fisheries were

Northern Norwegian fishing station. The fish are hung to dry on racks. The boats are small enough to be dragged ashore. Large vessels to carry the fish and provide accomodation for the fishermen are lying at anchor in the bay. (Photograph by Knud Knudsen, 1875.)

off the coast of Båhuslen (Bohuslän), which at that time belonged to Norway. Then, in the first half of the sixteenth century, the centre shifted to the seas off Trøndelag and Møre. Decline occurred after 1650 but then in the 1700s the fish returned in huge numbers and catches rose along the whole of Vestlandet's coast. Suddenly in the 1760s the herring shoals disappeared from the northern coasts of Vestlandet and from the 1780s from its southern coasts too. There followed 30 years with almost empty seas everywhere.

The long-term development of the population of coastal Norway was much steadier than the ups and downs of the fishing industry might suggest. We find few signs of full-time fishermen who followed the fish. Instead it was a case of peasants and crofters from a wide area who migrated to the fisheries in the winter months and returned to their holdings in the summer. This dual employment pattern made it possible to mobilize a vast labour force. At the same time, it was a better way of making use of the working year and gave the fishermen something (agriculture) to fall back on should the sea fail to offer up its riches.

The normal vessel used along the entire coast was an open wooden boat with a crew of 4-6. The building of these boats usually took place in the fjords where suitable timber was available. The three most important pieces of equipment required for the cod fishing were the hand line with one hook, the long line with many hooks, which could be left in the sea, and the seine net. The longline and the seine net came into use gradually over a lengthy period in spite of opposition. The reason for this opposition was that nets and longlines demanded more space and created confusion on the fishing grounds. But generally the fish were so close together and in such numbers that even the simplest of equipment gave good catches. The herring fisheries usually employed seine nets though larger trawl nets were on the way in during this period. All this equipment was made of imported hemp by local domestic industry and was relatively cheap. All in all, for those who wanted to take part in the fisheries, capital costs were moderate.

Originally the cod had been preserved by drying it on racks, producing stockfish *(tørrfisk)*. This was cheap, it facilitated the carriage to market, and it could be handled by the fisherman himself. Salting the fish could be done on any scale only when access to cheap salt from southern Europe came about in the eighteenth century. Gradually after that, more and more of the catch was turned into *klippfisk*, which involved both drying and salting. The change-over occurred first in southern Norway, where the climatic conditions for drying by the wind only were the least stable. The production of *klippfisk* demanded greater investment and more organization. Hence it was usually in the hands of the merchants. The fisherman was more of a raw material supplier. Salt was even more important for the exploitation of the herring stocks. The individual fisherman could hardly hold supplies of salt or organize the work. So here too the merchants took control of the processing. The more that salt was used for preserving the fish, the more the processing stage was taken out of the hands of the fishermen themselves. However, the great demand for barrels for the herring fisheries had a spin-off effect in districts with forests. The carriage of the fish to the exporting harbours usually took place on small cargo boats with a half-deck and sails. These boats came from rural areas, which thus took their share of the profits from the fisheries.

The water-powered gate saw opens up a new Norwegian resource

As with the fisheries, forestry was a Norwegian industry that could not have attained any size without the demand from an overseas market. Again we are dealing with a typical export industry, the difference being that the export of timber products did not take place to any considerable extent before the period under discussion. In fact, the take-off is usually associated with a breakthrough around 1500 for the water-powered gate saw. This made it possible to increase the output of that most sought after timber product, milled boards.

The internal colonization resulting from the growth of population in Europe reduced the area of forest. At the same time, the demand for wood products increased, with the great expansion of the building and shipping industries. The transport of such heavy goods of mass consumption was expensive. The densely populated areas around the North Sea turned, therefore, to Norway. The way was short and the supply apparently enormous. Exploitation came first where access was easiest, namely along the coasts from the Oslofjord to Bergen. One of the advantages Norway offered was the large number of rivers and streams that could drive the saws. In the purchasing countries, the situation was much more difficult. Complicated wind-driven or hand-powered saws had to be used. In addition to boards, foreigners were interested in a number of other timber products. Beams, for instance, were much sought after. Value was added by sawing and cutting, both skilled crafts. It would be wrong, therefore, to see the timber trade as purely an export of raw materials.

Regulating the timber industry

From the middle of the seventeenth century the growth of this new industry flattened out, and in some areas there was an actual decline. The coastal areas had had problems for a long time. In the southern parts of Vestlandet, the forests were all but razed. The heart of the industry moved north, with major areas like Møre and Trøndelag coming into production. Along the coast of Agder and in Østlandet resources had also been exploited to excess. But here felling could move further inland. The great natural waterways meant that timber could be floated over vast distances. But this was expensive since it involved clearing the rivers and setting up booms and it demanded a considerable labour input. The purchase, marketing and passage of the timber downstream also involved a considerable amount of organising. Timber prices had to be high for it to be worthwhile exploiting the innermost areas of Østlandet. It was not until the boom years around 1800 that the limits of felling reached the most distant of these vast timber resources. However, where felling was not profitable one could still produce charcoal or tar, both of which could stand the costs of transport better.

Ideally the sawmills should lie as close as possible to the exporting harbours so as to avoid having to float the fragile planks. This was the case with the waterways of Skien and Drammen. The timber from the upper Glomma, on the other hand, was carried by horse and sleigh from Øyeren to the sawmills at Skedsmo and Nittedal, and the dressed timber was carried from there to the lumberyards of Christiania.

Just when the over-exploitation of the forests came to be seen as a threat, prices levelled off or began to fall. In the short term, many timber exporters sought to compensate for the fall in prices by increasing production – something that certainly did nothing to improve the resource situation. In 1688 the authorities introduced the so-called sawmill licences. The right to export timber was restricted to a certain number of licensed saws and a ceiling was set on production. This resulted in a halving of output relative to the position immediately before their introduction. The regulations applied to southern and eastern Norway (east of Åna-Sira). In 1750 similar regulations were imposed on the rest of the country. The idea behind these licences was to stop the ruthless exploitation of the forests and to send prices up by restricting supply. Today's oil market has witnessed similar exercises. We do not have a comprehensive analysis of the experiment; however, in spite of dispensations and cheating over the quotas, it did lead to lower and steadier exports and a stabilization of production in the hinterlands of the individual export harbours. The system of licensed saws remained in place until 1860, but the quantity restrictions were removed in 1795.

The metal industries

The sources indicate that the first Norwegian mine dates from around 1500, but the great expansion of the metal industries did not come about until the first half of the seventeenth century. The works can be divided into three groups: iron works, which lay, for the most part, between Arendal and Eidsvoll and numbered in all around 20; copper works, which lay close together in an area of northern Østlandet and in Trøndelag and numbered around 10, with Røros as the most important; and finally the single, but impressive, silver mine at Kongsberg.

Unlike agriculture and forestry, the metal works made great demands on capital and craft skills. Towards the end of the period of union, a well-managed iron works represented a capital of 100,000–200,000 riksdaler. Most of this, in the early stages, came from Denmark, with the king in the lead, and from abroad. Governmental income from Norway was also ploughed in. Almost all the expertise also came from abroad, above all from Germany. This applied to both the management and the key workers. By the middle of the eighteenth century, some 8,000 people worked in the Norwegian metal industries, with around half of them in Kongsberg. After that numbers fell, first and foremost through a reduction in activity and finally owing to the temporary closure of the silver mine.

In assessing the importance of the employment in the metal industries one must not forget their wider impact. The works were heavy users of energy in the form of firewood and charcoal. The carriage of these, together with the ore and the finished products, involved the movement of great quantities over long distances. All this provided considerable secondary employment for the peasantry over a wide area. And the mining communities themselves were, of course, important markets for agricultural products.

Activity at the iron works stabilized during the eighteenth century. Access to ore was no problem, but charcoal burning made great demands on the woods in areas where the timber trade was also considerable. It was, therefore, difficult to increase output without raising the price of charcoal and so reducing the profitability of the mines.

Some specialist works were founded towards the end of the period of union: the salt works at Vallø near Tønsberg in 1739; the four glassworks of Nøstetangen and Ås (the 1740s), Hurdal (1755) and Hadeland (1762); and finally the cobalt works at Modum in 1776.

Shipping: a great Norwegian industry

The origins of Norway's shipping are obviously to be found in the long coastline, and the vast number of boats used for communications, fishing and trade, and not least the extensive overseas trade. In spite of this, the overwhelming bulk of Norwegian trade at the beginning of the seventeenth century was carried in foreign ships. Bergen was the only one of the few towns involved in foreign trade that had anything of a seagoing fleet. The authorities sought to rectify this by giving benefits to Norwegian merchant ships in return for the right to requisition them in wartime – the so-called ships for defence. Such arrangements were tried around 1620 and again in 1670.

From the middle of the seventeenth century events gathered pace. The English Navigation Laws of 1651 eliminated competition from third parties in the trade between Norway and England. A series of wars between the great seagoing nations of Holland, England and France gave the fleets of smaller countries the opportunity to gain entry. In 1670 Norway had some 240 ships totalling 22,000 net registered tons. Then followed an explosion. By 1696 the fleet had increased fourfold. It appears that this remarkable achievement was brought about with Norwegian capital. After the turn of the century trade conditions worsened and a certain decline occurred. The next period of growth took place in the second half of the eighteenth century, when the British fleet was hampered by international conflicts. Norway had about 500 ships in 1750. The number had risen to 1,600 by the outbreak of war in 1807. Its total tonnage was then 50 per cent greater than that of Denmark and Slesvig-Holstein put together.

The merchant fleet was based in the towns, and the greatest share was to be found in Bergen and the towns between Lindesnes and the Oslofjord. As one would expect, most of the fleet was taken up with carrying Norway's exports, principally fish and timber to markets in western and southern Europe. Usually the ships sailed in the summer half-year and were laid up during the winter. But from 1750 there was a rapid growth in the part of the fleet that carried cargoes between foreign countries and only seldom visited the mother country. Norwegian shipping was about to become an international service.

When war came in 1807, it is reckoned that around 12,000 Norwegian men were employed in the overseas trade. This was about twice the number that worked in the Norwegian mines. A considerable proportion of the seamen were unmarried and went to sea only in their youth. Like the servants in agriculture, they worked for low pay in conditions of near bondage.

Was Norwegian society richer?

Around 1500 about 150,000 people lived within Norway's current boundaries. Outside agriculture, fishing was the only significant livelihood. The export of dried fish financed large imports of grain. Three hundred years later the population had increased sixfold. Agricultural output had more or less kept pace with this, but the country still needed a considerable supply of grain. The fish stocks along the coast were better exploited, not least because herring in addition to cod were being caught. The Norwegian forests produced vast quantities of timber for export. Norwegian mineral resources were being exploited. Norwegians had won a leading position in international shipping. All in all we find an increase in the growth and diversity of the Norwegian economy.

The growth of population and the growth of the international market were undoubtedly the two most important forces behind this expansion. By increasing the input of labour it was possible to expand production in line with population. Heavy capital investment was required only in mining and shipping. Some of this capital came from overseas, but most of it seems to have been created in the Norwegian towns through the export trade in fish and timber. Native skills lay behind the growth of agriculture, fishing and forestry, while foreign expertise contributed much to trade and shipping and practically everything to the emergence of a Norwegian mining industry.

A contemporary attempt to calculate the income derived from the Norwegian export industries in 1805 gives an indication of the relative strengths of each. The export of fish was set at 2.7 million riksdaler; timber at 4.5 million; the products of the mines at 0.8 million; and the income from shipping at 2.0 million.

The value of Norwegian output was, then, far greater in 1800 than it had been in 1500. Less certain is the answer to how the average Norwegian fared during this period. For it is necessary not only to calculate output but also to reckon how much of it was taken by the state. Nevertheless it would appear very likely that average living standards rose. But of what interest is the average if the variation between the different members of the population had become greater? We have already seen that, just as the economy became more diversified, so did society. What implications did this have for income distribution and individual power?

11
Income and power

Compared with most other parts of Europe, Norwegian society in the years 1500–1800 appears egalitarian. The absence of a strong aristocracy is enough in itself to create that impression. But, as we saw in Chapter 9, the view from inside the country was quite a different one. For, during the union period, social groups became increasingly unequal. One aspect of economic inequality sprang from the control over resources. Who owned the land, the forests, the fishing boats, the sawmills, the mines, the ships? Inequality also resulted from fundamental differences in the rights and obligations of the various groups. In this chapter we shall be seeking the conditions that affected the degree of inequality in society.

The ownership of land down to 1660

Halvard Bjørkvik has estimated that just before the Reformation the Crown owned 7.5 per cent of the land; the aristocracy 13 per cent; the Church 47.5 per cent; and the remaining 32 per cent was in private hands. For the union period we have only one survey covering the country as a whole and that was based on the work of the so-called Land Commission of 1661. This shows the breakdown of the land tax (*landskyld*; more on this below) as follows: the Crown 31 per cent; aristocracy 8 per cent; Church 21 per cent; and 40 per cent in private hands.

It becomes immediately apparent that great changes took place between the two periods. First, the Crown lands had increased dramatically and at the expense of those of the Church. At the Reformation the king confiscated all the land belonging to the bishops, the monasteries and the nunneries. Only land belonging to the parishes remained

INCOME AND POWER 159

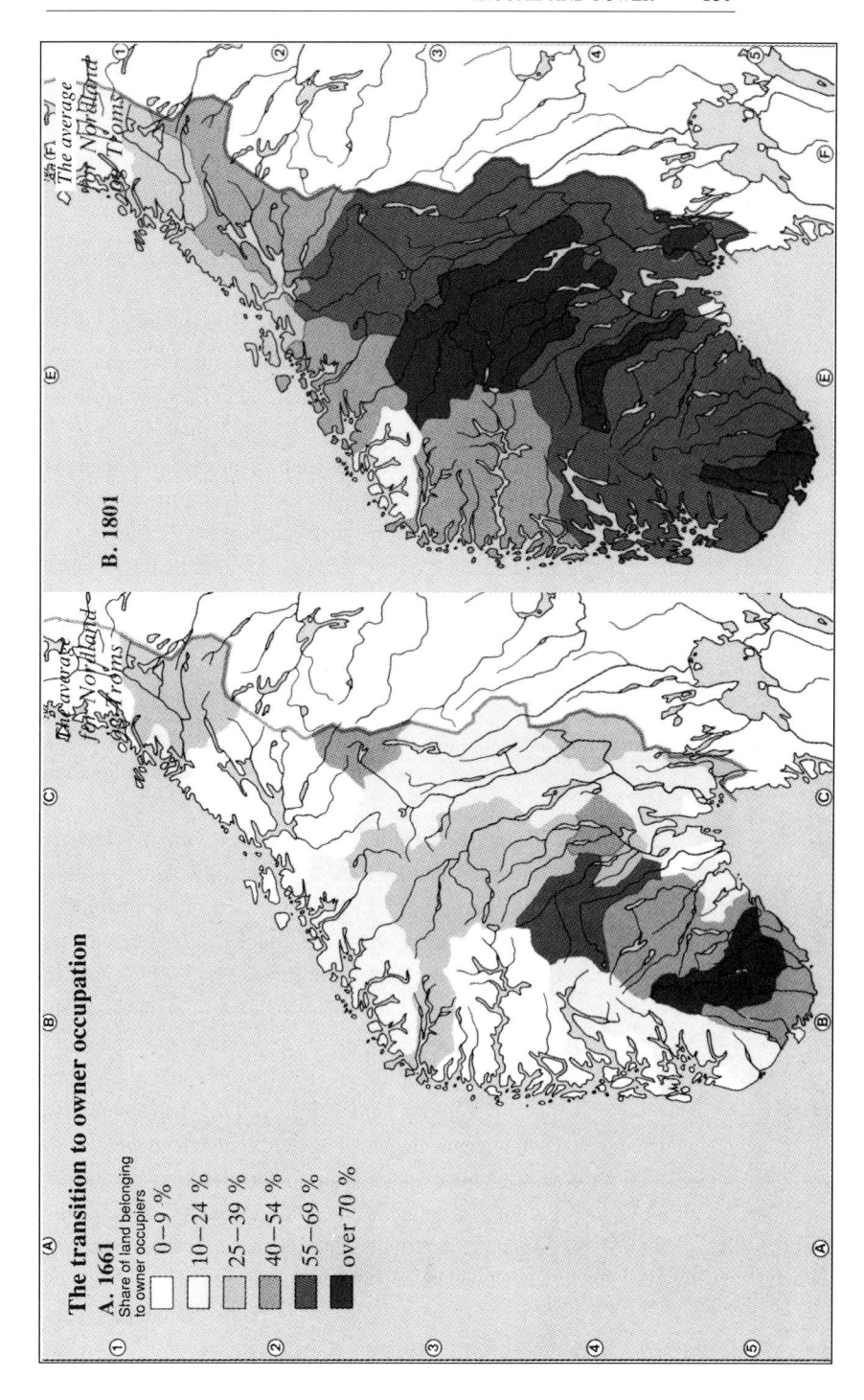

The transition to owner occupation
A. 1661
B. 1801

Share of land belonging to owner occupiers
- 0–9 %
- 10–24 %
- 25–39 %
- 40–54 %
- 55–69 %
- over 70 %

The average for Nordland
Troms

as Church lands, though in actual fact the king claimed these too. Second, land belonging to the aristocracy had declined from 13 to 8 per cent of the total, while that in private hands had risen from 32 to 40 per cent. An important explanation of this is to be found in the marked decline of the Norwegian aristocracy. Families died out or sank into the ranks of the peasantry.

What proportion of the privately owned land belonged to the peasants who farmed it? This we do not know for the medieval period, but from the 1661 material it would appear that about half (19 per cent) fell into this category. However the proportion varied widely from one part of the country to another – from only a few per cent in the north of Norway to 70–80 per cent in large areas of Agder and the western valleys of Østlandet. Thus only one-fifth of the agricultural resources of Norway in 1661 were controlled by the freeholder peasantry. The king, or one could say the state, held a good half.

Looking at the situation in the neighbouring kingdoms at this time, we find that a freeholder peasantry to all intents and purposes did not exist in Denmark. There, one-third of the land belonged to the Crown or was in public ownership; two-thirds consisted of private estates, most of which were held by the aristocracy. The situation in Sweden is less clear because much of the land was subject to dispute between the Crown and the aristocracy. The percentage of land held in freehold has been set at around 30 per cent in 1700 when the sale of Crown lands began. Thus, in all three countries the freeholder peasants made up a small group, though a much greater one in Norway and Sweden than in Denmark. What was special about Norway was that there the public lands were so much greater, and those belonging to the aristocracy so much smaller, than in the neighbouring countries.

The Norwegian peasant becomes a freeholder

About 1661 a host of changes began to appear in the pattern of land ownership. A constant shortage of money forced the king to sell off his public estates. In the first round of sales after 1660 it was the earlier Crown and monastic lands that were auctioned off. In the second round, after the Great Northern War in 1720, the rest of these estates followed. At this time too there occurred the notorious sale of land belonging to the parishes, a remarkable transaction that resulted in the

Norwegian churches becoming privately owned. The final round extended from 1821 onwards when the state sold the glebe land, previously part of the income of the parish clergy, though not the vicarages and rectories.

Did the sale of Crown lands lead to a system of private estates in Norway or to the beginnings of self-ownership by the Norwegian peasantry? In the first round after 1660 the king sold land in large blocks not primarily to the aristocracy but to burgesses and *embetsmenn*, (officers of the Crown), who saw it as a good investment. Only occasionally were the peasants involved in buying their own farms. But then something surprising happened. After a relatively short time the first generation of purchasers began to sell the land again and this time in small lots, direct to the peasantry. It was perhaps this development that led the Crown in the next round after 1720 to sell off land in small pieces, with the peasantry being given a better opportunity to bid. The sales after 1821 were deliberately designed to give tenants first refusal.

The causes of these changes in land ownership from the Reformation to the mid-1800s are not altogether clear. Why, for instance, did the king not allow the Danish aristocracy to share the spoils from the Catholic Church? Here one should remember that down to 1660 it was the upper ranks of the Danish aristocracy who elected the king and who tried to bind him by promises made before they would agree to his coronation. In the power struggle resulting from this, the landed estates in Norway represented a card that the king was reluctant to put into the hands of his opponents. So, when land sales became unavoidable after 1660, it was chiefly the burgesses in the towns who were given the opportunity to buy. Another explanation lay in the fact that Norway's basic industry – agriculture – was protected from exploitation in a variety of ways and was, therefore, less attractive as a source of investment. Many of the 'buyers' after 1660 were in actual fact royal creditors who were forced to take land instead of cash. Some were seeking control of the much more profitable timber industry, but this was achieved more effectively through the sawmill licences of 1688. The usual speculators moved their capital about as more profitable enterprises came on offer, e.g. the great shipping boom of the 1690s.

What made land in Norway relatively speaking so unprofitable? One reason was that, since the Middle Ages, the tenant had had a life interest in his holding. Another was that the *landskyld*, the yearly sum paid by the farmer to his landlord, had fallen dramatically since the

The attempt at a more thorough integration of the Sami people into Norwegian society began in the first half of the eighteenth century, with the Sami mission in the 1700s and the drawing of the border with Finland around 1750. However, the Sami managed to retain much of their culture and way of life. The photograph was taken by Knud Knudsen in 1875 and shows nomadic Sami at their summer camp near the coast.

Black Death and could not be raised without a lengthy legal process. To compensate for this, a couple of older dues were increased sharply and made permanent in the sixteenth century: one was a charge that a tenant had to pay when he took over a holding; the other had to be paid every three years. The landowner who lost through the fall in value of the *landskyld* sought to make good his losses especially through the charge made when a holding was taken over, but in 1684 the authorities put a strict upper limit on this – a limit that was broken only during the much more favourable economic conditions of a century later. Finally it is important to note the differences between Norwegian and Danish agriculture. The heart of the Danish estate was the large home farm, which the landowner ran commercially, on his own account, with labour services provided by his tenants. The thinly populated Norway with its tiny urban population provided far too small a market for such an activity and the scattered holding pattern made it difficult to mobilize an effective labour force from the tenants. This, together with the more important fact that there were far more promising opportunities on offer for the investment of capital in other Norwegian industries, meant that the Norwegian peasant after 1660 worked his way step by step towards becoming a freeholder and master of his own means of production.

The land ownership situation in Finnmark was unique. Here the land was said to be the king's demesne; privately owned land was scarcely to be found. Beginning in 1775, however, the authorities measured out, rated and gave away land. Not until 1863, when demand for land had become acute, did the state begin to take payment as a way of regulating access to it.

Ownership and control in the fisheries

Three factors made it possible to exploit the fisheries by means of small boats and simple equipment. First, there were vast quantities of fish; second, the fish came close into the shore; third, the seasons lasted but a short time. Usually the boat was owned by one man; but he and the other members of the crew provided equal shares of food and tackle. The catch was shared out equally, with one share going to the boat, i.e. the boat's owner. This relatively egalitarian system could break down if a crew member had nothing to contribute but his labour. In such a situation the boat owner also provided more of the fishing tackle and took a correspondingly larger proportion of the catch. However this occurred only rarely. Property rights could also be claimed for inlets from which nets were cast, or for good fishing spots near to land. But, in principle, operating from boats during the great seasonal fisheries was free for all.

In the traditional cod fisheries, the fisherman himself also took a hand in preparing the catch for market. He gutted the fish, hung it on the drying racks, and shared in carrying it to the harbours from which it was dispatched. The only capital of note was in the hands of those who owned the harbours with the huts in which the fishermen lodged and the racks on which the fish were hung.

During the course of the union with Denmark, herring fishing gradually increased in importance. At the same time, a larger proportion of the cod that was caught in southern Norway was converted into *klippfisk* (this involved both drying and salting it). In both of these activities a greater division of labour developed and a heavier concentration of capital. Salt was needed to preserve the herring and salt was expensive and had to be imported. It also required vast quantities of barrels and a mobile labour force to fill them. For these reasons the processing role of the business shifted from the fisherman to the merchants, who could more easily raise the necessary capital and organise it. Salt, good drying places and a mobile labour force were also necessary for the production of *klippfisk*. Thus the merchants gradually took a stronger grip on the industry and forced the fishermen back to being raw material suppliers only. This development occurred later in north Norway than in the south.

The merchants dominated the sales side of the industry throughout, with exports being wholly in their hands. The domestic market was less interesting, because most of the coastal population met their own requirements, while transport difficulties meant that only limited numbers living in the interior could be served.

The timber industry: from peasant hands to those of the urban elites

The control of the timber industry can be divided into three parts: control over the raw material (the standing timber itself); its processing (the sawmills); and its sale (the exporting). Down to the first half of the seventeenth century – the period when the coastal woods were exploited – the farmers dominated all three arenas. Even if four out of five peasants were tenants – far fewer in some of the most important forest areas – this had little impact on the amount felled. According to the law of 1687, a tenant could fell up to half the value of his *landskyld*, but the landowners did not pay much attention to this. It did not cost much to set up a water-driven saw and foreign timber buyers sailed into every fjord and inlet to deal with the farmers direct. In this way both income and profits were widely spread.

During this early period the Crown was also tempted to draw some income from the timber industry. The Crown had first refusal on goods put up for sale and could use this to get timber. Taxes and dues could also be demanded in the form of timber. As a major land owner the king could also establish sawmills in appropriate places. As early as 1545 a tithe was levied on the amount of planks produced privately, and the disposal of the timber coming into royal hands in this way was organised. Thus early in the seventeenth century many *embetsmenn* were involved in sawmilling and the timber trade on behalf of the king.

A dramatic change in the structure of the industry took place from the middle of the seventeenth century. For gradually, as the felling area moved inland, the peasants lost control of both the milling and the trade in timber. Capital needs and organizational skills were now such that only the richer merchants could supply them. The peasants were left with the basic resource, the timber itself, which the gradual change-over to a freehold system gave them control of. Only rarely, when it was necessary to coordinate or increase output, did the merchants buy up forests. This slight interest in the actual ownership of the woods indicates that the timber merchants had sufficient control through their monopoly of milling and sales.

This monopoly had the full approval of the Crown. The king and his *embetsmenn* withdrew from sawmilling and took their share of the profits through the tithe on the number of planks produced, the tax on sawmills, and above all from the export duty on timber. Collecting these dues was the easier the fewer sawmills and export harbours there were. From 1662, therefore, the merchants in the towns acquired the sole right to deal in timber with foreign buyers. In 1688 the number of sawmills operating for export was halved in Agder and Østlandet and each was allocated a maximum quota. The mills that were eliminated in this way were precisely the small ones that the peasants still held. Within a few decades the milling and the sale of timber, the two most productive of the three parts of the industry, were in the hands of the merchants.

The capital requirements of mining and shipping

Most mining operations, or at least the largest, were started by groups of investors whose share of the investment was rewarded by a corresponding share of the output. The king was a major investor, as were the better-off Danish and Norwegian aristocracy and merchant class. But a lot of the capital also came from overseas. During the difficult period for public finances immediately after 1660, some of the king's shares fell into foreign hands. But, by the early eighteenth century, ownership had stabilized along the following lines. The iron works, which were in general relatively small, were in the hands of single domestic owners, who were also responsible for their working. The copper mines were, on the other hand, still in joint ownership, though also with many Norwegian investors involved. The richer merchants of Trondheim were well represented here. The Kongsberg silver mines were owned by the Crown (i.e. the state) from 1683 till they were temporarily shut down in 1805.

The legal status of most mines and the articles under which they operated were laid down in individual agreements issued by the king. Tax or other incentives could be given by the state as a means of encouraging and promoting a mine. More interesting, from our point of view, was that the privileges accorded the mines also involved an infringement of the rights of other subjects of the Crown. For example, each mine was usually granted an area surrounding it, within which the peasants were obliged to fulfil certain duties. These could include supplying charcoal or other materials or so many days' haulage. These services were normally paid for, but at a fixed and usually low rate. It wasn't then just benefits that the peasantry derived from the mines; they also had to help subsidize them.

Most of the Norwegian fleet involved in foreign trade was based in the towns and belonged to their citizens. Not even during the shipping boom of the 1690s can we find much trace of foreign capital behind the building up of the fleet. Throughout our period, the system of part ownership (by which investors bought parts of each ship) was the usual form of ownership. In this way even small capitalists could invest in shipping and the great risks of the industry could thus be spread to some degree. The structure of ownership was, therefore, more democratic in shipping than in the mining industry. Everything suggests that the bulk of the very considerable capital required came from the surplus produced by the export of fish and timber.

The elite and the working masses

In the course of this chapter we have examined each industry in turn in order to find out who controlled it and how. The central themes have been ownership, labour and management. This has given us the opportunity to determine the links between the economy and the social groups.

A key distinction is clearly between, on the one hand, a large number of ordinary people and, on the other, a tiny economic elite. The former were to be found mainly in the country districts and it is they who carried out most of the physical labour within each industry. The elite was based in the towns and controlled almost all production outside agriculture (a few estates excepted), timber felling and fishing. The elite also controlled all significant forms of trade. The elite was found within the urban bourgeoisie and is usually termed the Norwegian 'upper bourgeoisie' or 'patriciate'. The group also embraced a proportion of *embetsmenn*, as we shall see later.

Within the mass of the population there were significant economic divisions. Indeed there was a great gap between the rich farmer from Hedmark, with his lands and woods, and the day labourer who perhaps did not even own the tiny cottage in which he lived. There were also great regional differences, e.g. between rich areas of Østlandet and Trøndelag and the typical smallholding areas of Vest-Agder and much of north Norway. One must not exaggerate the egalitarian aspects of Norwegian rural society, when it comes to either its social hierarchy or its regional pattern. Here Norway was little different from the rest of Europe.

What was special about Norway was that the populace generally was engaged in so many different activities. There were very few specialist farmers, or fishermen, loggers or seamen. Instead we find farmers and crofters who also were fishermen, loggers, hauliers for the mines, seamen, etc. The characteristic feature of the Norwegian labour force was that it had a hand in several enterprises. The main explanation for this, as we saw in the previous chapter, lay in the fact that so much economic activity was seasonal, and that the activities were well spread across the year as a whole. One finds two minor exceptions to this general rule: first, a core group of workers in the Norwegian mines were full-time craftsmen; second, a proportion of seamen also had no other occupation.

Looked at from a European perspective, one wonders why a country with such a well-rounded economy and extensive overseas trade was so little urbanised. The answer could be that Norway was a pure raw material producer. A closer look, however, shows this not to be the case. True, the country exported mainly bulk items with a modest value added – semi-finished goods, in other words. But the point is that much of the processing took place in the rural districts with the peas-

The Froland iron works was founded by Hans Hagerup in 1763 and extended by magistrate Hans Smith, who bought it in 1786. The royal licence needed to operate the works gives details of the area surrounding it, within which the peasantry were obliged to provide certain goods and services, e.g. charcoal. Even though the peasants were paid, the arrangement could be misused. The situation was exacerbated when the works' owner was also the local magistrate with power over the same peasants. Strong allegations of corruption and abuse of power were made against Smith during the Lofthus Rising of 1786–87. (Drawing by L. Berg, 1831.)

antry as the most important source of labour. The prime role played by the towns was as shipping points. This one-sided activity kept the towns small and worked against the emergence of domestic production of goods for a population with a larger than average purchasing power. The rich, but numerically few, members of the Norwegian patriciate made a good deal of their purchases of luxury goods abroad. Norwegian handicraft was left occupying a comparatively modest position.

Did the merchants exploit or provide a safety net for the peasantry?

From what we have said so far, it is clear that the most important relationship between the 'underclass' and the 'overclass' in Norway was not based on the control of the land. Such a relationship was to be found, but it was limited and was gradually wound down towards the end of the period of union. In this, Norway was markedly different from the rest of Europe. What was most important was the trade relationship that the majority of the general population had with the urban merchants. A smaller group, primarily the specialist workers in the mines and towns, were employees of that same upper class.

Most towns had the sole right to trade within a closely defined hinterland. Trade was, for the most part, organised in such a way that a peasant was tied to one, and only one, merchant in the nearest town. He supplied the goods he had for sale (fish, timber, etc.) to this merchant at a price determined by the latter. From that same merchant he took in return the goods he needed, primarily grain for his own consumption. It was difficult to move from one merchant to another and virtually impossible if a peasant was in debt. Those who have interpreted this trading relationship as an exploitative one have emphasized precisely this unlimited power of the merchant to dictate prices and to hold the peasant in debt permanently. On the other hand, the merchant depended on his customers for the goods he needed. The result was that he came into a personal and paternalistic relationship with them. The key to the situation was *credit*. The merchant had the resources to protect his clients against the worst effects of economic downturns, whether they were due to bad harvests, poor fishing at home or market problems abroad. But to be able to give credit the merchant required a long-term relationship with his customers.

We see, therefore, that the Norwegian common man had the benefit of two safety nets. First, his risks were divided between the various occupations he pursued. Second, buying and selling were so organised that the merchants in the towns were economically strong enough to provide credit in difficult times. This trading relationship undoubtedly had its drawbacks so far as the peasant was concerned, but broadly speaking it was a rational solution for a population that, after all, was struggling against the elements on the northern rim of Europe.

If this trading relationship was an exploitative one, we would expect to find dissatisfaction and conflict between the two parties. Not a few observers have expressed sympathy for the north Norwegian peasant fishermen, but there is no evidence that they or their compatriots further south ever rose in revolt against the Bergen merchants. One must go to Agder and Østlandet to find that. The best-known revolt is that of Lofthus in Agder in the 1780s, which was clearly directed at the merchants. It is noteworthy that these events came towards the end of the union period and occurred in years of extreme need. The uprising was more against the abnormality of the situation than against the system itself.

We know less about labour relations and nearly all that we do know is from the mines towards the end of our period. Was pay a matter of tradition; was it dictated by the employers; or did it reflect supply and demand? There is much to suggest that tradition was important. This prevented workers enjoying the good times, but it protected them against a sudden drop in earnings. A similar buffer against times of depression can be seen in the corn stores that were set up at many of the works. From these workers were able to buy food and other necessities at stable and, to some extent, subsidized prices. That we nevertheless find more unrest at the mines and metal works than amongst the peasantry can be explained by the fact that here the workers had little to fall back on should the enterprises employing them encounter difficulties. The mines generally sought to operate at full capacity and as a result were subject to major setbacks when markets failed or seams ran out and new ones were not discovered. The administration of the mines too was rather complex and this opened the way for mismanagement and corruption. Nevertheless, by international standards, working conditions at the Norwegian mines can be characterized as stable and reasonably good.

Everything considered, we must come to the conclusion that, in the relationship between the two major social groups, there is little sign of exploitation of the one by the other in our period. First of all, there was scarcely any of the feudal or manorial exploitation that was so common in the rest of Europe. Second, the relationship between the populace generally and the urban elite was dominated by trade not by the purchase of labour. In both these instances the parties were mutually dependent and there was little non-economic pressure. This leads us, however, to a new line of enquiry: how did the state relate to these great social groups? Was the exploitation carried out by the state itself? Who, in that case, used the state for their own purposes?

12
The state and its subjects

Let us, for a moment, put ourselves in the place of a typical Norwegian – a peasant farmer – at the end of the seventeenth century. Such a person would hardly be aware of belonging to a state or other large public body. Instead he would see himself as an underling, someone with few rights and many obligations, facing a foreign administration or power. His picture of this would be two-sided. In distant Copenhagen, the king and the central administration were to be found. He would not know much about either but he nevertheless regarded them with awe and they had his trust. At home, in everyday Norway, he dealt with the king's servants, *embetsmenn* like the priest, the collector of taxes and the rural magistrate. It is they who made demands on behalf of the authorities. Them he neither trusted nor liked.

Is this a realistic view or is it a caricature?

An analysis of the years 1680–91, a time of peace, shows that, of the total state income of Denmark-Norway, around 10 per cent went to maintain the king, his family and court (a body of some hundreds) in the capital Copenhagen; as much as 60 per cent of the budget was earmarked for the army and navy; and 10 per cent went to pay the king's *embetsmenn*. Was then the state essentially no more than a splendid court and an extravagant war machine?

At the end of the seventeenth century we estimate that the state had about 1,500 *embetsmenn* in its service in Norway. Of these, around 600 were military and 400 ecclesiastical. Seemingly the king's servants were there primarily to 'command' and 'indoctrinate'.

In other words, the state's role was a small one, and gave the impression of transferring resources from a poverty-stricken majority to a rich minority. This contrasts markedly with our own contemporary state, the job of which essentially is to allocate resources and distribute them more evenly. Naturally the question arises: was the seventeenth-century state in the hands of small social groups who used it as an instrument of exploitation? But if so, who were these groups? The king and the court aristocracy? The public officials? The military? In what follows we shall acquaint ourselves with the state of Denmark-Norway as it developed from 1536 to the end of the seventeenth century and with its consolidation after that. Then we shall look at its social basis. This will show that the simple caricature presented in these introductory remarks must give way to a much more subtle picture.

The constitutional position

Constitutionally the period of union falls clearly into two parts. Down to 1660 Denmark–Norway was an elective monarchy. When a king died, his successor was elected by the council of the realm and subject to conditions laid down in a formal agreement. Even if the eldest male heir was regularly chosen, the struggle over this agreement gave the council of the realm real power. On the council sat members of the Danish nobility, and even if the king, down to the 1640s, had the formal right of appointment, the council to all intents and purposes chose its own members. Council members occupied the highest posts in the state. Thus one can describe the regime as a 'monarchy of the nobility' or the 'council of the realm's constitutionalism' (see Chapter 7).

Formally other groups in society had the right to take part in the running of the state. The ordering of society into nobility, clergy, citizens and peasants had its roots in the Middle Ages. In Denmark, the representation of the peasantry was discontinued in our period, but not in Norway. In both countries the different orders were summoned to pay homage and swear allegiance to the kings and heirs apparent chosen by the council of the realm. Occasionally the meetings of the different orders were also used for more specific political purposes, as, for instance, the sanctioning of extraordinary taxes. But it was the king who called the orders together. When called, they seldom took the initiative. It was a Danish meeting of the different social orders in the autumn of 1660 that was the stage for the coup d'état that ended the power of the council of the realm and introduced the absolutist hereditary monarchy. The kingdom was in financial ruin after the wars of 1657–60, but the nobility refused to give up their time-honoured freedom from taxes and their other privileges. The proposal was made that the monarchy should be an hereditary one and, under military pressure, the nobility were forced to agree. With this the council of the realm, and the agreements it had been able to make with kings prior to their coronation, disappeared. A written constitution was created by the Law of the Realm of 1665. The king was declared absolute, with the following limitations: he should acknowledge the teachings of evangelical Lutheranism; give up none of his kingdoms and possessions; maintain the hereditary principle and his own absolute power.

The introduction of absolutism occurred suddenly and dramatically, but its origins went back a long way. Economic development had strengthened the bourgeoisie and weakened the aristocracy and the latter's monopoly of the top positions in the state had gradually been undermined. This is to be seen not least if one looks at Norway. Who ruled in this part of the kingdom on behalf of the king and the council of the realm? What level of resources did they manage to mobilize for use by the state?

Resources and administration

The income of the king first rose sharply when the ecclesiastical estates were taken over at the time of the Reformation. The reoccupation of farms deserted after the Black Death and higher rents gave further increases in income in the course of the sixteenth century. But the greatest growth came from taxes and customs dues. Apart from the tithe, the Middle Ages knew of only one other tax, namely the levy that replaced military service. But, when special circumstances required it, the king could negotiate with his subjects for so-called 'extraordinary taxes'. In the course of the sixteenth century such taxes were levied more and more frequently. The year 1625 marked the beginning of a period of continuously high taxation. Its imposition was closely linked to military activities. The extra taxes during the War of the Emperor of 1625–27 and the Hannibal Affair of 1643–45 were five to ten times as high as taxes during the years of peace 1615–20, and they never fell back to their previous level after these great surges. Customs duties on imports and exports had become a valuable source of income for the king in the course of the sixteenth century, but here again the great upsurge came in the following century. In the 1630s, customs rates were raised significantly, with those on timber exports providing the greatest source of income. In the course of somewhat over a decade, the income from customs dues rose between five- and tenfold, as did taxes. Thus overall we are looking at a colossal growth in what the state took of Norway's economic resources. Such a growth could obviously not take place without affecting the administrative apparatus.

The largest administrative unit in Norway during the sixteenth and seventeenth centuries went under the name of the *len* or county. It was in the charge of a lord lieutenant. After 1536 such men were drawn exclusively from the aristocracy and nine out of ten were Danes. The lord lieutenant's primary task was the collection of the royal revenue from within his county, i.e. taxes on land, the tithe, fines, other taxes, customs dues, etc. He also had military duties and the supervision of the legal system and the Church. We have already mentioned that the king's income rose dramatically in the course of the period 1536–1660. But how much of it found its way through the administrative system? The answer depended very largely on the conditions attached to the administrative appointments. The king's need to reward trustworthy servants drew him towards carving the country up into a large number of counties and giving them to lord lieutenants with the right to dispose of all the income. A strong monarchy, on the other hand, was best served by a few, large counties run on one of two lines. Under the first of these, the lord lieutenant provided the king with a fixed sum, the rest of the income being at his own disposal. Under the second the lord lieutenant had a salary and handed over the rest of the income to the king, after the accounts had been audited. Both these systems had their roots in the Middle Ages (see Chapter 7). The development we can identify during the aristocratic period down to 1660 was in the direction of larger counties and appointment conditions that gave the king a greater share of the vast increase in income. This in no way changes the fact that, throughout the entire period, the Norwegian counties were a major source of income for the Danish aristocratic lord lieutenants.

The beginnings of administrative reform

The lord lieutenants were, therefore, held in check financially while another development also served to weaken their position *vis-à-vis* the king. For a long time the lord lieutenants had used non-aristocratic servants called *fogder* in the administration of their counties. The *fogder* or bailiffs did the actual work of collecting revenues, acted as prosecutors and carried out sentences. Their administrative areas gradually took shape at a level beneath that of the county, the so-called *fogderi* or bailiwick. Because most of the conflicts between the government and its subjects came up in meetings between the bailiffs and the general public, it was necessary for the king to control the bailiffs too. Gradually the king broke into the patron–client relationship that the bailiffs and other lower officials had with the lord lieutenants. The bailiffs were transformed, as Rolf Fladby has so tellingly put it, 'from a servant of the lord lieutenant to His Royal Majesty's bailiff'. The king demanded loyalty from his bailiffs, could dismiss them and finally also took the right to appoint them.

In three important areas a strengthening or reform of the administration took place, each of which weakened the influence of the lord lieutenants. In the decades around 1600 an effective centralized legal system was revived in Norway. In the rural districts, the *bygdeting* (community assembly) operated, with the peasantry acting as jurors, helped and soon dominated by a literate and legally competent *sorenskriver* (rural magistrate). In the towns, the mayor and town council made up the local assembly. In the countryside, the *fogd* was the assembly's administrator; in the towns the *byfogd* had this role. One could, in the first instance, appeal from these courts to the country's Courts of Appeal, and from there to the High Court. Magnus Lagabøte's *Landslov*, from the thirteenth century, continued in operation. It was translated into Danish, expanded by the addition of new laws and published as Christian 4's Norwegian Code of Law in 1604.

The second area involved the collection of customs dues. About the same time that the authorities sharply raised customs duties in the 1630s, their collection was taken out of the hands of the *fogder* and transferred to a separate customs' service that was under the direct control of the king.

The third area concerned the Norwegian army. In the wars of 1563–70, 1611–13 and 1625–29 an attempt was made to use the old peasant call-up system, under the command of the lord lieutenants. This worked badly and in the 1640s the government began seriously to organise a Norwegian army with professional officers and peasant conscripts. In this way the aristocratic lord lieutenants, the military order of earlier times, saw themselves pushed onto the sidelines.

These are some of the early indications of an administrative development that created a coordinated service directly linked to the central administration in Copenhagen. The aristocratic lord lieutenants were forced to witness their power base in the local administration being limited and undermined long before the monopoly of power enjoyed by the council of the realm at the centre was shattered in 1660.

It is tempting to see a causal link here: new military technology and more frequent wars made greater demands on the national treasury. This meant a corresponding revenue had to be procured and the administrative apparatus had to be strengthened in order to accomplish the additional tasks of collection. The expanded administration disturbed the balance between king and council in favour of the former and led to the constitutional upheaval of 1660. There can be no doubt that there was a close chronological connection between the wars and the state's call on resources, and, as we have seen, the military was the major item on the national budget. But some things cannot be pressed into such a simple pattern, e.g. the great reforms in the legal system around 1600 or the monarchy's involvement in economic affairs. Perhaps we should regard the wars as temporarily accelerating a long-term trend, the hallmark of which was the greater involvement of the state in ever more aspects of social life.

The end of aristocratic rule?

The introduction of absolutism in 1660 was followed by major changes at all levels of the administration. The aristocratic *embetsmenn* in the central administration were replaced by 'colleges'. These were a kind of department. The officials they contained were each on the same footing, their job being to send decisions up to a higher authority. This arrangement implied a more professional approach to the allocation and treatment of affairs of state. The body nearest the king, the one that one would liken to a government, changed over time. In the period immediately after 1660 there existed a so-called 'state college'. Later came the council. Towards the end of the period of union, the king governed mostly with the help of his personal office, the cabinet. The absolutist monarchs ruled, in other words, through the

County boundaries in 1760

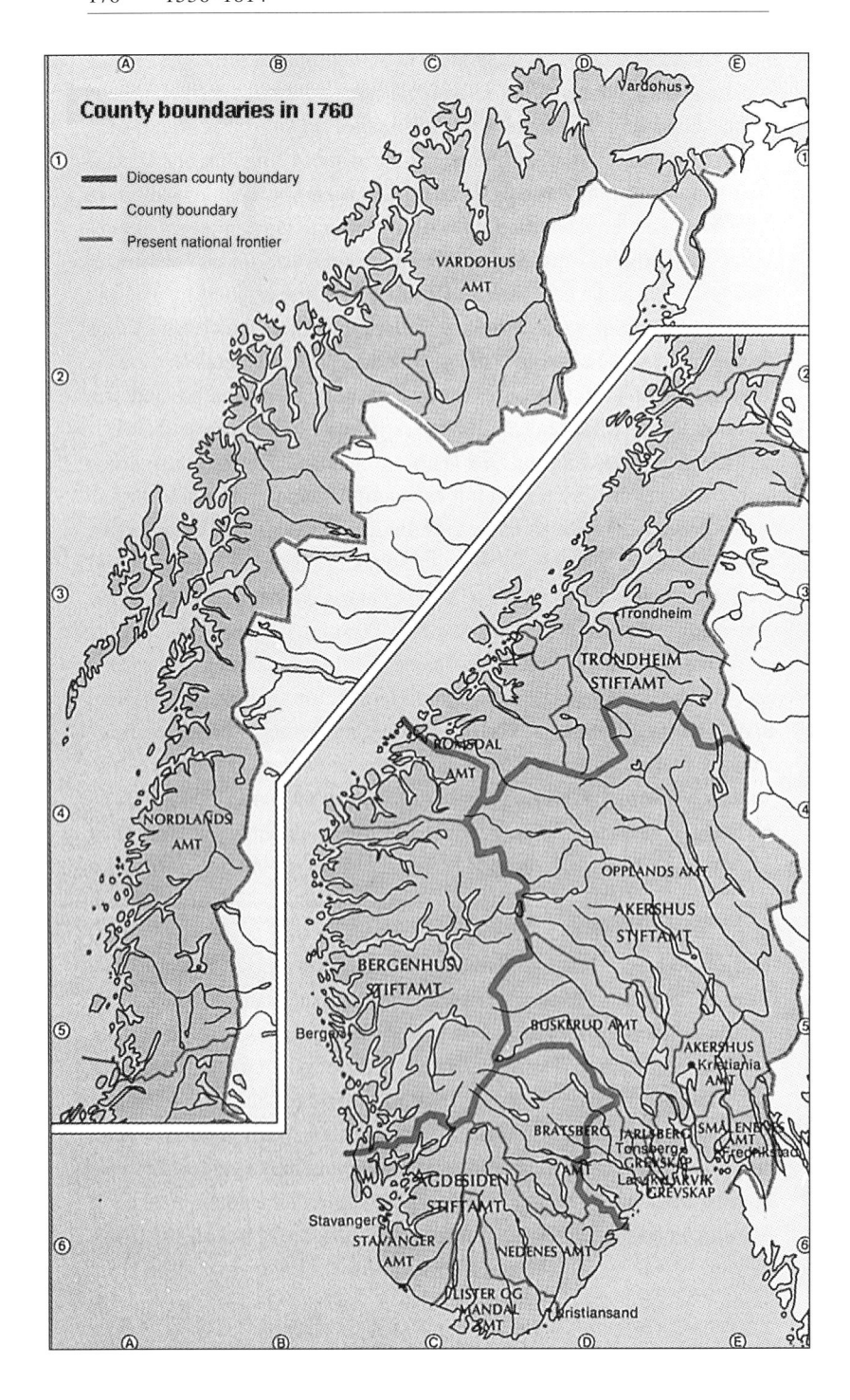

various circles of advisers they gathered around them: from the largest (the state college) to the smallest (the cabinet). For long periods, especially under weak kings like Frederik 5 (1746–66) and Christian 7 (1766–1808), the real power lay with this circle of advisers.

As for local government, the old lord lieutenantship was renamed, with few changes, as the *stiftamt* or 'diocesan county' (Akershus, Kristiansand, Bergenhus, Trondheim). Each was divided further into three or four counties, with the *stiftamtmann* ('diocesan county governor') taking charge of the largest. In addition to his tasks as an *amtmann* ('county governor'), he also supervised the other *amtmenn*, was responsible for the towns, and had duties involving the ecclesiastical administration, which he shared with the bishop of the diocese. Beneath the county level we still find a division into *fogderier* for the collection of revenue and policing, and another into *sorenskriverier* for judicial matters. In the 1660s there were 4 *stiftamt*, 12 *amt*, 55 *fogderier* and 65 *sorenskriverier* in Norway. By the end of the union with Denmark there were 16 *amt*, 45 *fogderier* and 54 *sorenskriverier*. Two *grevskap* (the property of a count) and one *baroni* (the property of a baron) were outside these arrangements. The number of parishes rose in the same period from around 260 to 350. All in all there existed a great degree of stability throughout the period of the absolute monarchy. The new government departments that emerged in the seventeenth and eighteenth centuries generally acquired their own administrative divisions and jurisdictions.

Where did power lie?

The lack of unity and coordination within the administration was striking and perhaps even deliberate – a divide-and-rule system that brought together the reins of control only into the hands of the absolute monarch in Copenhagen. When one investigates an issue and its progress, it nevertheless turns out that only occasionally did the central administration have the knowledge and the power to push through a political initiative of its own. The lead usually came from the local administration or from subordinates in Norway. In many cases it was the *stiftamtmenn* who stood out. The central administration in Copenhagen was by no means passive, but, for the most part, sought to fit proposals from Norway into existing law and practice.

Even if the nobility was pushed to one side by the coup d'état in 1660, it was by no means the end of the strong position its members had in the administration. They dominated the central administration throughout the period of absolutism and continued to have a virtual monopoly of top positions in Norway. Shortly after the introduction of the absolute monarchy, the king set up a new aristocracy of counts and barons, an aristocracy that could be used to reward both the old aristocracy and the rising bourgeoisie. In Norway, the aristocracy consisted of little more than empty titles with three exceptions: Jarlsberg and Larvik each became the domain of a count (together they now form the county of Vestfold) and a private estate in Sunnhordland was raised to the Barony of Rosendal.

The longstanding features can now be summarized as follows. First the state's call on Norwegian resources increased greatly down to the introduction of the absolute monarchy in 1660, with an especially marked increase after 1625. The tax burden increased and customs dues went sky high. For the rest of the period of absolutism the income drawn from Norway levelled out, at least if one looks at it in relation to the size of the population and the degree of economic growth. Parallel with the increase in the total tax burden, one can identify a marked growth of the administration in Norway during the seventeenth century, which culminated in the period of absolutism. The causes of this development are undoubtedly many and complex. The growth in the size and diversity of the society created the need for more services from the state, in both number and variety. An aggressive foreign policy and conflicts with other states claimed massive military expenditure. In the struggle between the king and the council of the realm, both money and the administration were used to tip power in the king's favour.

The *embetsstand*

Before we can examine this state in its relationship to groups in Norwegian society, we must recognise that the state itself created one of these groups during the period of absolutism, namely the Norwegian *embetsstand*. What was it that welded together the king's servants into an estate? The clergy in Norway contained throughout the whole period a considerable number of Danish born. The lord lieutenants and later the *stiftamtmenn* were usually members of the Danish aristocracy; few of them, in fact, set down roots in Norway. The *fogder* and *sorenskrivere* were to a great extent recruited from the Danish bourgeoisie. The German element was strong within the department of mines and especially so in the army. That such a strange and complex body could be welded so firmly together resulted from several factors. First, new recruitment on a grand scale stopped in the second half of the seventeenth century. Public service positions began to be hereditary and the families that had them set down local roots. Real estate and business activity contributed much to this. Second, socialization into the public service played a part. University education was required only for the priesthood. Not until 1736 was a law exam introduced for legal officers. Education and training otherwise occurred on the job itself via minor positions, and here family links, contacts and friendship were decisive. In the eighteenth century particularly the *embetsstand* enjoyed increased material prosperity and a rising social status, which led to an increased segregation, through inter-marriage and inheritance. Payment usually was a combination of salary, accommodation (a house and farm) and fees for various administrative functions. This last category rose dramatically during the period of absolutism as a result of rising populations in the various administrative areas. That the size of the group increased so modestly – from 1,200 senior officials in 1660 to perhaps 1,800 at the end of the period of union with Denmark – enhanced its exclusivity. No doubt the group mixed a great deal socially with the urban bourgeoisie to form an upper class; but in its official role it took on tasks that distanced it markedly from the other groups in Norwegian society. We shall now see how the state faced the two most important of these: the bourgeoisie and the peasantry.

The bourgeoisie: monopoly and competition

The preference accorded the towns and the urban bourgeoisie by the Crown stretched back well before the period of absolutism. From the Middle Ages the Crown had tried to weaken the strong position held by the Hanseatic merchants in Norway's overseas trade. This it succeeded in doing on occasion by shielding and supporting their native competitors. Two clear examples of this came in the sixteenth and early seventeenth centuries: first, the urban bourgeoisie achieved a considerable degree of internal self-government; second, they worked their way towards a practical monopoly of certain types of economic activity.

Nevertheless the first major breakthrough came about with the inauguration of the period of absolutism. In 1661 the king was acclaimed by his Norwegian subjects, and representatives from the urban bourgeoisie then put forward a series of requests. The king's answer came in 1662 with the so-called General Rights of the Towns. Amongst these was one giving the bourgeoisie the sole right to conduct trade and practise crafts in the country as a whole. Certain exceptions were made for some common crafts that were still to be allowed in the countryside as well as for barter between the peasants (generally tied to annual fairs and similar gatherings). Especially important was the monopoly of all import and export trade now granted to the towns and the requirement that only those who had acquired citizenship were to be allowed to engage in trade and crafts (the bourgeois employments). These general privileges went a long way to recompensing the bourgeoisie for the partial loss of local self-government they had suffered under the new regime. In the years that followed, the principles enunciated in the General Rights were incorporated in Letters of Privilege with which the individual towns were furnished.

The next great initiative to benefit the bourgeoisie was the introduction of the sawmill licence in 1688. As noted earlier the strict regulation of sawmilling was done in such a way as to promote the control of timber dressing by the bourgeoisie – in addition to the export trade in timber, which was already in their hands.

Nevertheless, from around 1700 it would appear that the tide turned. A series of conflicts arose in the early eighteenth century between members of the bourgeoisie in the established towns and others who had moved out and were conducting their businesses in the so-called *ladesteder* (literally, 'loading places'). Several of these eventually sought the status of towns proper, so introducing an element of competition into trade and trading areas. The authorities' attitude was clearly positive towards a breaking up of the marked geographical concentration of the bourgeois trades and they acceded to requests from *ladesteder* such as Arendal, Molde and Kristiansund. In so doing they at the same time challenged the powers of the upper bourgeoisie in the mother towns of Kristiansand and Trondheim.

Throughout the eighteenth century, time and again we see the authorities becoming involved in the regulation of trading relations between the bourgeoisie and the peasantry, from whom they bought timber and fish. The process began in 1697 with the reducing of the debt owed to the Bergen merchants by the peasant-fishermen of north Norway. More dramatic were the conflicts in Østlandet in the 1770s and in Agder during the Lofthus revolt of 1786–87. In both these cases the authorities listened to the complaints of the peasantry concerning their exploitation by the bourgeoisie. Also in the eighteenth century the government conducted a more and more open campaign against the urban guilds. These self-recruiting organizations of craft workers were now seen as obstacles to free competition, increased employment and cheaper goods. On the whole one notes that the repeal of the mercantilist regulations covering trade and industry, which took place at the end of the eighteenth century, met the demands of the Norwegian general public, whereas the urban bourgeoisie had mixed attitudes and had, to some extent, to see their interests set aside.

The peasants as taxpayers

It would appear difficult to argue that the authorities accorded the Norwegian peasantry the status of a privileged group in society all that time it made up the great majority of those subjects who bore the heaviest taxes and the greatest obligations of service. But in fact a development occurred from the end of the seventeenth century that must have given the peasants themselves a feeling that progress was being made in their defence of certain privileges.

First of all there was the question of the tax burden itself. Down to the introduction of absolutism in 1660 there had been a long-term trend towards sharply rising taxes. There was no proper system for tax assessment. An attempt was made to extract the same sum from each individual peasant (a poll tax), but gradually a certain degree of progression was introduced. The peasant farmers were sorted into several main groups according to the size of their holdings. It was not, however, until the 1660s that the breakthrough came: a tax system based directly on an assessment of the value of the output of each farm and holding. Since this assessment had not kept pace with changes in agriculture during the seventeenth century, the years 1665–69 saw the setting up of a land register where, in addition to the old valuation, information was collected that would form the basis of a new assessment. The old valuation was still used for assessing the rent tenants paid their landlords, while the updated tax assessment was the basis for calculating the amount of tax to be paid. From the 1660s then, most of the tax burden fell on the land and was paid by the peasantry according to a valuation that was reasonably just.

Historians generally now believe that the tax burden was stable, if at a high level, down to 1720, though it shot up dramatically during the war years 1675–79 and 1700–20. In 1723 a new tax register was produced that was designed to update the now almost 60-year-old register of 1665. But the case for greater fairness was, on this occasion, overshadowed by the fear of increased taxation, and, after lobbying on the part of the *embetsmenn* and opposition from the peasantry generally, the 1723 register was set aside. In 1746 the authorities ceased sending out an annual tax demand and in so doing accepted that in practice taxes and tax rates should remain fixed.

This changed after the national debt had risen enormously as a result of the military demands during the Seven Years War, 1756–63. In 1762 Denmark and Norway introduced an extra tax on the poll tax principle. The tax was to be a fixed sum to be paid by everyone over 12 years of age. The tax was strongly opposed in Norway. This opposition culminated in the 'Stril' riots (Stril are the inhabitants of the coastal region to the north and west of Bergen), when the peasants of the area called on the *stiftamtmann* and forced him to repay the tax. In the following years the authorities decided not to pursue the tax defaulters and abolished the tax altogether in Norway in 1772. Economic difficulties could have occasioned the revolt but the heart of the matter was political. The peasants refused to accept any other taxes than those they had traditionally paid. Not until the years after 1800 do we encounter a new attempt by the government to increase tax receipts in Norway – and this time with greater success. But the important fact to stress is that, as a result of gradually increasing prices and falls in the value of money in the course of the eighteenth century, the actual tax burden was reduced. The peasants had then quite a solid foundation for recognizing themselves as privileged so far as the payment of taxes was concerned.

Political and social benefits of the peasantry

While the towns had a considerable degree of self-government from the Middle Ages onwards, it is generally believed that the rural districts did not get it before the local government laws of 1837. This is not entirely true, as we have been able to show (Chapter 7).

From early times the church congregations had owned or at least had responsibility for the local church and the parsonage attached to it. The local population was obliged to select custodians to take care of the buildings and to manage the income. This gave the custodians a great deal of power over, for example, the parish priest's material living standard. When, in 1723, the king demanded the right to the churches and began to sell both them and the land associated with them, the custodianship duties attached to the church ceased, though supervision of the parsonages continued.

Representatives of the public also made their presence felt in the local judicial system in that they sat as jury members in the *bygdeting*. This judicial power became largely symbolic when the *bygdeting* came under the control of the *sorenskriver* from the end of the sixteenth century. But, with the major legal reforms of the 1790s, arbitration commissions were established to handle civil cases in the first instance, and here the peasants again gained a place as commissioners.

This marked the end, for the time being, of an important eighteenth-century development. In accordance with the provisions for setting up public elementary schools in 1739-41, each parish was to be responsible for its own schools. The administration of these schools was to be in the hands of a school board, of which the peasants were members alongside the parish priest. There is much to suggest that the peasants had the real power on these boards because they decided on the school's income. Between 1741 and 1790 each of the Norwegian dioceses set up its own system for dealing with poverty. The same procedure was followed as with the schools. Each parish had its own board with representatives from the peasantry, and, since the peasants were to pay the bulk of the poor rates, they got a corresponding say over the administration. Thus local self-government existed for individual matters before 1837. After a decline down to the church sales of 1723, self-government revived rapidly from the 1740s as new tasks were placed on it, and here the peasants secured considerable influence.

In addition to paying taxes and making a political contribution, the peasants also acquired benefits on the social front. As we have seen in Chapter 9, the growth of population meant that social equality could no longer be maintained. Down to the 1760s it was the government's policy that farms should not be subdivided. The reality usually did not live up to the regulations, but the policy that lay behind them could have contributed to the gradual channelling of population growth into a new social group – the *husmenn* (crofters). With the regulations of 1750 and 1752 the authorities approved this development. *Husmenn* got a certain amount of legal protection in the form of a contract and a tenancy for life on land they themselves had cleared. Those who took on a holding that had already been cleared could be treated much as their peasant landlords wished. At the same time, the peasants received an assurance that the tax assessment on their properties would not be raised as a result of the cultivation and improvements brought about by the *husmenn*. In this way the authorities signalled that the *husmann* system was to be a support for the taxpaying peasantry. (The land cultivated by the *husmenn* was not assessed for taxation, so they paid no tax either.) Another economic asset, of at least equal importance for the peasantry, was the cheap labour they were able to obtain in the form of young, unmarried servants. Besides the regulations on service that were to be found in the older legal codes, a specific injunction appeared in 1754. This enjoined 'unattached and unemployed people' to take 6- or 12-monthly service contracts at 'low wages'. This was intended to provide the peasantry with a cheaper labour force than if they had had to hire people at high prices, on a daily basis, during the harvest period. With these regulations covering *husmenn* and farm servants, the peasantry had received a clear message that they could exploit the social groups beneath them. It was now the peasantry's turn to feel themselves socially elevated.

A society in equilibrium?

The government operated in Norway through a social group that controlled and monopolized all government posts, namely the *embetsstand*. Despite the fact that this group had, through its geographical origins, its culture and its way of life, strong ties with the rising Norwegian bourgeoisie, the *embetsmenn* managed to maintain a certain distance between themselves and the business community. Thus it could be said that the regime did not settle all its power in Norway upon one particular social group.

This assertion must, however, be modified when seen within a time perspective. Down to the end of the seventeenth century – one can, in fact, set the dividing line in the 1680s – the government gave the urban bourgeoisie great political, and above all, economic privileges. The roles of *embetsmenn* and businessmen were frequently mixed. We note also that down to this period the peasantry were burdened with taxes and military services.

From the 1680s this long-term trend was reversed. The tax burden on the peasantry was stabilized and later gradually reduced. The peasants achieved a certain formal political influence at the local level (in addition to the de facto influence they already had). The sale of state lands was now arranged so that the peasantry had the opportunity to buy. And the peasantry got social privileges *vis-à-vis husmenn* and farm servants. The involvement of *embetsmenn* in business was restricted. And the authorities attempted, through the *embetsmenn*, to eject the bourgeoisie from their most privileged positions, for example, they encouraged competition in the country by supporting the *ladesteder* against the towns; they attempted to prevent the merchants from exploiting the peasantry in their trading relations; they opposed the privileges of the guilds and they responded quickly to the peasantry's demands for liberalizing trades and crafts at the end of the eighteenth century (the Lofthus revolt).

Even if it is obvious that the Norwegian merchant elite had great political influence, one can nevertheless assert that the resemblance Norway had to a one-class state in the seventeenth century had all but disappeared again by the end of the period of absolutism. The mainstay of the government was an *embetsstand* that, by the standards of the Europe of the day, was uncorrupt and impartial, and that in an effective way managed to balance the interests of the other groups in society.

13
Denmark and Norway

In Chapters 9–12 we have seen how Norwegian society developed demographically, socially, economically and politically, during the union with Denmark in the years 1536–1814. Only here and there have we cast a glance at the principal partner to the south. In this chapter, we shall give a general overview of relations between Norway and Denmark. Norway was the weaker partner in the union. In much of Norwegian historical writing since 1814, Norway too has been seen as the injured partner. The Danish connection has been examined from a formal legal, even a moral, perspective, which has created astonishment amongst historians south of the Skagerrak. Have Norwegian scholars seen a side of the picture that the Danes have missed? Or are they but spokesmen for a quickly roused and thin-skinned nationalism?

In the following pages we shall discuss relations between Denmark and Norway under three different headings: the cultural, the economic and the political. But before we attempt to judge the rights and wrongs of the case it is worthwhile remembering that, at the time we are speaking about, neither equality of esteem nor equality of treatment were held in much regard, in either social or political relationships. Quite the contrary, it was regarded as right and proper to take from the poor and give to the rich, or to let the strong exploit the weak. That Norway as the dependent, peripheral country should demand special treatment, even benefits, was foreign to the whole way of thinking. That is, perhaps, best understood if one sees Norway in the light of other contemporary European dependencies, such as Ireland, the Belgian provinces or Hungary.

The Danish language in church and school

Culturally speaking there is no doubt that Norway was affected the most by the union and at the heart of the cultural complex we find the language. Danish became the written language of Norway and engulfed the spoken language for large sections of Norwegian society. Paradoxically it was the Reformation that played the role of the Trojan horse for the Danish language in Norway. In other places, the mother tongue was used for new editions of the Bible, for hymns and for the liturgy. In Norway, however, Danish was used from the start. There were several reasons for this. The Reformation was set in motion by a foreign power and many of the new clergy, especially the upper echelons, were recruited in Denmark. But one should also not forget that in Norway the spoken language had been undergoing a process of change since the late Middle Ages. The Old Norse written language had, because of this, all but disappeared by the sixteenth century, with the result that there was actually no alternative to Danish. That an up-to-date Norwegian written language in the year 1536 could have stopped the change in the dialects (which has continued to the present day) appears unlikely. To blame Danish cultural imperialism is clearly wrong when one sees how German continued as the Church language in the duchies of Schleswig–Holstein, and Icelandic and Faeroic on the islands to the west.

The position of the Danish language in Norway was further strengthened in the sixteenth and seventeenth centuries by the large-scale recruitment to the urban bourgeoisie and the *embetsstand* in Norway from Danish and German linguistic areas. With these two social groups, Norway in effect got an upper class that both linguistically and culturally was strongly tied to the mother country in the south.

For the Norwegian-born general public, the language question first became a pressing one during the second, pietistic reformation of the eighteenth century. The practice of confirmation was introduced in 1736 and compulsory schooling introduced in 1739–41. Schools were to give children practice in reading as a means of acquiring a knowledge of Christianity; and all reading matter was in Danish. The gap between the Norwegian spoken language and the Danish written one was undoubtedly much greater in the eighteenth century than it is today, so that Danish had to be learned as a foreign language. This could have both hampered and slowed down the learning process, but with, perhaps, less negative effects for reading and understanding than for writing and self-expression. It must be stressed that not even in 1739 was there any alternative in Norway to written Danish and that it is by no means certain that the problem was much greater for children there than in, for example, Jutland.

A veneer of elite culture?

Throughout the entire period of union the Norwegian contribution to art and scholarship was modest. The few Norwegians who made a mark did so in Copenhagen and in a less than characteristic Norwegian form. At the same time, foreigners who travelled in Norway agreed that the upper layer of the bourgeoisie and the *embetsstand* maintained good contacts with the cultural life of Europe. This implies that the Norwegian elite were no more than consumers of imported cultural items. Art, for instance, suffered from the fact that the great patrons were in the capital or chose to get their culture from abroad. Scholarship suffered primarily because the seat of learning, the university, was situated in Copenhagen.

However, the fact that the elite culture was imported and never set down creative roots in Norway possibly led to the country's rich and varied folk culture being allowed to develop more freely and independently. When this culture was dragged into the light of day during the nineteenth century, Norway, within a Scandinavian context, was seen to be unusually well endowed. This is not to say that the Norwegian folk culture was incompatible with the characteristically Danish culture of the elite. It is, for instance, difficult to discover in the poetry of Peter Dass any artificiality in the link between the Danish language and the everyday life of north Norway, while the Danish hymns of Kingo and Brorson never stir the soul more deeply than when they are dressed up in Norwegian folk melodies. Nor does it appear that foreign influences on folk culture were less than in other countries – rather the reverse. So, if Norway was on the cultural periphery throughout the entire period of union with Denmark, it nevertheless carried a great and spirited promise of growth and development, both from within and from below.

The Norwegian peasantry had the rare skill of being able to combine foreign fashion with native colours and styles. Here we see the clothes from Heddal in Telemark taken from Norske Nationaldragter (Norwegian National Costumes), *published by Chr. Tønsberg in 1852.*

Taxes and transfers

There has been a lively debate surrounding the financial relations of Norway and Denmark from the eighteenth century onwards. The matter can be discussed under three headings: How did taxes and other public burdens weigh upon the subjects of the two parts of the kingdom? To what extent was there a financial transfer between them? What sort of economic policy did the government carry out in the two countries?

The century 1625–1720 was the great war era in Danish–Norwegian history. We have established that the tax burden rose sharply and that it remained at a high level between the wars. This was the situation in both countries. But did Norway have to bear a relatively larger part of the burden? On the basis of data from 1608, a year of peace, it has been estimated that Norway then contributed 10–15 per cent of the state's income. Data from the 1640s are of little use since it was a short and somewhat exceptional period of war. In the years 1676–99 Norway contributed 21 per cent of the state's income, Denmark (the kingdom itself) 54 per cent. The rest came from the duchies of Schleswig and Holstein and the other dependent territories. Calculations for the period 1731–71 and for the 1790s suggest that the Norwegian percentage moved between 24 and 29, i.e. somewhat higher than at the end of the seventeenth century. Roughly speaking one can say that Norway's contribution to the state's income rose from one-tenth to one-quarter in the course of the seventeenth century and remained relatively stable at about the latter level for the rest of the union period.

What kinds of income are we talking about? Customs dues accounted for around 35 per cent of the state's income in Norway. Most of this came from dues on exports, principally timber. Leaving out the somewhat exceptional Øresund tolls, the corresponding percentage for Denmark was only 10. However, it could be said that the Norwegian export dues were paid by the foreign buyers. But matters were not so simple. For the tolls quite clearly depressed prices and so hit the sellers. Nevertheless, the high percentage of the state's income that came from customs dues did give Norwegians an advantage. If we examine the rest of the state's income (essentially tax) and share it out per inhabitant, we find that the average figure for the years 1670–99 amounted to less than 1 *riksdaler* in Norway and over 2 in Denmark. Whether or not this was in Norway's favour depended upon how much the population generally produced or earned in the two countries. Our information on this is inadequate, but the general opinion is that most Danes were not twice as well off as most Norwegians.

The indications are, then, that the state drew less of its income from its Norwegian subjects than it did from its Danish ones. Because of Norway's more rapid population growth in the eighteenth century, the figures moved yet further in Norway's favour towards the end of the union period.

The picture as to the burden of taxation is not, however, quite com-

Equipping the Norwegian militia was a recurrent problem. But its capability improved gradually, and its self-confidence rose dramatically, especially after the clash with Charles 12 of Sweden's elite troops during the Great Northern War. Here we see an infantry man from 1728.

plete. A proportion of the transfers in the form of fees, tithes and administrative charges went directly to the *embetsmenn* in the two countries without going through any national accounts. These forms of income have not yet been researched. Besides, one must remember that the Norwegian peasants were subject to military service. The Norwegian army was a conscripted one, not, as in Denmark, for the most part enlisted (i.e. professional), while the bulk of the crews for the navy of both kingdoms were also Norwegian conscripts. Now it is very difficult to convert military service into monetary terms. Nevertheless it would seem that it constituted a considerable drain on the resources of Norwegian subjects in the years of war down to 1720, but was a relatively modest burden after that. Denmark too got a conscripted army in the eighteenth century as well as an enlisted one.

The next question concerns the use to which the income was put. Much of the state's income in Norway went to paying for goods and services produced there, but it is quite clear that there was a net outflow to pay for institutions in the capital that were shared by both kingdoms. Reasonably reliable data from the second half of the eighteenth century suggest that around half of the income entering the national accounts in Norway was drawn out of the country: this amounted, annually, to around half a million *riksdaler*. It would appear that the proportion of income transferred out of the country in the earlier years after 1660 was also around half. The palace and the upper echelons of society bought their goods and services in Copenhagen – here the grandiose buildings were erected; here the luxury wares were sold; here was all that was of significance in art and scholarship. Just what a loss this 'capital city effect' was to Norway can be seen in the rapid growth and prosperity of its own capital, Christiania, after 1814.

Economic policy

During the so-called mercantilist period down to the end of the eighteenth century, the government made many attempts to encourage trade and industry and to stimulate economic development. There were two periods of particular activity: the early 1600s under Christian 4 and the years 1720–60. Christian 4 set up trading companies and began the production of textiles in factory-like establishments. He gave them privileges designed to help them in competition with overseas enterprises. Not least he made a major effort in mining, with the silver mines at Kongsberg and the copper mines of Røros as the main examples. The trading companies and market-oriented production units were, for the most part, sited in Copenhagen, where the main purchasing power was to be found. But this did not hinder the will to invest in the development of Norwegian resources. Christian 4 has never been criticized for selling Norway short.

The government more or less followed the same principles during the next period of activity in the eighteenth century. Trade and the production of finished goods mostly benefited the capital, but the interest in Norwegian resources remained undiminished. Two features have, however, made this period a somewhat more controversial one amongst historians. The first of these was the transfer of the internal trading monopolies to Copenhagen. Trade with Finnmark, Iceland and Greenland was subject to a scheme designed to ensure that the inhabitants of these peripheral areas received the most essential supplies. In 1728–29 the trade with Finnmark and Greenland was transferred from Bergen merchants to those of Copenhagen and in 1733 the capital also got the trade with Iceland. In this connection it is easy to ignore the fact that the Bergen merchants had not found the trade to be a profitable one and that for a long period in the eighteenth century it sustained losses that had to be made good by the king himself. In 1726, Copenhagen was once again shown preferential treatment when it was given the right to warehouse goods without having to pay import duties until they were sold. But it is worthwhile noting that such privileges were later granted, in part, to provincial towns and that it has not proved possible to calculate just how valuable they were in monetary terms.

The second and more sensitive issue was the active support given to Danish agriculture. This, Denmark's staple industry, suffered a severe depression in the 1720s and 1730s. In 1735 the so-called corn monopoly was introduced. This gave Denmark the sole right to supply southern Norway (Østlandet and Agder) with grain. Historians have argued that this forced Norwegians to buy expensive and poor-quality grain and that Denmark did not manage to supply sufficient quantities when its own harvests failed. The corn monopoly was then blamed for the fact that Norwegians starved. Besides, this monopoly prevented a trade with other countries that were ready to supply grain in exchange for Norwegian timber. That the corn monopoly had certain negative effects cannot be denied. It should, however, be noted that many exemptions were allowed during the period it was in force (down to 1788). The monopoly probably also stimulated the cultivation of grain in Østlandet.

It is, however, more fruitful to see the grain monopoly as part of a larger set of measures. Goods produced in Norway enjoyed advantages on the Danish market, especially iron, salt and glass. The goal was to develop the internal economy by supporting the establishment of new ventures and by protecting them from overseas competition. Further, the government tried to encourage a certain division of labour between the various parts of the country and to knit them closer together into a tighter economic entity. So long as Norway had a wider spread of resources than Denmark, it is difficult to see how such an economic policy could seriously push Norway onto the sidelines.

Norway – a kingdom or a collection of administrative areas?

As we have seen, Norway, with the introduction of absolutism, was once more spoken of as a kingdom in its own right, on a par with Denmark. But this was in name only. The king and the central administration were Danish and ran Norway from Copenhagen. It is, therefore, more interesting to discuss Norway's status as a 'kingdom' in the light of the following questions: Was it possible to find administrative institutions of state whose framework was Norway as a whole? If so, just how independent of the capital were such distinctively Norwegian institutions?

The leading government post north of the Skagerrak was that of the viceroy. His principal job was to supervise the administration in Norway. At certain times, however, he was able to take somewhat more of a political course. Hannibal Sehested (1642–51) provides one example of this, as does Ulrik Frederik Gyldenløve (1664–99). In the years 1704–21 deputy viceroys were appointed. Their job was to chair a sort of Norwegian government in Akershus, the so-called *Slottsloven*. But in each of these cases a wartime situation prevailed that demanded quick decisions and the ability to act independently of the somewhat precarious communications with Copenhagen. With the stabilization of the overseas political situation after 1720, the position of the viceroy was correspondingly weakened. The position was unoccupied from 1739, held by a deputy viceroy from 1751 and was clearly left vacant after 1771. Contact now went directly from the central administration to each of the four *stiftamtmenn*. There was something paradoxical about the position of the viceroyalty: during its periods of importance it reflected both a strong central power and a Norway acting as a separate political entity.

Around the time of the introduction of absolutism in 1660, Norway's administration was divided into several departments, each of which had direct contact with Copenhagen. Several of these were exclusively Norwegian. This applied to the army, the postal service and the department of mines. But here too there was a tendency, during the following 150 years, to move towards smaller geographical divisions, which had the effect of weakening the joint Norwegian administration. A typical example of this can be seen in what happened to the legal system. After a reorganization in the 1660s Norway got a so-called *Overhoffrett* as more or less the final court of appeal (although it was still possible to appeal further to Copenhagen). In 1797, however, a further reorganization took place. Now each of the four *stiftamt* got its own court, from which appeals could go to the High Court in the capital.

There are grounds for believing that this tendency to put Norway's local government more directly under the central administration in Copenhagen expressed a wish for a greater unification of the various parts of Denmark-Norway. But it could also be seen as the natural result of better communications and a growing awareness of Norwegian conditions on the part of the central authorities. Hence an intermediary was no longer necessary.

In matters of legislation, however, the situation evolved somewhat differently. Christian 4's Norwegian Code of Law of 1604 marked a distinction between the two kingdoms. In spite of a strong desire to the contrary, this was repeated in the 1680s when separate Danish and Norwegian Law Codes were produced. In the Code of Christian 5, which came out in 1687, it is the section on the ownership and renting of land that is markedly different from its Danish counterpart. The law was constantly elaborated and updated by royal decree. There is no indication here of any active attempts on the part of the government to link the two kingdoms more closely together. Quite the contrary, it would appear that there was an ever-increasing awareness of the basic social differences between the two parts of Denmark-Norway.

Norwegian self-awareness

When interest in economic growth again developed after 1720, a literary genre was created that was to have considerable repercussions. Academically interested members of the Norwegian *embetsstand* and bourgeoisie began to produce topographical accounts of their localities. Gradually increasing in number, these accounts described the natural environment as well as economic conditions and contributed to a growing self-awareness. The authors all agreed that nature had richly endowed Norway and that the country was inhabited by an energetic, distinctive and independent race. Thus Norway was perceived as being very different from Denmark. When, in the 1750s, the authorities invited an open debate on economic questions, it immediately split into a Norwegian and a Danish section. It was not just that the two countries had different resources. There were fundamental differences in the basic industry – agriculture – and Norwegians were not slow to hold up their *odelsbonde* against the oppressed villeins of Denmark.

The first generally available national history of Norway appeared in the 1770s. Written by Gerhard Schøning, this publication enhanced a growing sense of Norwegian pride with its accounts of events before the union with Denmark.

Paradoxically it was the *embetsmenn* and the bourgeoisie, the two 'new' social groups in Norway, who, towards the end of the 1700s, began to see themselves as uniquely Norwegian. There is little evidence, however, of a corresponding attitudinal change within peasant society. This makes it difficult to use a concept such as nationalism, since this usually embraces all sections of society and includes language and culture. Contrary to the findings of Ernst Sars, it is difficult to identify specific aspects of Norwegian folk culture that found their way into the elite groups. Let us, therefore, rather talk of a growing Norwegian patriotism, a consciousness of feeling at home in Norway, of a Norwegian distinctiveness. It is important to stress that this consciousness was supplemented by the great respect accorded the indigenous population, the Norwegian peasantry. This respect forms the starting point for the much more marked cultural exchange that was to follow in the nineteenth century.

That there was little cultural exchange at the end of the union period should not surprise anyone. Norwegian society was clearly one of different orders or estates. In such a society there was little movement between the different orders, which were sharply differentiated one from another, not only in status and rights, but also in language and in material and intellectual culture. An open and more egalitarian political system had to be created before cultural integration could be speeded up.

Were Norwegians dissatisfied with the union?

To become politically dangerous, the growing Norwegian patriotism had to be linked to controversial political issues. During the second half of the eighteenth century such an issue developed over the demand for a separate university in Norway. *Embetsmenn* in Norway were notable advocates of this. They argued that to send their sons to study in Copenhagen involved them in considerable extra expense, since living costs were high there and temptations great. At the same time the Norwegian urban bourgeoisie were forever expressing a desire for their own Norwegian bank. Strong censorship in the country made it difficult to articulate such political demands, which the government immediately saw as a threat to the union. But, during the short period of press freedom under Struensee (1770–71), these grievances were aired in no uncertain terms. However, a long time had to elapse and a dramatic development take place before the central authorities acceded to the requests. A separate Norwegian university was agreed to in 1811 and opened in Christiania in 1813. And the way was clear for a separate Bank of Norway at the beginning of 1814.

The increased self-assertiveness on the part of Norwegians in the closing years of the union could give the impression that the two kingdoms were beginning to drift apart. But this is debatable. Administrative contact between Copenhagen and the Norwegian administration was probably never closer than in the years immediately before the Napoleonic wars, which reached Denmark-Norway in 1807. Economic contact between the two kingdoms in the form of shipping and the exchange of goods increased in scale, first under the stimulus of the monopolies on corn, iron, etc., and subsequently in the more liberal economic climate from the 1780s onwards. Even cultural contacts flourished more strongly and more freely around 1800 than at any previous time during the union. At the time when Norwegians were at their loudest in trumpeting the virtues of their *odelsbønder*, the government and progressive landowners in Denmark were inaugurating a gigantic agricultural reform that, in effect, was to equalize the position of the peasantry in both kingdoms just at the point when the union collapsed.

This suggests that it was scarcely a chronic dissatisfaction that broke the association with Denmark, no matter how critical Norwegians became subsequently. The association collapsed first because, in the course of 300 years, Norwegian society had grown large enough, rich enough and self-conscious enough to step into the ranks of independent states. A governing elite lacking in 1536 had finally developed. This elite saw itself as Norwegian, and this awareness, in the end, proved stronger than the close links with Denmark. Besides, there existed so little social injustice and exploitation in Norwegian society that the most important social groups could agree on an equal distribution of both obligations and benefits.

But the association ended too because the Oldenburg monarchy was drawn into a major European conflict in 1807 that, with one blow, opened up a serious crack within it. It then took only seven years before Frederik 6's dominion fell for ever.

14
The union collapses

In tracing events down to the dissolution of the union in 1814, it is difficult to ignore foreign affairs. It was, after all, events on the European stage that brought about the dramatic upheaval of 1814.

Throughout the entire period 1536–1814, foreign affairs were essentially a story of rivalry and war with the neighbouring state of Sweden. As foreign policy was the monopoly of the leadership in Copenhagen, everything was in place for a Danish dominance at Norwegian expense. To what extent then did the interests of the union partners coincide *vis-à-vis* their eastern neighbour?

Relations with Sweden

We can split up the period 1536–1814 into four phases, with dividing lines drawn in 1625, 1720 and 1807. Down to 1625 the two Scandinavian states were, militarily speaking, about equal. They fought for dominance around the Baltic and in Nordkalotten. Norway was drawn into this strategic game and experienced both the Seven Years' War (1563–70) and the Kalmar War (1611–13). On land, Danish military tactics involved war on two fronts, with attacks on Swedish territory from Skåne, which at this time belonged to the Danish Crown, and from Norway. As Norway's most densely populated area lay so close to the border, it was tempting for the Swedes to turn their forces against its most vulnerable neighbour. Military manoeuvres at sea were of key importance. However, down to 1625 there was no major shift in the balance of power between the two states.

The War of the Emperor in 1625–29 marks a turning point. In an attempt to help the Protestants and, at the same time, to pursue his own interests in north Germany, Christian 4 got involved in the Thirty

Years War. This resulted in great military losses and an ignominious political retreat. Worse still was the fact that the Swedish king immediately assumed the role of the vanquished Dane and won both land and influence in Germany. Now the Swedes not only had gained the upper hand in the Baltic but in so doing became an imminent threat to the Danish heartland. Swedish forces were now in a position to advance quickly into Jutland, cut off the islands and, if lucky enough to find the sea frozen in the strait between Denmark and Sweden, invade them too. In the two next wars – the Hannibal Affair of 1643–45 and the Charles Gustav Wars of 1657–60 – the Swedes took full advantage of their new position. Denmark lost all its territory in southern Sweden, and Norway had to give up Båhuslen (Bohuslän) and Jemtland–Herjedalen. Now Sweden could take over the strategy of a war on two fronts, with an army from the south against Denmark and by utilizing domestically based forces against Norway. In the wars that followed – the Gyldenløve War of 1675–79 and the Great Northern War of 1709–20 – the Swedes were gradually forced onto the defensive, but this was owing largely to an involvement with other, stronger, opponents than Denmark-Norway. These same conflicts demonstrated, however, that Norway was a theatre of war in which Swedish armies could operate without the direct involvement of foreign powers.

How did the Norwegians manage to defend themselves? To order the peasantry to hold arms and then to muster them, as had been done in the case of the Seven Years' War and the Kalmar War, proved to be an unsatisfactory arrangement. Thus a professional Norwegian army was officially set up in 1628 and began to operate as intended in the 1640s. The rural districts were grouped into areas (*legd*), each with the obligation of providing and equipping one soldier. An officer corps was created consisting mainly of Danes and Germans. These officers were spread around the country with the task of enlisting the soldiers and training them. For the last major military engagement at the end of the Great Northern War, in 1716–18, Norway was able to put almost 16,000 conscripts, as well as a number of professional soldiers, into the field.

Given a minimal level of leadership, equipment and provisions, the Norwegian farm boys put up a good show. Already by this time myths began to circulate around the Norwegian war effort, with frequent derogatory references to the Danes. There was a clear difference between the attitude the Norwegians had towards their own national, conscripted, armed forces and the opinion held by the Danes of the mainly foreign recruits who made up their land forces. It should also be noted that most crewmen in the joint fleet, which had its base in Copenhagen, were conscripted from the so-called *sjølegder* along the Norwegian coast, up to and including Trøndelag. There was no conscription in north Norway.

A neutrality that did not last

A turning point in relations between the two Scandinavian kingdoms occurred in 1720: a more peaceful period began. Sweden had come out of the last conflict weakened militarily and politically, while Denmark-Norway's desire for revenge disappeared. Apart from some minor episodes there was peace between the two powers down to 1807. The surveying of the border between Norway and Sweden around 1750 is an indication of the milder political climate.

The main aim of the political leadership in Copenhagen during this period was to secure the country from attack from the south. This was achieved by performing a clever diplomatic balancing act between the great continental powers. The core of this was the work involved in finding a solution to the so-called Gottorp question. A duke occupied the castle of Gottorp in Holstein. He was a member of a junior branch of the Danish royal family and controlled parts of Schleswig and Holstein. Through an inherited animosity towards the Oldenborgs, the Gottorp family represented a strategic threat to Denmark. The danger was heightened when the duke's family married into that of the Russian czar in 1725 and when another member of the family was elected heir-apparent to the throne of Sweden in 1743. From 1746 onwards, in an attempt to solve the problem, Denmark tried to align itself with Russia. A tedious period of diplomacy at last bore fruit in 1773 when the Gottorp duke was bought out of Schleswig-Holstein. Thus, from 1773 until 1807, Denmark-Norway held itself neutral with regard to England and France, and worked with Russia and Sweden to see that this neutrality was respected.

If the difficulties over the duchy were of little interest for Norway, there is no doubt that Danish neutrality gave Norwegian shipping and trade great advantages during the American War of Independence and the Revolutionary Wars. Great Britain was involved in both of these conflicts and lost markets to neutral countries. But when the Revolutionary Wars became the Napoleonic ones, the party was over. The neutral states were obliged to choose sides. Sweden chose England in 1805; Russia joined France in 1807. Then Great Britain made the choice for the Danish government an easy one. Fearing that the Danish-Norwegian fleet would fall into the hands of Napoleon, in August 1807 the British sent a large, combined land and sea force to Copenhagen. The town was besieged and the fleet captured. After this so-called 'rape of the fleet', the Danish king readily joined Napoleon.

It was a fatal choice. For the first time in 300 years the foreign policy interests of Denmark and Norway came into direct conflict. Denmark had allied itself with Napoleon because of its old fear of being invaded by land from the south. The price was the obligation to wage war along with France and Russia against Great Britain and its ally Sweden. The conflict with Great Britain would affect trade and shipping, while that with Sweden was to develop into a land war. In both cases Norway suffered far more than Denmark; 1807 inaugurated one of the worst crises in Norwegian history.

Living through the crisis years

The conflict with Great Britain led to Norwegian exports shrinking to almost nothing; essential grain imports were severely restricted and shipping met grave difficulties, even in distant waters. The pressure of the British fleet close in shore disrupted domestic goods traffic and cut most links with Denmark. At the same time, the Norwegian army was mobilized and moved to the eastern border. This necessitated large supplies of food and equipment to keep the troops on a war footing. Already in the summer of 1807 a government committee with four members and chaired by Prince Christian August was set up to govern the country in this tense situation. Christian August was already Commander-in-Chief of the Norwegian army in the southern part of the country.

Hostilities began on land in April 1808. Swedish forces reached the River Glomma but were repulsed and forced to retreat. During the summer the Swedes moved troops to the Finnish front where the Russians were attacking. The fighting then tailed off, though it was necessary to keep the troops at the ready on the frontier. To invade Sweden was all but out of the question. The shortfall in grain imports together with poor harvests at home brought starvation to much of Østlandet in 1809 and fatal epidemics of dysentery spread out from the insanitary army camps.

Things went badly for the Swedes on the eastern front. Russian troops advanced through Finland right into northern Sweden. In March 1809 Swedish officers engineered a coup against Gustaf 4 Adolf and put Carl 13 in his place. The new king had no children. In the summer, Christian August, the Norwegian Commander-in-Chief, was chosen as heir-apparent to the Swedish throne. In September 1809 the war ended in the east with a peace treaty ceding Finland to Russia. In December 1809 Sweden also made peace with Denmark-Norway. Accordingly, by the beginning of 1810 the internal Nordic conflict had ended, with the three governments in Copenhagen, Stockholm and St Petersburg all committing themselves to the side of Napoleon. By the autumn of 1809, Great Britain had eased the blockade. The crisis in Norway was over – for the time being.

The germ of a new development lay in the choice of an heir-apparent to the Swedish throne when Christian August died suddenly in the spring of 1810. The national assembly chose the French marshal, Jean Baptiste Bernadotte – now to be called Crown Prince Carl Johan. He was no puppet of Napoleon's but an independent and single-minded political strategist. He believed a retaliatory war against Russia would lead nowhere. Further he felt Sweden ought to give up Finland and annex Norway. He also realised that for this to succeed it was best to ally with Russia and Great Britain, rather than with France. The strategy was set in motion in 1812 when Napoleon went on the offensive against his former ally Russia. Carl Johan signed a treaty with the czar that, in exchange for military support against Napoleon, would give Norway to Sweden. The year after, a similar agreement was reached with Great Britain. In the summer of 1813, a Swedish army was sent to the continent to fight alongside the allies against Napoleon

To conquer Norway was a well-known and long-established goal of Swedish foreign policy. What was new were the means by which this was to be achieved: on the one hand, through agreements with the great powers and, on the other, through a campaign to get Norwegians voluntarily to change their union partner. From 1809 onwards, there were contacts between men of both countries at the highest level, with rumours of a liberal constitution for Norway and equal status in a union with Sweden. Such a future was also mentioned in the treaty between Sweden and Great Britain in 1813. But there was also another party east of the Kjølen (the mountains separating Norway from Sweden) that wanted Norway to be fully integrated into a Greater Sweden. Carl Johan himself was unclear on the issue.

The Danish government undoubtedly knew of the agreements Sweden had entered into with Russia and Great Britain over Norway. Frederik 6 made an approach to the allies in the summer of 1813 but it was too late. He therefore tied his country's destiny even more closely to that of Napoleon. In 1812 came the end of the breathing space Britain had given Norwegian shipping and foreign trade. The corn harvest failed again that same year. Even if there was as yet no war with Sweden, the crisis of 1807 looked set to be repeated. As in 1807, it was Norway that was the hardest hit. This time the king chose to send to Norway no less than his heir, Prince Christian Frederik. He took over as viceroy in May 1813. In the following 18 months, the two heirs-apparent – Christian Frederik in Norway and Carl Johan in Sweden – were to be the leading actors in a dramatic game over Norway's destiny.

The Peace of Kiel and the Norwegian rebellion

The Swedish reinforcements that arrived in north Germany in the summer of 1813 were incorporated into the allies' Army of the North. Carl Johan was put in command of this. He took part in the great Battle of the Nations near Leipzig in October, which Napoleon lost. The strategy now was to pursue the retreating French forces westwards, past Hamburg to the Netherlands. But in November Carl Johan suddenly swung his army north into Holstein. He drove back the Danish army there and forced the Danish king, Frederik 6, to sign the Peace of Kiel on 14 January 1814. In the fourth paragraph of the treaty, Frederik 6 ceded Norway to the king of Sweden. Norway, as a kingdom in its own right, should now enter into a union with Sweden. Carl Johan had never fully trusted his allies. Now he had seized the opportunity to secure his prize. He rejoined the march to the west, and in April the Army of the North stood outside Paris and sealed Napoleon's fate.

Reports of the Peace of Kiel reached Christian Frederik in Christiania on 24 January. He had come to Norway to frustrate the Swedish plans.

Now he decided to allow himself to be acclaimed king of Norway and to resist the transfer of the country to Sweden. To sound out the feelings of the people and, at the same time, to avoid meeting Swedish envoys, he set off for a visit to Trondheim in early February 1814.

It was obvious that public opinion was developing rapidly. Safely back in Christiania again, Christian Frederik called some 20 friends and important figures to a meeting at Eidsvoll on 16 February – the so-called 'meeting of notables'. Up to this point his plan was to take the title of king on the basis of inheritance and to maintain the union with Denmark. But at Eidsvoll he allowed himself to be talked into another way of proceeding: he was to agree to govern the country as regent until a popularly elected assembly should meet, give Norway a constitution and elect a king.

But Christian Frederik feared that the plans would be thwarted by the Swedes. He decided, therefore, that on the same day that elections for a national assembly were to begin – 25 February – an oath was to be sworn by members of the public in the churches: 'Do you swear to defend Norway's independence and to offer your life and your blood for the beloved Fatherland?' And, with hands upraised, the people were to answer: 'That we swear, so help us God and His Holy Word.' That this was a serious matter is evidenced by the fact that all persons of rank, together with 12 representatives from each congregation, were also to swear in writing.

The election was completed towards the end of March. Shortage of time meant that northern Norway was not involved. On 10 April, 112 popularly elected representatives met in a national assembly at Eidsvoll. By 17 May the new constitution was ready and Christian Frederik was elected king. Not only had Norway been restored as an independent state, it also had a constitution that gave political rights to an unusually wide spectrum of the people.

How had it been possible to set aside the Peace of Kiel in this way? Quite simply because the Swedish political and military leadership and the bulk of its military forces were engaged in the campaign against Napoleon on the continent during the late winter and spring of 1814. As Jens Arup Seip says: 'Sweden was not immediately in a position to grasp the prize Denmark had been forced to relinquish.' It was in this magical vacuum that Christian Frederik and the popularly elected representatives managed to create an independent Norway. But would it survive?

Independence – but in a union with Sweden

Already in April 1814 Carl Johan asked his allies for help to enforce the Peace of Kiel. A delegation of the Great Powers came to Copenhagen at the end of May to see if Frederik 6 had had any hand in the events in Norway. He was cleared of all suspicion. After that the delegation went to Christiania in early July. A British envoy had already been there a month earlier. He had clearly stated that Great Britain felt in duty bound to honour its promises to the Swedes. But he expressed sympathy for the Norwegian government and this raised Christian Frederik's hopes. The same happened with the delegation from the Great Powers: no giving way on the Kiel Peace but the promise of good conditions for Norway in a union with Sweden.

In the course of July the delegation began to mediate between Christian Frederik and Carl Johan. The latter had returned home to Sweden with his seasoned army at the end of May and then moved to the Norwegian border. An armed conflict was brewing. Carl Johan demanded that Christian Frederik should abdicate and leave the country immediately, and that Swedish troops should be allowed to advance to the River Glomma and occupy Norway's frontier fortifications. Christian Frederik said he was willing to call an extraordinary *storting* (parliament) and to offer his abdication to it. He would also accept that Swedish troops advanced to the River Glomma but not that they took over the frontier fortifications. That was where things stood when war began on 27 July.

The war turned out to be a disorderly retreat on Norway's part. Only at Kongsvinger was a Swedish force repulsed. As early as 3 August, Carl Johan made overtures to Christian Frederik for negotiations to take place. The war ended with the so-called Moss Convention of 14 August. With this the Swedes realized their military objectives. They had already reached the Glomma and now Christian Frederik promised to hand over the fortresses. Politically, however, Christian Frederik achieved almost all he had asked for before the war began. There were to be negotiations with a Storting about the conditions under which a union with Sweden should take place. With this Norwegians believed that the Eidsvoll constitution had been recognised de facto. Christian Frederik was to relinquish power immediately and abdicate as soon as the extraordinary Storting was convened. The only difference as regards the pre-war Swedish demands was that the abdication

The fortress of Fredriksten had time and again shown itself to be the cornerstone of Norway's defences against Sweden. In 1814 it played an almost symbolic role in the negotiations before and after the short campaign.

should now definitely take place and not be up to the Storting to decide.

The extraordinary Storting – in effect a new constitutional assembly – met on 7 October. Christian Frederik gave up the throne and the Storting revised the constitution with a view to a loose union and a weaker monarchy. By 4 November the new constitution was ready and the elderly Carl 13 was elected to the Norwegian throne. The link with Sweden was to last for 90 years.

The constitution

The Norwegian constitution was the most important legacy of 1814. For over 175 years, it has been the rock on which political life and the country's basic civil rights have rested. During this time it has undergone many changes, but none have shattered the underlying principles or the institutional framework created by the 112 representatives at Eidsvoll.

In actual fact, two constitutions were drawn up in Norway in 1814. The first was signed on 17 May and was designed for an independent

Norway. The second was completed on 4 November, the result of negotiations on the union with Sweden between Carl Johan and the extraordinary *storting*.

The May constitution was based on the principles of popular sovereignty and the division of powers. The king was to have the executive power; a representative assembly called the Storting was to legislate and set taxes, while judicial power was to rest with an independent judiciary. In the actual text, the constitution provides for a strong monarchy. The king was to appoint all *embetsmenn*, including the five cabinet ministers, and had the sole right to make war and peace and to determine foreign policy. The Storting was to be elected as a single body and on the basis of a broad franchise. That the Storting, once elected, should be divided into two chambers for the handling of legislation was of a practical nature and did not create any kind of a conservative 'upper house'. The Storting was to meet every third year. It had

The National Assembly at Eidsvoll as immortalized by Oscar Wergeland in the Storting's chamber in 1887. He was able to paint most of the representatives from contemporary portraits. Christian Magnus Falsen is seen reading out the proposed Constitution. Next to him sits the Secretary, Wilhelm F.K. Christie.

the right to legislate, to tax and to take up loans. It could impeach members of the government, of the Storting and of the High Court. The franchise for electing members of the Storting embraced all men over 25 years of age who were public officials, farmed taxed land or had, in the towns, property of a certain value. Some 30-40 per cent of all men over 25 fulfilled these conditions. Two-thirds of the members of the Storting were to be drawn from the rural districts.

The May constitution has been called the '*embetsstandens* constitution', not only because this group was chiefly responsible for drawing it up, but also because it laid stress on monarchical power, of which the bureaucracy was an instrument. It even gave *embetsmenn* security of tenure. The wide franchise meant that power was shared with a peasantry that, the *embetsmenn* believed they could manipulate to their own advantage in their campaign against the urban patriciate.

The November constitution rested on the same basic principles as its predecessor but the relations between the powers were now adjusted so as to provide a defence against the union partner Sweden. The king's control of defence and foreign policy was curtailed. The government got a greater degree of independence and the rules governing impeachment were tightened. The wide franchise was also maintained. The regulations relating to the actual union and to the joint institutions were placed in a separate Document of the Realm in 1815.

The two main actors

A central feature of the debate amongst historians on 1814 has been whether the changes brought about in this year resulted from short-term activities overseas (the Napoleonic Wars, the Kiel Peace) or from longer-term developments within Norway itself. It is difficult to say, other than that both were involved. The national assembly and the constitution would have been unthinkable had not Denmark-Norway become involved in the great European conflict of 1807–14 and the link between the two kingdoms shattered by Carl Johan on 14 January 1814. Yet there can be no doubt either that the seven years of crisis gave but an impetus to the patriotic and separatist tendencies that were already to be found in Norway. Without this crisis it would have taken longer for separatism to take hold, the result being that the secession would not have occurred until much later – perhaps in 1849, when the absolutist period in Denmark ended, or in 1864, when it lost the Duchies of Schleswig–Holstein.

Whilst admitting that the immediately preceding events were important, it is, at the same time, natural that one should be interested in the actors themselves. The two major players stand out. Carl Johan and Christian Frederik were both foreigners. It is difficult to avoid admiring the military and political skills of the French marshal who was heir to the Swedish throne and who laboured methodically and doggedly for four years to gain Norway as recompense for the loss of Finland to Russia. That he was forced to give the Norwegians the months from 14 January to 27 July 1814 to determine their fate themselves was obviously against his wishes. But on three decisive occasions in the course of 1814 concessions were made that can be traced back to Carl Johan. During the Kiel negotiations, Norway was at last referred to as 'a kingdom' and transferred to the Swedish king, not to Sweden. During the war in August, Carl Johan went a long way to meet the Norwegian political demands so as to achieve peace. During the negotiations with the extraordinary Storting, he again made great concessions in order to secure the essential goal: the union. Clearly all this took place under pressure from the Great Powers. But some historians have also noted his pragmatism and moderation, and even alluded to his radical past, during the French Revolution.

There is much more of a dispute over Christian Frederik. An older, nationalist tradition has depicted him as a puppet. His initial opposition to the Kiel Peace Treaty was in his own dynastic interest. Then, in February 1814, he was persuaded to put himself at the service of the Norwegians. But when there was work to be done in the cause of freedom during the summer and autumn of 1814, he proved to be not up to the task.

This picture of a 'stage king' has been sharply modified by recent work on events in 1814. Here it is appropriate to distinguish between his role before and after 17 May 1814. Support from Copenhagen underpinned the prince's central role as the initiator of the Norwegian rebellion. King Frederik 6 laid the groundwork for Christian Frederik's initiative by agreeing to the secession of Norway as a whole instead of piecemeal, and by sending large shipments of grain. Equally important for this reappraisal is the discovery of the prince's strong grip on the entire political process down to the constitution and the royal election in May. He exploited the patriotic and democratic mood of the country for his own interests; he manipulated information; he outsmarted his opponents; and he used supporters to influence the formulation of the new constitution in a monarchical direction.

This reappraisal of Christian Frederik as a politician is strengthened further when one comes to his role as the saviour of the Eidsvoll constitution. Here we must speak of nothing less than a completely new interpretation. He is depicted no longer as a failure, but as the loyal and self-sacrificial defender of the Eidsvoll constitution. He had to accept the war and the inevitable defeat, but through the Moss Convention managed to get the Swedes to recognise the constitution *de facto*. He also inspired the extraordinary Storting to rally round the constitution and not only to accept a minimum of concessions, but also to weaken the royal position before the union with Sweden was completed. One might almost say that this new interpretation makes Christian Frederik an 'out and out hero'. What remains, as something of a paradox, is that a politician of such dimensions should later become one of the dullest of Denmark's absolute monarchs.

Who was right in 1814?

Shifting more of the political initiative over to the prince in the Norway of spring 1814 is of consequence in two areas. On the one hand, it pushes 'the people' into the background – a matter of debate, as one school of historians would have us believe that 'the people' were the real driving force behind the independence process. On the other hand, it causes us to look with somewhat greater understanding on those who dared to campaign against the prince, even if this opposition was at the time subject to defamatory propaganda.

By getting the public to swear an oath during the election of February-March, the regent had tried to tie the entire population to his agenda for independence. Nevertheless a group emerged at Eidsvoll that was sceptical of the political line he was pressing. They were immediately branded as the 'union party', even as 'malicious'. Disagreement occurred, amongst other things, over the mandate for the national assembly. The regent argued that it was to provide Norway with a constitution – nothing more. The members of the opposition, on the other hand, believed that the assembly represented the sovereign people and could, therefore, take up any political question. They challenged the monopoly of power that in effect Christian Frederik enjoyed until an ordinary Storting could meet.

The demand for information and joint control applied especially to foreign policy, over which the regent wanted complete control. The opposition was of the opinion that to push the independence line against the wishes of Great Britain was to prolong the enormous economic problems of the years 1807–14. The opposition also believed that a union with Sweden was not incompatible with a considerable degree of Norwegian independence and a democratic constitution. But the regent was able to exploit the patriotic mood of Eidsvoll and the anti-Swedish feelings from the war years to crush the opposition minority. The majority chose independence, with Christian Frederik as king, without coming to grips with what would happen when this Norwegian king in turn inherited the Danish throne.

As 1814 ended the way the opposition actually wanted, one should perhaps congratulate this little group for its clearsightedness, rather than Christian Frederik and his loyal majority. But before one finally does so, one should consider a counter-factual question. Would Norway have got such an independent position in relation to Sweden and would the constitution have been so democratic, if the union had been established on the basis of the Peace of Kiel and not on that of the fight for independence under Christian Frederik? And would Norwegian nationalism have got the same conditions for its further development?

Part III
1814–1945
Rolf Danielsen and Edgar Hovland

15
The consolidation of the new state

After 1814 the country's history was again harnessed to the existence of a Norwegian state for the first time in 300 years. In 1905 this state freed itself from a personal union with the Swedish Crown and from limited institutional links with the Swedish state. The greatest trial for people and state came in the war years 1940–45. These difficult years resulted in an enhanced sense of national identity.

The Norwegian state's European territories took their final form when the frontier agreement was signed with Russia in 1826. The so-called 'Arctic ocean imperialism' of the inter-war years brought further territory in the Arctic and the Antarctic.

Christiania (since 1925 called Oslo) became the capital of the new state and the centre of the country's political life. With its base in the new university, the town also became a scientific and cultural centre. Christiania's position as the nation's capital gradually took on a physical form with the building of the royal palace and university in the 1840s, the Storting (parliament) in 1866 and the national theatre in 1898. From the middle of the 1800s Christiania replaced Bergen as the country's largest town and economic centre.

National independence and political freedom were, in the early years of the state's existence, closely related values. The fight to nourish and consolidate these values became a central theme of Norway's subsequent political life. The development of a political and cultural life of its own helped to bring about a growing feeling of natural unity in the new Norway. Administratively and economically, too, the country became as one.

Since 1814 Norway has experienced stronger economic growth and a greater degree of social change than at any time before in its history. The population increased from 0.9 million at the beginning of the nineteenth century to 2.2 million in 1900 and in excess of 4 million

The decision to raise a statue of King Carl Johan, the founder of the union with Sweden, reflected the strong pan-Scandinavian feeling in the 1860s. By the time the equestrian statue was ready to be placed in front of the palace in Christiania in 1875 – it had been produced by Norway's leading nineteenth century sculptor, Brynjulf Bergslien – the ideological message it was designed to express had lost its relevance.

today, in spite of a great wave of emigration from 1865 to the First World War. Throughout the whole of this period the old primary industries had been in full retreat relative to industry, trade and the service sector. At the same time, a majority of the population had moved from the countryside to the town. Also, in the course of the nineteenth century, Norway became one of the world's leading maritime nations. Economically, culturally and politically, the country became ever more closely integrated into the international community. The backward country on the periphery of Europe advanced to a position amongst the continent's most developed – economically and culturally. The bulk of the population reached a previously unthinkable level of welfare and prosperity. In the course of this growth, the state's role as an organizing and integrating factor in society became ever more significant.

Defence of the constitution

The constitution of 4 November 1814 provided the legal framework for Norwegian political life until 1905. Its first paragraph stated: 'The Kingdom of Norway is a free, independent, indivisible and inalienable realm, united with Sweden under one King.' The year 1814 not 1905 marks the birth of an independent Norwegian state. Admittedly an infringement of that independence lay in the fact that Norway did not have its own representation abroad; throughout the period of union, foreign affairs were handled by the Swedish foreign office (Chapter 19). The extent of Norway's independence – control of taxation, expenditure and legislation as well as the right to raise a national defence force – was nevertheless so great that the union of the two states was more personal than based on a comprehensive institutional arrangement.

The Swedish king had in 1813 promised the Norwegians a certain amount of self-government in a new union. However, what was achieved in the autumn of 1814 exceeded all that had previously been promised. Carl Johan's compliance before 4 November was due to shortage of time (Chapter 14). The overriding issue was to make the union an established fact. The conditions could be revised later when time allowed. It was not, therefore, to be taken for granted that the new state would enjoy a long life.

In 1818, Carl Johan became king and the upstart firmly established himself amongst the crowned heads of Europe. By this time Europe's political climate had taken an anti-democratic turn. The time seemed to be ripe for an attack on the Norwegian constitution. Carl Johan's plans aimed at cutting back the powers of the Storting to the benefit of the Crown. The revision of the constitution could be brought about in two ways: either by a coup d'état or by legal means; that is to say, by Carl Johan getting parliament, through persuasion, pressure and threats, to agree to changes in the written constitution, changes that would reduce Norwegian independence.

In the summer of 1821 the king mustered Swedish and Norwegian troops outside Christiania. At the same time, he briefed the Great Powers on his plans for the revision of the Norwegian constitution. All this suggested that a coup was being planned. However, the plans were halted and the king decided to take the legislative path. The proposals presented to the Storting in 1821 were wide ranging. They

The first Storting's chamber. Initially the Storting met in the hall of the Cathedral School – now reconstructed in the Folk Museum at Bygdøy. In 1854 the Storting moved to the auditorium of the University. Finally, in 1866, it was able to occupy the present Storting building, designed by the Swedish architect Langlet.

included, amongst other things, a demand that the king's power to delay legislation should be turned into an absolute veto; that the king should have the power to dissolve the Storting within the period established by the constitution for its deliberations; that *embetsmenn* (senior public servants who were graduates of the university or a military academy, who were appointed by the king in council, and who had enjoyed tenure), with the exception of judges, should be dismissable by the king; that the king should have the right to nominate the Storting's president; that changes in procedure be introduced, aimed at paralysing the Storting's powers of initiative; and that the Storting's power of impeachment should be changed so as to reduce its force.

The king's hopes of getting his plans realised were based on an expectation of Swedish support and the sympathetic understanding or help of the Great Powers. At the same time, he hoped he would split the opposition in Norway by playing on the traditional antagonisms between the *embetsmenn* and the peasants, and by assembling a group of supporters principally from amongst the *embetsmenn* by gifts and promises of advancement. None of these hopes were completely realised. Support within Swedish political circles was to some extent countered by the fear that, if Carl Johan came nearer to an absolutist position in Norway, his position in Sweden would be strengthened. No help from the Great Powers was forthcoming either.

After the fall of Napoleon the Great Powers wished to bring about a permanent peace by creating a balance of power in Europe that would make it difficult for any one power to aspire to a position of dominance. This meant that the new frontiers were drawn without regard for the idea that each nation should have a right to its own state. Democratic and nationally based uprisings were seen as a threat to the balance of power system and the Great Powers reserved to themselves the right to intervene against such uprisings, and in fact did so. Carl Johan's appeal to the Great Powers over the Norwegian question brought no response because a democratic and relatively independent Norway represented no threat to the balance of power in Europe. Indeed, in the case of one of the powers – Russia – a stronger Sweden, resulting from the incorporation of Norway, was not acceptable. The Great Powers' negative stance on Carl Johan's note of intent implied that their willingness to support Sweden on the Norwegian question ended the moment the union was achieved. That Carl Johan abandoned his plans for a coup d'état in 1821, and instead chose the legislative path, must, to a considerable extent, be ascribed to this lukewarm attitude of the Great Powers.

The attempt to sow the seeds of dissension in Norway also proved unprofitable. Carl Johan's intrigues and his appeals to the peasantry's traditional support for the monarchy contributed no doubt to the outbreak of an anti-parliamentary uprising in Østlandet in 1818, but it was soon suppressed. Many *embetsmenn* gratefully accepted the king's presents, but without allowing them to affect their votes in the Storting. The *embetsmenn*'s patriotically based opposition to the king's revisionary desires was to a considerable extent strengthened by their class interests. An attack on the constitution also threatened their position in Norwegian society. This applied in particular to the proposal to set aside their constitutionally guaranteed protection against dismissal (tenure). The split in the ranks of the *embetsmenn*, inherited from disputes at Eidsvoll (the seat of the constitutional assembly), was also quickly healed!

This combination of circumstances, all favourable to the new state, explains why a united front under the leadership of the *embetsmenn* in the Norwegian Storting was able to withstand Carl Johan's desire to weaken democracy and bring about a closer union with Sweden. The great crisis years were 1821 followed by 1824. Carl Johan put forward his constitutional proposals to each new Storting, as long as he ruled, but their rejection became, after a while, a formality. The attack on the new independence was thwarted.

The new constitution contained many ambiguities, especially with regard to the relative powers of the Storting on the one hand and the executive (i.e. the king and the government) on the other. A number of disputes occurred between the two when it came to putting the written constitution into practice. Drawing the boundaries in such matters came to dominate the work of the Storting during the first two or three decades after 1814 and was important for consolidating the position of the new state. The dispute over who should do what was also linked with the continuing conflict between the Storting and Carl Johan over the question of the revision of the constitution, and must be seen in that light. The compromises arrived at reflected the original stance of the Storting rather than that of the executive powers. This implied both a strengthening of Norwegian democracy and a consolidation of national independence.

Under the guidance of the *embetsmenn*

The main credit for the 1814 constitution must go to the *embetsmenn*, and it was they who led the defence of the independence it enshrined. They did so by virtue of their own position of authority and of their strong position in the Storting. The upwards of 2,000 *embetsmenn* made up but a tiny part of the electorate. In the light of the ruling that two-thirds of the members of the Storting should be elected from the rural districts, the franchise put political power potentially in the hands of the farming community. The strong representation of *embetsmenn* in the Storting was due, therefore, to the fact that other groups of electors gave them their support, in spite of partially opposing interests. This was partly because of their perceived authority and partly through the acceptance of established norms. In addition, the electoral process itself was hedged about by certain conditions that worked to the advantage of the *embetsmenn*. For example, in order to be entered onto the electoral register it was necessary to swear an oath of allegiance to the constitution, a practice in place until 1898. Many never took the trouble to anticipate this hurdle – an indication that the general public had little interest in national politics. Furthermore, organized electoral collaboration offended contemporary values, whilst in the years 1828–42 electoral law even forbad the use of ballot papers. The result was often a wide scatter of votes, which made it possible for more tightly organized groups to gain a representation far in excess of their numerical strength. Finally, up to and including the election of 1903, voting was indirect. The actual voters elected delegates to an electoral college, which in turn chose the members of the Storting. This meant that opposition groups, who made their presence felt at the first stage of the electoral process, for a long time allowed themselves to be manipulated in the electoral colleges, where the personal authority of the *embetsmenn* had a greater impact.

In spite of all this, the power of the *embetsmenn* was due primarily to the fact that they were without competition from other social groups. Unlike its neighbours, Norway had no aristocracy to occupy political positions of power. The political awareness of the peasantry was only weakly developed and the business elite, which had made its presence felt at Eidsvoll, was struck hard by the post-Napoleonic War economic crisis. The fate of Carsten Anker is typical. He had lived, as one of the country's richest men, at the Eidsvoll Works but had gone bankrupt in 1822 and died a poor man.

The *embetsmenn* milieu was characterised by a high degree of self-awareness and class loyalty. Thus they constituted a national class, whilst the peasantry and other economic groups were divided by conflicts of interest and regional concerns. That they could not be dismissed gave them security and, through their position in the executive, they had control over recruitment to their own ranks. Their intellectual superiority also enabled them to make their own, often self-interested values generally binding and morally supreme. They could, in the eyes of the rest of the population, and on the basis of their fight in the 1820s to preserve the nation, present themselves as the exponents of unity. Arising out of the new state's serious financial situation and the monetary policy pursued to meet it, an anti-bureaucratic opposition coalition of the peasantry and the urban elite seemed to be in the process of formation during the early years of nationhood. However, this broke down in the mid-1820s under pressure from the *embetsmenn*, whose national prestige proved too strong.

For the *embetsmenn* to maintain their position, however, it was necessary that, in the main, their rule should be accepted as a beneficial one. Malpractices amongst their own members were dealt with internally. Order in the money supply was achieved, though it involved a considerable national sacrifice. Inflation, which was in part a legacy of the union with Denmark and partly a product of the Eidsvoll guarantee, was brought under control and, through a compulsory levy (the 'silver tax'), the foundations were laid for a national bank, the Bank of Norway, in 1816. The bank was a private company down to 1949 and, though its top management was nominated by the state authorities, they did not attempt to control it. Its headquarters were in Trondheim until 1897. The reason behind these arrangements was to secure the bank's independence from the state. The Bank of Norway had a monopoly of the issuing of bank notes but also carried out normal banking business.

The rule of the *embetsmenn* was also progressive in the sense that, as we shall see later (Chapter 16), it led to a comprehensive modernization of Norwegian society. Through the laws of 1837, which established municipal authorities, local government was democratized. This area of administration had not previously been touched by the revolutionary events of 1814. In the longer term, the 1837 laws, like the franchise introduced in 1814, provided the opportunity for the transfer of power to other social groups at both the parliamentary and local level, but in the short term their primary purpose was to improve local administration.

The national identity

The *embetsmenn* constituted a national class also in the sense that they were instrumental in the establishment of a national identity for the new state. The institutional framework for a Norwegian state had been created in 1814. During the following decades nationalism was more securely established through an appeal to a common past and a common identity. Gradually this was introduced into teaching in schools and institutions of higher education. Undoubtedly the tastes and educational ideals of the *embetsmenn* left their mark on the image of the nation that evolved during this process of nation building. Nevertheless, such an image was necessary for the creation of a national identity inside the frontiers of the new state.

The generation of *embetsmenn* of 1814 had found in the Ancient World, as for that matter had their European contemporaries, ideals that coloured their sense of masculinity, rhetoric and art and, in part, their constitutional ideas. From the end of the 1830s and reaching a peak in the 1840s, there occurred a reorientation of attitudes away from the Ancient World and towards the Norwegian people. In the 1830s measures were taken to begin the publication of the Old Laws of Norway and the *Diplomatorium Norvegicum* (a collection of medieval documents). In 1839 the Public Record Office was set up, with Henrik Wergeland (the great national poet) as its first Keeper. Together these created better conditions for the writing of a national history, which was accomplished by Rudolf Keyser and P. A. Munch in the 1840s. They focused on the Norse Middle Ages, which they regarded as a period of national greatness, while a later generation of historians were at pains to show that Norway had held onto its popular freedoms in spite of its loss of statehood during the union with Denmark. Johan Sebastian Welhaven, who in the 1830s had written didactic poetry with themes from classical Greek allegories, turned in the following decade toward Norwegian nature and folk customs to find themes for his poetry. Already in the 1820s, I. C. Dahl had laid the foundations for a national school of painting, to be followed by Adolf Tidemand and Hans Gude, who went in for subjects from Norway's natural environment and folk life. The attempt by Ivar Aasen to create a new Norwegian written language with its roots in the spoken dialects was, at least initially, welcomed in academic circles. In 1844 the Society for the Preservation of Ancient Monuments was founded – its aim being to preserve the country's heritage of national and vernacular buildings. Finally, Peter Christen Asbjørnsen and Jørgen Moe published their first collection of Norwegian fairy stories in 1841.

The king and his council

The 1830s saw the peasantry entering the Storting in greater numbers. The development was the result of a growing political consciousness and a more liberal climate (cf. the July Revolution in France). It was also partly carried forward by a new popular movement whose leading activist was John Neergaard. The peasants in parliament did not form a coherent grouping or operate within an overarching political perspective. Rather, their interests were limited to the problems of immediate concern to peasant society, questions of tax and public expenditure, including public service pay among other things.

Through this, peasant politics acquired an anti-bureaucratic perspective. The incarnation of this 'old' peasant opposition was Ole Gabriel Ueland, a farmer, elementary school teacher, church deacon and parish constable from Rogaland. He sat in the Storting from 1833 to 1869. Even if the peasant opposition initially had little real effect on the *embetsmenn*'s hegemony, it nevertheless gave the dominant élite a shock and was a reminder of how precarious the foundation of their control of the Storting really was.

The relationship between the king and his government was also on the verge of change. The opposing forces in the constitutional conflicts of the 1820s were the Storting, on the one hand, and the king in his personal capacity, on the other. The government had found itself in a difficult and ambiguous position in the middle. When the Norwegian state was to be restored in 1814, a local administration already existed, but a central administration had to be built from scratch. Prior to 1814 the Dano-Norwegian monarchy had operated under the collegial system, with the king having direct access to each department of state or 'college' (so called because its members were of equal status). After 1814 each department was headed by a cabinet minister. However, the king now had access to such ministers only when they were assembled in cabinet.

With this system the constitutional fathers aimed to set limits on the personal power of the monarchy. The limits were stricter in the 4 November constitution than they had been in that of 17 May, because under the union with Sweden a strong monarchy posed a greater threat than one confined to Norway alone. The presence of other ministers in the cabinet isolated the king from the individual departments of state. At the same time, however, the fact that each department was headed by an individual minister made it easier for the Storting to ensure his political accountability. But ministerial accountability also strengthened the position of the government *vis-à-vis* the crown, in that it drew it closer to the Storting. Nevertheless, the early years of the new state *were* characterised by a strong personal monarchy. This represented a link with the pre-1814 situation. The king's personal power found expression in Paragraph 12 of the Constitution, by which the king was given the right to select his ministers, and in Paragraph 30 which allowed him to make the final decision in the event of disagreement between himself and the government. The ministers could, in such cases, absolve themselves from responsibility *vis-à-vis* the Storting, by appealing to the minutes, but they could not avoid giving the king's decision legal force by refusing to add their signatures to the decisions.

As, according to the Constitution, the king's person was 'holy' (that is to say, could not be made politically accountable), the conflict between the executive and the legislature took the form of a dispute between the cabinet and the Storting. Responsibility was made operative by parliament through the right of the Odelsting to inspect the minutes of government meetings. The Storting consisted of a single group of members elected at the same time. At the start of the session following an election, the Storting selected one-quarter of its members to serve in the Lagting. The Odelsting was formed by the remaining members. Although initially there was some idea of the Lagting operating as an upper house, this did not develop and the primary function of the two bodies was to ensure a bicameral consideration of all legislative matters. The ultimate weapon in the hands of the Storting was its right to impeach a minister. In such a case the prosecution was brought by the Odelsting, while the Lagting, together with the judges of the High Court, made up the court itself. During the period 1814–45 there were six cases of impeachment. The jurisdictional conflicts that arose could not hide the fact that once again the Storting and the king were confronting each other over issues of power. The government was obliged to perform a difficult balancing act between an ever-more confident Storting and a capricious and fickle monarch armed with great personal powers. But the government too was anxious to set limits to the monarchy's personal powers and to protect the national interest as against Norway's union partner. At bottom, Storting and government had a common interest, based on the fact that both these centres of power were dominated by the Norwegian *embetsmenn*.

Carl Johan had been aware that the cabinet represented a threat to his personal power and had, therefore, sought to weaken it. Right down to the end of the union, the government was divided into two sections. Three of its ministers remained permanently with the king in

Stockholm. One of them had the title of prime minister. The rest, 'the Norwegian government', was gathered in Christiania. Until 1856 the king's viceroy presided over them. Later the chair was taken by a senior minister who, after the abolition of the post of viceroy in 1873, took the title of prime minister. In the 1820s the king had tried to turn the Stockholm section into the centre of government, so that he could keep an eye on it. This was rejected by cabinet and Storting, and the tasks of the Stockholm section were gradually restricted to the protection of the Norwegian government's interests as against those of the king and the union partner.

The shift in power

After 1836 the king's involvement in Norwegian political life declined, in all probability the result of increasing age and the dashing of his hopes. This meant that the government was gradually able to free itself from the king's personal grip. The rights that the Constitution had granted to the executive power came to be exercised by 'the king in cabinet', i.e. by the government. During the closing years of Carl Johan's reign, the government moved in the direction of an independent, self-recruiting body; a development that was to continue under his successor, Oscar 1 (1844–59).

This process, taken in conjunction with the impact of the peasantry's entry into the Storting, meant that the *embetsmenn* came to look to the government as their natural stronghold, while the Storting was seen as a threatened outpost. At the same time, the advance of the peasantry led to a closer alliance between the upper echelons of urban society and the *embetsmenn*. While older political theory had emphasized popular sovereignty and the supremacy of the Storting, the result of this shift was an ideological adjustment that, with greater emphasis on the principle of the separation of powers, gave the government more of a leadership role in the life of the state. The shift, which was completed by the middle of the 1840s, found expression in an oft-quoted remark by Viceroy Severin Løvenskiold: 'Intelligence and wealth now look for protection to the royal power: a move now supported by all men of consequence.'

The newly won national independence was consolidated during the first three decades under the new constitution. And a *modus vivendi* was reached with regard to the union, which would be generally accepted almost to the end of the century. A central administration was built up and constitutional arrangements developed for regulating relations between the organs of state. The Norwegian '*embetsmenn* state' had acquired its classic form. The political centre of gravity was now the government, which on the one hand had forced back the personal power of the monarchy and on the other hand had maintained, over and against the Storting, its right to recruit its own members (though still formally appointed by the king) and to exercise the executive power's constitutionally guaranteed authority. This dualism in the life of the state lasted down to 1884.

16
Recovery and growth: the Norwegian economy, 1815–75

The independent Norway was born in a time of economic distress, with poor harvests, low stocks of food and other goods, and markets closed to Norwegian exports. The war had drained the reserves, produced inflation and created problems in the government's own finances. Compared with the golden years before 1807, the setback was dramatic. If, however, we take a look at Norwegian society some 60 years later, we find that the wartime losses had long been made good, the financial foundation for the new independent state firmly established, and a population that had doubled in size enjoying better material conditions. This process is the theme of this chapter.

Population growth and population movement

Norway was thinly populated in 1815, but during the next 60 years the population grew at twice the rate of the second half of the eighteenth century. The population increased from 0.9 to 1.8 million, which, relative to its size, was the fastest rate of growth in Europe, in spite of the fact that Norway lost people through emigration. The birth rate did not rise. The late age at marriage for women (26–27 years), which gave a short period of fertility within marriage, continued to be the most important regulator. What variations there were resulted from a peak in births reproducing itself when its members reached a marriageable age – an effect discovered by the pioneer Norwegian sociologist Eilert Sundt (1817–76) and known as 'Sundt's waves'. The faster growth was, therefore, the product of a sharp fall in mortality, a fall that proved to be a permanent one. After 1815 there were no more years of great crisis when deaths exceeded births.

Historians have put forward two sets of explanations for this: one economic, the other medical. Improved food supplies, resulting partly from greater production at home and partly from more regular imports, not only eliminated the great famines, they also increased the population's resistance to disease. The medical explanations range from compulsory vaccination against smallpox (1810) to the advent of a milder epidemic climate. The resolution of this dispute will come about only after more extensive enquiries are completed into changes in the mortality patterns of different age groups, social classes and regions.

Norway's nineteenth-century population explosion took place then because the chances of survival improved. Data from the 1820s suggest that Norwegian infants had a more solid grip on life than infants in other countries with which comparisons can be made. Lower infant mortality was probably, therefore, the most important reason why life expectancy in Norway was higher than in other countries.

There were great regional variations in population growth, brought about principally by migration. Internal migration consisted essentially of movement from the interior to the coast or to the far north. Mass emigration, which began in the 1850s, tapped the same source. Down to the mid-1860s emigration was especially marked from the inner districts of Hordaland and Sogn and the valley and mountain districts of Østlandet. During the next 10 years these areas were joined by the rich agricultural communities of Østlandet and Trøndelag.

Inside the country, people moved to both urban and rural districts. In 1815, some 11-12 per cent of the population lived in towns or built-up areas. The figure was still only around 15 per cent in 1845, though by 1875 the percentage had reached 25. The capital, Christiania, grew the fastest. This was the country's administrative centre and the port for a large and populous hinterland. Elsewhere, urban growth was tied to the growth of the export industries – fishing, the timber trade and shipping. Rural communities in which fishing, shipping or industry were important also experienced in-migration.

The shift in the settlement pattern mirrored the growth of, and change in, the Norwegian economy, which took off in the 1840s and which, together with emigration, prevented Norway from falling into the 'Malthusian trap' – whereby population growth chokes economic growth.

Agriculture: the basic industry grows

In 1801, around 85 per cent of Norway's population obtained its livelihood, in whole or in part, from agriculture. Most of the population growth down to 1850 had to find employment in the typical rural industries (agriculture, forestry and fishing). The agricultural population grew by 45 per cent to 1855, after which it stagnated and by 1875 accounted for less than 60 per cent of the total population of the country. Was it possible for agriculture to absorb so many without pressure on resources and falling productivity?

The number of holdings grew at about the same rate as the population, through subdivision and the clearing of crofts, while internal colonization resulted in the amount of arable land per head also keeping pace. The growth of productivity was crucial, for it meant that the net calorific output of agriculture almost doubled. The output of corn per

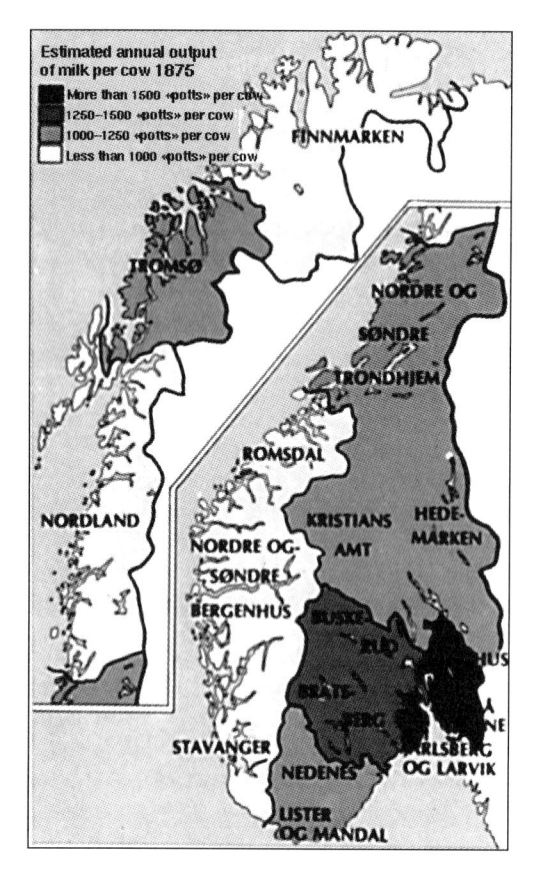

The annual output of milk per cow was regularly at its peak in those districts which had the best access to the growing urban markets. At the top lay the districts on either side of the Oslo Fjord. (A 'pott' is just under a litre.)

acre grew and, as the potato came to occupy an ever more important place, total output grew even further. Livestock production had a much lower growth rate. Despite this, the agricultural population as well as the nation as a whole was more self-sufficient and better supplied with agricultural products by the middle of the nineteenth century than it had ever been before. This does not indicate there was a massive pressure on resources. Output figures around 1800 are not without their shortcomings but still cannot obscure the evidence of real growth.

One searches fruitlessly for key changes in technology and management. However, better cultivation and new crops, especially the potato, partially explain this growth. Fallowing was given up. Heavy manuring and close sowing gave greater returns. The increased labour force made it possible to adopt more intensive methods. Wages remained stable until the middle of the century and rose slowly down to 1870.

The home market for agricultural products was greater towards the end of the period because an increasing proportion of the population had left farming. Better transportation made it easier to reach the market. Between 1855 and 1875 agriculture responded to market forces by placing greater emphasis on livestock production, especially in the neighbourhood of towns. Milk production rose by 50-60 per cent. Corn production stagnated and there was only a weak growth in the output of potatoes. This process of readjustment was led by some of the best agricultural areas of Østlandet.

Agricultural growth had a positive impact on the economy as a whole. One reason for this was that a smaller proportion of export earnings went to cover food requirements. Another was that the growth created a greater internal market as large sections of the agricultural population increased their purchasing power. The peasant economy, however, drew its strength from many sources. It is important, therefore, to look at those other activities that were combined with agriculture, in order to paint a complete picture.

Forestry and the timber trade

Peace in 1815 brought no new golden age for forestry. Quite the reverse, it marked the start of a major crisis. Norwegian timber met higher customs duties in its main market, Great Britain, and both the

Export of lumber 1836–1876, mill. cubic metres

Timber exports began to increase towards the end of the 1830s, and from about 1850 Norway gradually recovered its position in its traditional market, Great Britain. Generally good prices and a high value-added content helped timber exports account, on average, for well over 40 per cent of the total value of Norway's commodity exports for the years 1866–73.

price and the quantity exported fell sharply. Only in areas with low transport costs to the export harbours did it pay to continue cutting timber. The felling area shrank. Sales difficulties and falling prices set off an avalanche of bankruptcies and only a few of the major exporters survived.

Gradually, a greater emphasis on the French market replaced the loss of market share in Great Britain. In volume terms it did not take many years to reach the pre-war level, but prices were low. Not until the 1840s was there a real growth in demand and rising prices. During the period 1841–45 average annual exports amounted to 1.3 million cubic metres. The peak was reached in 1873 when 2.3 million cubic metres were exported.

Economic growth in western Europe, and especially in Great Britain, created the pressure on demand. Norway was again able to draw the full benefit from its favourable location with regard to the British market as the duties on timber were gradually reduced in the 1840s and 1850s. Great Britain again became the main market. The ground was laid for a new golden age.

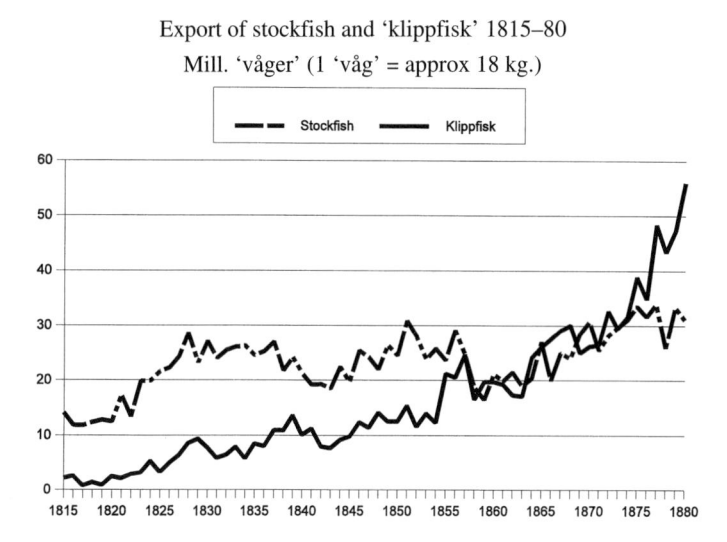

Export of stockfish and 'klippfisk' 1815–80
Mill. 'våger' (1 'våg' = approx 18 kg.)

There was a significant rise in fish exports, especially of klippfisk. *This created openings in new markets, first in the Mediterranean and later in Latin America.*

The post-war crisis struck not only the timber aristocracy, but also those who were associated with the business through felling, carting, floating and working at the saw mills and timber yards. The crisis also hit the forest owners, many of whom were peasants. As well as clearing the way for a larger group of exporters, rising, so to speak, from the wreckage of the bankruptcies, the crisis led to several forest properties coming into peasant ownership. The sale of state properties after 1821 also had the same effect. The price increases from the 1840s onwards worked in a positive direction, with higher real values and increased wages. The felling area was increased and the proceeds spread to new areas.

The fisheries and the export of fish products

The fisheries enjoyed a boom period after the war. A new influx of spring herring led to an expansion of 'fisheries Norway'. While the great cod fisheries were located from Sunnmøre northwards, the spring herring shoals swam into the coasts of Sørlandet and Vestlandet in the years 1808–70.

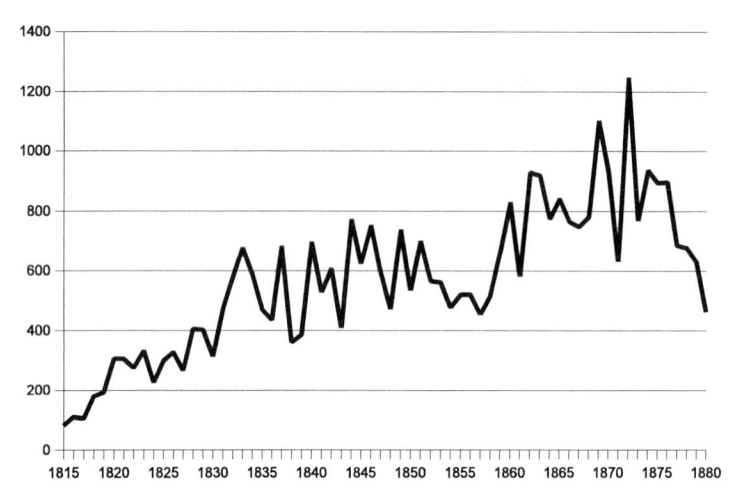

Export of salted herring 1815–80
1000 barrels of 116 litres

Until around 1870, spring herring dominated export sales. There then followed a short period when the 'large' herring caught off the coasts of northern Norway took over. But after 1875 'fat' herring were the main catch. The export of fish products in the years 1866–75 accounted for about 40 per cent of the value of Norway's commodity exports.

Most of the catch went for export. The export totals give, therefore, a good picture of the total amount of fish caught. Variations in the catch were great but, in the case of both herring and other kinds of fish, the long-term trend was upwards. Salted herring, cod liver oil and dried fish were the main products, but gradually the output of *klippfisk* (split, dried and salted cod) increased, so that towards the end of the period it accounted for well over half the total amount exported.

Norway also benefited from the fact that the herring disappeared from the coasts of Båhuslen (Bohuslän), for Norwegian herring could now take over the Swedish market and the markets previously supplied from Sweden. The growth of population in the rest of Europe meant an increasing demand for cheap food, and Norwegian *klippfisk* won a share of the market in the Mediterranean area. Norway did not, however, manage to enter the rich British market for fresh fish, with the exception of a few items of minor economic importance such as lobster, salmon and mackerel.

Sale prices for fish and fish products were favourable down to 1880, with the exception of a sharp fall in the 1820s. To some extent fish

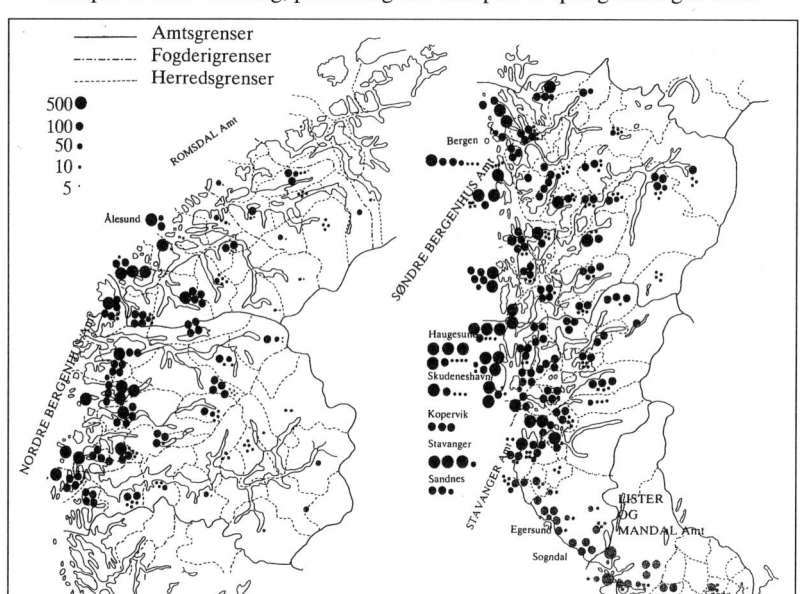

Participants in the catching, processing and transport of spring herring in 1868

In 1868 the bulk of the catch took place in the northern area. In total over 51,000 took part in the spring herring fisheries. Most came from the coastal communities, but a relatively large number came also from the interior. In the same season 21,000 men, from Finnmark in the north to Trøndelag in the south, took part in the cod fisheries off Lofoten; 14,000 more, in the spring cod fisheries off Møre. The total number of participants in the major fisheries taking place at any one time was around 90,000.

exports compensated for the loss of income from timber exports after the war and so contributed to a better trade balance. Fish exports, too, laid the foundations for the growth of towns and other built-up areas, especially in Rogaland, while the ancient fish-exporting metropolis of Bergen met strong competition from the *klippfisk* towns of Ålesund and Kristiansund. The geographical expansion of the production and export of fish gave rise to an expansion of the middle class, some members of which were in a position to invest in other businesses.

The blessings of nature together with increased participation – and not any great changes in technology – brought about the growth in

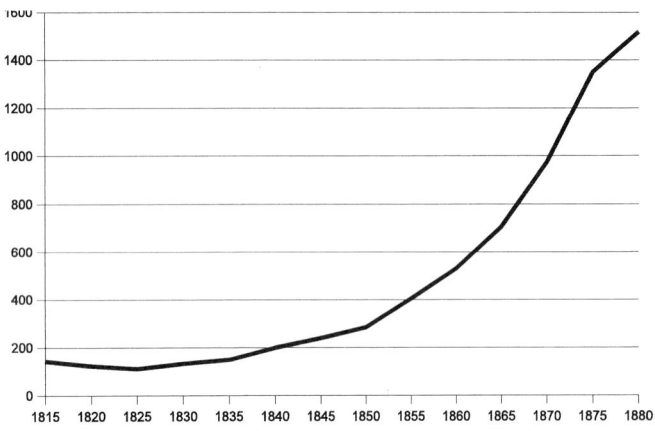

The Norwegian merchant fleet 1815–80
1000 net tonnes

From 1850 to 1880 the size of the Norwegian merchant fleet rose faster than total world tonnage. During the same period the average size of the ships in the Norwegian fleet rose from 77 til 185 tonnes net.

output from the fisheries. It was a case of coastal fishing from open boats. It is true that nets and the 'long line' were more widely used in the cod fisheries, and the seine or sweep net in the spring herring fisheries. In the 1860s approximately 90,000 took part in the great seasonal fisheries. Not only locals but long-distance seasonal migrants from coast and fjord communities travelled to Vestlandet for the herring fishing and to Lofoten for the spawning cod.

In just the same way as with forestry, the fisheries too were closely integrated into the peasant society. The peasants were fishermen. They also took part in the processing and transport of the product, and they produced a good deal of the necessary equipment, from boats to barrels. Export earnings had a very stimulating effect on peasant society. In many districts fishing was as important a source of income as farming and produced most of the cash earnings. The great seasonal fisheries fitted well into the agricultural year – as did forestry. There was little need for male labourers in agriculture in winter. Moreover, at sea there were fewer restrictions, such as property rights, than found on land. Thus the people without property were given the opportunity to establish themselves. The modest capital outlay could be met by credit from the fish merchant. The need for credit for fixed and working

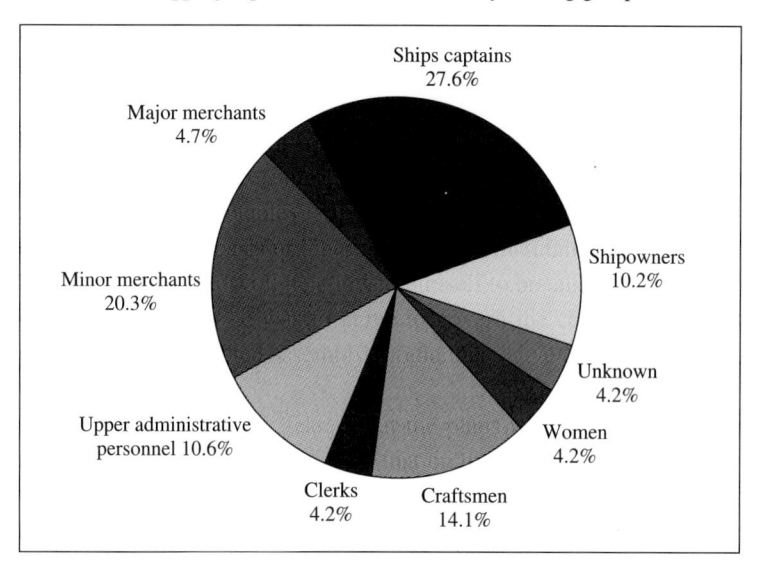

Shipping capital in Arendal in 1874 by owning group

- Ships captains 27.6%
- Major merchants 4.7%
- Minor merchants 20.3%
- Upper administrative personnel 10.6%
- Clerks 4.2%
- Craftsmen 14.1%
- Women 4.2%
- Unknown 4.2%
- Shipowners 10.2%

Investment in shipping partnerships in the towns of Sørlandet came not only from the economic elite, but also from the broad range of middle class occupations. Shipping was also closely integrated with shipbuilding and forestry in Sørlandet.

capital thus created strong bonds between the production and sales arms of the industry.

The shipping saga

Shipping was tied closely to overseas trade. The volume of exports determined the size of the fleet. Shipping found itself in difficulties after 1815 with the decline of the timber trade, which had required a large tonnage. The increased export of fish products no doubt reduced the effects of this. Nevertheless, the structure of the fleet changed dramatically over the course of a few years. The number of ships increased, but the total tonnage dropped sharply.

An uninterrupted period of growth began in the middle of the 1820s. By 1878 Norway had the third largest merchant marine in the world: 1.5 million tons net. Expansion was particularly marked from

1850 onwards. The ships were bigger and the fleet more productive as more ships were kept in operation the whole year round.

The growth in Norway's own export trade undoubtedly stimulated investment in ships, but the major stimulus came from the international shipping market. After 1827 Norwegian shipowners were allowed to compete on equal terms with the Swedish in the export of goods from Sweden. The export of Swedish timber grew strongly in the 1830s and Norwegian shipowners took on almost the whole of this trade. Before 1850 Norway had little of the trade between third parties. This made its breakthrough after the British repealed the Navigation Acts in 1849. Now Norwegian ships were in a position to compete for cargoes in the British market. Country after country reduced the protection provided for their own shipping, with the result that new markets were opened to free competition. At the same time, there was an explosion in international trade. Freer competition in a rapidly growing market for shipping services was exploited by the Norwegian shipowners.

It has been argued that Norway's major competitive edge was low freight rates. Importing second-hand ships contributed to low capital costs. By re-rigging, fewer sailors were needed. Norwegian seamen had to be content with poor food and low wages. Added to this, Norwegian ships did best in the transport of cheap bulky goods, where the speed of passage was less important. It would appear, however, that it was the complaints of competitors rather than a detailed examination of the situation that has produced the picture of next-best technology and low costs. Norway was undoubtedly a low-cost country compared with Great Britain, but the picture is not so one-sided when comparisons are drawn with other competitors. Besides, the strong internationalization of the shipping industry gradually led to a reduction in Norway's competitive advantage. There are, therefore, grounds for saying that it was because Norwegian shipowners built up an expertise in certain trades that they were more competitive.

Down to the end of the 1860s it was Europe itself that dominated international shipping, with a network of routes centred on Great Britain. Norway first got a strong position here in the timber trade, but also made itself felt in the corn trade from the Black Sea. In the 1870s the Atlantic trade with, among other items, corn, timber and cotton became important and in 1878 produced as much as 45 per cent of the gross freight income.

The expansion appears to have been financed by Norwegian capital mobilized through the joint ownership of individual ships. Though this capital was in more hands than in other countries, it was still too concentrated for one to be able to talk of a people's fleet. For a long time the shipping business had been an integral part of the activities of the larger trading firms, but towards the end of this period there was a clear tendency for it to be independent. Profits themselves gave a certain amount of elbow room for new investment and besides helped attract new capital into the business. Scarcely any activity in the country could give the same return.

The shipping industry was concentrated on the stretch of coast from Bergen to Christiania, especially Sørlandet. The towns along the coasts of Sørlandet, with their established tradition of shipping based on their own exports, were quick to exploit new openings in the market. Links with shipbuilding were close and the supply of experienced seamen considerable.

The expansion was based on a technology that Norwegian shipowners were familiar with – wooden ships under sail. The demand for capital was not insuperable and the joint ownership of individual ships was, for its time, an effective method of mobilizing it. Around 1870 the transition to steamships had reached an advanced stage in Great Britain, but Norwegian shipowners continued to use sailing ships. Bergen shipowners provided the exception. They had most of the country's modest fleet of steamships at the end of the 1870s.

Shipping was of great importance for the Norwegian economy. The number of seamen increased more than fivefold from 1840 to 1875, by which time there were approximately 50,000. The business stimulated shipbuilding and the fitting-out trades. In 1875 the building of wooden ships employed over 5,000 people and many other jobs were created in rope works, sail lofts and other handicraft trades producing shipping gear. Forestry too benefited from the strong demand for expensive, special-purpose items for the shipyards. The receipts from shipping also helped support a greater and more varied quantity of imports.

The first wave of industrialization

The sawmills were hard hit by marketing problems after the war. Glass and iron works lost a protected market in Denmark. Norwegian iron met much stronger competition from the British works, which now employed coal-based techniques for smelting. The iron industry enjoyed somewhat better times in the 1840s and diversified into the finishing trades, but lost out in competition with new workshops that were better placed in relation to the markets.

The 1840s heralded a new dawn in the industrial sector. There were, in 1850, around 12,000 people employed in industry; 25 years later there were 45,000. The expansion of the export trades led to growth in the traditional industries. For example, employment in ship building grew from ca. 1,000 to 5,700 between 1850 and 1875. The yards making wooden ships dominated the industry, which was, to all intents and purposes, a craft one. The development of the sawmilling industry took off in 1860 with the ending of the restrictions introduced in 1688. New steam-powered sawmills were built, while the modern steam-driven planing mills improved the quality of the finish and thereby the end-value of the product. The first mills for the production of wood pulp were established in this period, with the result that total employment in the timber industry rose threefold to almost 13,000 from 1850 to 1875. The new plants were generally bigger and operated the entire year, so that output increased more than the number of workers would suggest.

Textile factories and engineering workshops were a new departure. There were 5,000 employed in the textile mills in 1875, with about the same number in the iron and engineering industry. The latter was dominated by foundries and engineering workshops. Both the textile factories and the engineering workshops were important features of the modernization process. The textile factories turned out standardized mass-produced articles for an anonymous market. The machine shops, on the other hand, tailored their products to each individual customer. The market was small. Only later was there room for greater specialization.

Some of the conditions for the establishment of industry can be found in the home market. The import of cotton goods – both finished goods and yarn – increased, and Norwegian entrepreneurs saw possibilities for replacing imported goods by home-produced ones. The tariff of 1842 gave some protection to Norwegian enterprises, with lower rates for raw materials and semi-finished products than for finished goods.

The founders of the textile industry had, in most cases, a background in trade but were without technical knowledge. But now they were in a position to 'import the industrial revolution'. Great Britain had lifted the ban on the export of machinery in 1843 and machinery manufacturers began to develop their markets vigorously. They provided not just the machinery but also helped with the planning of the factories. They kept their Norwegian customers in touch with technical developments and obtained key personnel, skilled workers and foremen, who could train the Norwegian labour force.

The key to the success of the early textile industry was the import of 'the whole technological package'. The Norwegian factory owners could, as a result, concentrate on what they knew best, namely the commercial side. The engineering workshops were dependent on the import of machinery and technical know-how. Norwegians travelled to Great Britain to learn the production process. Production under licence was widespread and many workshops employed British artisans and engineers.

The advent of the textile industry in Norway was important enough, but for the future of industrial development, the engineering workshops were even more so. These engineering workshops made greater demands on technical competence. The training of Norwegian personnel, either in factories or in colleges abroad, was a precondition for a competitive engineering industry. In the new 'iron age', with its steam boats and railways, the machine shops played a crucial role, not only for repairs and maintenance, but also for adapting production equipment to meet specifically Norwegian requirements.

Industry occupied a very modest position in the Norwegian economy, judging from employment and output figures. Handicraft and petty industries employed twice as many people in 1875 as did factory-based industry. However, modern industry, especially iron and engineering, was of great strategic importance for transferring industrial production methods to ever more areas.

Modernization and liberalization

Expansion from the 1840s onwards was brought about not just through the growth of home and foreign markets, but also through changes in the framework for economic activities in Norway. These were partly the product of state initiatives and partly of new or modernized institutions that helped to reinforce the development of capitalism.

The Bank of Norway had the sole right to issue currency notes and, bearing in mind the experiences of the period during and after the Napoleonic War, took as its main task the prevention of inflation and the defence of the value of the currency. Silver redemption was, however, postponed and a long period of rising money values (deflation) followed. The silver fix of the *spesidaler* at par in 1842 gave a stable external value, which in turn gave greater predictability to foreign transactions and helped prevent good times being cut short by a rise in its value relative to other currencies. At the same time, the amount of notes in circulation was increased so that the problems of liquidity were less noticeable. With a convertible currency and an increase of money in circulation, the economy expanded.

Arrangements for providing credit were for a long time poor. The Bank of Norway and government funds provided the bulk of mortgages. The first savings bank was set up in 1822 and several others followed, but growth was modest before 1850. The first commercial bank came as late as 1848. The credit needs of trade and industry were met for the most part by private bankers and Norwegian merchant houses, which could, in turn, draw on their foreign connections. In periods of crisis, when the demand for short-term loans was strong, the lack of depth and flexibility in the Norwegian credit market was all too apparent.

In times of crisis the state took up loans abroad, which it passed on to industry and commerce. With the *Hypotekbank* (Norwegian Mortgage Bank) the state created in 1851 a credit institution that could draw foreign capital to the country and provide cheaper, long-term mortgages for the owners of real estate in town and country. The number of savings and commercial banks increased, and by 1875 the total amount loaned by banks and government funds reached 300 million *kroner*, a four-fold increase since 1850. The savings and commercial banks were responsible for 45 per cent and 20 per cent respectively, while the Bank of Norway, the *Hypotekbank* and government funds handled the remainder. The institutional arrangements for issuing credit had improved and were now such as to cover the needs of business, making it less dependent on foreign sources.

The development of communications in the broadest sense promoted growth and market integration. From the middle of the century both

The Bank of Norway's first bank note, 1817. The spesidaler *was divided into 5* ort, *and the* ort *into 24* skilling. *The* spesidaler *was tied to silver in 1842. The gold standard was introduced in 1873, with the daler as the main unit of currency. This was then divided into 4* kroner, *and the* krone *into both 30* skilling *and 100* øre. *The changeover to* kroner *and* øre *took place in 1875 when Norway joined the Scandinavian currency union.*

national and local authorities directed their efforts towards extending and improving the road networks. With this came lower transport costs. The postal services were also extended. A new postage system, together with reduced rates, brought prices down. The state took sole responsibility for the telegraph service and between 1855 and 1870 built a national network of lines, which at the same time linked Norway to an effective international communications system.

Postal traffic caused the state to pioneer the use of steam ships. The first steamboat was bought in 1826 and by 1855 the state owned 11. However, in 1857 it began to disband its network. The new policy was to subsidize private and local authority companies. Steamboats greatly improved the efficiency of goods transport, both along the coasts and on the great lakes. Steamboat traffic also led to greater public involvement in the development of harbours and quays. Through private and public initiatives, natural waterways were improved and several large canal projects further eased transportation in the rich forest areas.

It was the railway, however, that most clearly symbolized the new age. In 1854 the line between Christiania and Eidsvoll was opened. By 1875 there were 594 km of line in operation and decisions taken to build a further 1,000 km. The programme was completed in 1883. With the exception of the Christiania–Eidsvoll line, which was built and partly financed by a British company, the state was responsible for both the building of the railway network and its operation. Although both private and local authority finance was involved, the state took on the main burden. The development as a whole was not planned and, with the exception of that first line between Christiania and Eidsvoll, it was ahead of traffic needs. The state took up loans abroad and by doing so ensured that the investment in the country's infrastructure did not come into competition with businesses at home for the limited resources of the Norwegian capital market.

The tax system encouraged business. Direct state taxes were abolished in 1838. Customs and excise duties were the mainstay of government finance. Customs duties were gradually concentrated on those commodities that could not be produced in Norway: coffee, sugar and oil for lamps – the so-called 'revenue articles'. Taken together with higher duties on alcohol and tobacco, this meant that the burden of taxation fell on the general body of consumers.

The growth in the consumption of revenue articles made it possible to reduce the duties on fish and timber exports, so strengthening their competitiveness. To a considerable degree it was the interests of the exporters that determined the direction of customs policy, and in treaty negotiations the protection of the industries catering for the home market was a prime negotiating tool. By the middle of the 1870s almost all of agriculture and most of industry and handicraft no longer enjoyed tariff protection. The advantages accorded the export trades were to be paid for by stronger competition for the home industries.

The dismantling of the old privileges of trade and industry facilitated the setting up of new businesses. Enterprise, capital and labour could now go where prospects seemed promising without meeting legal obstacles. This process hit the towns and the town burgesses. A series of small built-up areas were given the status of towns, usually under protest from existing towns. The handicraft privileges were abolished in two stages, 1839 and 1866. The commercial laws of 1842 and 1857 trimmed the rights of town merchants so far as home trade was concerned, though they did not lose their sole right to send goods abroad until 1882. Handicraft workers and retailers established themselves in the countryside and both groups in the towns experienced greater competition. The handicraft trades were no longer protected against the setting up of new establishments. The abolition of the privileges previously enjoyed by the saw mills, the last great barrier, led immediately to many new companies being formed and a great expansion in the size of the industry.

The Norwegian state played a key role in the modernization process. Laws that dismantled privileges allowed enterprise and capital greater freedom of movement. Industry and commerce benefited greatly from low taxation and both customs policies and treaty negotiations strengthened the competitiveness of the Norwegian export industries. The state was also active in the creation of an institutional apparatus for the provision of credit, and played the main role in the development of the communications network, both of which helped to increase production and sales.

Economic growth and the standard of living

Changes in both output and the process of production occurred within each individual sector of the economy. But for the historian it is difficult to get a complete picture of the development over time as the sources are weaker, the further back one goes. Additionally, problems of measurement occur simply because a great deal of output never entered the market, but was consumed within the producer's own household.

The gross national product (GNP) is the economist's way of measuring the total output of goods and services. Figures for Norwegian GNP exist from 1865 onwards. In the period 1865–77 *real* growth was strong; that is to say, GNP per inhabitant grew. For the earlier period, 1815–65, we have little to go on. Simply to keep up with population increases, GNP must have increased by 50 per cent in the period 1815–45. But, at the same time, the level of GNP at the outset, in 1815, was much lower than before the war of 1807–14. The pre-war level was probably not reached, in real terms, and for the economy as a whole, before 1850.

Down to 1840 it was probably only in agriculture and fishing that output per head rose significantly above the pre-war level. From then onwards, growth became more general, the driving force being the timber and shipping industries. There was undoubtedly real growth in the Norwegian economy in the period 1850–75, but it is still not possible to say just when GNP per head rose above what it had been at the turn of the century.

Compared with most European countries, Norway in the 1870s was by no means underdeveloped, based on the level of GNP. In spite of their many failings, these figures do give a reasonable indication of the level of development. Measured in GNP per head, Great Britain was without doubt the leader, and Belgium, which also industrialized early, had a good lead over the majority of west European economies. Norway was on approximately the same level as Denmark, but ahead of Sweden and, in the period 1850–75, economic growth in Norway was probably faster than that of its neighbours.

The growth in the international market made it possible to exploit the country's resources more effectively. The growth of population in Europe increased the market for fish products, while economic growth stimulated demand for wood in many forms, from ships to buildings to telegraph poles, pit props and railway sleepers. The increase in international trade and freer competition gave Norwegian shipping almost unlimited room in which to grow. Norway managed to respond to the market signals because its entrepreneurs were at home with both the products and the technology required to produce them and because the demands for capital were surmountable. Overseas demand also matched well the country's resources and level of economic development.

Was the standard of living higher? It is not possible to give even a reasonably reliable answer to this basic question, and certainly not before 1850. The indicators are fairly crude. Down to the middle of the century, most people had to make a living within the peasant economy. Agriculture was the basic activity and the growth in output here satisfied the demand for food more adequately, as well as providing a foundation for a greater trade in agricultural products. Forestry, fishing, handicrafts and shipping were carried on in conjunction with agriculture and gave extra income. Across the board, incomes were no doubt higher in 1850 than in 1815. However, did all members of the rural economy benefit? Did perhaps the farmers enjoy ever-increasing

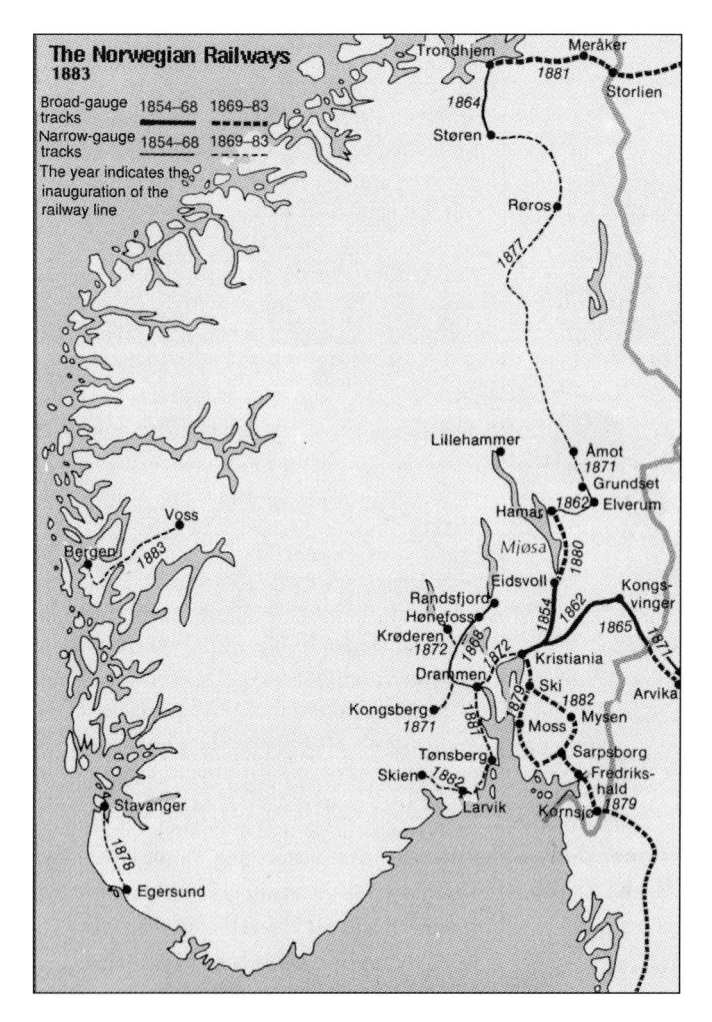

The early railways lines were built according to what has been called 'the Norwegian system'. Local interests, private or municipal, took the initiative and procured some of the capital. The State was then responsible for most of the capital needed for construction and was in charge of the building and running of the lines. In this way the issues of just what lines were to be built and when, were removed from the political process. The area round the Oslo fjord was well covered. But Trondheim, Bergen and Stavanger also got lines that tied them closer to their hinterlands.

standards, while those without property, the crofters and the day labourers, experienced worsened standards?

There were far more crofters and day labourers, both inland and on the coast. Their numbers reached a peak in the 1850s. But the number of farmers rose just as quickly, taking the country as a whole, and in Østlandet even faster. The proletarianization of the countryside did not, then, proceed further during this period. The number of crofters grew most rapidly in areas near the coast from Agder in the south to Troms in the far north. But here the crofter had a different role from that of his counterpart in the typical agricultural communities of Østlandet and Trøndelag. Here he was an agricultural worker with almost unlimited calls on his labour, low pay, and a holding without security of tenure. Elsewhere in the country a crofter was as secure as a tenant farmer and had few labour services. The crofters on the coast were also often independent fishermen or handicraft workers and were no doubt better placed than crofters in purely agricultural communities, where the competition for holdings depressed wages and led to an explosion in the services demanded of them. Thus there were great differences within the crofter community, both economically and in terms of social status.

Within the towns too there was no evidence of increased proletarianization. The group that was made up of labourers, ordinary seamen and servants increased in size, but at a lower rate than the broad middle layer of small traders, handicraft masters and journeymen, factory owners, white-collar workers and ships' masters. *Embetsmenn* and the richer merchants, who topped the social hierarchy in the towns, also declined in numbers relative to the rest of the urban population.

We may then draw the conclusion that, on the whole, the majority of farmers and the growing middle class in the towns experienced an improvement in their living conditions. Nor can there be any question of a general decline in conditions for those without property, even though variations from region to region were considerable.

After 1850, economic growth was clearly strong enough to bring about an improvement in living conditions. New workplaces were created and a stream of people seeking work moved from areas of stagnation to areas of growth, either within the country or overseas to the United States. Thus the system was not a closed one. 'America fever' grew steadily and over 100,000 emigrated there in the years 1866–73, mostly from rural areas. Farmers and their children were over-represented amongst emigrants, while crofters and day labourers occupied the same position amongst those who migrated within Norway. The labour market grew greatly and emigration helped to increase wages by reducing the numbers entering it. For the new groups of wage earners there was a weak growth in real income after 1850, while during the boom of the early 1870s wages rose sharply. Incomes were also raised by a more even distribution of work across the year. An increased consumption of groceries strengthens the impression of progress.

Incomes were skewed, both socially and geographically. Rural areas wholly dependent on agriculture and a long way from markets lagged behind and here it was the crofters and day labourers who occupied the worst position of all. These areas too had the heaviest rates of out-migration. And this, in turn, helped to break up the existing social structure.

Occupational diversity and social change

By the middle of the 1870s the Norwegian economy had become more diverse, although it was just beginning to industrialize. From about 1850 there had occurred a marked swing from occupations in agriculture, forestry and fishing towards handicraft and industry, as well as to transport and other services. The growth of built-up areas is one indication of this process, but even in rural districts there was an increase in the proportion of the population employed outside the primary sector.

It is impossible to give a precise account of the number employed in different occupations or economic sectors, partly because the data are inadequate and partly because many people were involved in two or more occupations. It is often impossible to decide which occupations gave the greater income. In 1875, over half of the working population (54 per cent) were employed in the primary sector. Of the remaining 46 per cent, some 19 were in handicrafts and industry and 27 in service employment of one sort or another. At the beginning of the century, on the other hand, around 85 per cent had been employed in agriculture, forestry and fishing. The totals are not without defects, but the shift between the main sectors is nevertheless clear enough.

The growth and change in the economy, together with the abolition of legal constraints on occupational choice, contributed to the opening of new career paths. Movement took place not just in a geographical sense but also occupationally and up and down the social ladder. The diversification of employment is difficult to grasp, especially in the countryside, because information on occupation in the early censuses is not adequately specified. It was felt to be more important to distinguish between freeholders, tenants and crofters than to elicit which employment produced the greater share of income. Handicraft, industry and shipping employed more people in the rural than in the urban areas in 1875 and many in the former areas had a smallholding or croft as well. Multiple employments were widespread.

Trading privileges were reduced, but the few general stores in the countryside were unable to eliminate the urban traders from their dominant position. The urban merchants had the sole right to import goods, and became wholesalers who supplied the small traders both in the towns and in the surrounding countryside. At the same time, retailing became more specialized and the number of shop girls increased considerably.

Handicrafts in the towns covered a wider range than in the country districts. The handicraft trades developed in different ways and in some of them great handicraft factories were established that imitated industrial production methods. Specialization, division of labour and mass production produced greater efficiency and, at the same time, broke down the old production system, thus opening the way for the employment of unskilled labour.

There were no insurmountable boundaries between handicraft and industry. Much of industry at this time was conducted without the use of machines and made little demand on power supplies. The towns, with around 40 per cent of industrial employment, concentrated on light consumer goods and machine shops. The modern textile factories were placed near their main markets, but here access to water power was crucial. Consequently the rivers near the great towns became the site of this industry. In Sagene near Christiania, the old workshop milieu along the Aker river was transformed into a modern industrial complex, while around Bergen industries were established alongside the tiniest of streams.

Social historians tend to see a static, closed society (a society based on rank), with strictly demarcated boundaries between the different social ranks, turning into a more dynamic class society. In the society based on rank, it was difficult to cross the boundaries of the rank one

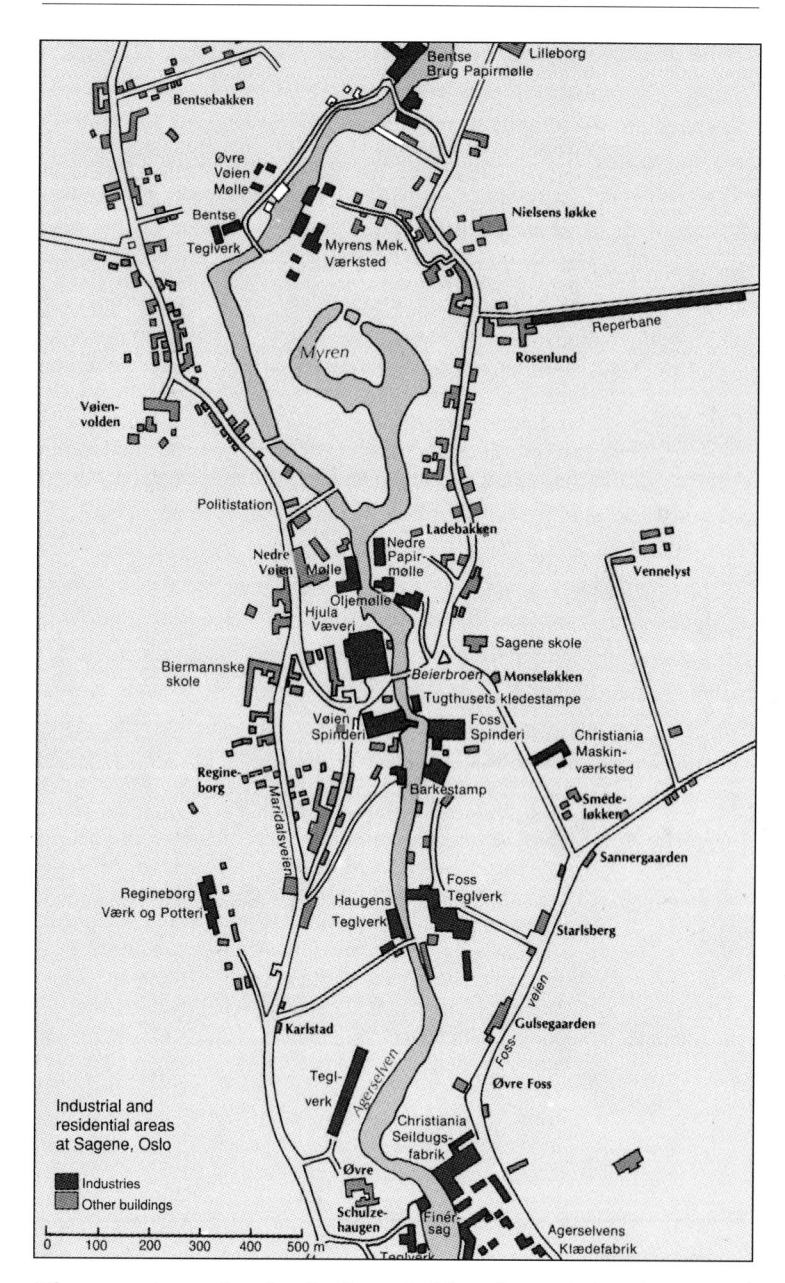

RECOVERY AND GROWTH: THE NORWEGIAN ECONOMY, 1815–75

The map shows the distribution of old and new industries around 1860 at Sagene near Christiania. Here the river Aker was the source of energy. Sagene was one of the dominant industrial areas of Norway during the first phase of industrialization.

was born into, and social ties were vertical. The relationship between the employer and his workers had a strongly paternalistic air about it – this applied to the handicraft master and his journeymen and apprentices; the farmer and his crofters and servants; and the factory owner and his workers. These bands of loyalty were, in the process of industrialization, replaced by horizontal ones between different groups that, economically, stood at the same level, belonging, in other words, to the same class. One's place in the social hierarchy was determined by one's economic position. Whereas the society based on rank was closed, the class society offered the opportunity for social advancement.

Norway can scarcely be described as a rank-based society at the beginning of the nineteenth century. The barriers between the different ranks were not solid enough for that. It *was* possible to pass from one to another. But, at the same time, it is clear that these opportunities were gradually increased, partly as a result of the removal of economic privileges, and partly because new development opportunities came into contention. Yet paternalism was strong and it was not until the end of the period that it weakened. Nor is it possible to point to any growth in solidarity amongst the workers at this time. All the same, the ideal types – a rank-based society on the one hand; a class-based one on the other – do say something important about the direction of change in this period.

17
The *embetsmenn* state: golden age, decline and fall

The period 1840/45–1870 has been called 'the classical age of the *embetsmenn* state'. The label suggests that these were years of considerable political stability. The earlier decades of conflict between the Storting and government made way for a period of mainly harmonious cooperation. The air of harmony did not, however, completely exclude stirrings of opposition within the Storting. For one thing, the peasant opposition that had established itself in the 1830s became a permanent feature. Ueland was a leading figure in the parliaments of the 1840s and 1850s. The other great peasant leader, Søren Jaabæk, first entered the Storting in 1845 and was to remain there until 1890. Jaabæk accepted Ueland's leadership for the first 10–15 years, though he was a more aggressive character; his anti-bureaucratic attitude came noticeably to the fore in the matter of the *embetsmenn*'s pensions. His attempt from the mid-1860s to organize an electoral alliance through the so-called 'peasant supporters' clubs', saw him overstepping Ueland's more moderate opposition strategy. Nevertheless, the peasant opposition kept throughout this period to its narrow agenda of immediate self-interest and an anti-bureaucratic stance. The peasants undoubtedly wished to curb the *embetsmenn*'s exercise of power, but did not seek governmental power or a leading role in national politics for themselves.

Towards the end of the 1840s a new opposition grouping entered the Storting. It consisted of three parts: the middle and lower ranks of business; handicraftsmen; and academics outside the ranks of the *embetsmenn*. Amongst these academics was the young solicitor Johan Sverdrup from Larvik. He was later to organize the opposition and to become prime minister in 1884. This new wave had its origins in the depression and the increased competition arising, in part, from the abolition of the old trading privileges. As for the academics, too many graduates had been produced for all to be absorbed into government service, i.e. to be *embetsmenn*. But the movement can also be seen as a distant echo of the storm that the events in Paris of February 1848 had unleashed over Europe.

The new opposition grouping attempted to build an alliance with the peasant opposition and took the first halting steps towards a tighter organization within the Storting, i.e. 'the men of freedom' in 1851, and 'the reform society' in 1859–60. But these attempts at collaboration failed. The most serious threat to the established regime, indeed to society as it was currently organized, came notably from forces buried deep within the populace and far outside the Storting, namely the Thrane movement of 1848–51.

The Thrane movement, named after its founder and leader Marcus Thrane (1817–90), represents one of the most remarkable outbreaks of popular protest in Norwegian history. Not until 70 years later, at the end of the First World War, was bourgeois society faced with a threat of such serious proportions. The Thrane movement was the first organized popular movement in Norway. At its height it had 414 associations with over 30,000 members. It began as a protest organization amongst workers, day labourers and craft workers in the towns. From there it spread to the crofters, landless agricultural labourers and petty peasantry in the rural districts of Østlandet and Trøndelag. In some neighbourhoods the movement was so all embracing that it could be seen as a revolt of the entire primary sector against both the bureaucracy and capitalist society. The movement could well have drawn inspiration from the wave of protest that spread across Europe. It also had features in common with the first English labour movement, the Chartists (1836–48). But, in the main, it should be seen as an expression of tensions deep within Norwegian society and of increasing population pressure, which, among other things, resulted in the crofter system reaching its peak precisely at mid-century.

There was a certain ambiguity about the movement's aims. On the one hand, its demand for one man, one vote can be seen as ultra-democratic. On the other, it believed in the old idea of the king acting personally to protect the interests of the common man. The latter found expression in a petition that was presented to the king in 1850. It bore 13,000 signatures. It was the revolutionary side of the movement, however, that provided the authorities with the opportunity to employ the force of the law. Thrane himself was imprisoned from 1851 to

1858 and spent the last 27 years of his life in America, an exile that ended in 1949 when his body was brought home to rest in grave of honour in Our Saviour's Cemetery in Oslo.

The reaction to this first revolt of Norway's underclass showed that the government was not only adept at passifying elements of the opposition, but was also prepared to use force when the danger appeared to warrant it. This vigorous response strengthened the government. Property owners, especially the better-off peasants of Østlandet, in fear of the threat posed by the movement, rallied strongly to the authorities. This change of direction sharpened a division that already existed between the peasants of Østlandet and Vestlandet on such matters as customs dues, and partially explains why attempts to establish a more positive opposition within the Storting broke down.

Modernization

How was it possible for the *embetsmenn* to hold on to power, in spite of the outbreaks of protest we have just described and their declining numbers in the Storting? The answer lies primarily in the political initiatives they took; initiatives so sweeping that, in effect, the *embetsmenn* can be said to have taken the country in hand and transformed it in accordance with their own ideals.

The personification of these initiatives was to be found in the 'twin stars' of Anton Martin Schweigaard and Frederik Stang, the shining lights of the *embetsmenn* state. Both born in 1808 and both lawyers, Schweigaard became professor of jurisprudence at the university in Christiania in 1840, while Stang quickly gave up a promising academic career to become a barrister. In their youth they participated in an intellectual movement (the *Intelligens*) that, in the 1830s, developed a programme that demanded among other things that the government, in close cooperation with the Storting, adopt a major proactive role. As leading politicians they had the opportunity to make this happen: Stang as a member of the government from 1845 to 1856, and from 1861 to 1880 its head, Schweigaard as a member of the Storting for the nation's capital and the government's chief supporter in the Storting from 1842 until his death in 1870.

They shared a common interest, namely to develop a practical programme of economic and institutional reform. In that way they typified a generation of university graduates who in the 1840s grasped the political and intellectual leadership of the country. They represented a reaction against the previous generation's vociferous patriotism. The practical goals of these men can be seen too in a scholarly paradigm shift that began in the 1840s. The most typical representative of this perhaps is Eilert Sundt, a pioneer of modern sociology whose intellectual inspiration is to be found in the perceived need for a thoroughgoing reform of Norwegian society. For Schweigaard, this need was expressed in a utilitarian legal theory – a reaction against the idealistic speculations of German philosophy – and an acceptance of the new liberal tenets of political economy. For the government, these new attitudes found their political expression in a comprehensive programme aimed at modernizing the whole of Norwegian society.

The two decades either side of 1850 formed a period in which, throughout western Europe, an attack was made on the legal, institutional and physical barriers that stood against the unrestricted development in the market of the new technology and forms of production. As we have seen (Chapter 16), in Norway this initiative was directed against the traditional business privileges, the towns' exclusive trading rights, import and export duties, and, more positively, advocated the state's involvement in improvements to communications. The *embetsmenn* felt, on two counts, that they had the moral right to define the true interests of the people and to lead the process just described: first, because of their traditional claim to represent the general interest, and, second, because of their belief that they were society's intellectual élite.

Business privileges and customs questions were entangled in a welter of complex conflicts of interest. That progress was made towards sorting them out was partly because the forces of liberalism proved the stronger and partly because the *embetsmenn* were able to provide a focus of stability around which the constantly shifting pattern of alliances could form. 'In fact the opposition was strong and many sided but its members had such conflicting interests that they neutralised each other. This left them vulnerable to being picked off one by one' (J.A. Seip). In getting rid of the privileges attached to the towns and their economic activities, the *embetsmenn* could always count on the support of the peasants. For free enterprise was something that lay close to Søren Jaabæk's heart. On the other hand, it says a lot about the strength of the *embetsmenn*'s position in Norwegian society that in one area, the monopoly of certain professions enjoyed by the univer-

Anton Martin Schweigaard (1808–70) and Peter Andreas Munch (1810–63) were schoolfellows together at the gymnasium *in Skien. Schweigaard, lawyer and politician, was the epitome of the Norwegian* embetsmann *class; Munch, the leading representative of the breakthrough in Norwegian historical research. Here they stand together in front of the Domus Media at the University of Oslo. The Schweigaard statue (in the background) was made by Julius Middelthun and unveiled in 1883; that of Munch, by Stinius Fredriksen, in 1933.*

sity educated, the privileges were untouched. Not until the political system changed in 1884 were the first tentative steps taken to making inroads in this area too.

The involvement of the state in the development of communications was a continuation of a powerful tradition of management from the centre, dating back to the union with Denmark. It was, of course, almost a negation of the reigning theory of liberalism. At the same time, it can also be seen as paradoxical that the *embetsmenn*, the upholders and executors of the state's authority, were the keenest supporters of an economic theory that accorded the state a relatively passive role when it came to involvement in economic affairs. J.A. Seip has shown that this ideological paradox was resolved in practice by what he has called 'the Norwegian system'. Under this, liberal theory was accommodated by waiting for private bodies or local authorities to come up with the initial ideas and capital, e.g. for railway projects; but then the state would help on the legal side and with further capital, as well as taking a hand in progressing the projects and running them once they were completed. This meant that the Storting was to some extent kept out of railway questions and, as a result, conflicts over allocations and priorities were avoided. This mixed form of initiative had a special significance for the relationship between central and local authorities as problem solvers.

Local self-government

The local government law of 1837 represented a compromise between the *embetsmenn*'s centralizing ideology and the peasantry's wish for the transfer of power to local bodies. The jurisdiction of the new popularly elected bodies was qualified by that still held by the state. The local authorities were enjoined to carry out certain tasks, for instance in the areas of education and poor relief, and could, by law, find new tasks imposed upon them. In this way, they served as the executive arms of central government. On the other hand, they could take upon themselves tasks in all areas where they were not expressly forbidden to do so, i.e. where they did not come into conflict with the jurisdiction of the central administration. In the long run, this restriction of authority turned out to be sufficiently accommodating as to permit considerable local political initiative. However, in the early decades of local government, considerable efforts were made to create a balance between local aspirations for self-government and the needs of the central authorities to keep the activities of the new organs within a national framework – in effect to accommodate them as smoothly as possible to existing administrative traditions.

Educational policy provides an example of how this balancing act worked out. Through the school laws of 1827, 1860 and 1889, the central authorities sought to raise educational levels in the elementary schools. But the power of the law was not the only mechanism adopted in order to achieve this. Those local authorities that cooperated in seeking to give force to the government's wishes were rewarded by extra funds. 'The combination of carrot and stick was a basic feature of the policy of the state *vis-à-vis* the local authorities' (Edgar Hovland). At the same time, the degree of freedom accorded to the local authorities made it possible, in connection with the development of communications, to accommodate the model described above as 'the

Norwegian system'. Thus, for example, local authorities were able to make a financial contribution to new railway developments or to steam ships operating within their local area. A High Court decision of 1861 ruled that such interventions were within the competence of local authorities.

We have seen how the *embetsmenn* class, with its roots in the governments of the 1840s onwards, was able to get Norwegian society to accept a comprehensive policy of economic modernization and adaptation. A major reason for the policy's success – and for the stability of the government – lay in the fact that it took place within a society enjoying economic growth and increasing material well-being. But the transformation of society that was dependent on this growth also brought about a progressive crumbling of the foundations of the old regime.

The constitutional conflict

On 9 March 1872 parliament accepted a constitutional proposal that would allow members of the government to attend its sessions and take part in its proceedings. On 7 May the king vetoed the proposal. Nine days later the Storting replied with a vote of no confidence. The government wavered momentarily but then, collecting itself together, decided to resist. Three of the more conciliatory ministers, who continued to believe that an accommodation with the parliamentary majority was possible, were dismissed. Thus a united front was established.

The confrontation in the spring of 1872 was the opening of a constitutional conflict that was not to be resolved until 12 years later – the longest, most profound and most comprehensive in Norwegian political history since 1814. Throughout the 12 years the conflict steadily escalated, with a corresponding reduction in the possibilities for compromise. After the government had withstood the first frontal assault, the opposing forces became locked in a form of trench warfare. The parliamentary majority tried with all the means at its disposal to make life for the government's ministers as uncomfortable as possible, in the hope that this would drive them from their cabinet posts. At the same time, the constitutional proposal admitting ministers to the Storting was brought forward again and again. In the spring of 1880, after the government had refused to accept the proposal, which had been accepted by three newly elected Stortings in a row, a further escalation of the situation came about. On 9 June the Storting stated that the admission of ministers to parliament should have constitutional effect without the agreement of the king. When this too was not accepted by the government, there remained only one weapon left: impeachment. When the elections of 1882 gave the parliamentary opposition a big enough victory to secure a majority both for the indictment in the Odelsting and for a conclusive verdict in the Lagting, the Court of Impeachment began proceedings in May 1883.

According to the thinking of the parliamentary majority, the court was a political body empowered to interpret the constitution. The main constitutional problem it was called upon to adjudicate was whether the Crown had the power to withhold its approval of a constitutional amendment put forward by the Storting. In other words, did a power of veto on the part of the Crown exist or not? On this point the Constitution was silent. From this, the government and its supporters concluded that its power of veto was implicit. The opposition, on the other hand, concluded that there was no veto whatsoever, i.e. that the Storting alone had control of the constitution. As expected, the court accepted the latter interpretation and, by judgments handed down in February and March 1884, Prime Minister Christian August Selmer, who in 1880 had succeeded Frederik Stang as head of the government, together with his colleagues in the cabinet were relieved of their posts. A coup d'état was contemplated by both the king and those supporting the government but, when it came to the point, no one dared. After a brief interlude with the so-called 'April Ministry', the king relented and on 26 June 1884 appointed a government under Johan Sverdrup, the leader of the parliamentary majority.

To the extent that the conflict between the parliamentary majority and the government became ever more acute, so it became more and more difficult to occupy a position of compromise between the two opposing forces. Eventually the centre groups dissolved and, in the voting on the 9 June resolution, practically all the representatives voted either for or against. Put another way, the Storting had divided into two parties. This was formalized in 1883-84 with the creation of the Liberals *(Venstre)* and the Conservatives *(Høyre)* as parliamentary parties and later of two national parties outside the Storting.

The result of the constitutional crisis involved not only a power shift, but also the demise of the system of government that had been in existence since 1814. A new system of government emerged. The

This statue of Johan Sverdrup (1816–92), the leading exponent of parliamentary government and the democratic breakthrough in the 1880s, was unveiled outside the Storting building during the celebrations for the 150th anniversary of the Constitution in 1964. It was made by Stinius Fredriksen.

duality in the life of the state of a nationally representative body, on the one hand, and a self-recruiting government (though still formally in the king's name), on the other, gave way to a unified system in which the Storting was the source of the government's power. This did not necessarily imply a weak government, though many at the time thought it would. For precisely because it had the confidence of parliament, a government could operate with increased vigour. With the organization of the two political parties, a foundation was laid for a new system, *parlamentarisme*, which could be strengthened and developed further. As an element in the great political settlement after the Court of Impeachment's rulings, the franchise was extended to include those in rural districts who could prove they had an annual taxable income of 500 kroner and in the towns of 800 kroner. Of the new electors, 45 per cent were officials in the private or public sector, and 38 per cent were workers. The extension of the franchise went together with a breakthrough in political mobilization in 1882. Political life was no longer mainly a preoccupation of an elite.

At the heart of the dispute from 1872 was the question of the access of ministers to the Storting. It may be difficult to understand why this reform would produce such a strong reaction on the part of the government and its supporters. In the last phase of the conflict, the question was no doubt reduced to a decision for or against parliamentarism. But, at the beginning, the consequences for political power were much less clear amongst its supporters. On the government side, however, it was quickly feared that ministers in the Storting would soon come under the influence of that body and that the government would lose its independence, when it came both to recruiting its members and to exercising its constitutionally guaranteed rights.

The question of the position of government ministers had originally been raised by the movement of intellectuals in the 1830s that went under the name of *Intelligensen*. The idea then had been that the reform would make it possible for the government to exercise a more powerful political leadership. It says much for the shift in political self-consciousness and the awareness of where political power lay, which had taken place in the intervening years, that in the 1870s it was the parliamentary opposition that mobilized in favour of a reform they had previously opposed, whereas Frederik Stang, who in his youth had been a spokesman for the reform, now, in his capacity as head of the government, was firmly opposed to it. From where had the Storting developed this new power consciousness?

The new power consciousness

For contemporaries it seemed that the relative political harmony of decades was suddenly destroyed by an unexpected squall at the beginning of the 1870s. Even as late as 1869 the government had optimistically recommended to the king to give his assent to a constitutional amendment for annual (instead of triennial) meetings of the Storting, despite the fact that one could well imagine that this reform would increase the Storting's influence. Nevertheless, we can assume that the conflict had some connection with a process of social change that had been going on for decades and that was of such a radical character that, instead of asking why the conflict occurred in the 1870s, the question should be asked why it did not occur earlier.

One reason the *embetsmenn* had been able to play a leading political role lay in the not altogether happy situation of a business community split on grounds of self-interest. The abolition of economic privileges in the 1850s and 1860s created the conditions for new constellations of interests. The most apparent expression of this tendency lay in the widespread creation of associations, which, beginning in the 1840s, has continued down to the present day. In the middle of the nineteenth century this 'spirit of association' was an important indication of society's growing self-awareness. This 'spirit' showed itself in the case of trade and handicraft associations almost as an automatic response to the ending of privileges.

The associations, especially those representing special-interest groups, created new divisions in society, but their main effect was that they established the conditions for united action across the the old boundaries, which had been based on function, locality and region. Common to the organizations, despite their different goals, was that they came to operate as training grounds for performing on the public stage and allowed people to take part in political activity. A number of the matters these organizations wished to pursue could be resolved only through political means. They, therefore, offered opportunities for entering political life. Around 1850, merchants and artisans came together in the towns to hold so-called 'trial elections' before the ordinary parliamentary ones. This was the germ of the system of organized nominations that had its breakthrough in the 1870s and 1880s, in the same way that the political parties can be seen as a step in the direction of the organizational society. The *embetsmenn*'s regime had its roots in 'an organizational vacuum' (J.A. Seip), in which the possibilities for channelling the views of the opposition had been few. In the 1870s this vacuum was in the process of being filled.

Parallel with this breakthrough in the setting up of organizations and partly in response to it, there developed a new public with new ways of exerting political influence. Most eye-catching was the number of new newspapers. Economic change was the prime mover here. The revolution in retailing, amongst other things to meet the demand for ready-made clothes, created in the 1870s an increased need for advertising just at the time when the old restrictive privileges in this field were dying out – in Bergen in 1863, Trondheim in 1876 and Christiania in 1882. Later, leading opposition newspapers such as *Bergens Tidende* (founded in 1868), *Dagbladet* in Christiania (1869) and *Dagsposten* in Trondheim (1877) expanded under the same head of steam.

Another characteristic feature of this new public was the political rally, which made its debut in the early 1870s and which played a great role in mobilizing the vote prior to the Storting elections of 1882. A more vigorous flow of ideas through new channels and in a more open society ended the dominance of the *embetsmenn*'s value system.

On the whole, 'the associations movement', the new press and the political rally were all evidence of a trend towards national integration based on the premises of the opposition. It is easy to see that the new communications must have helped break down regional barriers just as the expansion in popular education – to some extent the product of the legislation relating to primary schools of 1848 and 1860 – prepared the ground for political activity. Local government was also a very important training ground for political activity on the national stage. In the Storting of 1863, some 43 of the 55 peasant representatives had enjoyed mayorial office before entering that body.

In the evaluation of how general ideas were caught up and translated into actual policies, the question of the role of individuals will always be a matter of dispute. Is it the personality who creates the situation or the needs of the situation that draw forth the right personality – such as Johan Sverdrup, who was able to put himself forward as 'a business manager' for Norwegian society in its hour of need? It cannot be denied that Sverdrup's leadership from 1870 to 1884 contained an element of genius. For he combined a dogged strategic single-mindedness with a patient tactical flexibility within a personality that, at least with hindsight, provided the raw material for the creation of myths and a leadership cult.

At the same time as pressure from the opposition increased, there were clear signs that the social foundations of the old regime were crumbling. One expression of this was the loss of allies. The *embetsmenn*'s state rested upon an alliance of bureaucrats, businessmen and large farmers, especially farmers from Østlandet. A younger generation of merchants and businessmen who had worked their way up in the 1860s and 1870s seem, however, to have felt more attracted to the opposition. This applied particularly in the towns of Sørlandet and Vestlandet, while the conservatives still managed to hold on to their alliance partners in the capital, the towns of Østlandet and Møre and Trondheim.

It was amongst the lawyers – in the government, in the central administration and as county governors, that the hard core was to be found – the political élite of the *embetsmenn* class. During the closing decades of the regime, at the same time as the proportion of *embetsmenn* in the Storting was falling, there was an increasing tendency for the group's representation to be chosen from these higher echelons. Possibly this indicates a breaking down of the group's cohesion. A greater threat to the lawyers' dominant position came, however, from the new academic professions, which on the basis of their increased numerical strength and rising professional consciousness demanded their place in the administration: doctors, linguists, engineers, architects and agricultural experts – many of whom were inclined towards the opposition. The institutional solution to this competitive problem was to create new administrative units, based on specialist professions, which were placed outside the departments of state.

On to 1884

The political pressure on the old regime was, to some extent, maintained by the underprivileged who were demanding full citizenship. In 1859, those qualified to vote amounted to 7.63 per cent of the population, as against 7.59 per cent in 1882. Qualification for the franchise, as set down in the Constitution had, in other words, become tighter as a result of changes in the employment structure. At the same time, self-awareness amongst groups excluded from the franchise had grown. This applied in particular to the minor officials in public service, amongst them non-commissioned officers and teachers.

It is clear, all the same, that the conflict over the admission of government ministers to parliament began as, and continued to be, a conflict amongst the political élite, i.e. in parliament and in the section of the public that had long been politically active. The turnout at the elections of 1870, 1873 and 1876 was no higher than earlier. A slight change occurred in 1879 when 49 per cent of electors cast their vote, as against 46 per cent in 1873. But the real breakthrough came in 1882 with a turnout of 73 per cent, i.e. 72,000 votes, as against 42,500 in 1879. The 1882 election was the first in Norway in which strenuous efforts were made to mobilize the vote. Why the breakthrough came in just that year can be explained on two counts. First, the lines between the opposing forces were more clearly drawn, the arguments more polarized as a result of the resolution of 9 June 1880. Second, by narrowing down and simplifying the content of the constitutional conflict, it was possible to present it in the form of slogans with a high emotional content – for or against government by the people; for or against popular control of the Constitution.

To give a correspondingly simple explanation of the offensive against the old regime is not, however, possible. The question is to what extent it was a product of social changes, and to what extent the product of purely political factors, such as a growing spirit of cooperation in the Storting and Johan Sverdrup's brilliant leadership. These are still matters of debate. It is also difficult to perceive a social or class-based element in the change-over of political systems.

The two apparently solid bodies that now faced each other were, in fact, both coalitions embracing a wide range of economic and cultural interests. The Liberal Party *(Venstre)* comprised: elements from town and country; in south Vestlandet both Low Church and orthodox

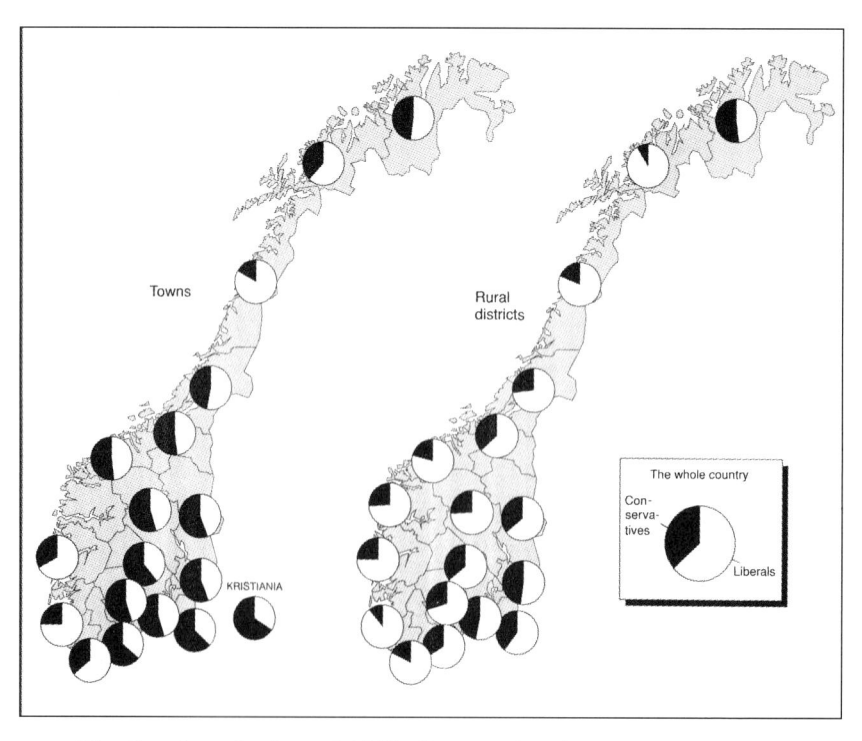

The Storting election of 1885. Support for the Conservatives and Liberals in the Storting election of 1885, by county and for the towns and rural districts.

Christians under the leadership of Lars Oftedal, a priest; and an urban group of free thinkers, providing a 'European' input. The Conservative Party *(Høyre)* embraced ultra-conservatives, who were determined to preserve the existing political system at all costs, as well as earlier moderates who in the 1870s had sought to achieve a compromise solution to the conflict. Occupationally speaking, the peasants formed the core of the opposition.

This last factor justifies the attempt to seek class interests behind the involvement of the peasantry. It is, however, somewhat problematic in this context that one finds in the counties round the Oslofjord – the area in which agriculture was most advanced – the greatest support for the Conservatives, though in the 1882 election the Liberals won here too. Added to this one finds it difficult to see specifically economic matters occupying a central position within peasant politics either just before or just after 1884. For this it is necessary to wait for events somewhat later in the following decade.

What held this heterogeneous opposition coalition together was its reaction against bureaucratic control in all areas of society – economic, social, cultural and institutional. The policies that they forced through immediately after the change-over of power provide an unambiguous testimony to a democratic revolt: the admission of ministers to the Storting; the extension of the franchise; the new conscription law; the law relating to *lensmenn* (bailiffs); the jury law of 1887; and the primary school law of 1889. In the decades down to 1884 Norwegian society had become so diversified and complex that the existing political system had come to be seen as too narrow to be able to articulate the needs of the different groups. The change in the political system involved a more open political exchange in which different interests could express themselves in new ways. But the change was not such that individual or class interests – the bourgeosie on one side, the peasantry on the other – found it easier to come out on top.

As an expression, 'the fall of the *embetsmenn* state' is in need of some modification. For it does not necessarily imply a general reduction in the social significance of the bureaucracy. It is more that the political change-over involved a role sharing between the political decision making institutions on the one hand – the Storting, the government – and the bureaucracy on the other. Previously the government had constituted the top echelons of the bureaucracy.

After 1884, the direction of development meant that more and more social matters were put under the control of the authorities. This occurred simultaneously with a tendency to delegate decisions to lower levels of the bureaucracy. And this, in turn, led to the strengthening of the bureaucracy in relation to the political institutions.

18
Modern Norway takes shape, 1875–1920

Towards the end of the 1870s, the forces that had fuelled the growth in the Norwegian economy appeared to be exhausted. An important resource, the spring herring, had disappeared from the coasts of Norway. The forests had been felled to such an extent that there was little chance of increasing exports of timber. Also competition from Norway's densely forested neighbours was becoming stronger. Shipping, that major growth industry, was in the process of being left behind in the competition with the steamship. And the home industries, which were virtually unprotected, were now exposed to fiercer competition from abroad.

Faced with this great challenge, continued growth was secured through a switch to new products and the modernization of the means of production, a process that was common to all sectors of the economy. Mechanization and industrialization, broadly interpreted, can be taken as the hallmarks of the period. In this phase of development, industry was the dynamic force in the process of growth and the transformation of society. Technological developments made it possible to create new industrial products based on traditional Norwegian raw materials. Besides, it paid to innovate and, with electricity as the source of power, a large electro-chemical and electro-metallurgical industry was developed. This was a decisive step in Norway's transformation to an industrial nation.

Lines of development

Initially the change-over, which began during a period of depression, led to stagnation in the Norwegian economy for a decade (1877–87), but there then followed a number of years of moderate growth, which

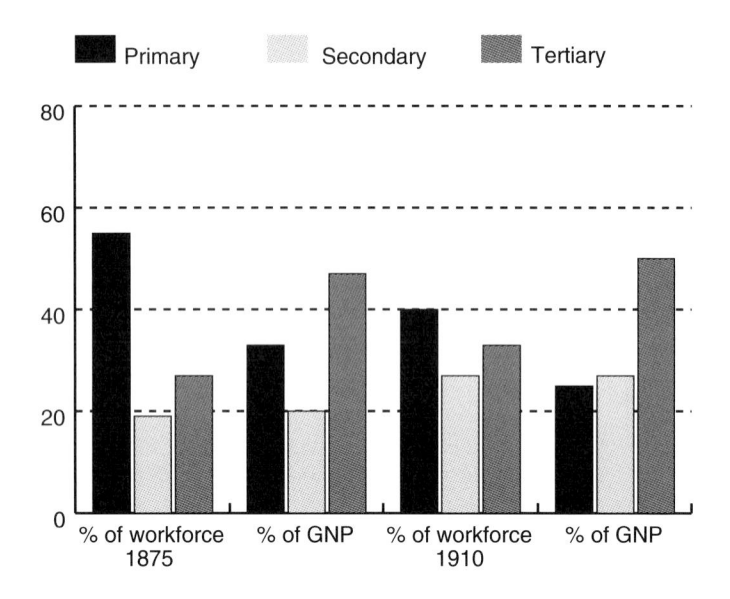

Working population by major sectors and the sectors' contribution to GNP 1875 and 1910

■ Primary   ▨ Secondary   ▨ Tertiary

The diagram shows the 'transfer dividend' achieved when an increasing proportion of the working population found employment in the more productive sectors of the economy.

merged into a period of rapid growth in the second half of the 1890s. A new depression (1900–1905) was followed by a very sharp upturn down to 1917, when the war made it impossible to maintain full-capacity working. The gross national product in 1920 was 133 per cent higher than in 1875, or, allowing for population growth, 75 per cent. Progress was clear, though in an international context rather modest – and undoubtedly lower than in Sweden and Denmark for the period as a whole. Denmark sailed passed and Sweden came up to the Norwegian level, measured by GNP per head.

The modernization of the economy resulted in more people being employed in crafts and industry, trade, communications and other services, while agriculture, forestry and fishing provided a livelihood for a smaller proportion of the population. Industry and services accounted for a steadily greater share of Norway's total output. The switch of capital and labour from the primary industries with the lowest levels of productivity accounted for some of the growth in output; the rest

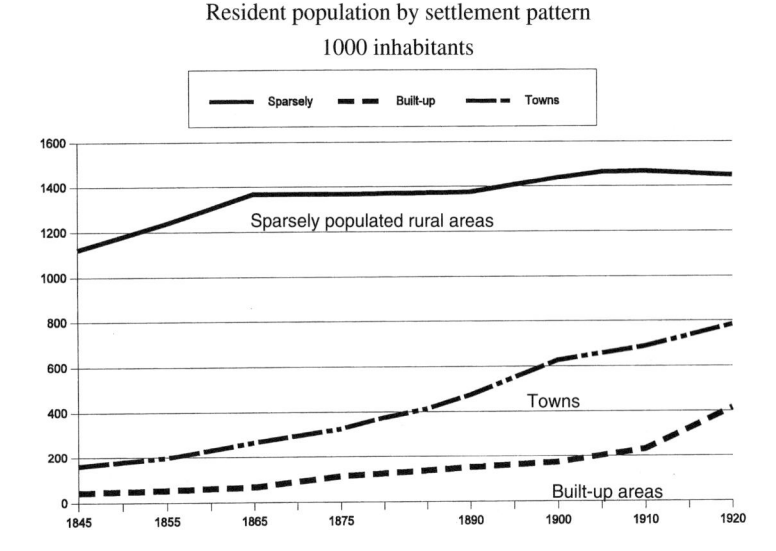

Resident population by settlement pattern
1000 inhabitants

Down to 1920 a major shift occurred in Norway's settlement pattern. The size of the population in sparsely populated areas was more or less stagnant. It grew rapidly, however, in the towns and built-up areas that, economically speaking, were akin to them, as a result of the strong growth in the secondary and tertiary sectors.

was due to a general growth in the productivity of the economy as a whole.

The excess of births over deaths remained high despite a decline in the birth rate. This decline, which began as a result of family planning, was offset by a sharp fall in infant mortality after 1890. People were also more mobile, though the pattern of migration remained very much the same. Towns and built-up areas expanded strongly, while the population of the more sparsely populated areas stagnated, indeed fell, relatively speaking. Down to about 1900 growth was highest in the urban districts, partly through a high rate of natural increase within the towns themselves, and partly through in-migration and the incorporation of populous suburbs. After 1900 the highest rates of growth were experienced by those built-up areas that had the settlement pattern and industrial structure of the towns but lacked their legal and administrative status. The population in towns and built-up areas rose from 440,000 in 1875 to 1,200,000 in 1920, i.e. from about 25 to 45

Overseas emigration from Norway 1861–1930

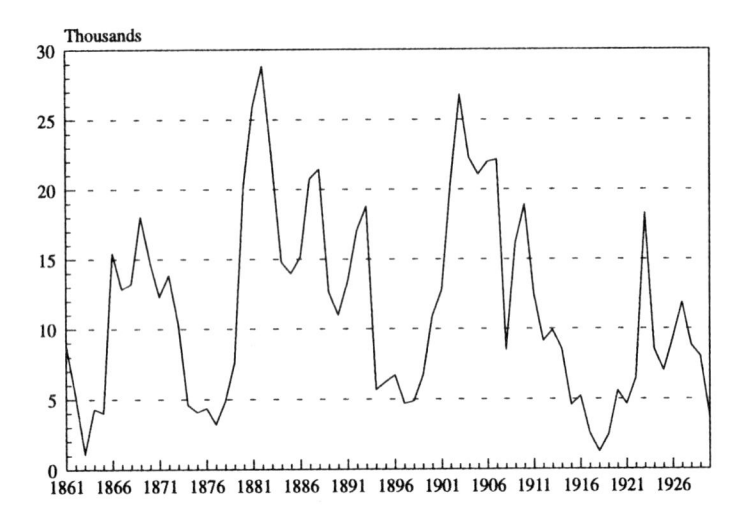

Norway had a very high rate of emigration throughout the period. North America was an important part of the Norwegian labour market, and the current of emigration was affected both by prospects 'over there' and conditions at home.

per cent of the country's population – a truly dramatic shift in the settlement pattern, which mirrored the changes in the economy and employment.

The flow of emigrants to America reached new heights, and was especially strong in the 1880s and the first decade of the 1900s. It also changed its character. Young unmarried men and women became the dominant groups, with the majority coming from the rural districts, though, in relative terms, emigration from the towns was occasionally higher. In total, half a million emigrated in the course of 45 years. Within Europe only Ireland had a higher emigration rate.

The pattern of emigration was influenced both by conditions within Norway itself and by prospects in the United States. Its intensity varied regionally and over time. The rise in the number of emigrants from Sørlandet and Vestlandet increased with the failure of the herring fisheries and the problems encountered by the shipping industry. A new feature of the emigration scene was that of the itinerant worker, who often made several trips across the Atlantic. America had definitely become an important part of the 'Norwegian' labour market and contributed to the rise in Norwegian wages. Without the safety valve of emigration, economic growth in real terms would have been lower and with it, living standards.

The growth in output contributed to a greater and brisker turnover. The household economy, in which output was geared, for the most part, to satisfying directly the household's own needs, lost ground to the market economy. Production had to be adapted to the market. This applied to all sectors of the economy, though the process of adaptation was at its most intense in agriculture.

A market-led agriculture

The demands of the market and the pressure of competition were the motivating forces behind the reorganization of agriculture. The peasants adjusted to the market and increased the production of saleable products.

Market demand was the result of structural changes and growth in the Norwegian economy. Between 1875 and 1920 the number of consumers rose by between 700,000 and 800,000 and they were better off. Milk consumption in the capital rose from approximately 1/4 of a litre per person per day around 1860 to 2/3 of a litre in 1911–12. Better communications – railways, roads and a veritable armada of scheduled boat services – made it easier to get goods to the markets.

The development of communications, however, brought with it tougher competition from abroad. Lower transport costs broke the 'monopoly' previously enjoyed by the grain-producing areas of the interior for supplying areas of deficit. From the middle of the 1870s grain prices fell substantially because supplies from the United States flooded the European markets. Grain produced in Norway could not compete in quality with imported rye because barley was not suited to the production of oven-baked bread – a new practice in Norway. The production of grain for human consumption fell and oats, the price of which did not fall particularly, increased its dominance, though mostly as animal feed. Old working methods continued in those rural districts unaffected by developments in communications. Thus it was advantageous for most peasants to buy cheap imported grain.

Price changes favoured animal husbandry, so that the bulk of output shifted to milk and milk products. Meat was considered to be a by-product. The total number of cattle remained more or less the same but, with better feeding, milk yields rose by 50 per cent between 1865 and 1920.

Working methods changed. Labour-intensive foraging in the mountains and outfields was not compatible with rising wages. Fodder increasingly came from cultivated meadows and fields. The area under agriculture declined, but the manuring of meadows and fields raised the output of hay and, besides, much more feed concentrate was now used.

Enclosures broke down common ownership, and collective working – the result of the strip system – declined. Property was better arranged, with a move away from a clustered dwelling pattern. This was in many places a precondition for fencing, ditching, clearing and the use of machinery and for new, more efficient farm buildings.

The horse and new horse-driven machinery replaced expensive human labour. This new technology was better suited to the cultivation of meadows than of fields, and Norwegian peasants proved to be more enthusiastic about mechanization than peasants in other countries. The mowing machine caught on quickly and was used even on small farms where the investment could hardly have paid off. Yet this, together with better ploughs and harrows, horse-drawn rakes, potato diggers and the racking for drying hay, now made of wire, amounted to a minor technological revolution. New species of plants, better suited to the Norwegian environment, also contributed to greater yields.

The peasant now became above all a primary producer, with processing and sales being taken away from the farm. Increased sales of milk to the towns and more efficient butter production, due to the separator, led to the establishment of a large number of dairies, most of which were cooperatives. In 1900 they numbered 845, but later amalgamations led to a concentration of the industry. In 1915 the dairies received 30 per cent of milk output and, together with the factories that produced canned milk, accounted for most of the modest exports.

Agriculture became more dependent on the purchase of equipment and other producer goods such as feed concentrate and artificial fertilizer and, as a result, was less dependent on a farm's own resources. Thus, pig and chicken farming, which relied less on the amount of land available, grew strongly. Agriculture was in the process of being 'industrialised'. This encouraged the growth of producer cooperatives, which helped keep the middleman's profits in the peasants' own pockets.

The change-over took time and many rural communities were untouched by it as late as 1920. The distance to markets, transport conditions and agriculture's place in the local economy determined the starting point and the speed of change. Where holdings were small and secondary employment the most important source of cash incomes, the process started later and in many areas did not occur until after the Second World War.

Adapting to the market evened out regional differences in working practices and production patterns. The sense of common interest was strengthened and the peasantry joined forces for the benefit of their class and industry. Cooperation offered the best possible way of exploiting the market. The Norwegian Farmers' Union (founded in 1896) was primarily concerned with articulating the industry's problems and making proposals for official governmental support. Protection for agriculture was the main demand, and modest duties on animal products were agreed in 1897 and again in 1905. The demand for a duty on imported corn – a source of acrimony amongst the peasants themselves – came shortly before the outbreak of the First World War.

The peasants also fought for restrictions on the production and marketing of margarine, an 'unnatural' industrial product and seen as the greatest of threats. The regulation of competition with industry over labour, land and forest resources was also sought. Measures were taken to create a stable labour force by providing cheap loans for housing with small plots of land. In practice, industry was barred from obtaining land and forests through the laws regulating the right to the use of Norway's natural resources.

Fishing and the fish-processing industry

The disappearance of spring herring from the coasts of western Norway forced the large organization involved in the catching, processing and marketing of the product to look for new spheres of activity. Fat herring from northern Norway became a sizeable new export item, and in the 1880s there occurred a shortlived, if hectic, herring fishery off Iceland and later in the North Sea.

Deep-sea fishing placed other demands on the boats. Sailing boats with decks were the first step, then came steam. Through funds earmarked for promoting salt water fishing, the state helped to spread the

Cod
Spawning and winter cod: December–April
Cod in pursuit of capelin: April–June
Iceland cod: March–September

Deep sea fishing
April–September also, to some extent,
November and December

Spring herring
Februar–April

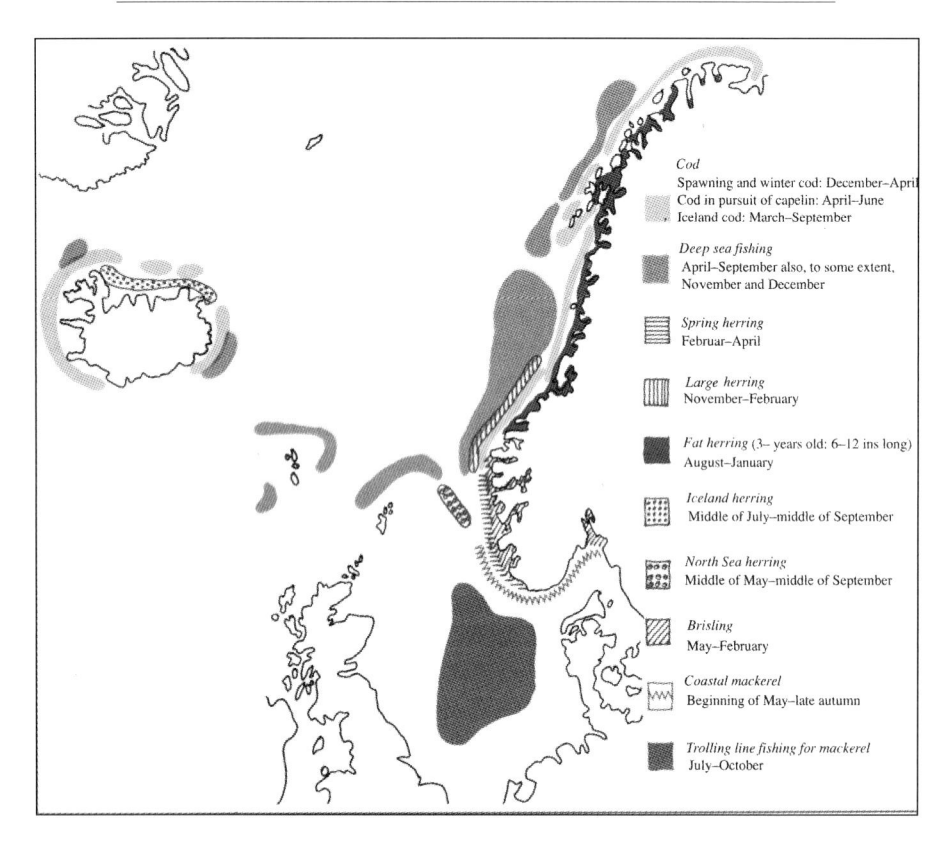

Large herring
November–February

Fat herring (3– years old: 6–12 ins long)
August–January

Iceland herring
Middle of July–middle of September

North Sea herring
Middle of May–middle of September

Brisling
May–February

Coastal mackerel
Beginning of May–late autumn

Trolling line fishing for mackerel
July–October

The map shows the most important fishing areas on the eve of the First World War. Fishing throughout the year was dominated by that in the seas near the coast, with peak catches being made in the winter months January–March.

new technology. Sunnmøre was the centre of the steam-driven fishing fleet, with Ålesund its main port. Steamships never achieved a dominant position in the industry but they were an important element. Investors outside fishing circles participated, and many salt water fishing ventures were organised as limited companies. The steam-driven fishing boats needed to be operational throughout the year, and transport, the bait trade and tugboat services for the herring fleet were the largest secondary sources of employment. As steam technology was too expensive for traditional methods of working in the industry (i.e. the combination of a small farm and a share in a fishing boat), it was a threat to the independent fisherman.

The threat diminished when, after the turn of the century, the petrol engine became sufficiently reliable. The engine was cheaper and could be mounted on a sailing boat. Within 15 years a revolution took place. By 1920 the motorized fishing fleet consisted of 8,800 decked and 6,000 open boats as against a mere 309 driven by steam. Mechanization involved a rapid and massive investment in new technology, with tremendous benefits for builders of wooden boats, as well as engine and equipment manufacturers. Even if some areas undoubtedly led the way, mechanization occurred over a broad front with the fishermen themselves as investors.

The advent of motor-driven boats increased mobility. Fishermen could now follow the fish more easily and safety was improved. Productivity increased with more seaworthy boats and more equipment. Mechanical aids for drawing nets and long lines reduced the physical effort required, and innovations with regard to equipment, such as the drift net and the purse seine, produced larger catches. All these technological changes created a more effective industry.

The great investments occurred because it was possible to fish throughout the year by moving from one fishing ground to another. Principally this was because a major herring boom commenced towards the end of the 1890s. Thus fishing for winter herring was followed in the summer and autumn by fishing off Iceland, or in the fjords for brisling and fat herring, which provided employment for most of the year. When prices were exceptionally high – as they were during the First World War – conditions were conducive to rapid mechanization. Just how many the industry employed can be estimated only very roughly, but the numbers undoubtedly rose between 1900 and 1920. Given that the fishing fleet was now operational over a greater part of the year, total man-hours worked no doubt rose considerably.

A wider product range stabilized the market and increased the value of fish exports. Exports of herring packed in ice rose steadily and on the eve of the First World War were greater than those of salted herring. Fresh herring fetched a higher price and also helped stabilize the market for salted herring. Herring was also used for fish meal and oil. The commercial fishing of sprats was started in north Norway in response to industrial demands there. At first production was concentrated on fish meal, but the breakthrough in producing edible fats out of marine oils made it possible to use herring and whale oils for human consumption.

The canning industry, with brisling-sardines as its most important product, grew ever more significant. Between 1903 and 1915 the number of factories trebled, employment (in man-hours) quadrupled and exports grew fourteenfold. The industry, centred on Stavanger, had major repercussions on a variety of support services, and created a modern, capital-intensive brisling and sprat fishery.

The mechanization of the fishing fleet and the industrialized processing of the raw material led to the fishing industry becoming to a greater extent part of the more purely capitalistic sector. Compared, however, with the timber products industry, the processing of the raw materials from fishing and whaling was but a modest affair.

Forestry and the wood products industry

After reaching a peak in 1873, exports of timber swung between 1.5 and 2.0 million cubic metres a year down to 1905 and then fell gradually to 1.0 million cubic metres by 1914. Domestic consumption, however, rose during this same period. For exports the industrialized processing of timber, from wood pulp to paper, was the source of the new growth. Grinding mills were used to transform timber into pulp, a product suitable only for producing coarse paper. The production of pulp by a chemical process (the sulphite process) made it possible to produce high-quality papers. The new technology brought down paper prices and this led to an enormous growth in consumption.

Stocks of timber suitable for turning into planks, battens and deals in the catchment areas of the Drammen and Skien river systems had fallen. However, with their surplus water power these areas now became the centre of the new industry. The pulp mills could process timber of smaller dimensions and so solved the raw material problem. The leap from sawmill to grinding mill was not great. The technology was comparatively simple and cheap. In the 1880s, Norwegian wood pulp produced by this process had a dominant position on the international market. Experiments with chemical pulp began in the 1870s and several mills were built during the following decade, but most suffered technical problems and low profitability. With the sulphite process, a breakthrough occurred around 1890. This process was more capital intensive than for wood pulp produced by the grinding mills and demanded a knowledge of chemistry and metallurgy. British capital

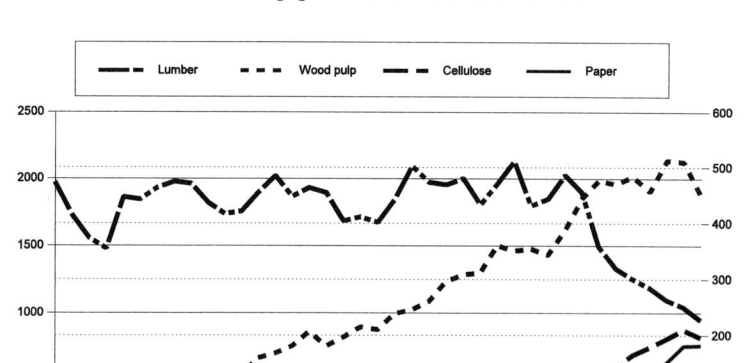

Export of lumber (in 1,000 cubic metres), wood pulp,
cellulose and paper in 1,000 tonnes) 1876–1914

The wood products industry grew strongly from the 1880s. Shortly after the turn of the century its export value was as high as that of timber exports. By 1914 it amounted to 80 million kroner *as against 30 million kroner for timber.*

and know-how played an important role in the development of both the chemical pulp and the paper industries in Norway, one example being that of the Kellner Partington Paper Pulp Co. Ltd., which built up the largest integrated concern in the industry: Borregaard.

By 1906 the timber products industry employed as many as the saw and planing mills together; by 1915 some 50 per cent more. Just before the outbreak of the First World War the new export products brought in twice as much as exports of timber. Because of pulp, cellulose and paper, the timber-based industries held their place for a long period as Norway's most important export business, with over 40 per cent of the value of total commodity exports.

The owners of the forests benefited from rising demand and higher prices. Spruce values rose substantially and it now paid to fell the smaller trees. The wood products industry also had a considerable impact on the Norwegian engineering industry. The pulp mills stimulated the production of turbines and grinding equipment. Firms like Myren and Kværner were able to compete internationally, and gradually the Norwegian engineering industry came to produce much of the more complicated equipment needed by the paper industry.

The process of industrialization

New industrial products based on raw materials from the primary industries increased value and contributed to forestry and fishing continuing to be the twin pillars of Norway's commodity exports. Although the wood products industry was the country's first large, modern export industry, there were, down to 1920, three other notable features of the industrial scene. First, the consumer goods industry, based primarily on the domestic market, increased its range considerably. Second, the country developed a new export industry based on its water power resources and partly too on its ore and mineral deposits. Finally, the process of modernization and industrialization gave a major stimulus to the industries producing capital goods, the growth of the iron and engineering industry being particularly marked.

Industrial development took place in fits and starts. In terms of numbers employed, three periods of rapid growth can be isolated; 1885–90, 1895–99 and 1906–16. In the years 1875–85 there was growth too in several important consumer goods industries as well as in the wood products, iron and engineering industries. Total employment in manufacturing industry rose from 48,000 in 1885 to 80,000 in 1900 and almost 160,000 in 1920. The whole industrial sector, including building and construction, craft and minor industries employed 300,000 by 1920.

The textile industry, which had developed a sizeable market in Sweden, suffered a setback when the Norwegian–Swedish 'common market' was abolished on the repeal in 1897 of the law *(Mellomriksloven)* regulating the trade between the two countries. From the turn of the century the growth industries were, above all, those producing ready-made clothing, shoes, foodstuffs, alcohol and tobacco. These consumer goods, in total, provided about 30 per cent of industrial employment.

Mining also experienced increased growth in the 1890s. New technology made it possible to exploit lower-quality iron ore and other mineral deposits. Foreign capital created new, vigorous mining communities (Sulitjelma and Kirkenes) and revived older ones (Folldal and Løkken). In 1909, as much as 80 per cent of the share capital in the mining companies was in foreign hands. The extraction of pyrites, copper ore, iron and nickel increased sharply. In 1902, ores, metals and minerals accounted for 2 per cent of commodity exports; in 1916 for 23 per cent.

Hydroelectric power was the foundation for the energy-demanding heavy industry that turned Norway into a major exporter of electro-chemical and electro-metallurgical products. Norway had considerable advantages on the energy side, but the power stations and industrial plants were bigger than Norwegian capital alone could cope with. Not only capital but processes and technology had to be imported. Saltpetre was the exception.

There was an acute need for nitrogenous fertilizer. A crisis in the world's food supplies was to be averted only by the production of massive quantities. A Norwegian invention, the Birkeland–Eyde method, took, as it were, nitrogen out of the air with the assistance of huge quantities of electrical energy. The foundation was laid for a new world product. Norsk Hydro (established in 1905) had by 1911 invested 100 million *kroner* in power stations and factories and by 1914 the export of nitrogenous fertilizer had reached about 75,000 tons per annum. It was Swedish, German, French and Canadian capital that made it possible for Norsk Hydro to expand so rapidly.

Because so much energy was lost in the process of transferring electricity from one place to another, the plants had to be placed near the sources of energy. The result was that industrial communities grew in previously almost uninhabited areas. Rjukan and Notodden, both owing their existence to Norwegian saltpetre, had by 1916 respectively 10,000 and 5,000 inhabitants. This energy-based industry created many communities that were dependent on the success of one or two concerns. Output embraced saltpetre, calcium carbide, cyanamide and aluminium, as well as different kinds of ferro-alloys and electro-steel based on scrap iron. A number of the factories began production just before and during the First World War, while the construction phase of others was at its most hectic actually in the war years.

Employment in the building and construction industry increased in the 1890s, but the Christiania crash of 1899 hit house building very hard. Activity increased again after 1906. The new industry, with its power stations, plants and dwellings, demanded vast numbers of construction workers. Employment in these industries was strengthened by greater public investment in the communications sector, in schools and hospitals, in water and sewerage and in the development of power stations for the production of hydroelectricity and the necessary distribution network. The number of construction workers rose to almost 60,000 by 1920, roughly twice as many as in 1910. With the building of power stations, great opportunities for growth opened up for the production of electrical equipment. The expansion of this sector came when large foreign companies established subsidiaries in Norway or went into partnership with Norwegian concerns.

The mechanization of agriculture and fisheries, together with the development of industry, also laid the basis for growth in the capital goods industries, especially in iron and engineering. The production of machines and machine tools, together with repairs, gave employment to a number of large and many small concerns. The growth of shipping also gave a new impetus to the shipbuilding industry.

From sail to steam

In 1878 steamships accounted for only 3–4 per cent of Norwegian tonnage, as against 50 per cent of Great Britain's. The fall in coal prices together with the triple expansion engine considerably reduced running costs, so that steamships were able to compete in more trades. Steam technology made new demands. Norway had neither coal nor steel and, even though Norwegian shipyards had experience in building steamships, they were both few in number and small. The import of ships was essential for a rapid development of a Norwegian fleet of steamships.

In contrast to, for example, Canadian shipowners, who pulled out of international shipping altogether and sold their sailing fleet, many Norwegian owners carried on as before. Down to 1891 the sailing tonnage remained at about the same level as in 1878, but then began to fall. Investment in steamships rose rapidly and in 1907 the steamship tonnage passed that of sail. By 1915 some 70 per cent of the tonnage was driven by steam. Already in 1897 steamships produced half of gross freight income. Income per ton net was annually three to four times greater for steamships than for sailing vessels.

There was a marked geographical shift in the industry. Bergen led the change-over from sail to steam. By 1914 the four leading towns –

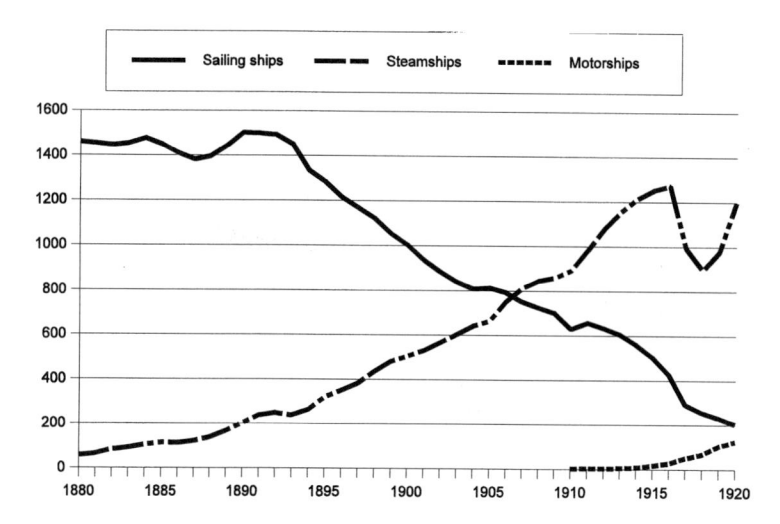

The Norwegian merchant fleet 1880–1920

The changeover to steam took place slowly and hesitantly, not in fact gathering momentum until the 1890s.

Bergen, Christiania, Tønsberg and Haugesund – had a good two-thirds of the country's steamship fleet. The stretch of coast from Stavanger to Kragerø, with 40 per cent of the sailing fleet in 1878, had, in 1914, a smaller share of the steamship fleet than the town of Tønsberg alone. The change-over to steam was the result of enormous investment in a few shipping districts, while the classic sailing ship area failed to make the readjustment.

The usual explanation for the inertia on the part of shipowners in Sørlandet is that they kept their sailing ships until all their capital was consumed and so lacked the financial base required for the change-over to steam. There are few studies of the profitability of the carriage of goods by steam or sail in the 1880s or 1890s, but indications are that sailing ships gave a reasonable return on investment. Many sailing shipowners bought cheap secondhand ships and in the 1890s this was reflected in the astoundingly high percentage of shipwrecks.

With the change-over to steam, shipowning was finally separated from commerce. The limited liability company was the usual organizational form. This made it easier to take a long-term view of the business and to build up reserves. It was a more modern way of conducting

Steam ships in 1914 according to home port

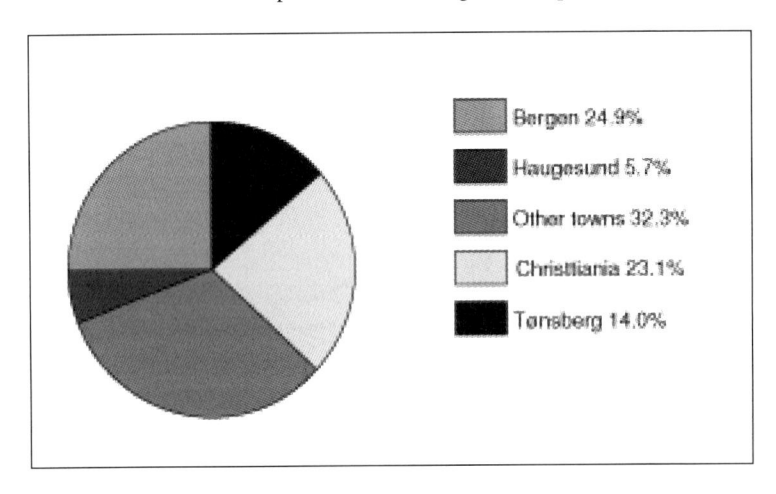

- Bergen 24.9%
- Haugesund 5.7%
- Other towns 32.3%
- Christiania 23.1%
- Tønsberg 14.0%

Bergen and Christiania were the dominant steamship towns. The towns from Stavanger to Kragerø failed to make the changeover from sail to steam.

a business than the shipowning partnership. The limited liability company made it easier to mobilize capital and to obtain loans. Ships were approved as goods on which mortgages could be taken out by laws passed in 1901 and 1903, and even savings banks issued loans to finance ships, taking shares as security. Long-term charters also made it easier to raise capital and loans, and made future earnings more predictable, so reducing the risk element. But, at the same time, such charters gave less chance of bumper profits. Norway was unable to compete on an equal footing with the great shipping nations in the growing liner trade (i.e. ships sailing on a regular schedule) because these protected their own fleets. As a result, less than 10 per cent of the Norwegian fleet was involved in this trade at the start of the First World War.

Shipping continued to be of vital importance for the Norwegian economy in spite of readjustment problems and times when cargoes were scarce and profitability weak. It had a significant effect on employment, with the shipowners placing many contracts for new boats and for repairs with Norwegian yards. Just under a third of the steamship fleet was built in Norway and that stimulated the shipbuilding companies from the 1890s onwards. Foreign earnings from shipping covered most of the deficit on the commodity trade with overseas and so made it possible to sustain a large and varied import of consumer and capital goods.

Commerce, banking and communications

Imports of goods more than trebled between 1875 and 1920, but the volume of domestic trade probably increased even more. For the old barter system was increasingly being replaced by a money-based system, which provided greater flexibility in commercial transactions. Employment figures give only a rough measure of the growth in commerce. Yet in 1920 it employed almost 90,000 people, more than three times as many as in 1875. Relatively speaking, growth was highest in the country districts, but there it had started from a very low base.

Commerce changed its character. A few large ports, such as Christiania, Bergen and Trondheim, handled more and more of the country's imports. This applied particularly to Christiania, which as a result got a greater share of the wholesale trade with other towns and the rural areas. Specialization in the urban retail trade had evolved even by the early part of the period 1875–1920. The old general store that provided most essential goods had been forced to give way to the many specialist shops. By 1920 even small built-up areas had a series of such shops. Large department stores, patterned on those overseas, were established, but the specialist store dominated the picture.

The communications network was increased and made more effective. The length of railway track was doubled between 1883 and 1920, while passenger and freight traffic rose more than sevenfold. There were more roads and they were of a higher standard. And by 1920 there were as many as 270 scheduled bus services. Even stronger growth had taken place in the case of scheduled boat services along the coast. These, served by smaller steamships, which covered local traffic, tied together the whole of coastal Norway. Trains and steamships also linked Norway with international markets. The distribution of goods was vastly improved. The state continued to play an important role in the communications sector through the state railways and by subsidizing boat and bus routes. The use of postal, telephone and telegraph services increased enormously. The domestic transport system as a whole employed around 65,000 people by 1920.

Banks and other loan-granting institutions increased both in number and financial strength. The volume of loans increased sixfold between 1875 and 1914. The savings banks continued to occupy a central position, even though the commercial banks had overtaken them by the turn of the century in terms of total assets. The growth of the banking sector was strong, but in Norway it was characterized by small units serving local markets and primarily meeting the needs of business for short-term credit. Norway lacked the large, solid investment banks that could play the role of entrepreneur. The banks were rarely involved in starting new companies. More often they had to convert loans into shares when companies were refinanced and reorganized.

Long-term capital for new ventures had to be obtained from other sources and the need for such capital increased strongly in shipping, timber products and the energy-based industries. Domestically this was organized via limited liability companies. Such companies took hold from the 1880s both for new ventures and for the reorganization of private firms previously operating as single traders or partnerships. Companies had great difficulty in obtaining long-term loans. Permission to use the bond market and to obtain loans from the newly established credit associations improved the situation somewhat.

Foreign capital played a key role in industrial growth after the turn of the century. There was a great import of capital, and foreigners acquired a direct interest in the ownership of Norwegian companies. In this, Norway was clearly distinguished from its Scandinavian neighbours, which also had large capital imports but usually in the form of loans. There is no doubt that imports of capital were a precondition of rapid industrialization in this period. In addition, the state and local authorities borrowed heavily abroad in order to build up the infrastructure of the country. Access to foreign capital meant that the scarce supplies of domestic capital could be used for other purposes, so giving the modernization of the economy greater breadth and substance.

The pattern of employment changes

A feature common to the industrialization of all countries seems to be a marked shift in employment between the main sectors of the economy. The total of gainfully employed rose by almost 50 per cent between 1875 and 1920, from a good 700,000 to well over 1 million.

The growth was about the same for industry and services, while the primary sector stagnated, its share of total employment falling from 54 to 37 per cent. Industry increased its share from 19 to 28 per cent, the service industries from 27 to 35 per cent. Most of the new workplaces were created in manufacturing industry, commercial activity and communications, together with the public sector.

Not only was the labour market larger, it also offered much greater variety, with new jobs and new career patterns. Significantly there were greater choices available to women, whose main sources of income in the pre-industrial period were domestic service or farm labouring. The increased choice for women did not lead to an increase in the proportion of women wage earners. The numbers remained relatively constant at around one-third of all women over 15 years of age – a rising tendency being replaced by a slight fall after 1900. The women in the workforce were young and unmarried, very few indeed remaining in paid work once they were married. Widows were the exception, seeking employment from necessity. This pattern did not change until after the Second World War.

In the first phase of industrialization, women took jobs in the textile industry. By 1920, a good fifth of the industrial workforce were women. They were to be found in almost all branches, but were especially numerous in areas such as textiles and clothing, canning, chocolate, tobacco and matches. From the turn of the century, however, service industries proved the strongest draw. By 1920 there were almost as many women in this sector as in industry, but they accounted for almost half (44 per cent) of the number of workers in it. With specialization in retailing, more and more women got jobs behind the counter, while in the hotel and restaurant business their dominance was all but absolute.

Women now took over the telephone service, as earlier they had the telegraph, while it was probably the typewriter that led to the great flow of women into offices. By 1920 there were over 20,000 women working in offices. This was over 40 per cent of the total employed there. Women were strongly represented in schools, while in the health service they had over 70 per cent of jobs, with midwifery and nursing being the typical female occupations. In total, some 15,000 women were employed in schools and the health sector.

Even if many obstacles to women's choice of employment were removed and admission to education broadened, few women managed to climb up the occupational hierarchy. Most kept to the bottom rungs of the ladder and had to be content with lower pay than men even when they were doing the same job. In spite of all the modernization, as many as 40 per cent of women in paid employment continued to be in domestic service or farm labouring in 1920.

The self-employed and the wage earners

Norwegian business was characterised by many small, independent producers. In 1920 they accounted for 26 per cent of businesses, as against 31 per cent in 1875. Numerically the largest groups were peasants, fishermen and independent working craftsmen operating on their own account. Ignoring grown-up children on the farms, the average peasant employed less than one worker. In craft businesses and commercial undertakings, 3–4 employees was usual. Even in manufacturing industry there were many small concerns, but 20 per cent did employ more than 50 people each in 1916. Large concerns were usually limited liability companies. In total, the self-employed numbered about 280,000 in 1920, and, even if a good many employed only themselves and occasionally took paid employment, the numbers who employed others was very large.

Wage earners, who had only their labour to sell, had by 1920 reached a figure of almost 800,000, an increase of over 300,000 since 1875. Increasingly, for the gainfully employed, wages were the only or the most important source of income.

Amongst wage earners, the greatest growth came in the white-collar sector. Here numbers more than trebled in the period 1875–1920 and by the latter date totalled almost 140,000. Blue-collar workers numbered around 650,000. Differences between the two categories came from the nature of the work done, conditions of appointment, payment systems, norms, aspirations and social attitudes.

The white-collar workers comprised a complex grouping, ranging from top management in both the private and public sector, to an extensive body of well-educated professionals in the middle, and to the rapidly growing subordinate staff in offices and shops. It was the professionals who possessed much of the expertise that played such a vital role in the modernization process. The bulk of the white-collar workers belonged, as a matter of course, to the growing middle class, but the distinction between the lower white-collar and manual workers was also clear.

The subordinates amongst the white-collar workers seem to have had more security of tenure than the blue-collar workers and greater opportunity to work their way up, either to a better position or to becoming self-employed. This fostered loyalty, but probably checked collective action in pursuit of better pay and conditions. The strategy employed by the specialist groups was to raise professional barriers, with a view to increasing their status and improving their market position.

As far as the blue-collar workers were concerned, the gap between top and bottom was not so great, though such a gap did exist. Indeed there was quite a gulf between the highly qualified workers with skills that took a long time to acquire and the unskilled day labourer who survived on intermittent, casual work. The skilled workers were sought after and in good times were able to improve their conditions on an individual basis. The unskilled had less to offer, got lower pay and were also more exposed to unemployment. Thus the interests of blue-collar workers were far from being uniform.

The blue-collar workers were mobile and labour turnover at their places of work considerable. Little is known about their life course and career patterns. They came from different backgrounds and gained their experience in different working environments, and their value in the labour market varied enormously. Nevertheless, they managed to develop a class identity that spanned the differences and made them a power in society. They were able to build upon a European-wide ideology that emphasized the common elements in their position as employees and which, at the same time, set them apart from other groups in society. They defined a common enemy, capitalism, that exploited them. Of decisive importance was their determination to change the existing power relationships, abolishing capitalism by revolution or reform. Within the Norwegian labour movement, the mainstream followed the reformist line.

The redistribution of the proceeds of production to the benefit of the workers was a central goal. The strategy was to confront employers directly in a worker-controlled labour market and to capture political power. The means was collective action.

The labour aristocracy – those skilled workers with the best chance of gaining control over the sale of their labour – provided the impetus for the organization of labour. The results of their endeavours carried the gospel of unity and solidarity to new groups. The National Federation of Labour (AFL) numbered 5,000 members when it was founded in 1899. By 1919 it had reached as many as 144,000. Persistence in building up the organization, firm leadership and discipline in the ranks made it possible for large groups of workers to improve their pay and conditions considerably. In the labour market, free competition was moderated through collective agreements between organizations representing the participants in that market. The Norwegian Employers' Confederation (NAF) was established in 1900.

State intervention

The state's role as the organizer of growth and development had to be supplemented by the roles of regulator and arbitrator. Modernization created conflicts between different industries, between groups within those industries and more generally between employers and employees. The conflicts were not new, but they acquired a greater range and intensity in that large weighty organizations were now in a position to exert greater pressure on the authorities.

From the 1880s, conflicts of interest on the tariff question, between those serving the export market and those serving the home market, were accentuated. Not until the agricultural and industrial interests came together, however, was it possible to move towards moderate protection in 1897 and 1905. Tariff protection was a stimulus to growth, especially for industries serving the home market.

The introduction of modern technology created problems in a number of industries, particularly in fishing. In many cases the state was forced to revert to regulations that protected the traditional fishing interests, amongst other things over the use of new equipment. For instance, whaling in deep-sea territorial waters off north Norway was forbidden after the fishermen of Finnmark had taken the law into their own hands.

Legislation regulating the rights to natural resources can be seen in terms of trying to preserve the traditional economic structure. Not only foreign but also Norwegian companies were, in practice, prevented from acquiring land and forests. The wood products industry was thus unable to control its supplies of raw materials. As to the major issue – the acquisition and exploitation of waterfalls and mineral resources – there was a shift from protection against foreign capital to the control of *all* large-scale capital. The desire to control the pace of industrialization and to avoid too rapid and radical a change in the economic and social structure coloured the *Konsesjonslov* of 1909 (this regulated the right to exploit natural resources, though it scarcely had the desired effect). The regulations in fact stimulated the Norwegian economy and helped reduce the burdens of the local authorities. For the regulations, which required the use of Norwegian workers and materials, and involved the obligation to help towards a solution of 'local' problems, involved mining concerns, builders of hydroelectric power stations and companies wanting to buy power. Established industries too benefited from foreign investment in the shape of collaborative agreements, which brought in new technology, know-how and capital. The law, moreover, secured for the state enormous assets when the concessions expired after 60–80 years.

The state also created regulations to improve working conditions and to protect employees against injury at the workplace. These undermined the freedom of action of businesses and increased their costs. In industry, limits were set on the employment of women and children and machinery was to be rendered safe. Compulsory accident insurance was introduced, to be financed mostly by the companies. Attempts were made to regulate shipping just as strictly. Loading lines, painted on a ship's side with a view to stopping it from being overloaded, and regulations covering manning and conditions on board were the main points at issue.

Conflicts in the labour market, with strikes and lockouts, which also had a serious impact on third parties, called for state intervention. The Liberal (*Venstre*) Party wanted to outlaw the main weapons of both sides and force them to settle their differences through compulsory arbitration. Opposition to this from employers and employees alike was so strong that the regulations introduced did not go that far. The system established in 1915 distinguished between legal and non-legal conflicts. Conflicts over the interpretation of a valid agreement between the parties was not to be allowed to disturb industrial peace, but should be decided in a special Labour Court. In conflicts over pay and working conditions there was to be compulsory mediation before strikes and lockouts could be started. The regulations, together with an interim law on compulsory arbitration, contributed to greater peace on the economic front.

GNP and private consumption per inhabitant 1865–1920
in 1910-kroner

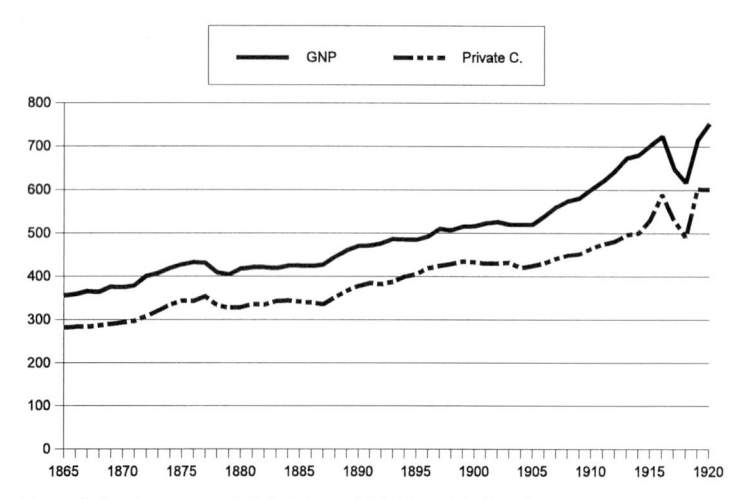

Growth in the years 1892–99 and 1905–16 helped secure better material conditions for the broad mass of the population. Also, welfare measures initiated by local and national government reduced the impact of income loss, due to accident, sickness or old age.

A more modern society

There were radical changes in the economy and as a result in the whole society in the period 1875–1920. The process did not evolve smoothly. Problems in the decade 1877–87, brought about by economic depression, were particularly important in slowing down Norway's development. Productivity increased in all the main sectors, at the same time that the two most important – industry and services – took on a greater economic significance. Both expanded in terms of employment, stimulated urbanization and contributed to the creation of the market, which accelerated changes in agriculture. The Norwegian economy became more tightly integrated and mutual dependence became stronger both between industries and between the different parts of the country. The strong growth in the sector of the economy oriented towards the market was a decisive step towards the economic unification of the kingdom.

It would appear reasonable to give industrialization major credit for growth and change in this period. The first important step was the building up of the wood products industry, the second the establishment of the power-based electro-chemical and electro-metallurgical industries. But, at the same time, industrial methods of production spread to new areas. Industry became more important in terms of both employment and output, while its repercussions on other sectors was very considerable.

Norway was not an innovator, creating new products and new technology, but rather a good imitator, which, starting with the straightforward importation of machines, processes, skilled labour and, to some extent, capital, was, after a time, able to carry the development further. The ability of mechanized industry to adjust and adapt shows how quickly the level of technological competence could be raised. This receptivity to new ideas has usually been explained by Norway's long tradition of overseas contacts. Rapid technological changes in agriculture and fishing would suggest that this receptivity was widespread, but the slow and hesitant change-over from sail to steam, and the comparatively slow growth of the shipbuilding industry during the period of expansion down to the First World War, point in the opposite direction.

The traditional export industries continued to play a significant role. In addition, towards the end of the period, rising exports came from the mines and the power-based industries. These new export industries were to set their stamp on the Norwegian economy for many years to come. As suppliers of raw materials and semi-finished products to other countries' capital goods industries, the Norwegian economy was highly exposed to trade cycle movements. The variety of goods exported increased. That Norway was now a more developed country was also mirrored in imports. The share of consumer goods fell, while that of raw materials and producer goods increased.

The Norwegian economy became more productive. Output increased much faster than the population. Investment took a greater share of the gross national product towards the end of the period, but nevertheless the growth in private consumption was considerable. In that the distribution of income was hardly more skewed than earlier, growth brought better material conditions to the broad mass of the population. Real incomes rose until the price explosion that occurred during the First World War. A better social security net further reduced the effects of loss of income brought about by sickness, accident or old age (see Chapter 19).

Large groups of the population must have felt the period to have been one of rising material well-being, with the threat of poverty receding. The evening-out of pay differentials between blue- and white-collar workers, which was clearly marked in the years before the First World War, increased during the wartime inflation. At the same time, the gap between the *nouveaux riches* and the wage earners became more apparent. This increased social tensions within Norwegian society.

There were inter-regional tensions too, based on the fact that growth had not been evenly spread. Norway's economic centre of gravity in this period had quite definitely shifted from countryside to town and from north to south. The dispersal of the new energy-dependent heavy industry did little to reduce the undoubted position of dominance in the Norwegian economy held by the southeastern part of the country. The gap between the industrialized areas and those dominated by the primary industries widened. Not, however, until the inter-war years did the problems of the Norwegian regions become really pressing.

The modernization of the Norwegian economy had taken a major step forward, affecting not just the workplace but other aspects of life too. It is easy to forget the countless large and small innovations that so reduced drudgery at work and in the home: the motor in the boats along the coast; the sewing machine; light from an electric lamp; and the new agricultural equipment. Even if such newfangled items were still not owned by everybody, they undoubtedly helped strengthen the general belief in further advances and a better future. The exhibition in Christiania in 1914, which celebrated the hundredth anniversary of the Constitution, was not only a demonstration of the cultural and material growth in Norwegian society; it was just as much a monument to an era and a generation that regarded the future with great optimism.

19
The political sphere, 1884–1918

After 1884 the political parties took charge of recruitment to political office in the Storting and the government, as well as for most town councils. Members of the Storting now lost their traditional freedoms, through being tied to national parties and programmes. Initially just the Conservatives *(Høyre)* and the Liberals *(Venstre)*, the two parties from the constitutional conflict, occupied the political stage. But the two-party system was soon replaced by a multi-party one. The Moderate Liberal Party, a right-wing splinter group of the original Liberal party, entered the Storting at the election of 1888 with 24 seats and remained there, though with fewer and fewer seats, until immediately after the turn of the century. In 1903, the Norwegian Labour Party, which had entered the political arena in 1887, won its first seats in the Storting, 4 in total, all from the far north of Norway. The *Frisinnede Venstre* – yet another right-wing splinter group from the Liberals – appeared for the first time at the election of 1909. Prior to 1884 it had been assumed that parliamentary government would be tied to a two-party system. Several parties meant that minority governments at times took over from the classic rule by a single party with a majority of seats in parliament. However, in spite of the increased competition for votes, it was the two original parties that dominated the system until 1918.

How could the two traditional parties dominate the system for so long? The explanation lies in the fact that, for a long time, the system operated with a limited franchise, mobilizing newly enfranchised voters was a lengthy process, and the electoral system itself favoured a two-party system. Down to 1919 a plurality voting system was in operation. Up to and including the election of 1903, there were no direct elections to the Storting. Elections took place in constituencies returning one or several members. From 1906 to 1918 there were

298 1814–1945

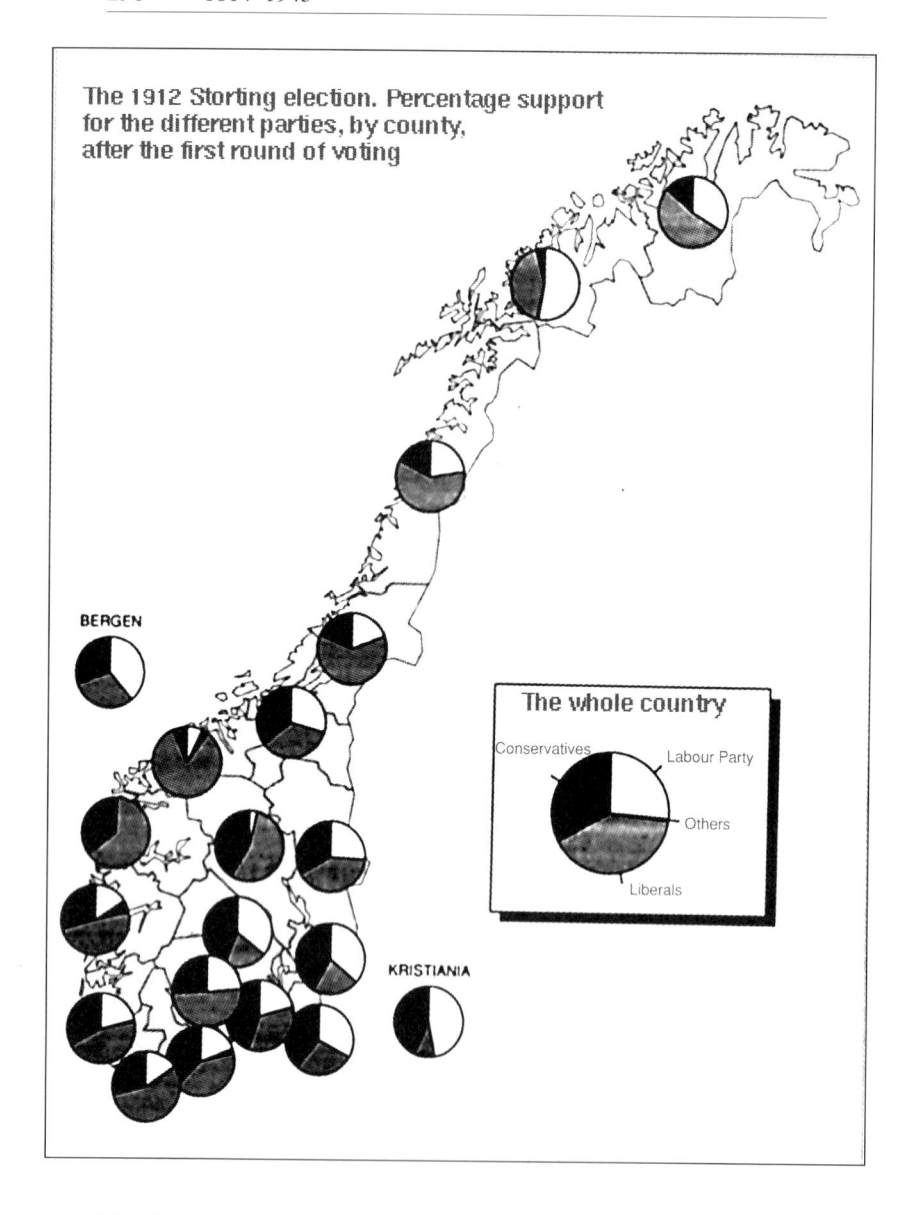

The 1912 Storting election. Percentage support for the different parties, by county, after the first round of voting.

direct elections in single-member constituencies, though with a second election if none of the candidates received an absolute majority on the first ballot. Both these systems, requiring a majority, favoured the main parties, primarily the Liberals, and so helped to preserve the two-party system. The most extreme example of this occurred at the election of 1915 when the Liberals (and its close allies the Worker Democrats), with 37.2 per cent of the vote, won almost two-thirds of the seats, whereas the Labour Party, with close to one-third of the votes, received only 15.5 per cent of the seats.

The second ballot, which was a part of the electoral arrangements introduced in 1905, did create problems for the major parties. This was because special-interest groups, such as the Teetotallers, the Church Party, the supporters of the Dano-Norwegian language (as opposed to that based on Norwegian dialects) and the Norwegian Farmers' Union, could all take part in the first round of voting, and then enter into negotiations with the main parties, before the second round, for the 'sale' of their blocks of voters to those candidates who would commit themselves to supporting the interest groups' specific programmes. These problems were not, however, so great that the main parties lost control. On only one occasion under the system of single-member constituencies, at the election of 1918, did one of these interest groups, the Farmers' Union, manage to enter the Storting – in this case with three seats.

More important for special-interest groups than the 'political channel' was the influence they could bring to bear by direct lobbying. The 1890s witnessed a breakthrough for national organizations representing professional and economic interests. These spoke for large or economically powerful groups. Demanding a say in national politics, by the turn of the century they had earned the right to be heard before the Storting decided on questions affecting their interests.

Changes in the party political system

The origins of the Conservatives and the Liberals were to be found in the constitutional conflict. The great Liberal coalition remained intact for so long that it effected most of the old democratic reform demands, the last being the jury law of 1887, which aimed at strengthening the popular element in the administration of justice. A division between the 'moderate' and the 'true' (if radicalized) Liberal supporters began, however, to open up immediately after the election of 1885. The disagreements were originally of a religious and cultural nature and emerged over the question of Church organization (Norway had a state Church) and the proposed honorary salary for the cultural radical, the leading novelist, Alexander Kielland. The 'moderates', who had their main support amongst the deeply religious populations of Sørlandet and Vestlandet, gradually, however, came to take a middle-of-the-road position on social and economic questions, e.g. on extending the franchise or the distribution of the tax burden. After 1887 the split in the Liberal Party resulted in the creation of a new political party, and Johan Sverdrup became prime minister of a minority government of the Moderate Liberal Party.

The 'true' Liberal Party, which again achieved a majority in the Storting at the election of 1891 and held it for the next decade, had to some extent renewed its appeal and changed its profile. First, the party came to take a radical line on the question of the union with Sweden; second, it formulated a socially radical appeal, expressed in its desire to introduce direct taxation; and third, it proposed that all men should have the vote. This last demand was met in 1898. The demand for a universal franchise for women was proposed at about the same time as that for men, but was not achieved until 1913, in spite of the fact that, from a party political point of view, it was a less controversial matter.

The new socially radical appeal of the Liberals found its clearest expression in local politics, however. While the party system broke through suddenly at a national level in 1882, the acceptance of party politics at local level has been a long-drawn-out process. It began over a century ago and even to this day is not wholly complete. Party political candidates were put up at local elections in most towns immediately after 1884, but it is difficult to distinguish a clear division on political lines between the Conservatives and the Liberals at this level. However, a change took place in the middle of the 1890s. The Liberals launched a new social welfare programme in Christiania, Stavanger, Bergen and Trondheim. Among other matters this contained demands for a reform of the poor laws and health care, for labour exchanges and for house building by local authorities. This radicalization, which for the first time created real divisions in local politics, was the product of several factors, though one in particular stands out: in the large towns the Liberal Party was under pressure from an organized labour movement that was beginning to put up its own candidates for election.

The Liberals' 'municipal socialism', as it was usually called, had repercussions on politics at the national level by contributing to a mood for more radical changes. The renewed appeal of the Liberals partly reflected a change in the composition of the electorate. The old Conservative and Liberal parties had their main support in the urban and rural districts, respectively. But in the 1890s the Conservatives became stronger in the rural districts, while the Liberals advanced in the urban districts, taking, in 1894, the Conservatives' two old strongholds of Christiania and Trondheim.

Towards the turn of the century many former Liberal supporters, amongst them merchants and industrialists, began to react against the party's radicalism and complained that the leadership had forsaken the old policy of economic prudence and become a party of expenditure. This complaint was pursued by old Liberal newspapers such as *Verdens Gang* in the capital and *Dagsposten* in Trondheim. This shift in traditional party attitudes resulted in an attempt, shortly after the turn of the century, to restructure the existing party system along social and economic lines – the old Conservatives and Liberals to be replaced by a 'non-socialist' party, on the one hand, and a 'socialist' party, on the other. Leading members of the Liberals, among them Christian Michelsen from Bergen (he was the prime minister of Norway in 1905 when the union with Sweden was dissolved), moved towards the Conservatives in order to bring about a realignment of the parties. The Conservative Party put all its strength behind a move towards a broad alliance of the non-socialists. The demand for alignment on the right had its counterpart in the appeal by the radical Liberal Johan Castberg for an 'alliance of all democrats' in Norway, i.e. a rapprochement between the socialists and the left wing of the Liberals. Both appeals assumed that the old Liberal Party would be broken up.

The movement for an alliance of bourgeois interests focused much of the unease felt in peasant circles and in their organization, the Farmers' Union, about the existing party system. In the course of the 1890s the special interests of the peasants became more sharply articulated, especially their demand for financial prudence in government and for tariff protection. This did not, however, lead, as it did in Sweden, to the creation of a political party at this point in time. In Norway such a party was not established until 1920. The demands for a separate peasants' party were deflected in 1897 when a provisional agreement was reached between the industrial and farming interests that made it possible to get through a tariff reform of a moderate protectionist nature. The rest of the unease was absorbed by the movement for party realignment.

A first step towards realignment was taken at the election of 1903. The Liberal Party lost votes both to the socialists, on the one hand, and to the Unity Liberals (the forerunners of the *Frisinnede Venstre*, which was organised in 1909) and the Conservatives at the opposite end of the political spectrum, on the other. For the first time since elections had taken place on party lines, the Conservative Party was able, with support from right-wing defectors from the Liberals, to muster a majority in the Storting – under the name of the 'Coalition Party'. This question of unity was to a considerable degree linked with common concerns about the maintenance of the union with Sweden. In order to understand this, the union problem must be examined in some depth.

The union conflict

Immediately after the constitutional conflict was brought to a conclusion in 1884, the union problem became ever more dominant – and remained so until 1905.

The union question had been a minor issue in Norwegian politics after Karl Johan's attempt to push through a revision of the Constitution had ceased in the 1830s. The union with Sweden had come to be accepted as part of the framework of the life of the nation. This did not mean that, from time to time, a certain dissatisfaction with the conditions of the union was not expressed. Around 1840 this dissatisfaction was mostly about symbols, e.g. that Norway's name should come before that of Sweden in the king's title on Norwegian coins, and especially over the question of a Norwegian national flag. From 1821 the Norwegian tricolour was used as the flag of commerce in European waters and from 1838 also on more distant seas. Naval ships, however, carried the Swedish colours, with a white cross on a red background in the top corner nearest the mast. In 1844, King Oscar 1 accepted the Norwegian demand for parity of treatment, so that the two countries came to fly their own national flags with a union symbol (a combination of the Swedish and Norwegian national colours) in the top corner nearest the mast. This union symbol remained on the flag of the Norwegian merchant marine until 1898 and on the official state flag until 1905.

The November Constitution had given the king the right to appoint a viceroy who would preside over the Norwegian government on his behalf. In Norway this was always interpreted as a mark of dependency. In 1859 the Storting annulled this, believing, after confidential negotiations, that the king would approve. After pressure from the Swedish authorities, the monarchy went back on its promise. In a famous address of 23 April 1860 the Storting rejected this Swedish assumption of a shared control of Norway's Constitution.

The conflict over the position of the viceroy was the most serious to date between the union partners, and was to cast a shadow over the following decades. In the short term, however, it was little more than a minor incident, in a period characterized by a desire for rapprochement on the part of both partners to the union. The 1850s and 1860s were the era of Scandinavianism.

Scandinavianism can be seen as an alternative to a distinctively Norwegian nationalism, and had as one of its ideological underpinnings the recognition that the linguistic and cultural differences between the three Scandinavian peoples were no deeper than the corresponding regional differences within, for example, France or Italy. A central political aspect of Scandinavianism was the recognition too that the existence of small countries was threatened by the Great Powers. The striving for German unification, which, among other things, had found expression in Prussia's attack on Denmark in 1864, supported this line of reasoning. Scandinavianism, which was also supported by the Bernadotte family for dynastic reasons, found expression partly in a desire for the unification of all three states, including Denmark, and for a closer union of Sweden and Norway, with the Swedes as the driving force. The desire for a revision of the conditions of the union was, however, also widespread in Norway. The Storting quickly removed the obstacle to a revision of the union contained in its address of 23 April 1860. A committee on the union was set up, with Ueland, the peasants' leader, amongst the Norwegian representatives. Its report, presented in 1867, offered, amongst other things, a joint cabinet that would deal with treaties and questions of war and peace.

The proposals were, however, rejected by the Storting by overwhelming majorities in 1871. One reason was probably that they became tangled up with the dawning constitutional conflict and, therefore, provided the opportunity for demonstrating opposition to the Stang government. But the main reason was that Scandinavianism, in spite of having recruited some of the earlier 'patriots', was more and more becoming identified with a general political conservatism.

The union committee's proposal for a joint cabinet would have given Norway greater influence over the foreign policy of the united kingdoms. Its rejection revealed a schism between those who were willing to pay a price for equal treatment, in the form of a closer union, and those who insisted on equality without any such admission. After the union committee's proposal had been rejected, the latter position was established as the view of the majority and became the official Norwegian line for the rest of the union period.

In the constitutional conflict down to 1884, relations between the two countries took something of a back seat. Nevertheless, it is clear that the conflict did have certain union overtones in that the dispute over the extent of the Crown's rights involved Norway's position in the union, as it had done in the 1820s. When the union question again became an issue in 1885, the initial reason was a Swedish initiative that involved the key problem in relations between the two countries, the organization of foreign relations. To understand the conflict that followed, we must first understand what this involved.

The period of conflict, 1885–1905

Foreign affairs lay in the hands of the king – not the king of Norway nor the king of the Union, but the king of Sweden. Under him was the foreign minister, a member of the Swedish cabinet. The Foreign Office was staffed by Swedish civil servants. Throughout the period of union, foreign affairs issues were presented in the so-called 'ministerial cabinet', which was a Swedish body. Initially, besides the king, the foreign minister and another Swedish minister had seats in this cabinet. From 1835 onwards, as a result of an act of Swedish courtesy, the Norwegian prime minister in Stockholm was also given a place, but only when matters pertaining to Norway were being dealt with. Day-to-day dealings with foreign powers were handled by two separate bodies – the diplomatic service and the consular service. The diplomats were appointed by the Swedish 'ministerial cabinet' while the consuls, whose job was to deal with trade and shipping matters, were, after 1836, appointed by a so-called joint cabinet – a joint Swedish–Norwegian body that if it met in Christiania had a majority of Nor-

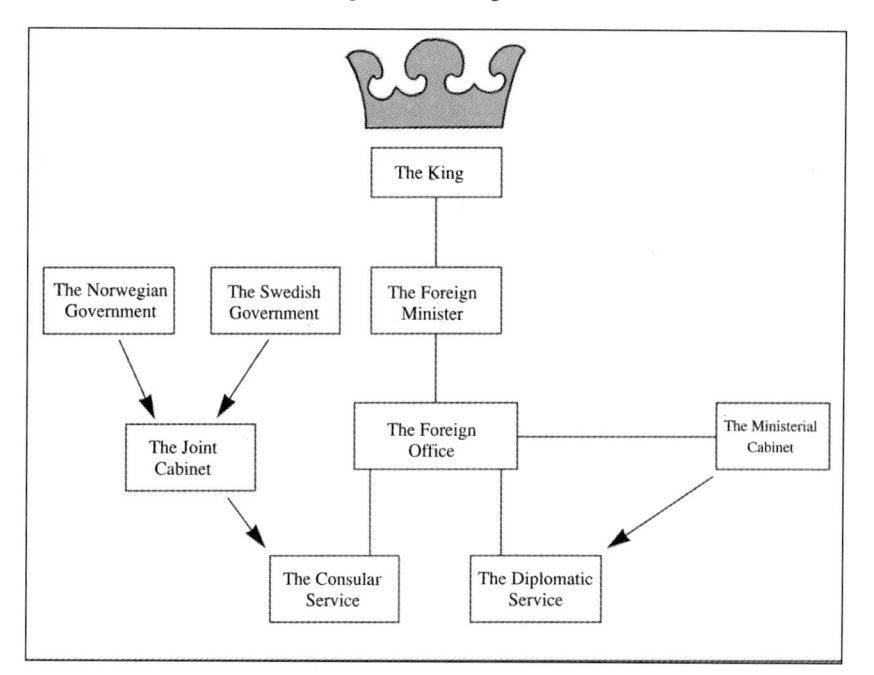

The direction of foreign affairs during the Union with Sweden

```
                          [Crown]
                            │
                         The King
          ┌─────────────────┼─────────────────┐
  The Norwegian       The Swedish       The Foreign
  Government          Government        Minister
          ↘             ↙                   │
        The Joint              The Foreign ──── The Ministerial
        Cabinet                Office            Cabinet
              ↘            ↙         ↘         ↙
            The Consular            The Diplomatic
            Service                 Service
```

wegian members while if it met in Stockholm it had a Swedish majority. So far as the system of appointment was concerned, complete equality prevailed within the consular service, and in the closing decades of the union there is no evidence whatsoever that Norwegian interests were in any way neglected as a result of the appointments that were made. A diplomatic career was, on the other hand, if not formally then almost exclusively in practice restricted to upper-class Swedes.

In 1885 the system was changed unilaterally by the Swedes. This started a chain reaction that led to conflict occurring throughout the entire system. As part of the growing democratization of Swedish political life, the number of Swedish members of the ministerial cabinet was raised from two to three, at the same time as its deliberations were brought more closely under the control of the *riksdag* (the Swedish parliament). That, no doubt unintentionally, emphasized still further Norway's subordinate position. Negotiations predicated on Norway's demand for equal representation proved abortive, because it proved impossible to reach agreement on a formula that would get round the sensitive question of the foreign minister's nationality.

The conflict over the composition of the ministerial cabinet led to the radicalization of political opinion in Norway on the union question. Before the parliamentary election of 1891, leading figures in the Liberal Party promised that, if their party won, they would, during the following parliamentary term, see to it that Norway got its own foreign minister. The Conservatives' alternative proposal was a joint foreign minister, who could be Norwegian or Swedish and who would be responsible to the governmental bodies of both countries. The voters gave the Liberal Party the majority it had asked for, but, in the event, in recognition of the realities of power politics, the party was reluctant to keep its promise. Instead, the Liberal Party took an alternative tack, directing its guns against the weakest link in the system with a demand for a separate Norwegian consular service to be created by Norway unilaterally. Politically, the question was of the highest priority during the first half of the 1890s. It provoked a series of serious political crises until, in 1895, the Storting had to give way, recognizing that the road to a unilateral Norwegian decision was, for the moment, closed.

The period of negotiation, which began in 1895, continued with some interruptions until the winter of 1905. The Swedish authorities eventually accepted a separate Norwegian consular service, though with the proviso that it should still be under the control of the Swedish Ministry of Foreign Affairs, whereas the Norwegian side insisted that a Norwegian consular administration should be established in Christiania under the control of the Norwegian government. No doubt the idea was that in this way the seed would be sown of a separate Norwegian foreign office, the first step, in other words, towards a complete change in the administration of foreign affairs. But this was a knot that could not be untied, only cut in two. That happened on 7 June 1905. The Storting's resolution of that date was based on the fact that the king, against the advice of his cabinet, had vetoed the statutory decision of the Storting to set up a separate Norwegian consular service. This was in defiance of the Storting's interpretation of the constitution, which allowed the king to exercise his constitutionally guaranteed rights only in agreement with his cabinet. When this was no longer the case, and when the king was not in a position to form a new government that would legitimize his position, then he was no longer king. Thus the union ended because the king, according to the Norwegian interpretation, was the only common tie between Norway and Sweden.

That Norway unilaterally gave notice that the association was at an

Christian Michelsen (1857–1925), shipowner and politician, was prime minister in 1905 and a driving force during the breakup of the union with Sweden. His fellow townsmen in Bergen thought highly of him, and their esteem is symbolized here by the size of the plinth. The statue was made by Gustav Vigeland and was unveiled in 1936

end created few complications in relations with the outside world. With the agreement reached in Karlstad in the autumn of 1905, the Swedes conceded, after Norway had made certain concessions, including the dismantling of newly erected frontier defences. The Great Powers had no vital interest in maintaining the union and in 1907 formally guaranteed Norway's territorial integrity as a state.

Why did the union collapse?

What broke the link after 90 years, in spite of the fact that, for much of the time, the union had barely ruffled Norwegian public opinion and had never been an obstacle to the economic and cultural development of the country?

The conflict over foreign representation began immediately after the government was brought under parliamentary control in 1884. This control did not, however, include the administration of foreign affairs. The Liberal government, which had a majority in the Storting, resigned over the disagreement with the king on the consular question, and was replaced by a minority Conservative government in the years 1893–95. In other words, the existing union blocked the free development of Norwegian parliamentary democracy. It is, therefore, possible to interpret union radicalism as an extension of the Storting's ambition to control political life, which had commenced before 1884. The union inevitably ended because it stood in the way of Norwegian democracy.

Earlier, the union had been defended on the grounds that it guaranteed the country's security and brought economic advantages. These arguments were undermined in the 1890s. After 1895 the two countries began to prepare for military operations against each other. Sweden's repeal of the law governing economic relations between the two countries – forced by a growing demand for protectionism in Sweden – ended the Scandinavian 'common market' in 1897 and hit certain sectors of the Norwegian economy very hard.

The main explanation of the shift of Norwegian opinion against the union must, nevertheless, be sought in the growing national self-consciousness, which rendered intolerable the country's subordinate position in the union. The cultural and material flowering of the second half of the nineteenth century – not least the fact that the Norwegian commercial flag fluttered over every sea – was a powerful stimulus to Norwegian national feeling.

Growing Norwegian nationalism was naturally a political issue to be exploited. In the first years after 1814 the appeal to nationalism was used by the dominant elite to reinforce its control as well as to establish the identity of the new state. By the closing decades of the nineteenth century, Norwegian nationalism had gradually acquired a more radical stance and was turned against the status quo. By demanding a revision of the union along radical lines, the Liberal Party was, from 1891 onwards, virtually able to monopolize the appeal to nationalism, winning, as a result, election after election. The Conservative Party, which believed that Norway's national interests were best served within the union and that the way to equality was through negotiation, was ever more conscious of the monopoly of power enjoyed by the Liberals. Above all, the party became, around the turn of the century, increasingly conscious that its policy on the union was an obstacle to the broad non-socialist alliance it wished to create. Liberal supporters who, on economic and social grounds, ought to join such an alliance stuck to their old party because of its policy on the union. Thus the Conservatives, after the turn of the century, gradually modified their

Henrik Ibsen (1828–1906) is one of the world's greatest dramatists and the leading representative of Norway's striking cultural advance in the nineteenth century. The statue in his birthplace Skien was made by Dyre Vaa and was unveiled in 1958.

unionist position and turned towards that held by the Liberals. This development was completed by 1905. The resolution of 7 June was taken by a Storting that, for the first time since the breakthrough for political parties, contained a Conservative majority. Given this, it is possible to argue that the union foundered because the Conservatives wanted to get rid of a question that had contributed to the Liberals' monopoly of power.

The Liberals' last heroic age

Once the union was dissolved, the Liberal Party lost its great issue. The prospects of restructuring the party system along the lines sought by the supporters of a joint Liberal–Conservative merger now seemed brighter. Christian Michelsen's government of 1905 felt called to lead this process and went into the election of 1906 with its own programme. The Conservatives consented to this strategy, and adopted a low profile. The result of the election showed just how unclear party divisions had become. For example, nine representatives were elected who supported both the government's and the Liberals' manifestos. The electoral statistics reveal that the election of 1906 was the only one since 1882 where it is not possible to distinguish clearly to which party newly elected members of the Storting belonged.

Nevertheless, it is clear that the election of 1906, much to the surprise of those supporting a merger between the two old parties, was characterised by a swing towards the Liberals, in that as many as 64 of the 123 representatives were elected on their programme alone. To this must be added 4 Worker Democrats, who belonged to the Liberals' left wing. The move towards the left becomes even clearer when taking into account the Labour Party's success. It made its first major breakthrough at this election, polling 16 per cent of the votes and obtaining 10 per cent of the seats. During the subsequent sessions of the Storting, the crumbling party walls were rebuilt and in 1908 the Liberal Party was undoubtedly reconstituted under its new leader, the shipowner Gunnar Knudsen. The collapse of those seeking a realignment of the political parties also found its expression when those elements of the Liberal Party that had broken away in 1903 formed their own party, *Frisinnede Venstre* (the National Liberals) in 1909 – a party that, it must be admitted, soon came to work closely with the Conservatives.

With the election of 1912, the Liberal Party entered a new heroic age, holding on to power right down to 1920. During the First World War the party was able to play a completely dominant role, partly because the Conservative Party was at its weakest at the elections of 1912 and 1915 and partly because, out of regard for the country's situation, the Liberal Party was able to enforce extraordinary crisis measures to protect its neutrality and its supplies, virtually without opposition.

Why did the realignment of political parties not take place, and how was it possible for a Liberal Party, split and outmanoeuvred during the closing years of conflict over the union, again to become the country's largest party? One attempt at answering these questions might well start with a model created by the political scientist Stein Rokkan that seeks to explain the unique nature of Norway's party political system. Rokkan focuses on two fundamental dividing lines or 'axes'. The first, which found expression in the establishment of the Conservative and Liberal parties, reflects contrasts of a regional or cultural nature – town versus country, centre versus periphery. The second axis follows the social division between privileged and unprivileged and found its expression in the rise of the Labour Party. According to Rokkan, what distinguished the Norwegian party political system was the fact that the second dimension developed before the first had been eliminated. The result was that the two crossed each other, giving rise to complex regional variations in party colouring. In applying this model to our questions, it becomes apparent that it focuses on issues of cultural policy that were particularly relevant in the period after 1905: the organization of the Church; liquor licence policy; the language conflict. All these made the realignment sought on socio-economic lines that much more difficult.

A second way of answering the question posed above, which does not exclude the first, is that the Liberal Party managed to unify the nation, so far as that was possible, on an issue that was to dominate Norwegian politics in the years between 1905 and 1914: how should one react to an invasion of foreign capital that could come to take possession of Norway's natural and economic resources? This question was tied up with another: should industrial capitalism enjoy a free rein in Norway or should the industrialization of the country take place under society's control? Once Norwegian waterfalls became a major source of energy, as the result of technological advances, and once foreigners began to show an interest in Norwegian forests and mines, such issues were no longer hypothetical. Indeed, in the years after the Boer War and the end of the union with Sweden, the source and control of capital could be seen as matters affecting the country's national independence.

From the political debate three main positions emerged: a liberal stance that would give a free rein to industrial capital; a 'national capital' position that would give preference to Norwegian capital; and a 'national democratic' position that, no matter what the nationality of the capital, would exercise control, partly by making the purchase of waterfalls, mines and forests subject to licence by the state and partly by provisions ensuring that installations created to exploit natural resources should, after a certain number of years, become the property of the state ('the reversionary right'). Whereas opinion in the Conservative Party and amongst the National Liberals was split, the Liberal Party managed to unite around the 'national democratic' option. This was also the position most deeply rooted in Norwegian public opinion, not least amongst the peasants. As one commentator noted after the

Liberal Party's great election victory of 1912: 'the peasants cast a radical vote from a conservative position.'

Seeking the middle ground

Attempts to restructure the Norwegian party system along more marked social and economic lines failed, but developments after the turn of the century were nevertheless characterized by a somewhat stronger polarization than earlier. This was due to the emergence of the Labour Party. The party won its first seats in Troms and Finnmark and, after the introduction of single-member constituencies, was able to score successes in the large towns of the south. In the elections of 1915 and 1918 the party won the support of almost one-third of the voters.

This impression of polarization is weakened, however, by the fact that both wings of the political spectrum took up moderate positions. The Labour Party was not a revolutionary Marxist one; until 1918 it held to a pragmatic reformist tradition. When the Conservative Party was set up as a party seeking electoral support in the autumn of 1884, it included an intransigent extremist grouping that would seek to commit the party to resurrecting the old political order, with a government outside parliamentary control. The majority, however, under the leadership of the party's founder and head, Emil Stang, the son of Frederik Stang, saw to it that the Conservatives adopted a moderate position, which resulted in it accepting, after a few years, the rules of the parliamentary game. Emil Stang formed the first Conservative government in 1889 after a vote of no confidence brought down the ministry of Johan Sverdrup. Later, this moderate stance found expression in the ability of the party to adjust its position on the union question and, after the election defeat of 1912, to accommodate itself to the aspirations of peasant society. This party, more strongly than the others, emphasized that social policies should always be formulated with regard to the ability of national and local government finances to support them, but it never rejected the policy of social reform.

The origins of Norwegian social policy lie in the major Labour Commission appointed by a unanimous Storting in 1885. A law on factory inspection in 1892 and a law on accident insurance for workers in 1894 resulted from its report. Health insurance followed in a law of

1909. These laws were under constant revision so that eventually they came to embrace all industrial concerns and the entire population.

The impression of polarization is reduced still further in that the powerful Liberal Party adopted a largely middle-of-the-road position in Norwegian politics. Throughout its entire history, the party has been subject to the loss of its right-wing elements – the 'Moderates' in the 1880s, Unity Liberals (later the *Frisinnede Venstre*) after 1903; the Agrarian Party in 1920; the Christian People's Party in 1933; and the Liberal People's Party in 1973. Yet, right down to the First World War, the party showed an amazing ability to rebuild itself. The Moderate Liberals, to be sure, became organizationally part of the Conservative Party after the turn of the century, but the bulk of its electoral support was probably taken back by the mother party. The National Liberal rebels made no permanent inroads into the Liberal Party's electoral support. Rather, in the years around and during the First World War the party stood as the upholder of social reform and conciliation, and won the sympathy of large sections of the population.

To sum up: Norwegian politics seen in a European context were characterized by a middle-of-the-road tendency, which found expression in party manifestos, strategies, and positions on particular issues. This tendency was probably a reflection of the country's relatively egalitarian social structure. This egalitarianism ran through the entire constitutional system. Whereas Norway from 1814 had had a one-chamber system, there existed in, for example, Sweden an upper house down to 1918 that in effect took care of conservative interests. The dream of creating an upper house in Norway appeared from time to time in ultra-conservative circles, the first time during the dispute over the king's powers of veto in the 1880s, the last in the 1930s, but it always faded away when it was realized that Norwegian society did not contain the social elements needed to support an upper house.

Because the Norwegian constitutional system had only a few, weak conservative guarantees and those that did exist were soon reduced, all political groups were dependent on the favour of an electorate that was based on an equal and universal suffrage. Compared, for example, with Sweden, where national political parties first came to be organized after the turn of the century and the first hesitant steps in the direction of parliamentary government taken as late as the years leading up to the First World War, political life in Norway had an aura of modernity.

20
The inter-war years

Presenting an overview of developments between the two world wars is no simple matter. Economic life was subject to stresses and strains that led to permanent changes in the capitalist system through cooperation between producers and an increased involvement of public authorities in the economy. Belief in the free market and capitalism's inbuilt ability to maximize the output of society's productive resources was weakened and events lent strong support to ideas for replacing the market's 'invisible hand' with a state that regulated and planned.

Crises yes, but growth too

Extremes are what usually stick in the collective memory, both in economics and in politics, and economic development in the period between the wars was rich in drama. Businesses went bankrupt, flourishing industrial centres saw virtually all activity cease, and the population was reduced to a diet of relief work or public assistance. Banks, the nerve centre of the productive system, staggered under the force of the depression.

Deflation created a nightmare for both the private and the public sectors. The pressure of debt set strict limits to the freedom of action of both national and local authorities. Making an accommodation with one's creditors, bankruptcies and foreclosures were effective instruments for the reduction of debt, but the process was painful. Deflation also contributed to a redistribution of wealth in society.

Long-term unemployment compounded the difficulties. In years of depression the unemployment curve rose like peaks above a 'plateau of inactivity'. Poor relief – with all its stigma – was the only means of survival for large groups of the population. In the worst year, 160,000

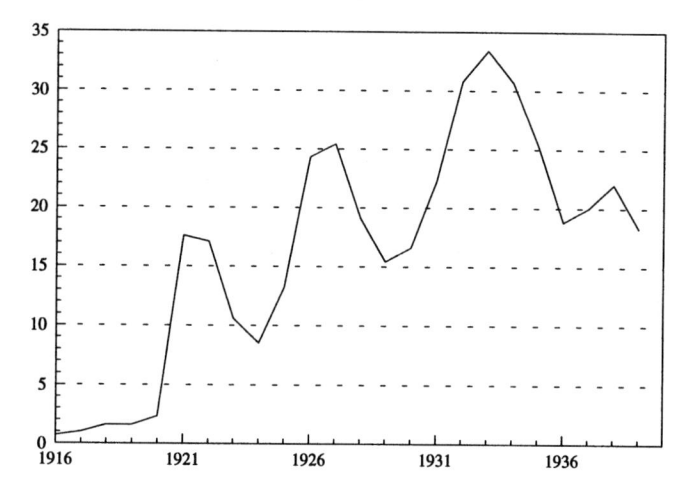

Unemployed trade unionists as a percentage of total membership 1916–40

The fluctuations in the number of unemployed mirrored that of the trade cycle in the inter-war years. But even in times of growth employers were unable to provide enough new jobs to employ the growing number of those seeking work. As a result, unemployment was on a rising trend throughout the entire period, but the total rate of unemployment was significantly lower than that among trade union members.

breadwinners collected money or food coupons from the poor law authorities, so becoming second-class citizens.

It is not difficult to catch sight of crises and the victims of crises during this period, but there is another and equally important side to the picture. The inter-war period was not one of permanent crisis. Quite the contrary, it was marked by an economic growth that compared favourably with that of earlier periods. The graph of GNP per head shows a sharp fall in 1921 and again in 1931. Each took three to four years to make good, after which, on both occasions, rapid growth was experienced (in 1926–30 and 1934–39). Total output of goods and services, per gainfully employed person, rose by 38 per cent between 1920 and 1939. Thus the Norwegian economy was more productive at the end of the period than it had been in 1920. This provided the basis for better material conditions for large groups in society, but not for all. That was the main problem.

Before 1920 there was a positive correlation between economic growth and the more fundamental changes in both the economy and the society. Growth and change were very much two sides of the same coin. Whereas previously growth had been sustained both from increased productivity in the different sectors of the economy and from the 'migration' of labour and capital from areas of low to high productivity, there were now only a few changes in the proportion of the labour force in the main economic sectors. The stream of migrants from the rural districts all but dried up and the growth of built-up areas ceased.

There were parallels to Norway's development in other countries. Because of its large foreign sector, the country was strongly affected by the international economy. Economic problems were imported, and fluctuations in Norway's development were, for the most part, the same as those in the other industrialized countries. But some features were peculiar to Norway, brought about partly by the structure of the Norwegian economy, partly by development during and immediately after the First World War, and partly by the policies that were pursued in the 1920s.

The wartime economy and the post-war boom

The war made a deep impact on the country's economy. Norway was dependent on the importation of vital foodstuffs as well as raw materials and production goods in order to keep the productive system fully employed. Norway's imports were subject to conditions imposed by the belligerent nations, conditions that came eventually to be very strict indeed. From 1917 on, the supply position became so tight that output fell and in 1918 food rationing was necessary. The demand for Norwegian goods and shipping services grew dramatically during the war but, in that Norway was dependent on supplies that Great Britain controlled, it was obliged to restrict its dealings with Germany.

Norway's neutrality was under increasing pressure from the belligerent powers and the authorities were forced to perform a difficult balancing act – making the necessary concessions to the British, who controlled its supply lines, without provoking the Germans into military intervention. Olav Riste has strikingly summed up Norway's position as that of the 'neutral ally'.

GNP and private consumption per inhabitant
1914–39 in 1938 kroner

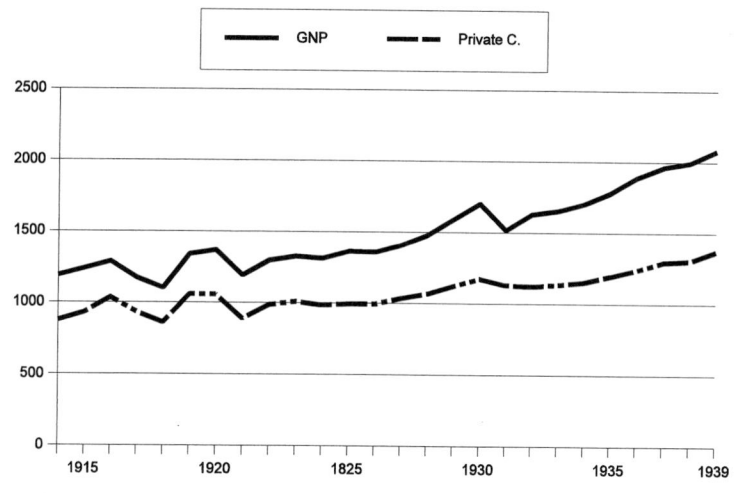

Taken as a whole, the inter-war years witnessed considerable economic growth. Even though a high proportion of GNP went to investment, private consumption per head rose by 30 per cent from 1920 to 1939.

The public authorities were obliged to intervene in the economy with regulations that were of quite a different order from those seen in peacetime. This had to be done in part indirectly by the business community's own institutions, which were made responsible for seeing that imported raw materials and production goods were not re-exported to the enemy, in either a crude or a finished form; and in part directly through intervention in both production and distribution. The state not only regulated prices and conditions of sale, but also forbad or demanded the production of certain goods. The state and local authorities ran businesses, and in individual cases the state invested considerable sums in order to secure production and sales at guaranteed prices. The First World War witnessed the apprenticeship of the interventionist state.

The main tasks were to prevent distress, maintain employment and control prices. There was no actual suffering while near full employment prevailed throughout the entire war. But the shortage of goods and the large money supply made it impossible to keep prices down. The strong rise in prices continued till the sudden downturn in the international economy in 1920, and by then Norway's price level was higher than that in most other countries.

The demand for shipping space increased enormously and pressure on the Norwegian fleet was increased by the sinking of large numbers of ships. Freight rates rose to unbelievable heights and income prospects led to an absolute fever of speculation in shipping shares. Share speculation was just one of the many expressions of a society awash with money during the First World War. The problem was to find sound projects to invest in. The number of joint stock banks increased sharply and working capital in these and the savings banks increased fourfold in the period 1914–18. The banks had problems in earning a good return on their capital and so had fewer inhibitions about investing in highly risky and speculative projects.

Easy credit, together with rising tax incomes, led the county and municipal authorities to undertake great investments in, among other things, power stations for producing hydroelectricity. The local authorities were able to free themselves from the state's control of borrowings by taking out short-term loans. The state itself contributed to increased pressure on the economy by granting large loans to national and local agencies in charge of supplies and through credit supplied to both sets of combatants by the Bank of Norway for the purchase of Norwegian goods.

The falling purchasing power of the *krone* at home contrasted with its rising value abroad. The balance of trade surplus led to a sharp rise in the value of the *krone* against both the pound sterling and the dollar. Large foreign currency reserves were built up by the Bank of Norway, and Norwegian shipowners too accrued hefty balances abroad. Norway took the step from a debtor to a creditor nation and a key concern like Borregaard was brought into Norwegian ownership. Foreign interests held a less dominant position in the ownership of Norwegian business by the end of the war.

The war was followed by an international boom, which had especially important consequences for Norway. Imports rose well above pre-war levels. There was a marked deficit on the foreign trade balance and suddenly Norway became a debtor nation again. All the credit balances were gobbled up by these imports. The value of the *krone* fell dramatically. Inflation was greater than in most other countries and continued for a time after the depression in the international economy had begun.

Crisis and convalescence

The downturn came in Norway during the late autumn of 1920. Its effects were dramatic. In the course of two years, prices almost halved. The bottom fell out of the freight market, and in the summer of 1921 approximately one-third of the tonnage was tied up idle. Net incomes from freight fell in 1921 to one-third of the 1920 level. The fall in commodity exports was also great. A number of the fishing industry's traditional markets were destroyed as a result of the war and revolution. The collapse in demand for products of the timber industry spread, with inevitable consequences for the forests, where production all but ceased. A falling value of the *krone* in 1921 reduced the effects of falling international prices for Norway's export industries, but a year later the crisis intensified when the *krone* began to rise.

Businesses were eliminated, or ceased or reduced production. Output prices fell, as did costs, but costs did not fall as much or, more importantly, fast enough. It was not possible to push down wages in line with prices. The workers vigorously opposed this and there were major conflicts between employers and employees, which reduced output considerably. In 1921 some 3.5 million working days were lost as a result of labour conflicts, in 1924 some 5 million. The victors were those workers who had a job to go back to after the clashes. Many had not. In 1921 and 1922 almost one in five trade unionists were unemployed and the state-supported unemployment scheme ran out of funds in the course of a few years. The ability and the willingness of the authorities to create relief work on a large scale diminished sharply.

The crisis spread to the banks. Debtors could not service their loans and the fall in real values meant that securities supporting the banks' commitments fell sharply or disappeared altogether. No doubt there was much speculation, but many solid customers had their problems too. A number of local authorities had difficulties because their tax revenues fell while their debt repayments remained stable and their social benefit payments rose. They too were no longer able to fulfil their obligations. The banks' losses came from many sources and they had to put up with runs, sometimes of panic proportions, from anxious customers who wanted to rescue their deposits.

The fear of a collapse in the credit system, with resulting consequences for businesses and workers, motivated the banking support

The dramatic fall in freight rates from 1920 to 1921 led to one-third of tonnage being laid up. The photograph shows ships laid up in Haugesund in 1921.

policy carried out by the Bank of Norway, with help from the government and some of the larger commercial banks. That support was not, however, sufficient to rescue the shakier banks. But, on the whole, the support policy mediated the worst effects of the crisis and assisted business.

The war, stock market speculation (1917–18) and the post-war boom created debt; the fall in prices and incomes created the debt problem. The repayment problems experienced by businesses and private individuals spread to the banks, and distressed local authorities, pressed by the banks, sought help from the state. The state, through a deficient accounting system, had contributed strongly to the inflation and had pursued a counter-cyclical policy in the deflationary period. Now, at last, it was presented with the bill. The series of handsome budget surpluses proved to be a fiction. The national debt rose from 357 million *kroner* in 1914 to 1,730 million in 1925. The state's financial crisis, which also helped establish a policy of financial orthodoxy for many years to come, was essentially a debt crisis.

The parity crisis and the international boom

The Bank of Norway declared that its aim was to restore the parity of the *krone*. The goal was decided upon in 1920, and there is broad agreement that the Bank's policy in 1921 and 1922 was a deflationary one. On the other hand, it is claimed that its policy of supporting the commercial banks during the years 1923–24 was a deviation from this line, though it is doubtful if the total volume of credit increased in this period.

Deflation eased from the beginning of 1923. The domestic price level rose and the external value of the krone fell. The rise in prices stimulated increased economic activity, while the export industries became more competitive again. Increased activity brought lower unemployment, but still only modest growth in total output. The desire to invest was weak, and sharp fluctuations on the foreign exchanges ('the quicksilver *krone*'), contributed to rendering all calculations uncertain.

The year 1925 heralded dramatic changes on the foreign exchange market. The external value of the *krone* began to rise so quickly that the task now was to put a brake on it, so as to limit the damage to business. The Bank of Norway tried, along with the government, to stabilize the exchange rate in 1926, but the attempt was half-hearted and had little effect. In the course of barely two years – from the beginning of 1925 to the end of 1926 – parity was almost reached, and on 1 May 1928 the *krone* was again tied to gold. Two factors were decisive in the rapid rise: first, increased exports; second, the fact that speculators drove up the value of the Norwegian currency, confident that parity was the ultimate aim of the Bank of Norway.

The rise of the *krone* triggered renewed deflationary pressure. The price level sank whereas costs did not fall to the extent needed to compensate for the rise in the *krone*'s external value. Exports were hit, while industries serving the domestic market met harder competition from abroad. The pressure of debt increased and unemployment rose sharply again. The parity crisis meant that Norway did not get the full benefits of the international boom from 1925 onwards. Growth was not stopped, but it was severely curtailed.

During the depression of 1921–22 it was the export industries that had been responsible for most of the fall in the value of output. In the second half of the 1920s it was these same industries that were responsible for its rise.

The Norwegian merchant fleet 1918–39

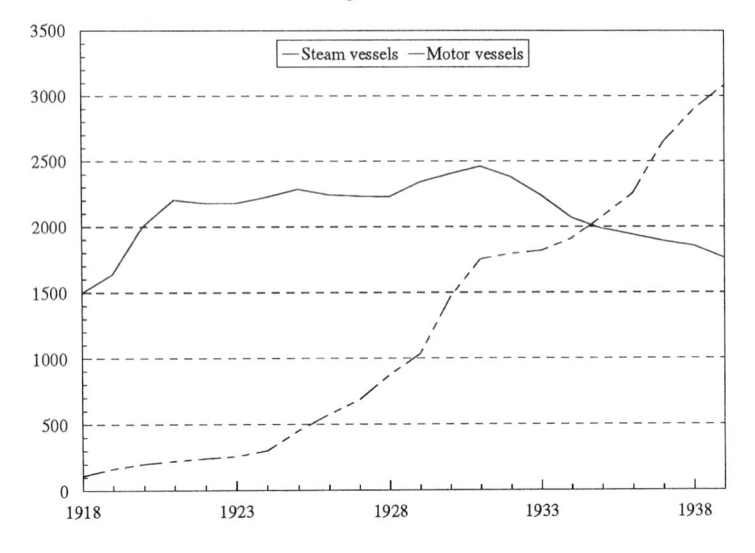

1000 gross tonnes

Whilst the changeover from sail to steam had been a slow one, Norwegian shipowners were quick to invest in oil-driven motorships. At the outbreak of the Second World War, Norway had the most modern fleet in the world, and had become the leading tanker nation. The combination of long-term contracts and considerable credit from the shipyards gave Norwegian shipowners good opportunities for expansion.

Within manufacturing, growth was especially marked in the electro-metallurgical and electro-chemical industries. Market conditions now allowed productive capacity to be fully utilized. Competitiveness was strengthened by new technology, which raised productivity and reduced energy consumption. In addition to Norwegian inventions such as the Søderberg–electrode and the Tysland–Hole furnace, new processes and production methods were imported, often linked to direct foreign investment in Norway. An example of this was the cooperation between I. G. Farben and Norsk Hydro over the Haber–Bosch method of producing artificial fertilizers.

In the 1920s the authorities interpreted the laws regulating access to Norway's natural resources in a liberal fashion so as not to drive foreign interests away from the many Norwegian firms with large refinancing needs. Highly specialized industrial centres were often totally dependent on one or two large concerns. It was the mining, the electro-metallurgical and the electro-chemical heavy industries that derived most benefit from foreign capital. This capital injection meant much in a period of low investment generally. Equally important was the access to new technology and to new production processes. Through their links with multinational concerns, Norwegian firms found access to markets easier. For, in a period of rising cartelization and international regulation of competition, it was not easy for a small producer to go it alone.

Shipping and whaling were the other growth areas. The fleet was expanded and modernized. Tonnage increased by 60 per cent between 1924 and 1931, and by 1930 Norway had the world's most efficient fleet because so many of its ships were oil-fired. Norwegian shipowners had also become leaders in the tanker market. The fleet was built up for the most part through the importation of ships. The growth in tonnage therefore had little effect on the Norwegian shipbuilding industry. Norwegian shipyards were not very competitive: they were expensive, had small slipways and were not in a position to offer the same favourable financial terms as their competitors. Swedish shipyards, for instance, were able to offer shipowners up to 60–70 per cent credit on new ships.

Whaling increased even faster than shipping in this period. Norway and Great Britain dominated the industry during the inter-war period. A series of technological innovations rendered the factory ships wholly independent of whaling stations on land. From 1925 to 1931 growth was astonishing. Norway produced almost two-thirds of the world's whale oil. In addition, Norwegian experts manned the whaling fleets of other countries. Expansion led not only to a collapse in the price of whale oil but also to the first catastrophic over-exploitation of a marine resource.

The growth of the Norwegian economy in the second half of the 1920s came in highly capital-intensive activities, where strong growth in output did not lead to much increase in employment. This helps explain why the unemployment figures were at record high levels during the parity crisis of 1926 and 1927 and continued at a high level in the 'good' years of 1928–30. The other important factor was the wave of rationalization.

The crisis of the 1920s had made businesses much more cost conscious. The goal of rationalization was cheaper production, i.e. lower costs per unit of output. Efforts spread across a broad front – from machines replacing expensive labour, to time and motion studies, different kinds of performance-related pay and new methods of cost control. A better-educated management, which sought to improve relations between the different factors of production and to achieve a better flow in the productive process, began to have an effect. Rationalization initiatives have been accorded some weight in explaining why industrial employment stood still in the years 1926–30 while output rose strongly.

The need for income and the growth of output

The peasants met falling prices and rising debts by increasing output, thus keeping up their gross incomes so as to be able to service their debts and more or less maintain their consumption. This response was linked to the fact that family labour was dominant. The reduction in hired help had begun before the turn of the century, and by the end of the 1920s as much as 84 per cent of the man-hours worked in the industry were provided by family members. By working harder, more could be produced without increasing wage costs. Besides, the prices of artificial fertilizer and feed concentrate fell more than did the prices of agricultural products. Thus the farmers tried to work their way out of the crisis – by producing more – but in so doing created new problems.

The war had strengthened the ideology of self-sufficiency. Norway imported a lot of grain, and during the war a corn monopoly was introduced as a temporary measure. However, after a break of two years it was made permanent from 1929 through the establishment of the Norwegian Grain Corporation. In the 1920s Norwegian harvested food grains received a subsidy. This was recouped by a charge placed on the total sales of food grains and flour throughout the country. In addition, the farmers also received a payment for the food grain they produced and consumed in their own households. But subsidies were not big enough to make much difference to the amount of grain produced; the peasants' main source of income was and continued to be from animal products, which were in effect protected through an increased tariff in the 1920s. Prices in Norway lay therefore above prices on world markets.

Towards the end of the 1920s milk production had increased to such an extent that the domestic market for cheese and butter became too small. So long as free competition prevailed, such an over-production would force domestic prices down to the level of export prices, i.e. the world market prices after freight costs. Tariff protection would, in other words, no longer have any effect.

Competition at home threatened to equalize the price difference between milk for direct consumption and milk used for producing butter and cheese. More and more producers could now reach the fresh milk market, thanks to better transport facilities, including lorries. The trend was quite clear. Increased supply drove the price down, with the inevitable consequence that it approached the same low price for milk intended for butter production. This meant hefty losses for those peasants who had previously dominated the fresh milk market. Losses would be greater still if the price differential disappeared altogether and if, in addition, the butter price fell to that obtainable on the world market. It was obvious: competition between the farmers must be abandoned and the market regulated.

The Great Depression

The slump in the world economy, which began in the United States in 1929, soon spread to Europe. The effects were felt in Norway as early as 1930 in important export trades, especially shipping, though it was not until the following year that the full force was felt. In the worst year, 1931, GNP fell 8 per cent relative to 1930. There then followed a period of weak growth until the 1930 level of GNP was again reached in 1934. From then to the outbreak of the Second World War the economy grew strongly.

Looked at in terms of national economic measures (GNP, etc.), the depression was less profound in Norway than in most other countries. The downturn was shorter and the upturn came earlier. The greatest impact was on investment. The fall in prices was less in Norway than in most industrialized countries, and from 1931 the price level began a weak rise. Parity, which had claimed such sacrifices, was given up after three years or so (1931) and, after a devaluation of approximately 10 per cent, the *krone* was tied to the British pound in 1933.

There are grounds for suggesting that the new stability in the price level was one reason for a lower level of conflict at the work-place. Apart from the major strike of 1931, fewer working days were lost in the 1930s than in the 1920s. Stable prices eased the rapprochement between employers and employees. This received formal expression in the Basic Agreement of 1935. Peace in the labour market also helped to turn the economy from depression to cautious growth.

The crisis of the 1930s had its greatest impact on unemployment. In 1933, one in three trade unionists were out of work and total unemployment has been reckoned by most people to have been in excess of 100,000. The details of the employment position (e.g. how many were on short time) is not known. In addition, there are grounds for reckoning on a certain amount of under-employment in the primary industries because there were fewer possibilities of combining agriculture with other sources of income.

Unemployment fell, but remained high even after economic growth became stronger in the second half of the 1930s. Growth created many new work-places, but not enough. The rise in the population of working age was very marked in the 1930s and now no relief was provided by emigration. Thus the explanation for unemployment in the good times too must be sought principally in demographic conditions.

Out of the crisis

Already in 1932 output began to rise slowly and from 1935 to the German occupation growth was considerable. Both the turn-round and the subsequent strengthening of growth owed much to the development of industries geared to the domestic market. The strength of the crisis brought about a transformation. A series of firms were literally 'forced' to create new products and many newly established concerns staked their fortunes on goods that appealed to the larger consumer groups. Furniture, cycles and electrical goods such as hotplates, stoves, lamps, irons and radios were some of the products giving the new industry possibilities for growth. More frequent changes of fashion stimulated the textile and clothing industries and there was a sharp rise in the number of new firms in some of the foodstuffs industries.

Domestic industry benefited both from increased tariff protection and from the devaluation of the early 1930s. Many new firms were established in the rural districts, and in Sunnmøre they did especially well, above all in the furniture industry. The new location pattern was a product of several factors: the development of small electric motors made it easier to establish small industries in rural areas with electric power; wages were lower in the countryside than in the towns, or, in the former, there was no troublesome labour movement; capital requirements were modest and there are many examples of workers investing in their own place of work. Finally, costs could be kept down to a level that helped contribute to the creation of goods for a mass market.

The campaign for the purchase of Norwegian goods was probably another source of protection. Vigorous marketing, through the use of advertising, made its break-through and helped channel demand towards the new products, so reinforcing the shift in consumption. The pattern had something in common with the one that characterized the United States during the boom of the 1920s. The widespread extension of electricity supplies down to the beginning of the 1920s helped both to create the conditions for the establishment of new businesses and to stimulate the demand for electrical goods.

A necessary condition for this development was buying power on the part of a comparatively wide range of consumers. Pay in real terms rose for those in work. It is more difficult to be certain about real income because short-time working and short-term layoffs were not unusual. If we take it that annual income rose, then ordinary working people had more to spend. Greater buying power amongst those with little inclination to save stimulated demand. An additional explanation of the increased demand for durable consumer goods lay in the reduction in household size from the end of the 1920s onwards. A lower burden of dependency could help shift buying power from life's necessities to items for a decent living. Finally, demand was shifted from imports to home-produced goods.

It is difficult to evaluate the role played by the public sector in the revival and growth of the economy in the 1930s. Stimulating the economy by expanding credit – the British economist Keynes' solution – was not taken up. Quite the contrary, there were budget surpluses and the national debt was reduced. It is true, however, that the public sector grew faster than GNP, especially in the second half of the 1930s.

Taxes and other forms of state income increased considerably. It is difficult to measure the distributive effect of the tax system, or of public investment and consumption, but it would, at the very least, be difficult to deny that changes in the profile of income and expenditure influenced effective demand in the economy.

Direct transfers from the public to the private sector were modest, but scarcely unimportant. In many rural districts, for instance, subsidies for clearing new land were an important cash supplement. But the major transfers of the 1930s took place without entering local or national government balance sheets.

The regulation of the market and competition

Agriculture, forestry and fishing were hard hit by the crisis. The effects were exacerbated because these activities were often operated in tandem. The bulk of the local authorities hit by the crisis were situated in Norway's more remote districts and were economically dependent on primary industry. Because the crisis struck key groups in bourgeois society, and because one of the props of the public administration apparatus, the local authorities, threatened to give way, the state had to do something to ameliorate the crisis. The main problem was to create profitable production.

The threat of a price collapse in the milk sector forced the peasants into organized action. Their strategy was to maintain separate markets with different prices. Fresh milk should have a high price because its consumption was little affected by price changes, but that meant a reduction in supply. In the same way, the cheese price could be raised by regulating production and thereby supply. The rest of the milk was to go to butter production. The system presupposed a complete control of supply and price equalization so that all producers got approximately the same price no matter what the milk was used for. Further, the losses sustained by the regulated export of butter surpluses at low prices was to be shared out amongst all producers.

The regulation of the market was unworkable without legal protection. In 1930 a modest sales tax on a number of agricultural products was introduced to finance organized marketing. The peasants were themselves able to build up the regional milk cooperatives that would be responsible for market regulation and the equalization of prices.

Varig glede og hygge
med
NORSK RIKSKRINGKASTINGS
FOLKE-MOTTAKER

Kr. 79.—
+ st. kr. 1.-

Rimelig
avbetaling

SELGES OGSÅ I SAMVIRKELAGENE

In 1925 a radio receiver cost 200 kroner. The state-sponsored 'people's receiver' of 1936 cost less than half that figure. Some 35,000 sets were sold. Price reductions, hire purchase and advertising campaigns served to channel demand towards new products like this.

But they had to have legal authority to impose an equalization tax on those producers who supplied the customer direct. This they obtained in 1931. In this way the direct suppliers were not able to undermine the milk cooperatives by keeping prices down. The equalization tax eliminated the free riders in the peasants' own ranks.

The regulation of exports was an increasing problem because of trade restrictions in the form of higher customs barriers and import quotas. The problem of over-supply was solved in 1931 by forcing the margarine manufacturers to blend their product with butter. All the surplus butter had to be bought by the margarine producers at above the world market price, thus creating not only a better market but an almost unlimited one. The blending of butter with margarine led to higher prices for the latter and so stimulated the consumption of ordinary butter. This created the basis for a further growth in output, which, in fact, occurred.

The regulatory system could not prevent a fall in the average price of milk – a consequence of the sharp rise in butter production, which paid the lowest price. By a tax on margarine (introduced in 1934) that rose inversely to the amount of butter blended with the margarine, extra funds were created to help equalize the prices between the different milk cooperatives. This system prevented a price collapse and created the opportunity for a rise in output, which together increased the income of the peasants. The regulatory system was extended to the sale of meat and pork. A major cooperatively based processing and sales agency made it possible to transfer a proportion of the middle man's profits to the production arm of the industry.

The marketing regulations evened out differences within the agricultural sector, but they also involved a major indirect transfer of income from the consumers to the peasants, through higher prices for agricultural products and margarine. To do this directly, and to the same extent, via the tax system would have been a political impossibility.

This crisis management was based on close cooperation between the state and industrial organizations, with the state transferring a number of activities of an official cum legal character to these organizations. The crises of the inter-war years created the system within which post-war agricultural policy developed. Taking into account direct subsidies for the reclamation of land, the purchase of artificial fertilizer and interest payments, together with various other initiatives designed to reduce the burden of debt, the conclusion must be that the policies created to overcome the crisis made a considerable contribution to increasing the incomes of the agricultural population.

A similar policy was pursued with regard to the fishing industry, but here the problems were more complicated because the industry was wholly dependent on the international market. Two approaches were attempted. First, the goal was to get the most out of the international market by creating a cartel for the export of dried fish *(klippfisk)*. Second, by organizing marketing boards for the sale of herring (introduced in 1928–29) the goal was to maintain separate markets with different prices for fresh herring, salted herring and manufactured products, while at the same time getting the most out of the markets offering high prices through restricting supplies to them. The principle was also applied to direct sales of white fish, but the law dealing with unprocessed fish generally, although passed in 1938, did not come into effect until after the war. The state had to give legal protection to the sales organizations. The regulation of the fishing industry was less effective than that of agriculture because the markets for fish were not controlled so easily. In any case, the arrangements for sales in the cod sector came too late to stabilize the economy of the fishing population of north Norway in the 1930s.

Manufacturing industry too was moving away from free competition. Whereas transformation and rationalization were offensive strategies in the campaign for market share, regulation of competition was the defensive one, since it involved a more or less strict sharing out of existing markets. Least effective were agreements on common prices, a price cartel. Sharing the market geographically and setting quotas for members' output – often with a joint sales organization – were much more successful strategies. There was no shortage of ideas about what to do.

Cartels usually have a conservative impact on the structure of firms, hindering change and leading, as a rule, to more expensive products by allowing the least effective production units to survive. In many cases, too, cartels put an end to the creation of new firms in the particular lines of business in which they operate.

The control of competition through the formation of cartels was very widespread in the capitalist world of the inter-war years. Norwegian exporters joined cartels via their contacts with international concerns, and Norwegian shipowners were involved in attempts to regulate the tanker market in the 1930s. The Bank of Norway tried to press individual branches of industry into so-called voluntary agreements, but several were forced into cartelization through special laws or under the guise of the trust law.

The Trust Control came, in the 1930s, to take a more sympathetic view of market regulation. Regard for the consumers and low prices gave way to the wishes of the producers, who wanted prices they could live with. Legislation was prepared that would give the authorities wide-ranging powers to require cooperation between producers and further structural rationalization in economic life. The initiative came to nothing but it was symptomatic of a paradigm shift. Order and planning were the new buzz words. Social benefit challenged profit as the ultimate goal of economic activity.

Patterns of development

The upturn in the second half of the 1930s was clearly different from the good years at the end of the 1920s. It is true that there were better times for shipping, and the modernization of the fleet was marked in the years just before the war. But the contribution of the export industries to growth was diminished. They were hampered by restrictions in international trade, customs barriers, quotas and bilateral agreements. The Norwegian economy became more insular.

Home industries, including building and construction, came to play a much more important role. The growth of both employment and output was much stronger here than in the export-oriented industries. This was to become a characteristic feature of Norwegian economic life in the years ahead. The small business element grew in importance and the average concern came to employ far fewer than in 1920. Manufacturing industry in the rural districts was clearly moving forward.

Agricultural output increased under cover of its strongly defended borders, but there were few changes in working methods and mechanization advanced much more slowly. Individual districts specialized in fruit and vegetables. Fur farming was a growth industry in others. There were major fluctuations in the fishing industry. Productivity increased in the herring fisheries but stood still in the cod sector. However it was low prices that created the greatest problem for the cod fishermen. Technological advance was modest and in parts of the industry there was a reversion to a more primitive level of fishing. One has to go a long way back in history to find so many men fishing with hand lines from open boats as there were off Lofoten when the number of participants peaked in the 1930s.

The picture is just as mixed when we come to look at material living standards in the inter-war years. In some areas progress was clear. For most groups of wage earners, real wages clearly increased. The working week was reduced considerably and large groups of workers had won the right to holidays with pay. There was also progress in housing standards and clothing.

On the other hand, real wages for agricultural and forestry workers fell and the army of unemployed did not share in the growing prosperity. And there were bad times for certain groups of fishermen. Worst of all were conditions for the cod fishermen of north Norway, but also in the rest of the coastal areas it was a matter of maintaining the status quo or barely that. There were major problems too in the forest areas. Differences between the regions of Norway became much greater. Rural Norway, or at least large parts of it, lagged behind. The division of farms and the creation of pioneer settlements increased the number of small-holdings that could not, on their own, provide a livelihood. Fewer opportunities for paid work and poor earnings from the fisheries reduced incomes from secondary employment. The large rise in the number of people in the working age groups, together with the fact that manufacturing industry and services failed to create enough new workplaces, led to many more people in the rural districts being wholly or partly without employment. They were pent up now – but ready to fly.

21
Crisis and war: from discord to unity

The political history of the inter-war years has a quality that distinguishes it clearly from the period before and the period after. In the years before 1918 and for much of the period after 1945, the power of government was based on solid one-party majorities in the Storting, whereas the inter-war years witnessed a parliamentary system based on minority parties, together with frequent changes of government. Before the First World War and after the Second, public opinion generally supported Norway's political institutions. In the inter-war years, on the other hand, the political system and traditional norms of political behaviour were challenged by powerful organized forces on the left and right of the social and political spectrum. The period was also marked by shifts and major conflicts within the party system. Amongst the non-socialist parties, the Conservatives replaced the Liberals as the largest party, forming the government three times in the period 1920–28. At the same time, the Labour Party emerged as a new power. In other words, the lines of Norwegian politics were redrawn. The system was also fragmented by the establishment of a number of new parties. Some were but one-day wonders. Others, such as the Agrarian Party formed in 1920, Norway's Communist Party (1923) and the Christian People's Party (1933), became permanent features of the system. Political life took place against a background of conflicts and upsets in the economy and the social system.

It is possible to divide the political history of the inter-war years into three sections, each with its own special characteristics. The first, 1918–27, is marked by a radical labour movement raising the flag of revolution for the first time on Norwegian soil. The threat was regarded as serious, but it was not serious enough to overshadow the Conservative–Liberal dichotomy that had dominated political life since the 1880s. The second period, 1927–35, which began with the Labour

Party's electoral breakthrough, is marked by a new alignment, with the labour movement on one side and the non-socialist parties on the other. The third period began in 1935 with an agreement, brought on by the economic crisis, between the Labour Party and the Agrarian Party. With the latter's support the Labour Party leader, Nygaardsvold, was able to form a government. With the formation of Nygaardsvold's government a period began that was to be dominated by a Labour Party that had come to terms with the existing social and political system; there was a new stability at government level, and a reduction in tension and division between the Norwegian political parties.

A revolution of the masses?

The key event marking the start of the political history of the inter-war years was a famous resolution carried by a majority at the Labour Party's annual conference in 1918. In this resolution the party reserved the right to lead a revolution of the masses, even if it did not have a majority in the Storting. The resolution was the result of a radicalization of the party, caused in part by difficult living conditions during the last phase of the First World War. The major source of inspiration for the resolution came from Russia's victorious Bolsheviks. Ideologically it represented a coming together of two traditions: a Marxist one, which had characterized the Labour Party's youth movement, and a syndicalist one, which in 1913 took on an organizational form as *'Den norske fagopposisjon'* (a faction within both the political and trade union wings of the Labour Party) inspired and led by Martin Tranmæl.

The threat of revolution forced the non-socialist parties, and bourgeois society as a whole, to consider how best to avert it. The result was two strategies that complemented each other. One was defensive. In part it aimed at winning time to carry out a comprehensive review of, among other things, the demand for the nationalization of parts of the economy. In part it made concessions, e.g. the new electoral law of 1919, which brought the number of parliamentary seats won by the Labour Party more in line with the number of votes cast for it; and the NAF (the Norwegian Employers' Confederation) was willing to go a long way towards meeting the demands of the trade unions during wage negotiations. In 1919 the Storting, unanimously, gave legal backing to the 8-hour working day. The second strategy was more

During the union with Danmark, the Norwegian language was supplanted for administrative and literary purposes by the very closely related Danish language. The upper classes in the cities even spoke Danish, but with a Norwegian accent. In rural areas, however, the old language survived in a variety of different dialects. During the nationalist movement in the 19th century, the self-educated genius Ivar Aasen (1813–1896) created a national standard for written Norwegian rooted in Norwegian dialects. The supporters of this standard (called landsmål, *later* nynorsk*) demanded that it replace Danish as the Norwegian national language (called* riksmål, *later* bokmål*). The Conservative Party (*Høyre*) was associated with bokmål, while the Liberal Party (*Venstre*) was associated with* nynorsk. *Since 1885, the two languages have had an equal official status. For the past decades, the Norwegian linguistic conflict has decreased, mostly because the two languages have become more similar. This cartoon from 1919 illustrates the significant role of the language problem in Norwegian politics, even at a time marked by the impending threat of a socialist revolution.*

aggressive and looked to the use of force should the worst come to the worst. It included, amongst other things, surveillance and infiltration, secret military planning and the systematic preparation of measures designed to take the sting out of mass strike action.

The effectiveness of these measures was never tested, since it was clear already in 1920 that the labour movement's revolutionary fervour was beginning to ebb away. The economic recession hit both the trade union and the political wing of the movement. Trade union membership had risen to 144,000 by 1919. At the same time, the trade unions forced through an agreement on collective wage bargaining and the legal protection of the right to strike. For Tranmæl and his 'revolutionary programme', however, the trade unions had another task, that of storm-troopers in the war to overturn society and create a socialist state. But the economic crisis of 1920 and the depression that followed defeated this goal. In the course of four years, membership was reduced by 60,000. At the same time, the political wing of the movement split apart, principally as a result of relations with Moscow. The Labour Party joined the Moscow-dominated Third International (the Comintern) in 1921 and as a result the moderate wing of the party broke away and formed the Norwegian Social Democratic Labour Party. When the Labour Party resigned from the Comintern two years later, the left

'Now then, how far have you come with the Revolution in Norway?'
'For the moment we're fighting about how to spell it!'

wing split off to form the Norwegian Communist Party. The election of 1924 thus witnessed three labour parties fighting each other.

Fearing revolution, the Conservative and the Liberal parties cooperated over preventative measures. When the threat diminished, the two parties reverted to their traditional dominance of Norwegian politics – but for a brief period only. To some extent the old battles continued to be fought. Even as late as 1919, when the fear of revolution was at its height, the president of the Storting, Tveiten, a Liberal, asserted that 'Temperance and the Language' were 'the two most important planks in the party's platform'. The language question, which had already been brought into Norwegian politics before the turn of the century, reappeared as a result of the controversial orthographic reform of 1917. As for the liquor question, it caused more conflict than any other in Norwegian politics during the first half of the 1920s. A temporary prohibition on alcohol sales (with the exception of beer and table wine) was brought in during the war and made permanent after a referendum in 1919. The prohibition of fortified wines lasted until 1923, while that on spirits lasted until a referendum in 1926.

The alcohol question not only involved ideological and socio-political antipathies. It also affected economic policy and national finances. Reprisals from the wine-producing countries hit sections of Norwegian trade and industry, especially shipping and the cod fishermen of north Norway. The treasury was hit by the loss of taxes on alcohol.

The decline of the centre party, the Liberals, was to some extent an expression of the increasing polarization of Norwegian society. Its support of prohibition accelerated the process, while the Conservative Party, which opposed prohibition, benefited. The Liberals also had to bear other burdens. During the first half of the 1920s the Conservatives focused on the need to restore the country's finances. And since the Liberals had had a majority in the Storting and had formed the government during the First World War when the foundations of the crisis had been laid, the Conservatives had no difficulty in allocating responsibility for it.

The national financial crisis and the debt problems of the local authorities were caught up in the difficulties over parity, all of which added to the complications surrounding relations between the non-socialist parties The political wing of the Norwegian Farmers' Union, the Agrarian Party, was established in 1920, the result of a build-up of dissatisfaction at the way the Conservatives and Liberals had looked after the interests of agriculture. The new party made a breakthrough as early as the election of 1921, with 17 out of 150 seats. This hit mainly the Liberals, while the Conservatives hoped for a new right-wing coalition partner. But the rise of the *krone*, which hit agriculture hard, eliminated the dream of a permanent understanding. Instead, a gap opened between the Agrarian Party on the one hand and the Conservatives and Liberals, who both supported the parity option, on the other.

A Labour Party majority?

The specifically Norwegian depression, a direct result of the return to parity, provides much of the explanation for the Labour Party's triumph of 1927. Earlier that year, the Social Democratic Party, which had split off from Labour in 1921, returned to the fold. Together they won 59 of the 150 seats, as against 32 three years earlier. In addition to this, the Communist Party won 3 seats. There was a real possibility that, at the next election, the political wing of the labour movement would win a majority in the Storting.

The Conservative Party was hardest hit by the defeat of the non-socialist parties. It had had to carry the burden of government during a difficult period and lost the battle over its top priority, the reconstruction of the national debt and the restoration of the nation's finances. The ending of prohibition also resulted in many voters who had supported the Conservative Party because of its anti-prohibition stance leaving the party. The election marks a turning point in the political history of the inter-war years. After 1927 the traditional Conservative–Liberal division gave way to a division between the socialist and the non-socialist parties. Immediately after 1918, bourgeois society had braced itself to meet mass revolution with force. The possibility of this had diminished. Now the threat was of a society turned socialist by legal means. Such a threat could be averted not by calling in the police or using military force, but by the mobilization of political resources, by arguments and by appeals to the electorate.

The highest priority then for the non-socialist parties was to stop the socialists gaining a majority at the elections for the Storting in 1930. In their campaigns, and particularly that of the Conservatives, the Labour Party was branded as revolutionary and, in spite of having withdrawn from the Comintern in 1923, one that was still loyal to Moscow. This appeal in itself indicated that the non-socialist parties were playing down their own internal differences. This was most noticeable in the reduction of hostilities between the Conservatives and the Liberals. In the case of the latter, this was expressed in the support the party gave to a 1930 proposal for electoral pacts. This arrangement allowed parties to support each other during a parliamentary election by adding their votes together and then sharing the seats pro rata.

The rapprochement of the Conservatives and the Liberals was made easier by the fact that issues that had previously divided them either had disappeared from the political scene or were of less importance. This applied, among other things, to the language and alcohol questions, especially, in the case of the latter, after the ending of prohibition. The Conservatives made the strongest appeal for an anti-socialist alliance. As late as 1927 the party had competed with the Liberals for governmental power. After 1927 it came to terms with the fact that it must support minority governments of the Liberals and the Agrarian Party until its ultimate goal, a non-socialist coalition government, could be achieved.

The election campaign of 1930 was one of the most vehement ever conducted in Norway and election day itself was marked by a massive mobilization of the vote for the non-socialist parties. The Labour Party lost 12 of the 59 seats it had won in 1927, while the Communists were swept out of the Storting altogether. The greatest success was enjoyed by the Conservative Party, which increased its total of seats from 31 to 44.

The Labour Party's defeat was caused not by a loss of votes but because the opposition managed to mobilize all its supporters. At 77.6 per cent, turnout was the highest since the introduction of the universal franchise for men. Especially noticeable was the female turnout, which was 10 per cent higher than its previous peak of 64 per cent in 1924. One must assume that the Conservatives' appeal to such values as the home, the family and Christianity, set against the Labour Party's internationalism and alleged atheism, had been particularly effective in bringing out the female vote.

That the differences of opinion between the non-socialist parties began to reassert themselves, especially between the Agrarian Party and the Liberals, after 1930, as compared with the previous parliamentary session, owes something to the fact that Labour's crushing defeat reduced the fear of a socialist transformation of society. As a result, the non-socialist parties had again gained a greater opportunity to argue amongst themselves. Added to this, the economic crisis of the 1930s drove new wedges between the parties. Measures designed to limit production and regulate sales were among the ways of countering the crisis to which non-socialist politicians could, for the most part, agree to give legal backing. Nevertheless, the demand for direct intervention in the economy by the state in the form of subsidies and grants to encourage employment grew steadily stronger, first in the

Labour Party, then in the Agrarian Party. For most Liberal and Conservative politicians, however, it appeared that the, as yet, unsolved national financial crisis set limits to the state's ability to help, even though it was realised that subsidies and increased public consumption would act as a stimulus to economic activity. The Liberals had the greatest reservations. The Conservatives' reservations lessened after a while, principally because their main aim was to maintain a non-socialist government. They, therefore, felt the strongest need to accommodate the views of the Agrarian Party. But the Conservatives' attempts to mediate between the Agrarian Party and the Liberals were in vain. On 15 March 1935, Johan Nygaardsvold formed a Labour Party government, having reached an understanding with the Agrarian Party on state grants to meet the crisis.

A crisis agreement and a relaxation of tension

Labour's formation of a government came as a shock to bourgeois society, but it was soon apparent to everybody that the new party of government had, in major areas, little in common with the party that in 1918 had proclaimed mass revolution and internationalism. This new orientation became obvious when, for example, the party joined in the celebrations of Norway's National Day on 17 May bearing national flags and banners. In the 1920s the Labour Party's internationalism had appeared highly provocative and had given national values a more conservative colour.

The Labour Party's decision to rally round the symbols of nationalism strengthened national integration and re-established the traditional link between nationalism and political radicalism. In its revolutionary phase during the 1920s, the Labour Party had tried to set up its own cultural organizations and to create a labour athletic association. These attempts were abandoned towards the end of the 1930s. Already, in its opening statement, the government made quite clear that it would give priority to solving the problems arising from the economic crisis, and that it would not challenge central bourgeois values such as a stable currency and sound finances.

The question of the content and timing of the Labour Party's transformation, from a revolutionary to a 'reformist' and national (as opposed to international) party, is one of the most controversial in the history of the Norwegian labour movement. Some would have it that a gradual adaptation to bourgeois society began immediately after the party resigned from the Comintern in 1923. Stages along the way included the reunification of the party in 1927 and Hornsrud's brief Labour Party government the year after, a government that did not have a majority in the Storting and that, therefore, indicated that the party had given up its traditional opposition towards taking power without a parliamentary majority. That the party took a step to the left before the election of 1930 by omitting from the manifesto the declaration that a popular majority would be a precondition for a socialist transformation of society, represented in this context only a temporary deviation from an obvious trend.

Others contend that the shift took place in 1933, when the party went to the poll under the slogan 'Work for all' – a return to practical, pragmatic reform policies, which gave the party a breakthrough in the rural areas and as many as 69 out of 150 seats in the Storting. The sudden reversal was, if one accepts this line of argument, the product of people's expectations of an active campaign against the crisis and the party leadership's fear of fascism and Nazism, which, in Italy and Germany, had demonstrated their ability to mobilize the working masses during an economic crisis. Those who support this line of reasoning point to the reunification platform of 1927, which still gave room for the basic elements of the revolutionary Marxism of class conflict, and draw attention to the deep divisions between the classes that emerged in the strikes and lockouts of the 1920s, arising from the employers' wish to force wages down to a level that matched a deflationary situation. However that may be, it is clear, with hindsight, that the Labour Party's revolutionary orientation represented only a brief episode in its more than 100-year history.

The party's strategy for its fight against the crisis was formulated in Colbjørnsen and Sømme's 'Three-Year Plan' of 1933 and the party's own emergency programme of the following year. The main feature of the emergency programme was a considerable increase in funds for public works such as road and railway building and land colonisation. The agreement on crisis measures reached with the Agrarian Party in 1935 involved policies of particular interest to it, such as grants for agriculture and forestry as well as for the fishing industry. These exceptional grants were to be funded by increased national taxes including a new sales tax.

In principle, these measures represented little that was new, when seen in the light of the policies of the non-socialist parties. The difference lay in the size of the appropriations. In other words, it was a matter of degree. All in all, the measures indicated a marked growth in the state's ambitions in regard to the running of the economy, but even so in 1935 this represented no question of principle. State involvement in this direction had long been on the increase.

The precedent had been created during the First World War when businesses had been subject to regulation by the state. In the 1920s a new offensive had been undertaken. A temporary state-run grain monopoly introduced during the war was made permanent in 1928. From the beginning of the 1930s the Storting gave legal authority for a series of measures that forced businessmen to collaborate on both production and sales. A basis for solving the debt crisis of the local authorities and of agriculture took legal form in 1928 and 1934. This made it possible for the state to be involved in the negotiations over, and the writing down of, debts. The idea that, before 1935, bourgeois politicians were incapable of dealing with economic problems is a myth. That the Labour Party had higher ambitions in this regard is, however, another matter. After 1935 there followed a series of new state initiatives. The government also tried to secure a general authority to enforce cartelization, but in this it was stopped by the non-socialist majority in the Storting.

The second half of the 1930s was marked by strong economic growth, which also brought benefits to the majority of the population. Was this improvement the result of government policy, or of the economic upturn that had begun before 1935? Economists tend to support the latter explanation, but this does not conflict with the view that the policies that were carried out did affect the sharing out of the new prosperity, e.g. in the form of considerable cash payments to exposed groups such as smallholders and fishermen.

At the same time, a wave of social reforms increased the well-being of the population. The financial crisis of the 1920s slowed social reform, at both the national and the local level. The formation of Nygaardsvold's government released new initiatives. The sickness insurance measure of 1909 was extended to cover new groups. A law embracing benefits for the disabled came in 1936. A compulsory scheme for unemployment insurance was established in 1938. The law on worker protection was revised so as to include new categories of workers. The question of old-age pensions had been on the political agenda since the 1890s. A solution seemed to have been found at the end of the First World War, but a law of 1923 was never put into operation. In 1936, however, this most important of all insurance questions was finally resolved. After this series of reforms, which came into being within a short period, Norway was one of the leading countries in the social policy area. Though no doubt there were conflicts between different interests and of an ideological nature over peripheral elements in the benefits system, the reforms enjoyed an overwhelming consensus, which helped strengthen the impression of a relaxation in tension between the parties.

Nygaardsvold's government continued as a minority one after the elections of 1936. That it, in contrast to the other inter-war minority governments, nevertheless continued to exist was due to the fact that down to 1937 it was supported by the Agrarian Party and later, on all major matters, by the Liberals. Even the Conservatives gradually came to realize that no alternative to the existing government was to be found. This parliamentary support from the non-socialist parties is itself evidence of the government's moderate line. Not only did the socialist slogans of the 1920s cease, so too did earlier indications that the plans to meet the crisis would involve budgeting for a deficit and increased borrowing, as recommended by the British economist John Maynard Keynes. The growth in public expenditure after 1935 gave no indication that the norms of orthodox finance had been set aside.

The pragmatism and moderation of the Labour Party made an important contribution to the reduction of political tension that characterized the second half of the 1930s. The Basic Agreement of 1935 between NAF (Norwegian Employers' Confederation) and AFL (National Federation of Labour), described as the 'Industry's Constitution', contained an overarching system for solving conflicts. It showed that, as in the political arena, so at the workplace, levels of tension had eased. Moderation was on the increase too within the non-socialist camp. The clearest expression of this was the defeat of the right-wing 'activists' at the beginning of the 1930s. The threat of revolution and the state financial crisis sparked off a demand in the 1920s for a non-socialist coalition as a prerequisite for a more energetic style of government. The demand was taken up in circles where extra-parliamentary political tendencies, even the demand for a 'strong man', were in evidence. The right-wing activists amongst, for instance, *Frisinnede*

Venstre and the Fatherland League raised the demand for tougher treatment of the labour movement. Implicit in this demand lay a criticism of the Conservatives for being weak and irresolute. The activists then posed a particular threat to the Conservatives. But they were crushed at the beginning of the 1930s, not least owing to the Conservative Party leader C.J. Hambro's implacable attitude. Vidkun Quisling's National Socialist Party, formed in 1933, was no more than an echo of the much stronger activism of the 1920s. The party got only 2.2 and 1.8 per cent of the votes at the elections of 1933 and 1936, respectively, was never represented in the Storting, and was able to attract a certain amount of public attention only because of its bizarre political style.

The basis for the formation of Nygaardsvold's government was the economic crisis and the resulting problems. From 1937 onwards these issues became less important. Instead, questions of defence and security came to the fore of Norwegian politics. This takes our account to the greatest catastrophe to have struck Norway in recent times. It was fortunate indeed that its people were able to meet this catastrophe far more united than they had been 10 years earlier.

Norway's war

During the Crimean War and the conflict between Denmark and Germany in the middle of the nineteenth century, Norway and Sweden had been drawn closer to the area of European tension. Otherwise the country had remained on the periphery of power politics ever since 1814. Suddenly, however, at the turn of the year 1939–40 Norway, which previously had been all but invisible so far as Europe's military strategic history was concerned, became the focus of the strategic deliberations of the four warring great powers: Great Britain, France, Russia and Germany. During the Winter War in Finland, Norway was perceived as a political staging post for action by the western powers against Russia. With the ending of the Winter War in March 1940, Norway was left as a goal for Germany's strategic ambitions at sea. The occupation of Norway following the invasion of 9 April 1940 was not the result of a German victory in a race with the western powers. Rather the German attack was, in strategic terms, an achievement of such a high order, and involved such daring, that it was considered unthinkable – even from the point of view of the western allies. With a sudden, coordinated movement, which, with the exception of the sinking of the cruiser Blücher in the Straits of Drøbak (in the Oslofjord), was carried out without significant losses, every major Norwegian harbour from Oslo to Narvik was brought under German control in the early hours of 9 April.

The German invasion plans had also sought to paralyse Norway's political life by getting hold of the king and the government. These plans were frustrated by the sinking of the Blücher. As a result, the king, the government and the president of the Storting, C.J. Hambro, got extra time to discuss matters. The outcome was a decision to carry on the fight. In a meeting at Elverum, the Storting empowered the government to 'take care of the kingdom's interests'. Thus a constitutional basis was created for exercising the powers of government in extraordinary circumstances. The authority given at Elverum was not formally voted upon, but its legitimacy has never been doubted, either then or subsequently, by any official Norwegian authority.

The decision to fight the Germans was taken in a situation that, from a military point of view, must have appeared all but hopeless. Confusion reigned. The country's most important harbours were in enemy hands. Many arsenals had been lost. Mobilization, on the basis of those remaining, was slow to start. Much of the navy was out of action with the loss in the early hours of 9 April of the ancient iron-clads, *Norge* and *Eidsvoll*, in the harbour of Narvik. Norway's defensive forces were also in poor shape. The soldiers who were fighting in 1940 had between 48 and 84 days' basic training and virtually no modern equipment. The navy had barely been updated since the turn of the century.

Defence questions had been a peripheral issue in Norwegian politics throughout almost the entire nineteenth century. Nevertheless a (by Norwegian standards) not inconsiderable rearmament had taken place in the 1890s, as a result of the dispute with Sweden over the union. This high level of preparedness continued after 1905, which meant that the country was able to mount an effective defence of its neutrality during the First World War.

Immediately after 1918, however, with no enemy threat in sight, a rapid disarmament took place. A minimum level was ratified politically through the defensive measures of 1927 and 1933. In the latter, which Otto Ruge, Commander-in-Chief in 1940, had been involved in designing, arrangements were made for raising the level of prepared-

The cruiser 'Blücher', which was sunk on the morning of 9 April 1940 by artillery and torpedo fire from the Oscarsborg fort in the Drøbak Sound. It was one of Germany's newest and largest cruisers. On board were the staff and divisions that were intended to occupy Oslo. The sinking of the 'Blücher' made possible the escape of Norway's political authorities.

ness – partly by a gradual increase in the training period and partly by extraordinary measures to be taken when a 'far-sighted foreign affairs leadership' warned of a new threat.

None of these arrangements were completely successful. As the international situation became more critical from the middle of the 1930s, questions of defence became more and more important in Norwegian politics and were the main reason why the stability of the government after 1937 came to depend upon an understanding between the Labour Party and the Liberals. These two parties stood for the least possible expenditure on defence. The Agrarian Party favoured a little more and the Conservatives considerably more. No political party, however, proposed a budget that came anywhere near the level deemed necessary by the military experts. The extraordinary appropriations granted in 1937 and after came too late to have any particular effect. Behind the complex pattern of reasons for these attitudes looms not only the Labour Party's traditional scepticism with regard to the military, but also a general psychological block created by the economic and financial crises of the inter-war years.

In spite of the fact that some assistance from British forces arrived by the middle of April, the campaign in southern Norway was over by the beginning of May. In north Norway, on the other hand, Norwegian, French, British and Polish units, after being initially repulsed, were gradually able to take the offensive and they recaptured Narvik on 28 May. Here the campaign did not end until 7 June and then only because allied forces were withdrawn in order to be used against the German offensive in France. In this situation the government was confronted with far-reaching decisions. There were four possibilities: total surrender; to continue the fight without the troops of the western allies; the setting up of a neutral zone around Narvik under Swedish occupation, which should divide German-occupied Norway from a free Norway; and finally the option that was chosen – to continue the war from outside the country's boundaries. The surrender terms agreed in Trondheim on 10 June applied only to the forces on Norwegian soil.

From a neutral to an ally

The engagement of the western powers in the war in Norway was not due to prior agreements, but a result of spontaneous decisions on both sides. Not until it continued the war from British soil did the Norwegian government bind the country's destiny to that of the western allies. This decision involved a break with Norway's time-honoured foreign policy.

Right from the 1880s Norway's politicians supported a policy of neutrality for the united kingdoms of Norway and Sweden. When Norway gained full control of its foreign policy in 1905, neutrality was raised to the level of a dogma. Since 1855 Norway and Sweden had had guarantees of protection from the western powers, Great Britain and France, because of a treaty signed in November of that year. This protection was replaced in 1907 by an agreement whereby France, Great Britain, Germany and Russia guaranteed Norway's territorial integrity. This agreement did not, however, hinder Norway's continued neutrality. By joining the League of Nations in 1920 Norway deviated from its traditional line. But when Norway in 1938 reserved its position *vis-à-vis* the League's decisions on sanctions, the country's traditional neutrality was reinstated.

Since 1905, however, Norway's position on neutrality had been supplemented by an implicit understanding that in the last analysis

Great Britain would protect the country's independence. This 'implicit guarantee', which had also influenced Norway's defence planning, meant that, after the autumn of 1939, Norway – if the worst came to the worst – must not allow itself to become involved in the war on the opposite side to Great Britain.

Of decisive importance for the government's choice in June 1940 was the position of the merchant fleet. The Norwegian merchant fleet, at 4 million tons gross, made up 7 per cent of the world's tonnage, while as much as 18 per cent of the world's tanker tonnage was in Norwegian hands. Besides, the Norwegian fleet was the most modern in the world. After 9 April some 85 per cent of the fleet managed to keep out of German hands. As was the case in the First World War, the bulk of Norwegian shipping was already in the autumn of 1939 contractually placed at the disposal of the allies' war effort. On 22 April 1940, the entire fleet in foreign waters was requisitioned by the Norwegian government and later managed by the Norwegian Shipping and Trade Mission (Nortraship) in London.

The merchant fleet created the economic foundation for the government's existence; it strengthened the country's reputation amongst the allies and it represented Norway's most important contribution to the common war effort. Three thousand Norwegian sailors paid for this with their lives. Armed forces too were created on allied soil and from 1943 in Sweden too. During the war years Sweden also accommodated a body of Norwegian refugees numbering more than 40,000 individuals. The armed contribution overseas cost 1,100 dead, mostly amongst naval and air force personnel.

While the government in flight through southern, then through northern Norway, and finally in London, tried to conduct the war on Norway's behalf, a political game took place in occupied Oslo regarding the country's fate. Vidkun Quisling, the leader of the political faction, the National Socialist Party, had already on 9 April proclaimed himself prime minister of a new government that was willing to cooperate with the occupying power. An 'administrative council' was formally appointed by the High Court on 15 April to take charge of the occupied territories. But with Hitler's appointment of a Reichskommissar, Josef Terboven, on 24 April the council was placed under the Germans' civil administration. The Germans' repudiation of Quisling in favour of the administrative council involved an attempt to secure the cooperation of legitimate Norwegian institutions. These attempts reached their climax during the negotiations that took place that autumn over the state council. The goal was to set up an alternative government in opposition to Norway's lawful government and to give it a veneer of legality, i.e. with the cooperation of the Storting.

Nazification and resistance

The first months of the occupation had been marked by confusion, defeatism and a resigned acceptance of German demands. The presidents of the Storting, during the negotiations over the state council, asked the king to abdicate. However, on 25 September the negotiations broke down. This led to the removal from office of the administrative council, the prohibition of parties other than the National Socialist Party (NS) and the appointment of ministers by the Reichskommissar. With this the situation was clarified and the lines were even more clearly drawn by the 'official ceremony at Akershus' on 1 February 1942 when a 'national government' was established under the control of Terboven and with Quisling as 'minister president'. A programme for the Nazification of Norwegian society was drawn up. Gradually a resistance movement developed, at first spontaneously, later with secretly organized civil and military wings and in accord with the Norwegian government in London.

The Nazification of society's public institutions and voluntary organizations began as early as the autumn of 1940. At the turn of the year 1940–41, elections for local councils were replaced by appointments, with all powers of decision making given to the mayor. Attempts were made to get rid of civil servants in national or local authorities or force them into NS. In the spring of 1942 the bishops and clergy resigned their posts. Many teachers were deported to Finnmark, in the extreme north of the country. Of great significance was the fight over Norwegian voluntary organizations, for it was here that the Germans and NS suffered their greatest defeat, and because large sections of the public were involved. First came the sporting and religious organizations. Gradually more organizations joined, and in May of 1941 some 43 national organizations protested at the Nazification of Norwegian society. A moral standard for these conflicts had already been set in December 1940 when the High Court resigned in protest against the violation of the principles of a state governed by law.

The protests of the voluntary organizations led to their legal administrations being replaced by Norwegian Nazis. The NS strategy behind these changes was the laying of a foundation for an occupationally based 'national council', which, in line with the model of a corporate state, would replace the Storting. The answer to this was the building up of secret organs of leadership, which meant that the organizations could continue to function as constructive bodies in Norwegian society and even, to some extent, compensate for the disappearance of the political institutions. Pressure on Norwegian society also found expression in terror and executions, the setting up of internment camps and deportation to concentration camps in Germany. It was the Jews, however, who suffered most. Of around 1,850 Norwegian Jews, 759 died in German extermination camps.

The resistance movement gradually took on a military dimension. The military operations of the Norwegian underground began in 1942 and were especially important during the last year of the war. Intelligence activities – both those of domestic origin and those involving agents sent from abroad – made a major contribution in the battle against the German navy and the German supply lines along the coast. From the end of 1942 and beginning of 1943, the Communists ran their own active guerilla and sabotage operations.

The increasing scope of the resistance movement created the need for coordination. Considering that the leadership operated in secret and with communications difficult, it necessarily had a self-constituted character. 'The Circle', which began in 1941, had its roots in Oslo's middle class. 'The Co-ordinating Committee' (KK), of the same year, was more broadly based in the large voluntary organizations. The Circle and KK together formed a civilian resistance movement with the Chief Justice of the High Court, Paal Berg, as its constitutional spokesman. This body was recognized by the Norwegian government in London in 1943 and in the spring of 1944 assumed the leadership of the Home Front. At the same time, a separate leadership for the military resistance movement was formed. This was ultimately responsible to the Commander-in-Chief (Defence) in London. From the turn of the year 1944–45, the Home Front's leadership included both civilian and military leaders. The Communist resistance movement, however, remained – or was kept – outside.

It is quite natural that the resistance movement, both at home and abroad, should occupy a central place in the history of the war years.

But the balance sheet also contains items on the other side. Military resistance in Norway itself started late and developed in close alliance with activities in the war zone abroad. And only a relatively small part of the population was involved at the most exposed level. The police and the press soon succumbed to Nazification. The reorganization of the local authorities met little resistance. Much of manufacturing industry worked voluntarily, or under various degrees of pressure, for the German war effort. NS increased its membership from 7,000 in the autumn of 1940 to a maximum of approximately 40,000 three years later. And 5,000–6,000 Norwegians joined the German armed forces.

The war caused a good deal of material damage. Half the merchant fleet was lost. Productive resources were worn out. Built-up areas and towns like Elverum, Molde, Kristiansund, Bodø and Narvik were virtually destroyed in the war of 1940. The scorched earth policy perpetrated on Finnmark and north Troms at the turn of the year 1944–45 was a national catastrophe. Everyday life was for many marked by terrorist fears and material privation. On the other hand, the situation was not anarchic. National and local authorities conducted their business according to their well-established administrative traditions. In everyday life, the German occupying forces behaved, for the most part, in a disciplined fashion.

Break and continuity

The question must be answered whether novel post-war developments had their roots in the war years. The war marked the end of Norway's policy of neutrality. After a short bridge-building phase, Norway in 1949 aligned itself by treaty to the western powers. The wartime experience prioritized defence for the first time since the turn of the century. And there was a growing understanding that the future of the Norwegian people would continue to be influenced by events on the continent and in the wider world arena.

Political life returned to normal in the summer of 1945 without complications. The basis for this was the national solidarity and the support for free political institutions that had developed during the war years. But it is also apparent that this was a continuation of tendencies that had appeared before 1940. The notion of national unity must, however, be qualified in the light of the 60,000 individuals and their families who suffered legal and social penalties after the war because of their wartime activities. This legal action created wounds that over 50 years later are still not completely healed.

The war ended unemployment. In spite of shortages, full employment meant that many people were able to obtain benefits previously unattainable, e.g. education, while at the same time wartime inflation reduced the burden of personal and municipal debt. The destruction of towns and cities and the deterioration in capital equipment created an enormous need for post-war reconstruction. National solidarity and the wartime experience provided the opportunity for solving this task through a united effort and under the direction of the state. Paradoxically, the war marked a turning point in the welfare of the people, ending the poverty that had previously been the lot of many Norwegians.

Part IV
The years since 1945
Tore Grønlie

22
Reconstruction, radical change or continuity?

In Norway, 1945 was a year of jubilation. As early as 7 May, the first flags were raised with the news of the German surrender on the continent. The day after – liberation day – marked the end of five years of occupation, privation and sacrifice. National Day celebrations on 17 May proved to be an overwhelming display of national unity. The festivities climaxed when an exultant populace welcomed the king home on 7 June.

The devastation of war and the problems of reconstruction

The celebrations were soon replaced by a sombre reality as Norwegians confronted a ravaged land. Some 20,000 homes had been destroyed. The military operations of 1940, the air raids and other acts of destruction had severely damaged many towns and built-up areas, especially along the coast. In Kristiansund, 2,100 flats had been destroyed, in Bergen 1,300. A scorched earth policy by the Germans in Finnmark and north Troms after the Russian invasion of 1944 had resulted in almost every building being levelled to the ground. The country's recuperation and ability to create new wealth were hampered because much of the means of production and communications were either destroyed or worn down. Roads and bridges had been blown up; factories were in ruins or suffering from lack of maintenance; ships had been sunk; fishing boats burned. There was a lack of raw materials and other supplies, and businesses were cut off from their traditional markets.

It is not difficult to understand that contemporaries focused on reconstruction as the economic and political task with the highest priority. Attention was almost wholly concentrated upon the *destructive* effects of the war and on the need for a disciplined, collective effort in the service of reconstruction. The tone was set by a book from an

On 7 June 1945, forty years to the day after the dissolution of the union with Sweden and five years after he had left Tromsø, Haakon 7 again set foot on Norwegian soil, to enormous acclaim. The King personally had been the rallying point for the resistance movement. His firm stand did much to ensure that Norway came out of the war with her sense of national unity enhanced.

influential group of economists that appeared in May 1945: *What the war cost Norway*. Their main conclusion was that the war and the occupation had cost Norway and Norwegians some 17.5 billion pre-war kroner.

The calculations indicated that the loss of capital was greatest (30–60 per cent) in the most important export industries, namely shipping and whaling, the fisheries and parts of manufacturing industry. Manufacturing output was only half what it had been before the

Kirkenes, 1945. In the 1940s reconstruction was the overarching problem. Finnmark and northern Troms had been burned to the ground after the Germans' scorched-earth policy ahead of the Russian advance. Elsewhere many towns and built-up areas had been heavily damaged. As it happened, the country's productive capacity was restored to its pre-war level within a few years – much faster than expected. The rebuilding of homes, however, took longer – in some places, 10–15 years.

war; mining output only one-fifth. The experts believed that, under favourable conditions, 'reconstruction' – the lifting of production and consumption to pre-war levels – could be accomplished in the course of five years.

Contemporary politicians were also engaged with other problems associated with the liberation and reconstruction. Many feared serious unemployment. The country had suffered heavy unemployment before the war. During the war, 140,000 people had either worked for the Germans or taken part in military activities at home or abroad. Everyone was now coming back to an economy that was operating well below its potential. The politicians also feared inflation. The Germans had withdrawn 11 billion kroner from the Bank of Norway during the war. Money had accumulated in banks or was put away privately since during the war there was little to buy. Lots of money and few goods could unleash a massive increase in prices. Additionally there was the fear that the post-First-World-War experience would be repeated. A short boom followed by a new downturn would, at worst, lead to a lengthy depression. An influential Swedish book that prophesied this had the appropriate title: *A warning to the peace optimists*.

Post-war history viewed as 'reconstruction'

For contemporaries, the problems of reconstruction and the political and social efforts required to solve them were the central issues. It was to be expected that the first 'histories' of these days should be written at the time by people directly involved in the events. Historians came later with their analysis of the recent past. And when they did it was also to be expected that their accounts would be heavily influenced by the understanding contemporaries had of the issues. Time must pass before one can put events into longer lines of development and analyze them from new perspectives and different points of view. The reconstruction view of post-war history was, therefore, a dominant one for a long time.

Post-war reconstruction was, however, but a short episode in the life of Norwegian society. National output and private consumption reached pre-war levels by the end of 1946. Manufacturing and fishing reached pre-war levels by 1947, agriculture by 1948. And even the country's exports had by 1947 a larger share of the national product than they had had before the war. It was the reconstruction of war-damaged homes in the north and west that took the longest time.

The experts were also wrong in other areas. There were no employment problems of any magnitude. Quite the contrary, there was a shortage of labour that resulted in the economy being run below its potential. Policies had to be changed so that investment could be concentrated on activities that gave the greatest output for the lowest labour input. The problem of inflation continued to be threatening, but it was held in check by rationing and a strict regulatory system that was kept in place until the early 1950s. The expected post-war downturn did not appear either, and the fear of depression shared by economists and politicians alike wore off by the end of the 1940s.

The problems of reconstruction gradually faded into the background by the beginning of the 1950s. But the reconstruction mentality continued for a long time. The same attitudes and qualities were required to build the new Norway as to reconstruct the old, it was thought. A marked increase in production was the only possible way to general welfare and social security. A major problem was industry: it was underdeveloped and productivity was too low. The solution was that everyone must work harder and more effectively; wealth must be created before it could be shared. The 1950s were, therefore, in many ways 'the age of restraint' in Norway's post-war history. Those years were dominated by campaigns for increased productivity, hard work, moderate pay settlements and restraint on the part of the state in carrying through radical social reforms. Economic growth in the 1950s was less than it had been in the 1940s or was to be in the 1960s. A minor economic setback in the years 1957–58 could still remind people of the crises of the inter-war years. The car – that symbol of prosperity above all others – remained rationed until 1960.

The decade of economic optimism

The 1960s were the first decade of general prosperity in Norway. Gradually people became occupied with matters other than reconstruction, productivity campaigns and moderation in all things. Now interest was focused on the strong and continuous growth in output, on economic prosperity and on the sharing of that prosperity. At the centre of political attention stood the ever more important influence of the state on society, its contribution to the growth of the economy as well as its role in directing it. People were especially interested in the sharing of the prosperity and the building up and further development of the Norwegian welfare state. Contemporaries noted the political stability, the agreement of all parties to the principles of the welfare state – and prophesied the 'death of ideology'.

The 1960s were not just the first decade of prosperity. It was also, more than anything else, 'the decade of optimism' in Norwegian political and social life. Many – including politicians and experts – believed that business cycles were a thing of the past and that minor deviations from stable economic growth could be compensated for by the appropriate economic policy. Growth would continue. The question was how strong it would be and how its fruits should be shared.

Nor was there any great argument over the distribution, so long as everybody came out better than before. Towards the end of the 1960s a debate arose as to whether it was any longer necessary to go for growth or whether society should consciously decide to aim for 'nil growth'. The debate is best understood in the context of the dominant contemporary view, namely that economic growth was all but automatic and permanent.

The economic and social conditions of the post-war period were regarded by people in the 1960s as something fundamentally new in the country's history. Post-war Norway represented a complete reversal of the conditions of earlier times. To the extent that thoughts on the inter-war years played any part in contemporaries' views of their own times, it was as a negative mirror-image of the trouble-free contemporary scene. The strong economic growth of the post-war years was set against the much slower growth of the inter-war period: the post-war stability was contrasted with the depressions of the 1920s and 1930s. The full employment of the 1960s was compared with the long queues of unemployed in 'the hard 30s' and the peaceful labour market compared with the great strike years between the wars. Social stability and a more egalitarian society had replaced the class war of the 1930s. Political stability and consensus, loyalty towards the system and national unity had replaced political splits and confrontation, revolutionary ideology and anti-parliamentary tendencies.

Contemporaries were also interested in why things had gone so well in the post-war period. What had the business community and the politicians now done right that they had handled so badly in the inter-war period? Many came to believe that the good times were due to the active involvement of the state in directing the economy, together with Keynesian economic policies.

Contemporary history: a case of radical change or continuity?

Those who, towards the end of the 1960s, first began to write Norway's post-war history were also affected by the society's focus on the here and now. In general they viewed the post-war years as a unique period in Norwegian history. They found their explanations within the timescale of the period itself and used the inter-war years more for illustrating the converse, than as a basic element in the analysis of the post-war era. Both contemporary opinion and historical comment shifted in the 1950s and through the 1960s. Post-war Norway was now seen as a period of radical change, not merely one of reconstruction.

It is now time to put a question mark against this view of the post-war period as well. The historian is constantly being influenced by new research. And the post-war historian has been strongly affected by new knowledge on the inter-war years. We know today that those years witnessed not only stagnation, crisis and distress, but also change, new growth and social advancement. But historians are also influenced by their own times. The 1970s and 1980s saw the return of economic problems, new ups and downs in the economy, social problems and unemployment. Basic questions are being asked about the role of the state in society and the effectiveness of economic policy and of economic management. The 1960s' belief in continuous growth and steadily increasing welfare received a death blow in the 1970s and 1980s. At the same time, there arose a new interest in the inter-war years' problems and in the parallels between that period and our own times.

It was not necessary to abandon completely the reconstruction view of the post-war years in order to consider one that stressed the revolutionary aspects. This interpretation was just no longer acceptable on its own. And it is scarcely necessary completely to discard the radical change perspective in order to open up the possibility of seeing the post-war years in yet another light. But the majority of historians now feel it is necessary to look further back in time, *past* the radical change that is known to have occurred and *past* the reconstruction that was also an important element in Norway's recent history.

Starting with new knowledge, it is now necessary to question the revolutionary perspective. Was the strong growth really *just* a post-war phenomenon that began in the period of reconstruction and continued with the expansion of output after the war? Perhaps the post-war period has not been as novel as the radical change perspective presumes?

The historian of the post-war period is now also searching for the long lines in history. Perhaps the roots of post-war growth, general well-being and political stability will be found precisely in the crises and conflicts of the inter-war years? And were there, even during wartime, positive developments that point towards economic growth and the welfare state?

23
A quarter of a century of growth

The years from 1945 to 1973 differ from both the inter-war period and the war years in being characterized by strong and – above all – stable growth. If we focus our attention on manufacturing industry alone, this period is also clearly different from the one that followed. For it was from 1945 to 1973 that Norway experienced the longest continuous period of growth in its modern history. GNP rose annually by an average 5 per cent. Compared with the rest of western Europe, this was about average. The fastest growth occurred in the period immediately after the war – with 20 per cent growth in the years 1946–48. Growth was weaker in the 1950s, but became especially dynamic in the first half of the 1960s. GNP fell in only one year – 1958 – and then by a mere 0.1 per cent. Between 1946 and 1970, Norway's population grew from 3.15 to 3.9 million. Even when this annual population growth rate of 0.6 per cent is taken into account, economic growth was strong.

Population and work

Three aspects of the post-war growth in population stand out as being especially important. The first is the high and stable number of births: 60,000–65,000 annually, with a peak of 70,000 in 1946. These large cohorts – they were some 20,000 above the low point of the 1930s – were caused above all by a lower age at marriage and a fall in the number of unmarried, as compared with the mid-1930s. The second feature of note is the ageing of the population. This had its origins in the fall in mortality of the birth cohorts from the years 1880 to 1920, together with the fact that a smaller proportion was lost to the country through emigration. The number of people over 70 years of age increased from 130,000 in 1946 to 325,000 in 1970, a much larger

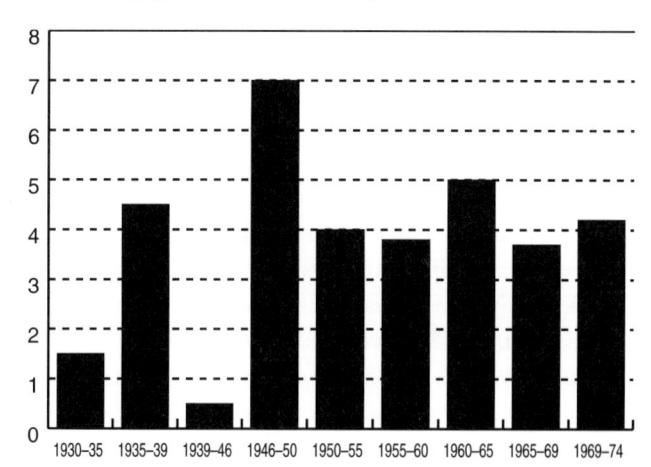

Yearly growth in GNP – fixed prices. Percent. 1930–74

Period	Growth
1930–35	1.5
1935–39	4.5
1939–46	0.5
1946–50	7
1950–55	4
1955–60	3.8
1960–65	5
1965–69	3.7
1969–74	4.2

increase, relatively speaking, than occurred in other age groups. Both these developments had a great impact on the expansion of the welfare state (Chapter 24).

The third feature – a much more complex one – is the very modest growth in the working population. Total employment grew by barely 200,000 man-years over a period of 25 years, no more than in the single decade 1930–39. The workforce grew in the 1940s and again in the 1960s, but stagnated completely in the 1950s. This occurred in spite of economic growth and a shortage of labour for much of the period. Economic growth could possibly have been even stronger had labour not been so much of a bottleneck. The cohorts from the inter-war years that now reached the working age groups were, for the most part,

Working men and women over 15 years (16 in 1970 and 1980) as a percentage of all married and unmarried men and women, 1930–1980

	1930	1946	1950	1960	1970	1980
All women	30	27	26	24	25	27
Unmarried	57	59	62	56	46	32
Married	3	4	5	10	20	28
All men	88	87	87	83	75	61
Unmarried	86	82	84	72	61	47
Married	93	93	92	91	84	71

part, small. In the 1940s and 1950s this was to some degree compensated by the tendency for young people to prefer well-paid work to continued schooling. But this proved to be a temporary phenomenon. In the 1960s the large post-war cohorts entered the labour market. But then a sharp fall occurred in the male activity rate because more and more chose to stay on at school and, in any case, the time spent in education grew longer.

The growth of the economy and the modest additions to the labour force meant that Norwegians were spared unemployment of any significance. Generally, the annual average number of wholly unemployed was 15,000, or 1.5 per cent of the employed population. Only during the brief downturn in 1958–59 did unemployment increase, but even then the yearly average rose to scarcely 25,000. What unemployment there was had either a seasonal or a geographical character. North Norway and a few other districts had higher totals. Unemployment also rose in the winter.

In view of the tight labour market and low unemployment it might appear strange that the activity rate amongst women remained low for such a long time. Indeed, the proportion of women whose income from their own labour was their most important 'means of support' was lower between 1946 and 1970 than it had been before the war. It sank from 30 per cent in 1930 to 24 per cent in 1960. The reason for this was that a higher proportion of women were married and it was only very rarely that married women were gainfully employed. By 1970, however, the proportion of married women who had work outside the home increased sharply. But this was neutralized to a very great extent by the fact that the activity rate amongst unmarried women fell sharply, as increasing numbers undertook education and training. However, part-time working by women increased significantly – thus by 1972 some 45 per cent had paid work.

From scarcity to affluence

Economic growth led to a marked increase in material well-being. The average pay – in real terms – more than doubled. A vivid impression of the growth in affluence can be gained by examining just what was consumed. Shortly after the war, the average household used more than two-thirds of its income on necessities such as food, clothing and accommodation; by the beginning of the 1970s, less than half. In the 1940s almost 40 per cent went on food: 25 years later, less than a quarter.

Expenditure on the home showed only a small increase. Nevertheless it is here that the explosion in living standards of the first 25 postwar years can best be observed. The average household lived at the beginning of the 1950s in a flat with three to four rooms. If one includes the kitchen, then each household member had one room each. If the family lived in a town, water was provided (95 per cent in 1946), but if the family lived in the countryside there was a 50–50 chance that water had to be carried into the house. The 'average household' probably had an electric cooker (70 per cent in 1952), but very few had a water heater (27 per cent). The 'average *town* household' had, as likely as not, a toilet but not a bath (59 per cent and 30 per cent, respectively, in 1946). But the family in the countryside had neither (under 10 per cent in 1946). The household had no fridge (4 per cent in 1952), no washing machine (15 per cent), no vacuum cleaner (20 per cent), and no freezer. On the other hand, it did have an electric iron (84 per cent).

By the 1970s the average family home had an extra room, so that each family member disposed of 1.5 rooms on average. The chances were that 'our household' now had all the installations and facilities mentioned above (73 per cent had a bath, 70 per cent a toilet, 90 per cent hot water). That expenditure on the home did not rise more, in spite of the rise in standards, was due to official controls and subsidies and to a significant fall – relatively speaking – in the price of domestic equipment.

Private transport, leisure gear, visits to restaurants, hotel stays and package holidays experienced an almost explosive increase. At the beginning of the 1970s, Norwegians used almost as much money on these things as they did on food. One-seventh of consumption went on the purchase and running of a private car, an item that was not to be found in the statistics of consumption immediately after the war. The number of cars increased twelvefold between 1949 and 1974. In the 1940s there were more than 50 people per car, by 1974 fewer than five.

Living standards are not to be measured simply in terms of consumption. Norwegians got more holidays and more free time. From 1936 all had the right to nine days' holiday. In 1947 this was increased to 18 working days and in 1964 to four weeks. The standard working week was gradually cut, from 48 to 45 hours in 1959 and to 42.5 in

1968. Towards the end of the 1950s it was usual for industry to shut down at noon on Saturday. After an interim period with a free Saturday every other week, a five-day week was introduced for most occupations around 1970.

There are no systematic enquiries into leisure pursuits before 1970, so it is not possible to know precisely how free time was used. But many spent more and more time at their country cottages. In 1970 there were 190,000 holiday cottages in Norway, one for every seven houses. Almost three-quarters of these were built after 1945 – often by the owner in his recently acquired leisure time. Immediately after the war, holidays on the Mediterranean or the continent were the privilege of the few. In 1974, 160,000 Norwegians went on holiday by charter plane. In the inter-war years radio had become the entertainment and communications medium. In 1941, 470,000 radio licences were issued. By 1974 the total had trebled to 1.3 million. The number of radio receivers was much higher. Norway acquired television in 1960 – one of the last countries in Europe to do so. In the course of the next 15 years TV could be received in most parts of the country and 1 million licences were being issued.

Industrialization and the service society

Economic growth has been closely tied to the development of the Norwegian industrial society, later the service society – or, as it is often called, the 'post-industrial society'. Norwegian industrial output increased four- to fivefold between 1946 and 1973, with a yearly average growth rate of 6 per cent. The strongest growth of all took place in the years 1946–50. During the 1950s, growth was relatively modest, but then it surged again, especially in the early 1960s. More and more people became industrial workers. Just before the outbreak of war, industry supplied around 250,000 man-years of employment; at its peak in 1974 the figure reached 420,000.

In the years immediately after the war, it was the industries that served the home market that grew the fastest. The food and drink industries led the way, but were soon followed by the textile and clothing industries, together with the iron and engineering industries. The demand for food, clothes, shoes and various other consumer goods such as furniture, stoves, pots and pans, and radio sets was almost

Industrial workforce. Thousands of man-years 1920–82

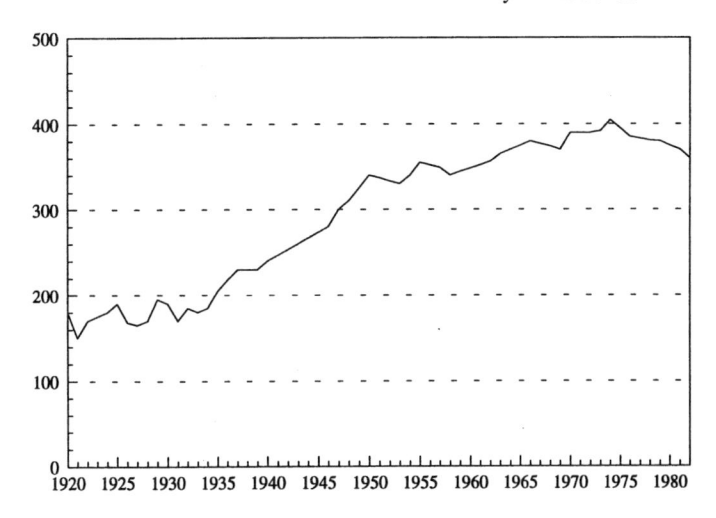

Industrial production, yearly average of growth rates 1920–83

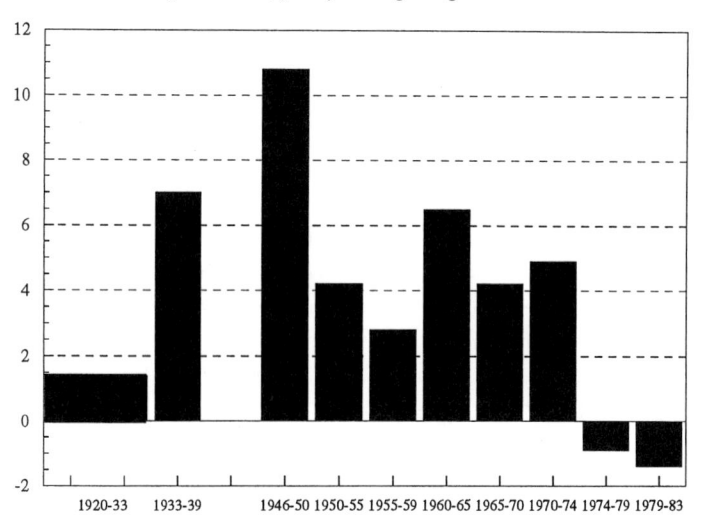

unlimited. Strong Norwegian import controls and currency regulations, together with export restrictions in other countries, protected home industries from foreign competition.

From the end of the 1940s, the fastest-growing industries were those serving the export markets. The chemical industry and the new smelting works now grew rapidly, not least with the establishment of new large-scale industrial concerns and new towns. Norsk Jernverk in Mo i

Working population by major sectors 1865–1980

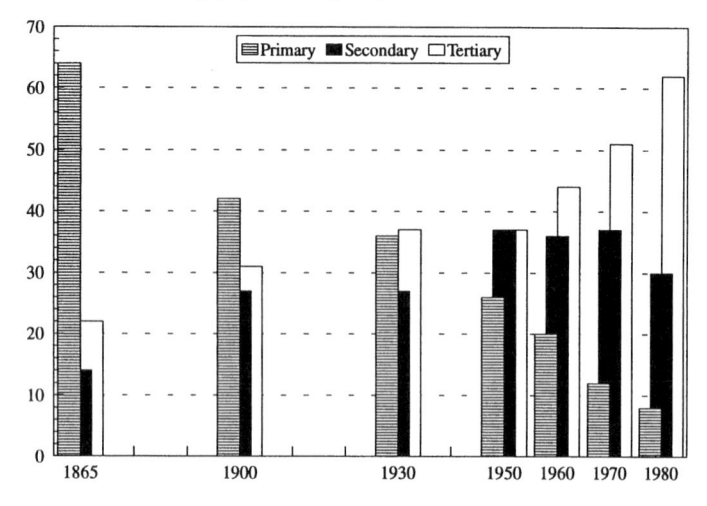

Rana, the state aluminium works in Årdal and Sunndalsøra, together with Elkem's in Mosjøen and Norsk Hydro's ammonia factory in Glomfjord, were some of the most important. The industrial development of the 1950s and parts of the 1960s was reminiscent of the years before the First World War – heavy industry producing semi-finished products for world markets using cheap Norwegian water power. At the same time, growth more or less stopped in the industries that pro-

Employment (in man–years) in the service industries, as a percentage of total employment, 1950–1980

	1950	1960	1970	1980
Retailing	9,1	11,4	13,0	15,0
Financial, insurance and business services	1,3	1,7	2,3	5,8
Public administration and defence	4,2	5,6	6,1	8,2
Public and private services	6,7	8,9	13,6	20,9
Personal services	6,3	5,5	4,9	3,0
Transport (including shipping)	9,7	11,8	10,0	9,0
All services	37,3	44,9	49,9	61,9
Primary and secondary sectors	62,7	55,1	50,1	38,1
	100,0	100,0	100,0	100,0

duced consumer goods for the home market and which had been strong in the early post-war years: the food and drink industries, leather and rubber, and not least the textile and clothing industries.

Dividing industry into that serving the home and that serving the overseas markets became less relevant in the course of the 1960s. Most branches of Norwegian industry now produced for an international market, while those that previously had served the home market now faced competition from abroad. Amongst the earlier home market industries that now grew by venturing into the world market were shipbuilding and the timber and furniture industries. Another industry that came to prominence during the 1960s was graphics. Centred in the towns, its growth resulted from the new service society's need for the dissemination of information and marketing.

Shortly after the war, the primary, secondary and tertiary industries each supplied about the same amount of employment. In spite of the fact that the secondary sector employed more and more people, it did not strengthen its relative position after the beginning of the 1950s. Since that time, the service sector has become the great generator of employment, in Norway as in the world generally. By the beginning of the 1970s almost half of all employment in the country was to be found in the service sector – with its approximately 750,000 workers.

The group that grew the fastest was in public and private services. By 1970 they provided more employment than the retail trades, which had been the biggest. Within public and private service, it was the former that grew the most, with the educational and health sectors taking the lead. Public administration, defence, retailing and financial services were also growth areas. It was only in shipping and 'personal services' that employment fell: in the first because of the increased size of ships, severe rationalization of work at sea and an increasing use of foreign seamen; and in the second because paid housework all but disappeared as an occupation. With this a traditional form of female employment was gone. Nevertheless, the impression remains that the growth of the service industries increased the possibilities for female employment. Several of the industries that grew especially fast took a high proportion of women. In 1970 women accounted for more than 80 per cent of the employees in the health service, for 50 per cent in education and for 40 per cent in retailing. This was similar to the pattern in 1920. In addition, after 1970 more and more married women entered employment outside the home.

Urbanization

A significant growth in the populations of towns and built-up areas was both a cause and a consequence of the growth in industry and services. In 1970, 1 million more people lived in urban areas, while 250,000 fewer were in rural areas than had been the case 25 years earlier.

The process of urbanization can be observed at several levels. *Nationally* the process of concentration manifested itself through the strengthened position of the area around the capital Oslo. This was also the only part of the country to experience strong and stable net in-migration, with a gain of 60,000 people in the 1960s. North Norway, on the other hand, experienced strong out-migration, with a loss in the same decade of more than 30,000 people. This part of the country lost people to every other part.

Regionally the tendency towards concentration led to the eight largest urban areas increasing their share of the total population from 37 to 46 per cent in the years between 1950 and 1970. Around 1960, these eight centres had between them more than three-quarters of the country's population growth. Most of this, however, came not from in-migration but from the fact that the excess of births over deaths was especially great in the large towns.

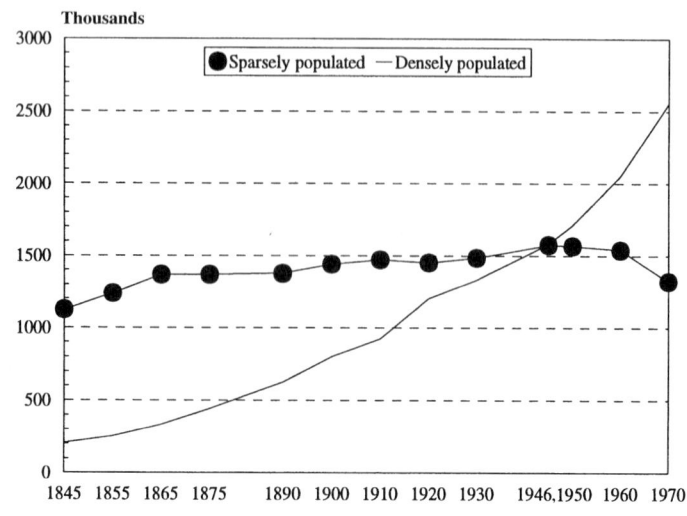

Resident population 1845–1970

Relatively speaking, the *local* concentration was even more marked than the regional. Throughout the entire post-war period rural centres and small towns have grown strongly, not least as a result of the amalgamation of many district councils and the growth of public and private services. In both the 1950s and the 1960s it was the built-up areas with 1,000–2,000 inhabitants that grew the fastest, while the smallest centres stagnated.

Urbanization had a great impact on the cultural scene. Gradually, more and larger areas became built up. Urban growth took place, for the most part, at the expense of the agricultural areas of sparsely populated neighbouring authorities. A demand for better housing led to the built-up areas around the larger towns growing several fold. But it was developments in communications – above all private car ownership – that made it possible for housing areas with an 'urban feel' to develop some distance from the great centres of employment. More and more people became commuters.

The primary industries: a technological revolution

Urbanization and the growth of urban employment have been both a cause and an effect of widespread changes in the traditional occupations of rural and peripheral areas. Shortly after the war ended, almost one-third of the labour force was employed in agriculture, forestry, fishing, sealing and whaling. By 1970 the proportion was down to one-ninth. More than one-quarter of agricultural holdings – 60,000 in total – were abandoned between 1949 and 1969. In the 1960s, 12 holdings disappeared *each* day. This affected the cultural landscape too. To some extent it was as if the country had returned to the later Middle Ages, with a renewal of the 'deserted farms problem'. In certain isolated places, nature again took over the fields and meadows that had been cleared with so much effort. But more often the land was absorbed into a neighbouring farm and the houses became holiday homes. The total area under cultivation fell by less than 10 per cent. In central areas the family often continued to live on the holding even though the farmer himself took another job. Sometimes he continued as a 'hobby farmer' on the side. Above all the labour employed on the individual farms fell – in agriculture itself to about one-third of its pre-war level by the early 1970s. The situation in forestry and fishing was broadly similar.

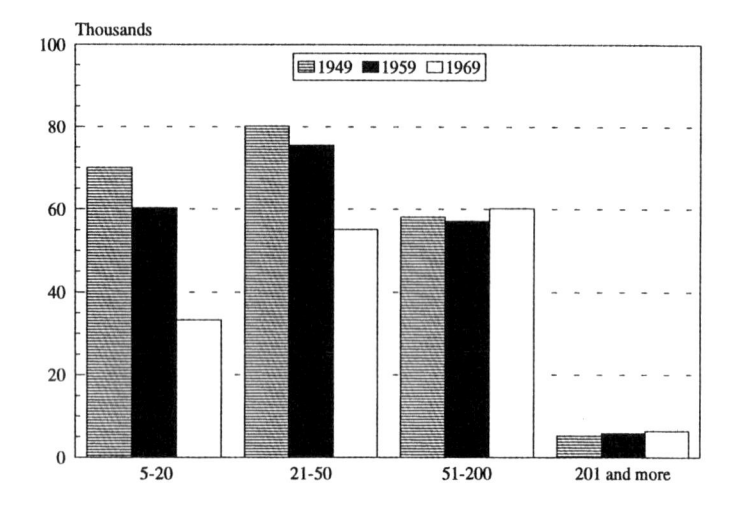

Number of agricultural units by size in *dekar* (1000 sqm)
1949, 1959, 1969

The primary industries did not experience lower output, except for forestry where there was a slight decline in production. Hay and meat production were 20 per cent higher by the end of the 1960s than they had been immediately before the outbreak of war, while milk production was 10 per cent higher. Agricultural growth was limited by the size of the home market. Growth in the fisheries output was much

The total agricultural labour force and per 1000 dekar 1929–1974

Year	1000 Man–years	Man–years per holding	Man–years per 1000 dekar
1929*	341,6	1,64	34,3
1939*	353,5	1,65	33,9
1949*	308,4	1,44	30,6
1959	229,3	1,16	22,7
1969	166,3	1,07	16,9
1974	122,9	1,02	13,6

* *It is assumed that in 1929, 1939 and 1949 some 60% of labour on the farm went to agriculture, the rest to forestry and work in the home (this was the situation in 1959).*

stronger. The average catch at the beginning of the 1970s was almost two and a half times greater than it had been at the end of the 1940s. Here exports dominated. Eventually the enormous catches threatened the fish stocks, in the case of herring as early as the late 1950s.

These developments had their origins in the technological revolution that occurred in the primary industries. In agriculture, the use of feed concentrates more than doubled and milk yields per cow almost trebled. The number of tractors in Norway grew tenfold between 1949 and 1969; the number of milk machines did likewise. Forestry was revolutionized by the introduction of the chainsaw in the course of the 1950s. By the end of the 1960s there were perhaps some 50,000 such saws in use. In the fisheries, the development was characterized by the switch from coastal to deep-sea fishing, from seasonal to year-round fishing, and from fishing as a part-time occupation to a full-time one. In 1948, only 20 per cent of fishermen had fishing as their only job; by 1971 the figure had risen to more than 40 per cent. Here the development was propelled by the switch to larger boats and more efficient labour-saving gear such as the trawl and the seine net. It was also stimulated by the creation of a significant fish-processing industry in both public and private hands. But the units of production continued, on the whole, to be small both in agriculture and in the fishing industry.

The reasons for growth

Twenty-five years of steady growth and fundamental changes in the economy, flanked by difficult periods before and after, make it necessary to discuss the reasons for growth. Contemporaries – especially, perhaps, those who had links with the party in government – stressed above all the effect of the new economic policies of the post-war era. These laid great emphasis on planned economic growth: high investment; priority given to highly productive and capital-intensive businesses, as in industry and shipping; productivity gains; rationalization and efficiency. We would rather stress the interplay between policy, productivity increases and international stimuli.

Norway never developed a planned economy of the type the Norwegian Labour Party outlined in its most ambitious manifestos at the beginning of the post-war period (Chapter 25). Still, economic policies did play an important role. This is seen most clearly with regard to industry and power production. Industry had the highest priority and the government made great efforts to channel investment to it. This occurred most directly through the state's own industrial activities, especially within the aluminium, iron, steel and mining industries, frozen fish production and, at the beginning of the 1960s, the chemical industry too. All these belonged to the great growth industries from the start of the 1950s.

The state also stimulated industrial growth in the private sector. This took place particularly through large-scale investment in the building of power stations by public authorities. The power was delivered to industry on long-term contracts at favourable prices. Energy resources were Norway's greatest competitive advantage on world markets and for a long time were thought to be unlimited. Not until the end of the 1960s were conservation issues raised seriously.

The state also employed subsidies and tax breaks as incentives for industrial growth, growth that for a long time was considered to be an unqualified asset. Down to the second half of the 1950s it was the state's own enterprises, together with the larger private Norwegian companies, that were favoured. Then the government started a campaign, under the leadership of the one-time UN General Secretary Trygve Lie, to attract foreign investment capital to Norway. An earlier scepticism regarding large-scale foreign enterprise, which had its roots in the period of large-scale industrial growth around the beginning of the century, gave way in the face of an almost unqualified enthusiasm for further industrialization. Oil refineries in Tønsberg and Stavanger, and aluminium works on Karmøy, Lista and Husnes are all products of this campaign.

Regional policy, which especially from the end of the 1950s took on a significant role, was also essentially an *industrial* policy. It involved public support in the form of subsidies, financial arrangements and the expansion of the infrastructure. There can be little doubt that this policy too contributed to significant growth in and spread of industrial activity throughout the 1960s and into the early 1970s.

Productivity increases occurred in all branches of economic activity. This, too, was to some extent a result of policy. Immediately after the war the Labour Party government sought to direct at first hand the rationalization of the industrial structure through the decisions of a planned economy. The results of this were scarcely dramatic. But, at the beginning of the 1950s, the government placed great emphasis on the increase of productivity through cooperation between the public authorities, the trade unions and industry itself. A Norwegian Productivity Institute was created and American methods of time and motion studies and the improvement of working processes were adopted. There is every reason to believe that the marked improvement in industrial productivity throughout the 1950s was, to a considerable extent, the product of this political offensive – and perhaps particularly of the intense campaign for increased effort on the part of the workers, which the leaders of the labour movement conducted amongst its own supporters. Later, rationalization and improvements in productivity were encouraged above all by increased international competition. Improvements in efficiency were not, however, sufficient to prevent serious new productivity and structural problems in industry – especially the timber-processing industry – in the 1960s.

A conscious political line also contributed to the structural rationalization of the primary industries. The authorities wanted to move towards a farming sector that could be self-sufficient and to this end encouraged the growth of larger farms, with increased mechanization and specialization, through subsidies and other measures of support, which were usually dependent on the size of output. In fishing, larger units were encouraged by favourable financial and other benefits for fishing boats, the easing of restrictions on the use of trawlers, and the industrialization of the receiving and processing end of the industry.

It would be wrong, however, to see the rationalization of agriculture and fisheries and the flight from the land as simply the product of political decisions. To a great extent they were spontaneous and unprovoked. The flight from the land was a natural feature of a growing economy. There was undoubtedly an excess of labour on the farms – primarily because industry in the inter-war period had not managed to maintain and create sufficient workplaces. As a result the urbanization of Norway had temporarily ceased. The excess of labour was increased by rapidly increasing mechanization. At the same time, the towns and built-up areas attracted people. Expanding industry and services offered secure year-round work and higher wages. The towns, too, could offer a range of service and cultural attractions that were not available in the country districts – not least of which was education for a rural youth hungry for knowledge. Migration was as much a quest for the opportunities the town could offer as a flight from the countryside.

Economic growth in the built-up areas was needed if people were to be attracted to them. But at the same time the influx of people was a pre-condition of the continued growth of industry and services. For much of the 1940s, 1950s and 1960s there was a shortage of labour. It has been generally accepted that the transfer of labour from the primary to the secondary and tertiary industrial sectors has contributed to economic growth, because the last two sectors have been more productive than the first. The transfer has produced a 'migration dividend'.

Norwegian exports and imports as a percentage of GNP

	1930	1950	1970	1982
Exports	15,6	17,0	19,5	31,2
Imports	24,3	29,5	29,4	27,5

Many people explain post-war growth as a result of the marked increase in international trade and the gradual involvement of Norway in this trade. The contrast between the liberalization of world trade after 1945 and the thoroughgoing protectionist climate of the inter-war years is striking. After the First World War, new states in Europe emerged and as a result new customs barriers. The crises contributed to countries isolating themselves through the protection of their own industries and attempts at self-sufficiency. Since 1945 the development has gone in the opposite direction, first through cooperation over the Marshall Plan, the Organization for European Economic Coperation (now Organization for Economic Co-operation and Development, OECD) and the General Agreement on Tariffs and Trade (GATT), and later through the European Free Trade Association (EFTA) and the European Community (EC) (Chapter 26). There can be little doubt that the liberalization bias contributed to growth. In the 1950s it was precisely the export industries that expanded the most. Norway exploited its comparative advantage – as it had done around the turn of the century – by using its own resources and cheap water power. Norwegian shipping expanded with the increase in international trade, and in the 1960s the involvement in EFTA provided the opportunity for a shift to exports by several industries previously confined to the home market. It is true that other industries met problems through the increase of competition in the home market, but, in general, internationalization had an undoubtedly positive impact throughout the 1960s. At the same time, agriculture retained its protected position in the home market.

Growth in world trade followed the growth in, and liberalization of, the world economy. Nevertheless, it is impossible to ignore the political decisions taken by individual countries. The integration of Norway into the international economy – for the government a desirable development – was the result of a political decision. Self-sufficiency, with its roots in the 1930s, had been a relatively strong attitude in the immediate post-war years. After 1947, the government chose to gamble almost everything on an export-driven industrialization. The government also chose to cooperate with the Marshall Plan and subsequent free listing (i.e. a reduction in the number of industrial products subject to quota restrictions) in the 1950s. And at the beginning of the 1960s the government initiated a further expansion of the energy-demanding export industries, e.g. the aluminium industry, while at the same time, through EFTA, opening the whole of industry to free competition.

Crisis, war and growth

Growth and industry-friendly policies; increasing internationalization; productivity increases and the transfer of labour – these are important for an understanding of economic growth. But at least the first two of these factors applied only from the 1950s onwards. It inevitably took time before the priorities of the 1940s could lead to increased output, and internationalization occurred but gradually. Not until the 1960s can one see the full effects of the interaction involving the state's own power and industrial enterprises, the drive for productivity improvements, the use of foreign capital, the aggressive regional policies and internationalization. But we know today that the strongest growth took place in the first five or six post-war years and was over by the beginning of the 1950s. And there was also a far greater growth in industrial employment between 1931 and 1950 than in the next 20 years or so – 170,000 man years as against 80,000.

In order fully to understand the economic growth of the post-war years, it is necessary to go back to the war and even further to the crisis years at the beginning of the 1930s. Then there was neither labour migration, an expansionist economic policy nor an internationalization of the Norwegian economy. Yet the foundations of the new industrial growth were laid down during the depression. The depression destroyed time-honoured methods, but at the same time prepared for the new. Small enterprises grew up based on a new but simple technology (electric power) and new products, e.g. furniture, stoves, kitchen utensils, bicycles, sports equipment and tools. A not inconsiderable rise in real wages for the majority who were in work stimulated an emerging 'consumer society'. On this basis industry was already on its way out of crisis *before* the war – and it was this growth that continued, in a stronger form, in the years after it.

The war itself also stimulated economic growth. Above all it eliminated important obstacles to growth. Unemployment, which had haunted society like a nightmare and caused serious social tension and conflict, disappeared. In 1938, some 60,000–70,000 people were without work – about 20 per cent of all trade union members. After 1942 there was, in effect, no unemployment. Bergen had had 4,000 registered unemployed in 1938: 10 years later only three adults were receiving benefits.

Unemployment disappeared for many reasons. Many people found work directly from the Germans on building and construction sites, air strips, roads and fortifications. Others worked in businesses that, in whole or in part, were based on supplying the Germans or German-dependent activities. In general, the special circumstances of the war led to a considerable fall in productivity and this too gave more jobs. The public sector, especially those parts of it tied to supplying, regulating and rationing, expanded strongly. Many people were taken out of the ordinary labour market into military or subversive activities. Many left the country. Others were imprisoned. Shortly after the war the labour market was 'normalized'. But this did not bring about new unemployment. Now all available labour was drawn into home market industries, which enjoyed virtually unlimited demand, or into the work of reconstruction.

Debt was another social problem that had cast its shadow over economic and social initiatives for most of the inter-war period. The problem had already eased in the course of the 1930s and virtually disappeared during the war. The rise in prices made debt easier to bear. At the same time, the large amount of money in circulation, together with price controls and rationing, led naturally to the paying off of debts for private individuals, businesses, farmers and local authorities. In agriculture the average debt, measured as the proportion of debt to total assets, fell from 40 to 20 per cent. The debts of local authorities were reduced by almost 40 per cent, at the same time as their income almost doubled. Many local authorities came out of the war completely free of debt. Income could now be directed to consumption and the improvement of social standards and investment in business activities instead of the payment of interest on, and the repayment of, old loans.

Also during the war there occurred a considerable growth of capital and capacity within industry. This growth was important for the post-war expansion. The expansionist Keynesian economic policies – based on public investment and unbalanced budgets – that the Labour Party had been so keen on had not been implemented during the 1930s. However the Germans' building activities and the abundant supply of money during the war helped to boost the growth of the economy in the same way that Keynes had believed should be brought about through the political mechanism. The effects were extended and strengthened by the requirements for post-war reconstruction.

In addition there was substantial technological development and reorganization within industrial concerns. New products and processes took shape, partly in response to German demand, partly under the shelter of special circumstances created by the war and through the absence of overseas competition. After the war these were to form the basis for rapid industrial growth. German building activities during the war also created enduring assets: roads, railways and airports, power stations and industrial concerns. The airport at Gardermoen was built, the Sørlands railway was completed. The building of the Årdal aluminium works with its associated power station had come a long way by the end of the war. The country's largest industrial firm, Norsk Hydro, became Norwegian – and semi-public – through the confiscation of German shares. Today one wonders if the material losses brought about by the war were not exaggerated in 1945.

A two-phased picture of growth

Perhaps on the basis of the above, it can be suggested that Norwegian growth occurred in two phases – each with its own explanation. The industrial and economic growth shortly after the war can be seen as an extension of the period of growth that was started by the reorganization and regeneration that took place during the depression of the early 1930s. This growth continued under the stimulus of the special demands created by the war and the subsequent reconstruction. 'Transformation' and 'demand-led growth' are key concepts here. The growth was supported and made possible by the rapid restructuring of the primary industries and the migration of labour from the countryside to the towns. This explanation leaves room for a reconstruction perspective on economic growth, but emphasizes continuity above all else – the link with the interwar years – and, paradoxically, the close ties between growth and depression.

The second kind of growth – that seen throughout the 1950s and above all in the 1960s – has a more revolutionary feel to it. Now it was the new industries based on production for export, together with the service industries that grew the most, while new urban societies and the development of built-up areas followed in their wake. The tempo of change in agriculture and fisheries accelerated; mechanization continued apace. In order to understand this growth it is necessary to examine the links between policy, the continuing movement of labour to the expanding industries and, not least, the growing internationalization of the Norwegian economy. It was to a very great extent a different kind of growth from the growth that had carried the developments from the 1930s and throughout the 1940s. Yet even in the 1950s and 1960s it is not difficult to see the links with earlier periods of the country's history. Water-powered heavy industry, the industrialization of exports; together with foreign capital, are reminicent of the major industrial expansion shortly after the turn of the century.

24
The welfare society

In the course of the 1950s and 1960s Norway become a welfare society. The majority of the population had the opportunity to secure a good steady income through their own efforts. Both welfare and material goods were relatively evenly distributed throughout society. At the same time a comprehensive apparatus of health and caring institutions together with a safety net of social benefits provided security against a loss or lack of income. The growth of the welfare society was dependent upon economic growth, and to a considerable degree the former kept pace with the latter. Thus growth and welfare, and the politics associated with them, have been considered as two sides of the same coin throughout the entire post-war period.

Many countries have become welfare societies in the years since the Second World War. What, above all, has characterized the Norwegian welfare 'model' is the especially high aspirations regarding the creation and maintenance of full employment, a strong egalitarianism, and an adherence to the 'principle of universality', whereby the services of the welfare state were for all and not just for the groups most in need. In addition, the welfare services have been for the most part provided by the public authorities.

Increased public involvement

Perhaps the most characteristic feature of the welfare society has been the development of a large and expanding public sector together with the active involvement of the state in society's development. An ever larger proportion of Norway's national product has been distributed through public authority budgets. Whereas the central and local authorities in 1939 disposed of barely 20 per cent of the national prod-

The politics aimed at economic growth strengthened the tendency of outmigration from the rural areas. But the abandonment of holdings and the shift away from peripheral areas would have occurred anyway. And, at the same time that the authorities stimulated centralization, they introduced measures of support for smaller farms.

uct, the share had more or less doubled to 40 per cent by 1970. Ten years later the public share had risen to 50 per cent.

The central and local authorities played several different roles in the development of the welfare society. As previously discussed, the public authorities contributed to economic growth, partly through their own economic activities and partly through the pursuit of policies designed to stimulate growth generally. The public authorities were themselves in many areas the greatest suppliers of welfare benefits. In other areas, they sought, through cooperation with other bodies, to provide benefits that were both cheap and widely available. Both the national and local authorities contributed to a levelling process in society by a comprehensive redistribution of wealth from the strong to the weak. To an increasing extent also, the authorities sought to regulate the activities of the private sector, so as to hinder or prevent its having a negative effect on individuals or groups, or on society as a whole. Through these multifarious activities, the public authorities became a major employer. In 1950, barely 200,000, or one-fifth of all wage earners, worked for national or local authorities. By 1970 the total was 335,000, or between one-quarter and one-third of all employees.

Policies for welfare and economic growth

The authorities often pursued several goals at the same time. The policies for growth aimed at increasing employment, general well-being and economic strength so as to support welfare developments. In return, welfare policy was inspired by a wish that it should contribute to growth. At the same time growth policies created welfare problems, which in turn made it desirable that arrangements be made to limit their effects.

Political initiatives were frequently contradictory. There are numerous examples of this. The desire to industrialize and to move labour to the towns created depopulation problems, which were met by regional political initiatives. These limited mobility, contrary to the initial policy aim. The attempt to increase agricultural efficiency by increasing farm size went hand in hand with measures to support small farms in outlying areas. Subsidies for building large, technically advanced fishing boats, and other subsidies based on the size of the catch, increased productivity, but at the same time increased inequalities in the industry. Other measures – such as the minimum income – sought to counter this.

The principle of universality for all welfare services and benefits helped to eradicate the stamp of social inferiority long associated with support from public funds. But, at the same time, the impact on economic equality was much less than it would have been had the welfare benefits been confined to those who needed them most. Public initiatives and services often, therefore, pulled in different directions. But the welfare society developed through such conflicts and the difficult choices that had to be made between contrasting aspirations and effects. The main tendency, however, was for an increase in welfare and security for all, and an ever-greater social equality in a country that, from an international perspective, was already egalitarian.

The equalization of incomes

It is difficult to measure the equalization of incomes with any degree of certainty. The statistics are inadequate, saying more about hourly wage rates and scales than about actual earnings. Methods of calculation have also changed over time. Additions to pay in the form of free or cheap accommodation, food or fringe benefits are difficult to estimate. It is easier to measure pay in the public sector, which has fixed scales, than it is in the private sector, and easier to determine the income of workers than of directors. There are, as well, considerable differences within occupations and industries. It is difficult to calculate the effect of taxation and even more difficult to say anything certain about the impact on income and assets of inflation and the taking-up of loans.

The main impression is, however, that incomes were equalized across a broad front. Between 1935 and 1950 the gap between the incomes of industrial workers and those of white-collar workers in the public sector narrowed, though the change has since become less clear. Nevertheless, measured in net pay after tax, the equalization process continued in the 1950s and 1960s. A civil servant who in 1950 had a disposable income 80 per cent greater than that of a worker, 25 years later had one that was only 60 per cent greater. The incomes of workers in agriculture and forestry came closer to those of industrial workers, at least down to 1950. Agricultural incomes grew much more than did hourly rates in industry. In the mid-1960s, full-time fishermen came to earn more than industrial workers. The hourly pay of women in industry in 1946 was 60 per cent that of men; by 1970 it had risen to 75 per cent. A married couple living on an old-age pension in the early 1960s disposed of an income barely 30 per cent as great as that of an industrial worker. Ten years later the percentage had risen to 45.

Housing

Of all welfare benefits, housing received the promptest attention from the public authorities after the war. Before the turn of the century, housing needs were perceived as one of the most urgent social problems – especially in the largest towns. The problem was exacerbated by the destruction and lack of new building during the Second World

War. Increased numbers of marriages and especially high marital fertility from 1944 to 1948 added to the problem as did migration to the towns. In 1945 the housing shortfall was put at 100,000 units. Five years later it had risen to 125,000. Of this latter figure, 45,000 were to be found in Oslo, Bergen and Trondheim. The shortage of housing in the towns acted as a brake on urbanization. The housing shortage became a permanent problem in post-war Norway.

Attempts were made to ease immediate needs by temporary expedients, e.g. reconstructing German barracks and official requisitioning of rooms in the homes of people who were deemed to have more than 'necessary'. In 1950 there were still between 5,000 and 6,000 requisition orders in force in Oslo, Bergen, Stavanger and Tromsø. This unpopular regulation was not completely done away with until the mid-1950s.

Rents were firmly controlled by the authorities, as, in many cases, was the sale of houses and plots. But it was, above all, new building that received most attention. Again the authorities took a major role in the actual production of new homes as well as in planning and financing them. To some extent local authorities built houses for rent; though it was only in Bergen that their role was substantial – here 20 per cent of all new homes were being built by the local authority down to 1955. More usually, the local authorities concentrated on obtaining and regulating building sites and then building the roads and other necessary infrastructure. For a long time they took little payment for this, which meant that house building received a considerable subsidy.

Most important of all, however, was the contribution made by the authorities to the financing of house building and to the regulation of the housing market. The National Housing Bank was set up in 1946. It became the most important instrument in the government's policy of building new homes. The bank gave cheap loans with long repayment terms, liberal depreciation allowances, and various other forms of interest relief and support. Deposits on new homes were modest and could, in many cases, be partly or wholly dispensed with if one did some of the work involved in building them, e.g. painting, general labouring. The bank also fixed maximum sizes and standards, the result being that official support was given only for good, but simple, homes. By the middle of the 1980s the Housing Bank had financed 875,000 homes, two-thirds of all the homes built after the war, and occupied by 2 million Norwegians.

In sparsely populated areas it was mostly detached houses that were built and any organization of the building process – outside public regulations and financial support – was seldom necessary. In towns and built-up areas, however, the building process itself had to be organized. The national and local authorities decided to use building co-operatives. As members of a 'house owners' co-operative', the occupants themselves administered the dwellings they owned in common. The actual building too was organized through a 'house building co-operative', whose members included those seeking homes, and the homes were shared out on a first-come, first-served basis. Members of the housing co-operative had first refusal on the purchase of used homes, the sale price of which was fixed officially. These housing co-operatives gradually came to dominate the building of homes in the towns; indeed they often had a near monopoly. In Bergen, they built more than 30 per cent of flats in the second half of the 1950s, around 40 per cent in the early 1960s and 70 per cent down towards 1970. 'Social house building' came eventually to be almost totally identified with the large blocks of flats created by the urban housing co-operatives, the financing of which was virtually wholly in the hands of the Housing Bank.

This co-operative building of homes was 'private' in the sense that those who lived in them also owned them – albeit collectively. This contrasts with local authority building that took place on a considerable scale in Norway from before the First World War onwards – as well as in several other countries. But the housing was very much 'public' in the sense that it was publicly financed and the authorities used the co-operatives as a part of their building policy. The local authorities were also often active in setting up and running the co-operatives, they favoured them by allocating plots, and they could demand a greater or lesser share of the flats for their own purposes. The freedom to choose one's home was limited in many places. Especially in the towns it was necessary to go via the housing co-operative's waiting lists, whether one wanted to or not. It is, therefore, reasonable to see house building as an example of the mixing of private and public activity that was such a characteristic feature of the development of the welfare society.

There can be little doubt that co-operative housebuilding was a great leveller. In the towns, the old division between those who owned and those who rented became less marked. The vast majority were lift-

The housing shortage was one of the great social problems of the 1940s and 1950s. Co-operative housing was given a high priority by the authorities. In the large towns, cooperative housing societies found a place to build with the creation of the new 'satellite towns'. At Lambertseter, outside Oslo, homes for 18,000 people were built between 1950 and 1958.

ed up into the ranks of the owner-occupiers. In the new estates of co-operative housing, all shared ownership – and status. The flats were all built to the same plan and were of equal size. Entry depended on one's membership number in the housing co-operative. The flats in each project were shared by drawing lots, which put the worker and the university graduate on the same landing. The quality of housing was raised substantially throughout the entire country. Internationally speaking, the standard was very high indeed. In rural districts and small towns, the Housing Bank financed 'a detached house for everyone'. In this way the new housing contributed to the evening out of differences between town and country.

However, at the same time, this social housing development had unthought of consequences. Cheap loans, tax relief on interest payments, inflation and a sharp rise in the value of fixed property led to a rise in the value of the assets of those who had built their *own* detached houses with the aid of Housing Bank loans, while those who were members of cooperative housing developments had no tax advantages and had to sell their homes at a price fixed by the authorities. When building land in the towns was reserved for the blocks of flats built by the housing cooperatives, the better-quality detached homes were built in the neighbouring local authority districts. Paradoxically this had the effect of creating new 'smart areas', quite the opposite of the egalitarianism sought after. Also, the new built-up areas in the rural districts and small towns took on a markedly uniform character as a result of the standardization produced by the Housing Bank and the manufacturers, who created a limited number of house types.

Education

Educational opportunities increased in number and variety, almost entirely organized and paid for by the public authorities. In 1950, scarcely 10 per cent of public expenditure went on education. Ten years later the figure was 15 per cent and in 1970 some 17–18 per cent. The number of teachers rose from 40,000 to 70,000 between 1960 and 1970. In 1970, as many as 800,000 – 20 per cent of the population – were in full-time education. The growth occurred through a massive expansion of the educational system at all levels. There were many reasons for this expansion. The large number of children born in the years 1944–48 had to be found places in the primary schools in the course of the 1950s. By the beginning of the 1960s they had reached the post-primary stage; they moved into the sixth forms in the first half of the 1960s, and after that into the universities and colleges. Urbanization dramatically increased the need for new school building.

The 'educational explosion' meant first and foremost that opportunities improved for a steadily larger proportion of the population. The growth in the number of pupils and students was far greater than the growth in the size of the cohorts from which they came. Gradually, education beyond the minimum required by law became a popular good. In 1962, two-thirds of all 15-year-olds were at school; by 1970 almost all. From 1955 to 1970 the number of students holding university entrance qualifications trebled (from 4,000 to 12,000) as did the number of university graduates. In 1970, there were 30,000 university students as against 5,000 before the war.

The educational explosion was propelled by an expanding society's need for a well-educated labour force, together with the wishes of both the private and public sector for ever more specialist skills. Specialization and the increased demands for vocational training also made it more difficult to go straight into work after a basic schooling. But an equally strong motivating force was the desire of the young and older generations for education as the way towards better-paid jobs, higher social prestige and a more satisfying life. The educational explosion was also the clearest expression of the increased social mobility in Norwegian society.

Educational policy also had two goals: to raise the level of knowledge of the people as a whole, and to contribute towards a more egalitarian society – culturally, socially and economically. From the end of the 1950s the gradual introduction of nine years of obligatory schooling added two years to the previous total. This was also an expression of the comprehensive idea: each generation should go to the same school and receive the same education. Only through a common schooling could the old social distinctions be broken down. Gradually, the comprehensive school replaced the earlier 'grammar' and 'secondary modern' schools (the former serving the academically inclined, the latter those who sought a practical, vocationally oriented education). The idea of streaming, by ability or subject, in the comprehensive school was abandoned. In the 1970s the grammar and vocational schools (these followed after the nine years of compulsory schooling) were amalgamated. The idea was to pursue the goal of a single school for all. But here integration proved much more difficult. The old forms continued much as they had done, though now under a joint name.

The rise in living standards made it both natural and possible for the young to go to school instead of to a job. At the same time, school fees, which had had to be paid by pupils of the grammar schools, were abolished, thus removing a burden that had been heavy indeed for many parents. The state set up a body in 1947 that provided cheap loans for pupils receiving post-compulsory schooling and for university and college students to help pay their maintenance costs. In a period with low interest rates a strong growth of real incomes, and rising inflation, to have to finance one's education through loans was no great source of anxiety.

The regional expansion of educational establishments also had a levelling effect. The building of new schools in rural district centres both strengthened and increased the range of educational opportunities. The post-compulsory schools, which previously had been confined to the towns, were now extended to new regional centres. The transfer of these schools to the new county administrative units emphasized that they were to offer opportunities for all, not just for young people in the towns. The country got three new universities, one for each region: Bergen in 1946, Trondheim and Tromsø in 1968. In 1969, the first three of a new system of regional colleges of higher education were opened – in Kristiansand, Molde and Stavanger. The country also got many new teacher training colleges. Gradually, Norway developed what was probably the most decentralized higher education system in the world.

The drive towards educational equality also had a gender dimension. In 1950, 40 per cent of those obtaining university entrance qualifications were women; in 1975 the percentage was 50. In 1950, 16 per cent of university students were women; 20 years later, 28 per cent were. And the trend continued: in 1970, women accounted for 35 per cent of new students. But there were still significant gender differences in the type of education received. In 1972, some 61 per cent of male pupils seeking university entrance qualifications were taking science courses, as against 69 per cent of females who were studying arts courses. In 1970, the proportion of women at the four universities had reached 40 per cent, as against only 7 per cent in those institutions of higher education devoted exclusively to business and engineering. Women featured prominently in pharmacy, languages, teaching and psychology, but their numbers were relatively small in theology, law, economics and the sciences.

The dramatic growth of education undoubtedly led to greater equality, but it is difficult to say by how much. On the other hand, it had a negative effect. The development of central schools often led to the closure of small schools in outlying districts. 'School commuting' became widespread. When the schools disappeared, the quality of life of small communities was reduced and the conditions for maintaining population worsened. This was especially true if with the school went the local shop, post office, bus and boat connections. Paradoxically, too, the expansion of education contributed to the impoverishment of some areas, even whole regions, in another way. Clever pupils who got their basic education locally travelled to the largest centres for their higher education. And there was a clear tendency for them to stay in their new environment. For here were the specialist jobs they had trained for; something that was not the case in the districts from which they had come. The imbalance was rectified to some degree by the strong growth in the service industries – and perhaps particularly in the public sector – towards the end of the 1960s.

Social benefits

In talking generally about the welfare society it is, perhaps, above all the ever-increasing degree of social security that is thought of first. Almost all of the social benefits have been provided by public authorities and into them has gone an ever-greater share of the country's resources: 7 per cent of net national product in 1948; 17 per cent in 1970. Old-age pensions were introduced in 1936. But, otherwise, almost all social support provided from the public purse before the war was collected together in one catch-all item: *forsorg* – the care of individuals in need of assistance, for one reason or another, who were provided with the minimum necessary after a thorough examination. After 1945 two lines of development emerge clearly: first, a shift from means-tested benefits to universal benefits and, second, a move to a more institutionally based provision of services. The one followed the other to some extent: the 1950s and 1960s saw the drive to universal benefits at its height, while the institutionalization of care did not really get under way until the mid-1960s. The continuing high rate of economic growth meant that ambitions for social care could also continue to rise – from necessary help in times of crisis, to a reasonable living standard for all via social insurance, and finally to institutional care when financial support alone was no longer enough.

Universal benefits should be for all who fulfilled certain standard conditions. The system gradually expanded with one benefit after another. Family allowances came first – as early as 1946 – though strictly speaking this was not a benefit but a subsidy for all families with children. Then came child allowances in 1958; disability allowances and rehabilitation support in 1961; widows' and single mothers' benefits in 1965. The principle of universality was carried through when health insurance was made obligatory in 1957 and the means test for old-age pensions was abolished in 1959. Gradually the various benefits were amalgamated. Thus in 1960 a general occupational injury benefit replaced all the work-related benefits. In 1967 a new administrative system *(Folketrygden)* was set up and by 1971 all the previous individual schemes were co-ordinated through this system.

The new benefits covered gradually more and more of those in need. In 1946, about 140,000 people were in receipt of pensions in Norway – about 4–5 per cent of the population. Of these, just under 110,000 were old-age pensioners, the rest being war pensioners or those suffering occupational injuries. By 1970, 590,000 were in receipt of pensions, a good 15 per cent of the population. Old-age pensions still formed the largest group – 335,000. This increase was a product partly of the abolition of the means test, partly of a reduction in the age at which pensions could be drawn, and partly of the above-average growth of the older age groups. Disability pensions were also now claimed by large groups who had previously fallen outside the system. In 1970, 130,000 people were in receipt of disability pensions.

With full employment, the numbers in receipt of unemployment benefit, which had been introduced in 1938, were small: only 8,000 in 1970. Compared with the situation before the war, there were also few in receipt of national assistance. A new social security law of 1964 replaced the old Poor Law, which dated back to the turn of the century. In 1970 only about 40,000 people required this help. To all intents and purposes this was now a supplement to the total range of benefits. All these benefits led to a more egalitarian society, in that more and more people who had previously been without an income now had a reasonable one. In addition, the actual benefits grew strongly, more so than average earnings.

For the first 10 years after the war, hospital building by no means matched requirements. Not until well into the 1950s did construction increase and not until around the mid-1960s was the number of hospital beds, relative to population, greater than before the war. The growth in the number of doctors per hospital was especially marked in the first half of the 1960s. And it was then that the *quality* of the medical services really began to expand. There was a sharp increase in specialization and the hospitals absorbed virtually all the rise in the number of doctors. Towards the end of the 1960s the building of nursing homes escalated. There were several reasons for this: the large increase in the number of elderly people; developments within medicine, which made long-term nursing both possible and necessary; and changes in settlement and family patterns, which made nursing within the family less common. About the same time too, a strong growth began in the institutionalization of other welfare services, not least the treatment and care of the handicapped. The increasing number of married women in paid employment also stimulated the development of creches and kindergartens.

While social benefits were wholly a public matter, the institutionalization process was one welfare area in which the private sector played a part, often led by voluntary organizations. The leading role of the public authorities remained unchallenged. But early in the 1960s it was still the case that private hospitals had 20 per cent of hospital beds. The initiative for expanding the new institutional care, which came towards the end of the 1960s, was often taken by humanitarian or religious bodies, even if their financing was for the most part from public funds. Here, therefore, is yet another example of the mixed management existing within the welfare society. Not until the hospital law of 1969 was responsibility for hospital building and administration put entirely into the hands of the county authorities.

Equality and the regions

One of the most characteristic features of the development of the Norwegian welfare state – not least in an international context – was the greatly increased drive for regional equality. Most attention here has been directed at what is usually called 'regional policy'. By that is generally meant those measures designed to strengthen and expand economic activities, above all industry, in the outlying areas of Norway. The first major initiative was the *Nord-Norge Plan* (Northern Norway Plan) of 1952. A development bank for north Norway was created from which loans and loan guarantees could be provided as supplemental financing when other sources had been exhausted. In special circumstances it could be used to buy shares. A company's own investments in the area were tax-deductible and there were especially favourable depreciation allowances. In addition, measures were taken to improve communications, expand power supplies and develop vocational training in north Norway.

The special priority given to the north of Norway lasted until the end of the 1960s. The goals of the plan were met – at least to some extent. The region's share of the national product increased slightly, as did total employment. Many new jobs in both industry and services were created: 23,000 in the years 1950 to 1960. The stimuli benefited above all towns and central places. The traditional economic activities of the outlying areas – fishing and agriculture – witnessed in this same decade a loss of 17,000–18,000 jobs. But this was in line with expectations. It was generally felt that the situation in the region could be improved, relative to that in the rest of the country, only by investing in the most productive areas of economic activity. Necessarily this meant strengthening the centres at the expense of the truly peripheral areas and occupations. The outlying regions were to become stronger by strengthening central places *within* them.

The contemporary view that the Northern Norway Plan had been a success was important for the continuation of regional policy at the beginning of the 1960s – and on a broader geographical front. The Trøndelag Plan and the Unemployment Fund's development plan of 1956, together with the Northern Troms Plan the year after, were all steps on the way to a national development plan for the regions. In 1960 the Regional Development Bank was set up, based essentially on the methods applied in the Northern Norway Plan. By the beginning of the 1970s these were being supplemented by investment subsidies, which varied from region to region. The setting up of the Regional Development Bank took place at a time of a great political campaign for the extension to and expansion of industrial activity in the regions of Norway.

The idea of 'growth centres' dominated thinking on regional policy and growth from the middle of the 1960s. Such centres were to be created by concentrating resources on the economic development of regional and local nodal points. These would attract migrants from the *real* periphery, and would also form barriers against a more extreme centralization focused on the largest urban areas. Banking on 'centres in the periphery' or 'decentralized concentration' was an attempt to maintain the main features of a dispersed settlement pattern. The Regional Development Bank, for the most part, used its resources in line with this strategy of stimulating a high degree of local centralization. Building for Industrial Growth Ltd. was set up in 1968. This company provided infrastructure and built industrial units for rent by interested companies. This initiative was a product of the same basic thinking that had already been adopted in the Northern Norway Plan.

There can be little doubt that regional policies did help considerably to even out or slow down the emergence of inequalities between different parts of the country. They came, however, under constant criticism for not benefiting the most peripheral areas. But it had never been intended that regional policies should provide support for every single economic activity or maintain an unchanged settlement pattern. Regional policy was always an element in the general policy for growth *as well as* in policies aimed at reducing the differences between regions. Ideally, growth itself should have reflected regional interests. When this did not happen to the extent judged necessary, the public authorities sought to prevent too negative an effect on the regions without going so far as to place too great an obstacle in the path of growth itself.

This double goal was a permanent feature of economic policy generally. Industrial, agricultural and fishing policy always included features aimed at growth and others that aimed at evening out differences between the regions. Industrial policy aimed primarily at growth throughout the entire post-war period. The state's own enterprises were an element in the drive towards the growth of output. But, at the same time, industrialization had a strong regional impact because a great deal of the resources required were in coastal and peripheral Norway. The aluminium industry went after the power in Årdal, Sunndalsøra, Mosjøen and Husnes. The iron industry sought ore and power in Rana. The fish-processing plants located in the fishing ports of Finnmark and north Troms. In these cases there was no difference between growth and regional policy. From the end of the 1950s there was a more conscious adoption of regional industrialization. Even so it was seen as a contributory factor to the overall goal of industrial growth.

A central aim of agricultural policy was equality with manufacturing industry. There can be little doubt that the most important means for achieving this were increased output, rationalization and efficiency so as to develop and strengthen 'self-sustainable' holdings. Yet at the same time measures were taken to even out differences between holdings, by strengthening the weaker, outlying ones. Marketing regulations created in the inter-war years were developed further after the war, with the aim of evening out prices, and consequently incomes, between different parts of the country. Already in 1945 special subsidies had been introduced for milk producers in the fjord and mountain areas, and in north Norway. In 1952 a general operating subsidy was introduced for smaller producers.

The hefty subsidies for grain producers made it more profitable to produce grain on the large farms of Østlandet and central Norway. This helped maintain the large differences in agricultural incomes. But, at the same time, the change-over to grain in the central agricultural areas made it possible to continue the production of milk and meat in peripheral Norway without a destructive over-production that, in the next round, would have led to the abandonment of precisely the least favoured holdings.

As with industry and agriculture, there can be little doubt that the fisheries policy has aimed above all at growth and rationalization. The living standards of fishermen and fishing districts were to be improved by increasing productivity. Larger vessels would give employment and better pay throughout the year. Processing plants in north Norway would provide a stable market and regional employment opportunities. At the same time, however, subsidies were introduced to help the weakest, for example via the provision of a minimum income. Legislation, subsidies and regulations all thwarted the growth of excessively large, highly capitalized units. On the whole, there can be little doubt that economic policy since the war has contributed to evening out regional differences and – from an international standpoint – upholding a highly decentralized settlement pattern.

Least attention has perhaps been paid to the levelling effects of welfare benefits provided through the various local authorities. Yet possibly these have been the greatest levellers of them all. Local authority institutions are themselves to a great extent local and regional mechanisms for distribution and redistribution. The whole system of local government went through a major reform in the 1950s and 1960s. Small authorities were amalgamated, usually with a built-up area or town as their new centre. This was the first comprehensive reorganization since the introduction of local self-government in 1837. Most of the amalgamations took place between 1962 and 1965. The number of local authorities decreased from 744 to 454. At the same time, the county authorities were transformed. From merely providing support for the rural local authorities, they became independent regional authorities with a distinctive role between the state, on the one hand, and the local authorities, on the other. The towns were brought under the jurisdiction of these authorities in 1964. Down to the mid-1970s they gradually acquired political and administrative organs based on direct elections and with their own income from direct taxation.

Øvre Årdal in 1968. Towns developed almost from scratch around the large new heavy industry plants. From the end of the 1950s there was widespread agreement that the most important method of maintaining the population of Norway's remoter regions was through industrialization and the development of centres of growth.

The amalgamation of local authorities brought about centralization. Small, previously independent authorities were joined together – often against their will – and important tasks were transferred from the local to the county authorities. The aim was to create units that could look after themselves and be more effective welfare producers and administrative agents of the state. A greater degree of centralization around a local hub was seen as necessary in order to strengthen the welfare opportunities provided in the most peripheral areas. By international standards the process of amalgamation was modest. For example, in Sweden the number of local authorities was reduced from 2,498 to 282 between 1945 and 1974. The idea behind the new county authorities was to create a political and administrative unit at the county level that could provide high schools and health care opportunities, both of which necessarily required a comparatively large population base, that were as widely accessible as possible. Without a strong administrative

State subsidies in kroner per inhabitant in rural, urban and county municipalities 1950–1974. (Fixed prices, 1966 = 100.)

	Rural municipalities Abs. Nos.	Index	Urban municipalities Abs. Nos.	Index	County municipalities Abs. Nos.	Index
1950	189	100	200	100	23	100
1966	297	157	244	122	115	325
1974	598	316	346	173	183	798

unit at the county level, it would not have been possible to maintain a local authority structure based on generally small units.

To a great extent, the equalization at the regional level was brought about by subsidies and transfers both from the state and between one authority and another. The arrangements were of two main types: special subsidies for a particular purpose, and general subsidies, often called 'tax equalization'. In 1974 there were 150 subsidy and reimbursement transfers between the state and local authorities in the national budget. Special subsidies were graduated according to economic means. For example, at the end of the 1960s the state provided subsidies for local authority primary schools that varied between 25 and 85 per cent of their running costs. These special subsidies have had a marked levelling effect. Thus, in 1974 local authorities in rural districts received 70 per cent more in subsidies per inhabitant than did urban authorities. For their high schools, Sogn and Fjordane, Nordland, Troms and Finnmark got 75 per cent of their running costs covered, while Oslo had to be content with 35 per cent.

The 'tax equalization' system also had a levelling effect. Shortly after the war the system was extremely modest: 4 million *kroner* in 1947/48. By 1972 the sum transferred exceeded 1 billion *kroner* – in fixed prices some 60–70 times greater than 25 years earlier. Until the early 1950s virtually all this money went to north Norway. After that, the system can best be seen as an income subsidy for regional local authorities generally, and above all for the smaller ones. In 1968, four out of five local authorities together with all the county authorities (with the exception of the central Østland counties), received support. Many authorities in rural areas received in subsidies as much as or more than they themselves raised in taxes and dues.

Equalization payments received from the state as a percentage
of tax income by municipalities of different size, 1974

	Size of population			
	<5000	5–25 000	25–60 000	>60 000
Equalization payments as a percentage of tax income	26	12	3	1

Overall, the reduction in differences between the regions is obvious in the years 1945 to 1970. Whereas in 1950 the average income for personal tax payers in Finnmark was just about half of that in Oslo, by 1970 it had risen to three-quarters. The inhabitants of municipalities dominated by service and industrial activities in the 1940s earned about twice as much as people living in agricultural areas. By 1975, the difference had fallen to 60 per cent.

Local authority welfare and the leveller state

This chapter has consciously focused on the development of a welfare *society* in Norway. At the same time it has consistently stressed the major role played by public authorities in bringing welfare to all. Most often, the role played by the *state* is stressed. The fact that the very term 'welfare state' has achieved such a dominant position is evidence of this role. The expression emphasizes welfare as a common national good, at the same time as it emphasizes the role of the state as the central provider and distributor of welfare. The local authorities are usually seen as providing an instrumental or supportive service for the state. The local authorities are understood to be necessary to ensure that national services are distributed locally.

There is, of course, nothing wrong in stressing the instrumental role of the local authorities *vis-à-vis* the state. Over the long term, the state has increasingly decided, through laws and regulations, both what tasks the local authorities shall accomplish and the means by which they should be carried out. Through more detailed regulations as well as subsidies and rebates the local and national administrations have been tied more and more firmly together under the state's leadership. Nevertheless, it is quite proper to emphasize the *interaction* between the state and local authorities in both the production and management of welfare services, and not least local authority initiatives in this context. For in many spheres there was a welfare *authority* before there was a welfare *state*.

Often the local authorities pioneered aspects of the welfare state. In the post-war period as well, local authorities, on their own account and using their own resources, have taken important welfare initiatives. This is especially true in the social sector. In the 1940s and 1950s local authorities displayed a broadly independent involvement in social benefit issues by giving supplements to centrally organized benefits, and even more importantly, by creating their own benefits. Some 200 local authorities had introduced local benefits for the disabled, for widows and for single mothers several years before the state legislated to make them national. Around 1960 more than 90 per cent of the country's population lived in these local authority areas. Gradually, the image of the local authorities changed from that of poor relief dispensers to providers of benefits. The role of the state in the development of welfare benefits was to act primarily on behalf of those authorities that could not themselves manage to mount a welfare offensive, and to develop and legislate for a national administrative and financial apparatus. In this way, what had been local became national. In the process the local authorities were gradually reduced to being appendages of a state-run welfare system.

The 'nationalization' of welfare benefits meant that in many cases the local authorities were relieved of their financial and administrative responsibilities. This, however, gave them the opportunity, throughout the 1960s, to direct their efforts into new areas: from providing monetary benefits to providing institutional care. Here, too, the state followed with rules and regulations that were common to the nation as a whole. Strong local authorities played similarly pioneering roles in other areas, such as in education and hospital management. In many ways then the welfare society appears as a dynamic interaction between local authorities strong on initiative and a state anxious to spread the benefits as evenly as possible. In many instances too, voluntary, religious and humanitarian organizations have played important roles in this game. Voluntary organizations have initiated important social undertakings, often with local authority support. In the next stage the initiative has been taken over by the local authority. Not until the third stage has the state, or perhaps the county authority, made an appearance.

Welfare society – change or continuity?

It is not difficult to argue the case for novelty when it comes to judging the development of the welfare society after 1945. Such a perspective must be founded above all on a view of the welfare society as a whole. Never before had welfare been pushed forward along such a broad front as in the decades after the war, with simultaneously ambitious programmes for house building, education, social security, welfare-oriented economic policies and the reduction of differences between the regions. It is also necessary to look at the level of welfare benefits, and at the shift from support as a necessity provided at a minimum level to the general acceptance of the ideal of a welfare benefit in the shape of a living standard acceptable to all. The post-war years also saw the acceptance of the idea of welfare benefits as a right – and not a form of charity. The principle of universality was also accepted, i.e. that the right to benefit was for the many rather than the few. The public involvement in the development of welfare was of a completely different magnitude from before. And welfare was 'nationalized' in the sense that the arrangements and services increasingly came under the leadership of the state. Thus, publicly provided benefits should, in principle at least, be the same throughout the country.

Nevertheless, the element of continuity must also be stressed. Most individual items in the development of the welfare society had long traditions. The benefits offensive in the 1950s and 1960s was not the first, but the third in Norway. The first lasted from 1894 until 1923. The second started after the Labour Party took office in the middle of the 1930s. It is natural to see the post-war developments as a continuation of those started in the 1930s. Perhaps it is more accurate to see the welfare developments in Norway as a continuous process, with parts of the 1920s, 1930s and the war years separating themselves out as socio-political interruptions in the reform process. Thoughts of social rights and universality have been linked with most socio-political offensives. What was new after the war was perhaps above all the broad political agreement on the principles for building up the welfare society. The idea of the comprehensive school had made its political breakthrough in Norway as early as 1920. As for house building, the larger local authorities had played a major role from before the First World War and cooperative housing was known from the inter-war period.

The symbiotic relationship between growth and welfare policies had emerged early in the 1930s when the attention of the labour movement was gradually shifted from the distribution to the creation of wealth. Through its new economic policies the government had already, to a considerable degree, taken responsibility for income growth and distribution in the primary industries. The development of welfare arrangements via a dynamic interaction between private organizations and local and national authorities also has long traditions in Norway. So too have subsidies and rebates with differential effects. From 1930, the tax equalization system had signalled increasing support for the principle of regional equality. The proactive state first took a dominant position in social development after 1945. But the basic ideas for this were already in place before the war.

25
A state in search of co-operation and consensus

In sharp contrast to the inter-war years, political and parliamentary life was for 25 years after the war characterised by a remarkable degree of stability. The Labour Party was in office until 1965 with one brief break. Nevertheless, throughout the entire period the two major political groups – the socialist and the non-socialist – were of roughly the same size. Fringe parties at either end of the political spectrum had little or no support and there was never any serious challenge to the political system. The immediate post-war years were characterised by the unity of wartime effort, the Joint Programme of 1945 and co-operation over the problems of reconstruction. On the other hand, the years 1947–53 were marked by new conflict between the socialist and the non-socialist parties. This was especially true in the case of economic policy, the planned economy and enabling legislation. The Labour Party wanted massive industrialization under the leadership of the state, an administration armed with strong powers to direct a planned economy, and far-reaching authority for the state's management bodies. For their part, the non-socialist parties defended the primary sector and small businesses. They feared 'creeping socialism' and were sceptical about the frequent official interference into the affairs of the business community. They defended the authority of the Storting and the rights of individuals against an expansive governmental and administrative force.

The major argument over the planned economy culminated with the debate on proposals for new price and rationalization legislation in 1952-53, but ended in something of a draw. The Labour Party abandoned its strongest control mechanisms, while the non-socialist parties accepted a far more proactive state than previously. Conflict over economic policy gradually subsided at the same time that there was more agreement over the main features of welfare policy. This growing con-

The parties' share of votes and number of seats at the Storting elections of 1945–1989

Party/Election list	1945 % of v.	1945 seats	1949 % of v.	1949 seats	1953 % of v.	1953 seats	1957 % of v.	1957 seats	1961 % of v.	1961 seats	1965 % of v.	1965 seats	1969 % of v.	1969 seats	1973 % of v.	1973 seats	1977 % of v.	1977 seats	1981 % of v.	1981 seats	1985 % of v.	1985 seats	1989 % of v.	1989 seats
A	41.0	76	45.7	85	46.7	77	48.3	78	46.8	74	43.1	68	46.5	74	35.3	62	42.3	76	37.2	66	40.8	71	34.3	63
H	17.0	25	18.3	23	18.6	27	18.9	29	20.0	29	21.1	31	19.6	29	17.4	29	24.8	41	31.7	53	30.4	50	22.2	37
KrF	7.9	8	8.5	9	10.5	14	10.2	12	9.6	15	8.1	13	9.4	14	12.3	20	12.4	22	9.4	15	8.3	16	8.5	14
Sp	8.1	10	7.9	12	9.1	14	9.3	15	9.4	16	9.9	18	10.5	20	11.0	21	8.6	12	6.7	11	6.6	12	6.5	11
V	13.8	20	13.1	21	10.0	15	9.7	15	8.8	14	10.4	18	9.4	13	3.5	2	3.2	2	3.9	2	3.1	–	3.2	–
NKP	11.9	11	5.8	–	5.1	3	3.4	1	2.9	–	1.4	–	1.0	–	–	–	0.4	–	0.3	–	0.2	–	–	–
SF	–	–	–	–	–	–	–	–	2.4	2	6.0	2	3.5	–	–	–	–	–	–	–	–	–	–	–
SV	–	–	–	–	–	–	–	–	–	–	–	–	–	–	11.2	16	4.2	2	4.9	4	5.5	6	10.1	17
DLF	–	–	–	–	–	–	–	–	–	–	–	–	–	–	3.4	1	1.4	–	0.5	–	0.5	–	–	–
ALP/FrP	–	–	–	–	–	–	–	–	–	–	–	–	–	–	5.0	4	1.9	–	4.5	4	3.7	2	13.0	22
RV	–	–	–	–	–	–	–	–	–	–	–	–	–	–	0.4	–	0.6	–	0.7	–	0.6	–	0.8	–
Andre	0.3	–	0.7	–	–	–	0.2	–	0.1	–	–	–	0.1	–	0.5	–	0.3	–	0.1	–	0.4	–	1.4	1
Total	100	150	100	150	100	150	100	150	100	150	100	150	100	150	100	155	100.1	155	99.9	155	100.1	157	100	165

A   – The Labour Party
H   – The Conservatives
KrF   – The Christian People's Party
Sp   – The Agrarian Party/The Centre Party
V   – The Liberals
NKP   – The Communists
SF   – The Socialist People's Party
SV   – The Socialist Left Party
DLF   – The Liberal People's Party
ALP/FrP   – The Progressive Party
RV   – The Red Alliance
Andre   – Others

sensus peaked at the beginning of the 1960s. The political parties had never come together on centre stage to the extent that they did then. In the 1960s the reins of government were taken over by the non-socialist parties. But this did not lead to great changes in the policies that had been pursued or to a more confrontational political climate.

The economic and social crisis of the inter-war years resulted in the demise of the idea of market self-regulation. Greater support was given to the idea of a proactive state – a state that would regulate economic activity, thus preventing destructive competition, and plan and direct economic life so as to encourage the growth of output and withstand crises. The socialist and non-socialist parties continued to disagree over the extent and form of the state's involvement. This division continued to be an important psychological and symbolic dividing line in Norwegian politics. But the proactive state became a reality, inspired too by widespread support for the ideal of a society providing for the well-being of all its members.

The proactive state was based on widespread participation. Increasingly, all parties in the labour and business world, as well as other organizations, were drawn into both the formulation and implementation of political decisions that affected their interests. The development led to the interweaving, on a considerable scale, of public and private sector administrative bodies. Gradually the state emerged as a force for achieving co-operation and consensus, with its policies and their implementation aimed, among other things, at providing solutions that could be accepted by as many people as possible.

Labour Party dominance and non-socialist divisions

After a short interval of coalition government in the first summer of peace, 1945, the Labour Party held a majority in the Storting. Majority government had not been seen since 1918. The war led to the radicalization of Norway – as it did the rest of western Europe. The relative size of the non-socialist and socialist forces of the inter-war years was reversed. The left in politics regularly achieved over 52 per cent of the vote at all elections down to 1965 – about 10 per cent more than in 1936. The Labour Party was dominant for most of the period. At the first election after the war the Communists got 12 per cent of the vote, but their support was quickly reduced through internal divisions and conflicts with the Labour Party during the introductory phase of the cold war. A new party appeared in 1961 – the Socialist People's Party (SF) to the left of the Labour Party, above all because of differences over foreign and security policy.

The Labour Party never received more than 48 per cent of the vote, but that was enough to give it an absolute majority of seats in the Storting at every election from 1945 to 1957. Its greatest majority was attained at the 1949 election when it won 85 of the 150 seats. But, after the election system was changed in 1952, its majorities became bare ones indeed. With the new challenger taking 2.4 per cent of the vote and two seats in 1961, the majority was lost. Now the Labour Party and the non-socialist parties had 74 seats each. The Socialist People's Party held the balance.

The ruling party also enjoyed great internal stability. Einar Gerhardsen was prime minister from 1945 to 1965, with the exception of the years 1951-55 when Oscar Torp took over and 1963 when the non-socialist parties had a brief period of office. Gerhardsen's authority was strong and his leadership of the government and the ruling party uncontested. There was a remarkable stability in other positions too. Haakon Lie, party secretary, had tight control of the party machine throughout the entire period. Halvard Lange was foreign minister for the same 20 years and Trygve Bratteli moved between key positions in the party and the Cabinet. On the list of ministers many appeared repeatedly, some serving in several departments.

The governing party's position was strengthened through its close cooperation with the powerful trade union movement. Industrialization and the resulting growth in the industrial workforce, together with a successful policy for economic growth, brought increased membership of the trade unions. Members affiliated to the National Federation of Labour (renamed LO in 1957) increased from 350,000 in 1945 to more than 550,000 twenty years later. Konrad Nordahl led the organization with great authority during the entire period. The party and the trade union movement were bound together by collective membership in the party for trade unions that wished it, hefty sums paid into party funds by LO, reciprocal representation on each other's executives and strong personal links. LO stressed the need for responsible policies in line with the priorities set by the Labour Party government. Important and difficult issues were discussed and clarified by an inner group consisting of the more influential figures. At the top was the Joint

Committee, consisting of chairmen and deputy chairmen in LO and the Labour Party, a powerful body for co-ordination and problem solving. An expanding and centrally supported Labour Party press, backed by LO's financial strength, was a powerful organ for party and trade union policies as well as for the government line.

The Labour Party and the trade union movement operated as a single disciplined body. The leadership had drawn the lessons from the destructive schisms of the inter-war years. They therefore laid great stress on finding collective solutions that would unite conflicting interests or wings. But a strict line was also taken with opposition groups or actions at grassroots level that appeared to pose a real threat to the policies of the leadership, or that would weaken the impression of unity. The Cabinet also followed a tough line with regard to the party group in the Storting. Here too discipline was strong. Individual representatives rarely took an independent line – and never if the party's majority was at stake.

Against the disciplined unity of the Labour side stood a sharply divided non-socialist opposition. The split actually increased just after the war in that the Christian People's Party broke through at national level. At the same time, the Conservatives, Liberals and the Agrarian Party all stabilized with a lower number of parliamentary seats than before the war. The Liberals suffered the greatest setback. The Conservatives continued to be by far the largest of the non-socialist parties with somewhat under 20 per cent of the electorate behind it, while the other three had around 10 per cent each.

For a long time the dissension between the non-socialist parties continued as it had before the war. The Conservatives and the Liberals were old adversaries. The Agrarian Party – which in 1959 changed its name to the Centre Party – and the Christian People's Party were founded essentially because of dissatisfaction with the non-socialist policies, especially those of the Liberals. Even an attempt at 'co-operation in the centre' towards the end of the 1950s ended in failure. The need of the parties to project themselves in order to win the favour of the electorate was felt more strongly than the need to construct an alternative coalition government.

A 'one-party state'?

It was this total picture that, early in the 1960s, inspired Jens Arup Seip's thesis of the 'one-party state'. Seip claimed that Norway's system of government in the period 1945–63 was totally dominated by one party, the Labour Party, and that this governing party played a dominant role in relation to the organs of government. The decision-making process within the party had – he believed – clear similarities with the authoritarian centralism of the one party states in the communist world. The thesis had, for a long time, a great influence on scholars and others who were concerned with the post-war system of government. How valid is it seen from today's viewpoint and subsequent research?

Most scholars now would agree that Seip overemphasized the Labour Party's dominance of Norwegian politics. The party's majority was usually very small and its leaders could never feel certain that they would secure a majority at the next election. The party did not pursue provocative policies and it was usually prepared to compromise. It rarely forced a policy against the combined opposition of the non-socialist parties. There were few bitter parliamentary exchanges. To a considerable extent the Labour Party followed the centrist tendency that was traditionally strong in Norwegian politics. Characteristically, towards the end of the 1950s all parties were broadly in agreement on economic policy, regional policy and social policy. That accords badly with the notion of a 'one-party state'. Besides, the 'one-party state' paradoxically went into decline just at the point it seemed to be at its height. It would scarcely have done that had it been built on a firm foundation.

Seip also exaggerated the leading role of the party. During the Labour Party's 'heroic age', it was the Cabinet that was clearly the policy-forming body – not the party machine. On the other hand he is undoubtedly right in saying that the government, in co-operation with key personnel in the central administration, exercised a strong leadership over the Storting. The Labour Party's stable parliamentary majorities did not give the same latitude for independent political initiative in the Storting that the weak minority governments had done during the inter-war years. The popular view of a party and a trade union movement characterised by authoritarian internal discipline remains, though it must be modified. Several examples can be found of a leadership fighting the opposition with barely democratic methods. But this was hardly the general rule. And the internal controls must be seen against a background of a strong sense of common interests and culture between the leadership and the grass roots of the movement. Probably the strong internal discipline and the willingness to cooperate with others outside the party should be regarded as two sides of the same issue. Unity in the Labour Party and the trade union movement was necessary if the government was to pursue a policy of compromise and co-operation.

The King's Bay crisis and a non-socialist government

The Labour Party's monopoly of government was broken in the summer of 1963. It was then that the four non-socialist parties formed a coalition government for a brief period under the leadership of the Conservative Party's leader John Lyng. After four weeks, Einar Gerhardsen, with a new Labour Party government, was able to take over the Cabinet offices again. But the Lyng government contributed to eradicating the obstacles in the way of organized non-socialist co-operation. The parties had demonstrated that they both could and would come together to form a government. In 1965, the four anti-socialist parties participating in the election offered a joint alternative government for the first time. The election produced a relatively clear majority of seats for the non-socialist parties – 80 as against 70 for the Labour Party and the Socialist People's Party. The four parties formed a government under the leadership of the Centre Party's Per Borten.

The change of government was not the result of fundamental or increasing disagreement over which policies should be pursued. Earlier differences over both economic policy in general and industrial policy in particular had been toned down. Nor was there any disagreement over the new regional policy. Even over the issue of the state's role in the economy, the differences were less than before. It could even be argued that the political rapprochement between the non-socialist and the Labour parties was a necessary pre-condition for the non-socialist coalition, because disagreement between one or several of the latter and the Labour Party usually brought into the open, or emphasized, differences within the non-socialist camp.

Nor was the change-over the natural culmination of a steadily closer co-operation between the non-socialist parties, with the aim of captur-

The departure of Einar Gerhardsen; the arrival of John Lyng. The Labour Party's monopoly of government was broken after eighteen years, twenty-eight if one includes the coalition governments of the war and immediate post-war years. The Gerhardsen government fell on 23 August 1963, because of a vote of no confidence supported by the non-socialist parties and the Socialist People's Party. The Conservatives' John Lyng formed the first non-socialist coalition government. Four weeks later Einar Gerhardsen was back in office as prime minister.

ing power. In the years prior to 1963 all attempts at organized co-operation had broken down. After the election of 1961, party alignments in the Storting were unclear. The entry of the Socialist People's Party into the Storting led both to an attempt at co-operation between the Labour Party and individual non-socialist parties and to a wide-ranging truce between the Labour Party and its opponents on the non-socialist side, in order to prevent the new party from getting too much influence. But, in the last analysis, it was the non-socialist parties and the Socialist People's Party that together brought down the government.

What brought about the change of government in 1963 was more a clash over the style of politics and the way it had operated than over content; more the result of the opposition's need to demonstrate its political integrity and desire for power than of a systematic and purposeful effort to create a coalition government.

It all started with a tragic accident in the state-owned coal mines at King's Bay on Svalbard in November 1962, which claimed the lives of 21 miners. The report of a committee of enquiry, the contents of which became known in June of 1963, was strongly critical of those responsible for the management of the mines. In August the non-socialist parties put forward a vote of no confidence, which they carried with the support of the votes of the Socialist People's Party. Gerhardsen's Labour government resigned.

The overt grounds for the opposition's motion of no confidence was the government's failure to follow up a Storting resolution of 1956 on special safety precautions at King's Bay, arising from the death of 43 coal miners in previous accidents. The government argued on its side that the opposition was exploiting a tragic accident in its pursuit of government office. It would on the whole seem reasonable to say that the opposition had the better of the argument. The dispute involved a matter of parliamentary principle, namely the duty of the government to inform the Storting and to implement its instructions. But at the same time it was also a question of power. The opposition parties were also guarding the Storting's rights, as an element in the defence of their own influence, against a government whose power was growing and that was increasingly arrogant in the exercise of it. Both opposition groups believed that the government had shown little respect for the Storting or for the basic rules of the parliamentary game.

The campaign for a planned economy

Central to the political debate in the immediate post-war years were questions relating to the government's planning and handling of the economy. Historians too have been preoccupied with both the content of the politico-administrative system employed to run the economy and its development. The Labour Party came to power in 1945 hoping to run the country according to the principles of a planned economy. The party believed that the economic crisis of the inter-war years had demonstrated that the business community was not, on its own, able to create a stable and secure economy. On the other hand, the productive efforts of the combatants in the Second World War had shown what it was possible to achieve through targeted planning and organizing.

The Labour Party based itself on the new economic thinking that

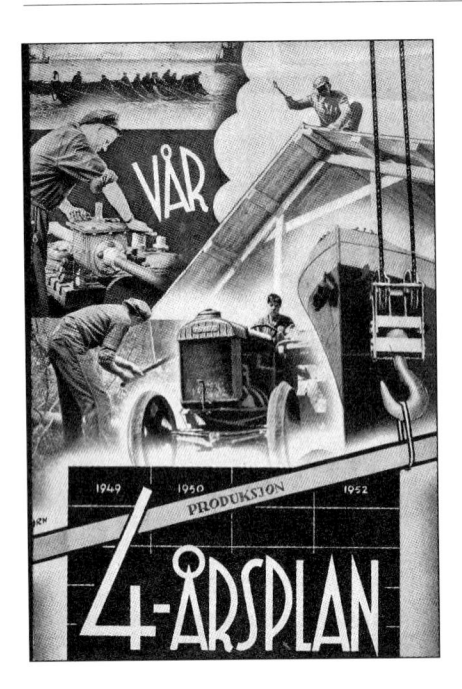

The 'planned economy' was one of the great slogans of the 1940s. The first national budget was presented in 1947; the first long-term plan, the year after. Both instruments were to be permanent features of economic policy. The campaigns to develop a decision-making apparatus for a planned economy and for directing the structural development of industry were less successful. The pamphlet was published by the Labour Party in 1948.

argued that it was possible to run an entire society's economy in principle along the same lines as a household or a business. The minister of finance, Erik Brofoss (later trade minister), was the leading representative of a group of young, dynamic economists who quickly took over key positions in politics and the administration. Through an annual national budget the politicians were to get an overview of the natural resources, labour force, productive capacity, market conditions and foreign economic situation. They would thus be able to take decisions on consumption and investment and the priorities to be accorded to different sectors of the economy. The first complete national budget was presented in 1947. It was supplemented in the following year by a four-year plan.

In order to improve economic planning, the government wanted to supplement the established parliamentary system with a system of decision-making bodies suited to a planned economy. A production committee was set up in each individual firm, after an agreement in 1946 between the National Federation of Labour and the Norwegian Employers' Confederation. A law of 1947 created industry-by-industry committees which were to plan and co-ordinate the development of production in each individual branch of industry or business. A

National Economic Co-ordinating Committee, set up in 1945, was to give the government advice on the most important economic questions. This committee hierarchy was designed to take decisions on all questions of production and rationalization, and on the setting up and closing down of individual concerns. The same idea – to lay a foundation for the direction of output and the structure of firms – lay behind the interim price and rationalization legislation of 1947, and the proposals of 1952 to make this legislation permanent. Similar thoughts had lain behind an unsuccessful campaign for a new trust law and a law on the creation of financial reserve funds made up of contributions from industry in the 1930s.

The planned economy's management structure never operated as intended. The production committees became joint bodies where the management and employees of individual firms consulted on questions of productivity and working conditions. The industry-by-industry committees became general bodies for consultation and co-operation between the authorities and business. As planning bodies they were unsuccessful. But, as joint organizations concerned with productivity questions and with channelling government support for industry, they operated satisfactorily. The National Economic Co-ordinating Committee was characterized by sharp conflicts of interests between the parties represented on it and was abolished in 1954. The most wide-ranging provisions of the interim price and rationalization legislation were not implemented. As the result of the debate of 1952/53, the draft law on rationalization was shelved, while at the same time the Storting agreed to a relatively moderate price law.

From detailed regulation to liberalization

Norway never developed a co-ordinated planned economy via a specially designed decision-making apparatus. On the other hand, in the immediate post-war years the Norwegian economy was regulated in detail by the ordinary state administration. These regulations must be understood principally against a background of needs and problems associated with post-war reconstruction. They were employed as necessary in order to prevent uncontrollable inflation, to contribute to a socially just distribution of the scarce supplies of goods, and, not least, to direct resources so as to attain the fastest possible reconstruction.

The 'sugar queue' at Svinesund (the border between Norway and Sweden) in the spring of 1952. Sugar-rationing lasted in Norway until September 1952. So when the Swedes raised the quota to as much as 10 kilos, the rush of sugar-hungry Norwegians was enormous.

The regulatory system developed during the war was maintained and supplemented by new measures. 'The stabilization line' involved firm controls on prices and conditions of sale. Wages were held in check by moderation and strong internal discipline on the part of the trade union movement, and by compulsion in the case of disputes. Most common articles of consumption continued to be rationed for a long time – bread and milk until 1949; meat, cheese, coffee and sugar until the summer of 1952. New construction and extensions were dependent on permits, material quotas and licences for foreign currency. Exports and imports were regulated in fine detail, the starting point being a regard for foreign currency needs and those of reconstruction. But these detailed regulations were also gradually wound down between 1948 and the early 1950s.

Three questions in particular have been asked about the development of the system for directing the economy. The first is why the detailed regulations were abandoned, even though the party of government still wished to direct the economy? The second is why Norway did not get a decision-making system appropriate to a planned economy as was assumed at the outset? And the third concerns the nature of the planning and administrative system Norway got instead.

Some scholars have seen the winding up of the system of detailed regulation as the government abandoning a planned economy and returning to a pure market economy. This view undoubtedly exaggerates detailed regulation as a management tool, at the same time as it undervalues those instruments that took their place. A comprehensive system of detailed regulation was scarcely ever thought of as a permanent tool. The rationing of consumption goods and building materials was unpopular and difficult to administer. In many cases its effectiveness was doubtful in a planning and management context. Regulations could be a direct obstacle to a real planned economy in that the regulatory bodies got bogged down in questions of detail and were never able to find the time for co-ordinated planning. Seen in such a perspective it is not surprising that they were abandoned as demand eased and the needs of reconstruction were gradually satisfied.

The liberalization demands that followed the Marshall Plan (1947) and the subsequent membership of the OEEC (Organization for European Economic Co-operation) also exerted a strong pressure on the regulationary system (Chapter 26). In order to get aid, Norway had to commit itself to freeing overseas trade through the so-called 'free list system', which was put into operation in 1949. But by giving up import and export controls the government also lost its mastery over the cornerstone of its regulatory system.

There is little doubt that the government wanted a permanent decision-making apparatus for a planned economy that would conduct an active policy of rationalization and restructuring. In fact this was not put into operation as planned, nor did the government involve itself directly in the restructuring of industry. What were the reasons for this? The idea of a decision-making apparatus for a planned economy was based on two foundations: first, the constituent parts of this structure should be able to make authoritative decisions but, second, should do so in co-operation with the affected parties and their organizations. The industry committees, the National Co-ordinating Committee and the production committees were never thought of as state bodies issuing directives, but were seen, collectively, as an institutional framework for a planned economy that would function with the co-operation of all parties concerned. It was soon apparent that co-operation was not possible, especially regarding the implementation of comprehensive planning. The Norwegian Employers' Confederation (NAF) was prepared to go along with the creation of production committees only if their role was limited to questions of productivity and working conditions. In establishing industry committees it was clear that neither the Norwegian Federation of Industry nor leaders of the different industries were prepared to co-operate in making these proper planning bodies. Co-operation with industry in the Economic Co-ordinating Committee broke down as soon as it began to deal with the national budget and the full range of economic policies.

Besides, the goals of reconstruction and a general expansion of output always took precedence over any form of long-term planning. Here, too, the state was wholly dependent on industry's ability and willingness to expand. The result was that the desire to plan could be pushed only as far as industry was willing to go. The same applied to any possible plans the state might have to bring about the rationalization of industry by compulsion. The position of industry was strengthened by the opposition of the non-socialist parties to the more extreme encroachments of economic planning. Besides, it was not only non-socialist politicians, industry's organizations and individual firms that were sceptical. The trade union movement was on the watch too for any negative consequences that the intervention of economic planning in the industrial structure might have on employment. Thus, for the government to take direct responsibility for the rationalization of firms and for closing them down involved a heavy political strain in relations with its own supporters as well.

Running the economy in the 1950s and 1960s

In running the economy at the beginning of the 1950s, the main task was to find instruments that were acceptable under new freer international market conditions, and, at the same time, to lay the foundations for co-operation rather than confrontation both with the opposition and with industry. The system of economic management developed in the 1950s and 1960s has not been as thoroughly researched as the detailed regulatory system and economic planning initiatives that were replaced. We can, therefore, comment on only the most important features.

Annual national budgets as well as long-term planning programmes were here to stay. These documents attempted to give a total overview of the country's economy as the basis for politico-economic decision making. But they got more of a predictive and less of a planning character than had originally been assumed. At the same time, the level of ambition became more realistic. Economic planning came above all to consist of attempts at strengthening positive movements in the economy and in markets and at counteracting the negative. Thoughts of an overall plan relatively independent of international market conditions were abandoned. On the other hand, methods and techniques both for drawing up forecasts and for calculating the effects of different measures steadily improved.

It has been generally accepted that, at the beginning of the 1950s, a basic shift occurred in economic policy making from the use of direct to indirect measures. The authorities abandoned regulations, embargoes and licences, which directly affected output and sales. Instead, the main emphasis was placed on financial and credit mechanisms such as taxation, limits on investment and borrowing, together with terms for loans. These had an indirect effect in that they set general limits that industry had to deal with, while not controlling activity directly.

It is undoubtedly true that there was a reduction in the number of direct measures, notably those tied to the setting of prices, rationing and the control of foreign trade. This was especially the case with the deregulation of the production and sale of industrial goods. The government definitely placed greater emphasis on broader and more indirect political and administrative measures. It is easy, however, to exaggerate the whittling away of direct regulation and the gap between direct and indirect measures. In practice, planning and management measures contained elements of both.

In general, the government from the 1950s onwards relied mostly on the control of credit as the means of directing the economy. This was done partly by trying to control the total volume of credit according to the economic situation, and partly by channelling credit, on favourable terms, to sectors and industries to which the government gave an especially high priority. This was achieved both through influencing the private credit institutions and through the state's own banking system. In 1952 a law was passed obliging the banks to deposit some of their reserves with the Bank of Norway. The law was brought into effect in 1955. At that time the state and the private credit institutions also entered into an agreement that set a ceiling on the banks' loan book. From then on such agreements were made annually. In 1965 a separate monetary and credit law was passed that gave the authorities general permission to regulate the amount of credit via loan quotas and the control of liquidity.

A comprehensive system of state banks was an important part of the administrative system. Their share of total bank loans to industry and private individuals rose from around 25 per cent in 1946 to 45 per cent in 1976. The Housing Bank itself had in 1970 more than half of the loans provided by all the state banks put together. The first 11 million *kroner*'s worth of loans made in 1947 had by 1971 turned into as many billions worth. Other important state banks were the State Bank for Agriculture, the State Bank for Fishing, Norway's Local Authority Bank, the State Bank for Educational Loans and the Regional Development Bank. Several of these institutions were long established, though now their activities increased substantially.

By using its banks, the state sought to promote its social, distributive and economic aims. At the same time, the state bank system as a whole was an important means of directing the state's general economic policies. In 1954, limits were introduced on the total to be loaned by all the state banks put together and a fixed budget detailed what could be loaned by each. From 1966 onwards the loans were co-ordinated via a common credit budget.

Individual industries and social areas continued to be subject to tight and detailed regulation, the most regulated being undoubtedly the primary industries. Agriculture was protected against competition from abroad through either a total or a seasonal ban on imports of products that were of economic importance for Norwegian farmers. The state's grain company continued to have a monopoly on the import of grain and flour and also bought up all Norwegian-produced grain. Conditions of sale and prices were for the most part subject to detailed regulation. A large number of supportive measures, some direct some indirect, affected production, income and sales. In 1982 there were 130 measures of this type. Subsidies for consumers were

The decade 1948–1957 was the boom time for the winter herring fisheries. In 1956 as much as 1.1 million tonnes were landed. Then the stocks collapsed. In 1961 the catch had fallen to 70,000 tonnes. The picture is from the fishing grounds at Rundøy off Ålesund in 1957.

used in varying degrees to influence price and income conditions both inside and outside the industry. Since 1952 relations between the state and the agricultural industry have been regulated by the Basic Agreement for Agriculture and by biennial agricultural agreements. The agreements fixed the overall income level and determined the parameters for income distribution within the industry itself.

The fishing industry, too, was subject to more and more regulation. Direct fish sales were conducted by the fishermen's own co-operative organizations, which had a legal monopoly. The building and operation of large fishing vessels – especially trawlers – were subject to licence. When resource problems emerged, catches were regulated strictly by means of quotas. This happened first with the herring fisheries but, as the problem became a general one, the system was applied to almost all kinds of fish. The fishing industry, too, gradually began receiving support of one kind or another – in the form of cheap loans for vessels, price supports and help with bait and equipment. In 1964 a

Basic Agreement was entered into with the fishing industry, following the pattern of that for agriculture. Subsequently, further agreements were made between the state and the industry.

Another area in which the previous post-war regulations were steadily expanded rather than abandoned was that covering building and development. The arrangement that demanded building licences for homes and business premises was maintained and expanded to include holiday cottages. The Housing Bank determined in some detail the size and shape of all homes on which it made loans, i.e. the majority. The Bank for Agriculture did the same for farmhouses and farm buildings. A new planning and building law of 1965 gave markedly extended powers to the authorities in matters to do with building and land development. The Shore Plan law of 1971 imposed a general ban on building within the shore zone. The sale of agricultural properties became increasingly dependent upon official approval.

Finally, it is important to note the vastly increased potential for economic planning and direction that lay in the steadily growing public sector. As indicated earlier, a greater and greater share of society's resources was disposed of across public budgets and so placed under the decision-making authority of elected politicians. And the public authorities were themselves active participants in many important sectors of society – in the entire welfare area, in economic activity, in the granting of loans and in transport.

'Organized capitalism' – 'the corporate state' – 'the segmented state'

As already mentioned, there is no historical account of Norwegian economic planning and management. Nor is there a generally accepted overall term for the system itself. A commonly used term such as 'mixed economy' conveys little more than that the system combined the right to private property and the formation of free markets, with public ownership and management. Some historians have stressed the international market oriented aspects of the Norwegian economy and the contrast between the detailed regulations and the planning ideals of the 1940s and the subsequent liberalization. They are eager to underline that the economic system in the 1950s and 1960s was still basically a capitalist one. Fritz Hodne uses the term 'reformed capitalism', and Edvard Bull Jr. 'organized capitalism'. Others are principally concerned with the development of concrete planning and management measures and less interested in their departure from the original thoughts and ideals. They are inclined to emphasize the development towards planning and direction in steadily more areas. Trond Bergh asserts, therefore, that the economic planning elements in the economic system were strengthened.

Perhaps the most characteristic feature of the Norwegian planning and management system is precisely the differentiated use of politico-economic measures. In one respect there are several parallel politico-economic systems with clearly differentiated planning and control profiles. There is a large public sector providing the foundation for a strict and detailed direction along politically determined lines – even if, in practice, this has not been fully exploited. In some industries – above all in agriculture and fishing – and in some important welfare areas, such a term as 'the regulatory economy' can be appropriate. Least controlled and directed have been the export industries and those subject to international competition. The public authority's function as a regulator of the economic cycle may provide the basis for the term 'manipulated economy', while the state's activity in relation to industry leads one to think more of a 'facilitated or stimulated economy'.

The discussion so far has focused on the system of policy and direction exercised through political parties, popularly elected bodies, the government and the administrative apparatus. There is, however, agreement amongst scholars that the political system, to an ever-increasing degree, has become marked by the direct participation of organized interests in the political decision-making process. These organizations share in the committee work and express themselves on questions that affect their interests; they negotiate among themselves and with the state; and in several instances the exercise of official duties is directly handed over to them. Our review of the economic management system has produced several examples: the credit agreements of the 1950s and 1960s were agreed in the Co-ordinating Committee, set up in 1951 with representatives from the Finance Department, the Bank of Norway, the Bank inspectorate and organizations representing the credit institutions. Agreements covering agriculture and fisheries were entered into after negotiations between the state and the organizations representing those industries. Regulation in the pri-

The major interest groups have obtained a steadily increasing power in society. Most 'visible' and 'audible' are their activities in the great pay and income negotiations. On the left, we see Tor Aspengren of the National Federation of Labour (LO), and on the right, Kaare Selvig of the Norwegian Employers' Confederation (NAF) coming to an agreement on the settlement for 1972, after the intervention of the national labour arbitrator, Preben Munthe. Increasingly, the larger interest groups have obtained the right to share in, or express an opinion on, most matters affecting their members' interests.

mary industries was largely carried out by the farmers' and fishermen's own organizations and sales administrations.

This development has led to a growing relationship of mutual dependence between the representative organizations and the authorities. The National Federation of Labour (LO) in 1936 had representatives on 16 permanent official committees, boards and councils; in 1951 on 90; and in 1966 on 202. In 1970, organizations covering the whole country had 1,900 representatives on official councils and committees. Organizations representing labour and industry accounted for 90 per cent of these. And almost all organizations said that government departments and directorates provided their most important contacts. Negotiation and co-operation between affected parties had been an important part of the intellectual background to the initiatives in the direction of a decision-making structure for economic planning in the immediate post-war years. This structure never came to operate as intended. But the presupposition that representative organizations would participate was realized, if in a more indirect and less formalized way.

The term 'corporate' is often applied to a state in which special-interest bodies have a strong influence. The development of the corporate elements in the Norwegian state management system is still not well surveyed. But several scholars have commented upon the relationship between traditional parliamentary politics and the role of the organizations. Political scientist Stein Rokkan called the two decision-making systems 'democracy by numbers' and 'corporate pluralism'; and, more pointedly, asserted that 'votes count but resources decide'. With that he implied that to vote at an election determines who will sit in political positions, whereas political content is decided by negotiation between the authorities and the strong organizations. With that, too, he believed he was also able to explain why there was so little disagreement in parliamentary politics: the interests the opposition represented were, to a great extent, taken care of through the other channel of influence.

Edvard Bull Jr. goes at least as far in scaling down the significance of traditional democratic party politics and of the national assembly. But he shows little interest in separating or balancing the powers of the different decision-making processes. For him the most important feature is what he calls a 'top people's partnership'. Important decisions are taken jointly between elites in the organizations, the civil service and politics, for the most part independently of the official political apparatus. The system is undemocratic because decisions are taken against the interests of – or at least over the heads of – ordinary people.

Scholars who took part in a major research project of the 1970s into the sources of power in Norwegian society, on the other hand, were especially concerned with the relationship between the different decision-making channels. They coined the phrase 'the segmented state'. By that they meant that the political system can be seen as a collection of sectors or decision-making arenas that are relatively clearly separated from each other – for example, the fisheries segment or the communications segment. Participants from politics, the civil service and the organizations operate within each segment. The segments each have their own special rules and routines for exercising policy, and the participants often have common interests, at least when compared with the participants in other segments, with whom they compete for resources. The model focuses – as does Bull's – on a partnership of interests, but these researchers find no proof of a systematic conflict of interest between the elites and the grass roots. The idea of a segmented state has consequences for an assessment of the possibilities for a joint politico-economic management system. Segments with a stable constellation of participants and procedures ought to provide a good basis for managing a sector. On the other hand, the co-ordination or linking together of the segments, so creating one comprehensive politico-economic management system, must remain problematic.

Post-war politics and management – a new system?

The post-war years have seen major changes in the Norwegian political system. There is a sharp contrast between the fight in the 1920s between parties loyal to the system and the revolutionaries, and the party-political consensus of the 1950s and 1960s. There is a great difference too between the parliamentary instability of the inter-war years and the stable parliamentary majority governments of the post-war years. The proactive state with its far-reaching ambitions is often thought of as a post-war phenomenon, 'the corporate state' too.

But on issues of politics and management there is every reason to emphasize the elements of continuity as well. The basis for the new majority parliamentarism was established by the strong growth of the Labour Party in the early 1930s and through the party's switch from a revolutionary ideology to a proactive reformism. There is nothing especially novel either about the broad consensus. As stated earlier, a characteristic feature of the Norwegian political system is precisely its strong centrist tendencies. The rapprochement between social groups and between political parties that came about in the 1930s and the Crisis Agreement of 1935 can be interpreted as expressions of this. The Crisis Agreement was at the same time an agreement between socialists and non-socialists and an agreement between town and country in Norwegian politics. The Basic Agreement in the same year involved a similar coming together of the two sides of industry. The war strengthened national unity and contributed towards a social radicalization. The Joint Programme of 1945 was an expression of both these tendencies.

The consensus in the broad centre of Norwegian politics was strengthened in the 1950s and 1960s. There was broad agreement about the expansion of the welfare state. Regional policies also had a unifying effect. All parties sought the support of the same body of voters. Strong economic growth laid the foundation for an increased well-being for all. There was less need of the contentious redistribution of wealth from rich to poor. The move towards a 'corporate state' can naturally, too, be interpreted as an expression of centrism and consensus. When the conflicts in a society are small it is natural and easy to allow 'all' to share in the shaping of decisions, at the same time that participation and consensus are important values in themselves. In addition, direction, in part, by those subject to it has a long tradition in Norwegian politics. For example, the regulating of the primary industries, which began in earnest towards the end of the 1920s, was above all a matter of self-regulation.

The breakthrough for politico-economic planning undoubtedly belongs to the post-war era. But its roots too can be found in the 1930s – in the Labour Party's policies to meet the crisis, in the impulses from Keynes' work, and not least in the development of a strong and expanding economics milieu at the University of Oslo, which, under the leadership of Ragnar Frisch, decided to seek practical instruments for economic planning based upon a scientific foundation.

26
Norway – a hesitant internationalist

A characteristic feature of post-war Norway is the country's growing involvement in the international community. Norway has increasingly been drawn into international commitments. At the same time, international relations and decisions have had a steadily greater influence on Norwegian politics and the Norwegian economy. By the middle of the 1960s, Norway, as a state, was involved in more than 60 international organizations. Most of these organizations had been established after 1945. Above all Norway became integrated into the western industrialized world. Several historians have emphasized the country's place in this, 'the rich man's world'.

The majority of the important collaborative organizations with Norwegian participation have been economic in nature, often tied to international trade and its liberalization. Amongst these were the OEEC (Organization for European Economic Co-operation) – later expanded and renamed OECD (Organization for Economic Co-operation and Development), GATT (General Agreement on Tariffs and Trade) from 1948, and EFTA (European Free Trade Association) from 1960. But with Norwegian membership of NATO (North Atlantic Treaty Organization) in 1949 the country entered into a binding agreement with other states involving co-operation on security policy. Throughout the 1950s and especially in the 1960s Norway's relations with the developing countries became steadily more important.

In spite of the country's strong image in the field of international co-operation, Norway has rarely been an enthusiastic protagonist of international organization. The government was usually cautious and hesitant, and more often than not joined because of the dangers or drawbacks of staying out rather than the advantages of going in. What Great Britain chose to do was always important. And, within the limits set by the international organization, the government always sought to maintain as much freedom of choice as possible. 'Special arrangements' were the order of the day. In other cases – as in that of the European Community (EC) – Norway chose to stay out. This cautiousness reflects the ideals of neutrality and independence, which have remained strong in a country that was late in getting its freedom. It reflects, too, the constant dilemma of small states: on the one hand, a strong need for the benefits and protection derived by co-operating with strong allies, whilst, on the other, a fear of being swallowed up or overwhelmed – or of provoking third parties.

Bridge building, cold war – and NATO

The cold war, together with the potential threat from the Soviet Union, led Norway to join NATO in 1949. After the war, Norway had again sought to remain free of alliances by adopting the so-called 'bridge-building line'. The main assumption underlying this was that the wartime co-operation between the United States, Great Britain and the Soviet Union could be maintained in the post-war world. The United Nations, as the new international organization for solving conflicts, was to be the cornerstone of Norway's security policy. The country sought to pursue an active role as mediator in this and other international bodies, thus preventing conflict. In the immediate post-war years there was no realistic alternative to this policy of non-alliance. In practice, the 'bridge building' was both cautious and low key. Norway was more concerned not to provoke the Great Powers than to go in actively for bridge building between east and west.

This bridge building has, among other things, been characterized as an 'interval marked by a certain lack of clarity regarding Norway's external political situation between east and west' (K. E. Eriksen). But the country's defensive link with the west was never in doubt, despite this lack of clarity. Relations with Great Britain were especially good: Norwegian military personnel were trained in Britain; the bulk of military equipment came from Britain; and the Norwegian forces of occupation in Germany (after 1947) were under British command. The military collaboration between the two countries was one of co-operation in peace-time with a view to mutual aid in the event of war. There was scarcely any thought of a neutral Norway if war should break out or a security crisis develop. In this respect Norway was clearly in a very different position from that of neutral Sweden. Relations with the United States were initially less trusting, with doubts arising about American capitalism and anti-communism. On the other hand, relations with the Soviet Union were even cooler. Many in the labour movement felt a positive ideological attachment to the Soviet state. But for most people the Soviet Union was looked upon as a potential enemy, even if anti-Soviet views were less widespread in Norway than in most western countries. And when those directing Norway's foreign policy felt they had to take sides on issues on which the USA and the Soviets had different views, they usually ended up in the western camp. An American summing up of Norwegian foreign policy in 1946 stated bluntly: '[it is] pro American and pro British as much as it dare, pro Russian as much as it must and pro United Nations as much as it can.'

The rationale for the bridge-building policy gradually disappeared after 1947. The development of the cold war showed that the assumption of continued cooperation between the victorious powers was no longer tenable. The American aid plan for Europe – the Marshall Plan – and Norway's participation in the economic co-operation surrounding this contributed to a strengthening of Norway's orientation to the west and was, as a result, a step towards NATO. But a tangible alternative to neutrality first appeared in January 1948 with a proposal from Britain's foreign minister, Ernest Bevin, for a west European defence alliance, to be joined perhaps by the United States and other countries.

Most of Norway's non-socialist politicians, together with leading figures in the Labour Party, supported this new line from the beginning. Others, including the foreign minister, Halvard Lange, wanted to see how the situation developed. Neither the Swedish nor the Danish Social Democrats saw any reason to give up their freedom from alliances. There was a strong desire to prevent a split on security policy within Scandinavia. Nevertheless, Norway definitely gave up the thought of a going-it-alone neutrality in the course of the spring of 1948. Threatening developments on the international scene necessitated this stance. The communists took power in Czechoslovakia in February/March. The greatest alarm was caused by the Soviet demand for a military aid agreement between Russia and Finland, together with reports in March that Norway would be offered a similar agreement or a non-aggression pact.

The choice was now between joining an Atlantic alliance or a Scandinavian defence union. The international developments of February and March 1948 together with Norway's exposed position caused the United States to support the plans for an alliance. On the other hand, Sweden proposed a Nordic defence pact in order to prevent a schism in the region and to avoid being isolated. Negotiations on defence arrangements for the region took place at three meetings in January 1949, in Karlstad, Copenhagen and Oslo. Sweden wanted a free-standing Nordic defence pact, whereas Norway wanted a Nordic pact linked with – or having explicit guarantees from – the emerging western alliance. The Danes proposed an alternative solution, in the form of a free-standing Nordic alliance supplied with weapons by the western powers, but which would not exclude the possibility of help from other countries in the event of an attack on the region. The Swedes and the Danes wanted first to form a Nordic alliance and only then to explore the possibilities of military equipment and support from the west. They believed the risk of a rejection was slight since the United States would, in any case, support Scandinavia. But Norway wanted a complete assurance of American weapon supplies and military support in the event of war. The lesson of 9 April 1940 indicated that such support could not be improvised but must be arranged in peacetime. The Americans for their part made it clear that, in the event of a shortage of weapons, what there were would be sent to their allies – in the first instance. The Nordic negotiations collapsed and in April 1949 the Storting agreed to negotiate for membership of NATO.

NATO – continuity or change?

Membership of NATO did represent a break with Norway's traditional security policy. For the first time in peacetime, Norway entered an alliance involving mutual commitments. It was also a clear breach with the country's policy of the inter-war years, in that Norway was now clearly willing to defend its freedom by force, through a considerable build-up of its military strength.

Nevertheless, the change is less clear than it would appear. Membership of NATO emphasized Norway's long tradition of looking westwards to the Atlantic. Norway' neighbours, Sweden and Denmark, had always had a much stronger commitment to the European continent. As we have seen, Norway's relations with the western powers during the First World War were so close that it was later to be dubbed 'the neutral ally'. The neutrality policy of the inter-war years had always been predicated on the assumption that Great Britain, in its own interest, would come to the support of Norway in the event of a threat to its freedom. And, during the Second World War, Norway was tied to the Atlantic powers, while the western orientation was relatively obvious too during the 'bridge-building' period.

What was new about the situation towards the end of the 1940s, in comparison with that of the inter-war years, was above all a belief that the threat was quite different. In the 1920s and 1930s practically no one thought an attack on Norway was likely, but during the initial phase of the cold war the threat from the Soviet Union was regarded as very real indeed. At the same time, it was considered unrealistic for Norway to avoid being involved in the case of war between the Great Powers. In such a situation it was clearly not enough to rely on the implicit support of the western powers. Novel too was the fact that the United States now stood out as Norway's main source of support. The shift marked an adjustment to the new economic and power political situation. Europe was in the process of being divided into areas of interest for the two superpowers, while Great Britain was on the way to becoming a second-rate power. America's atomic weapons now replaced the British fleet as the main guarantee of Norway's security.

A cautious ally

Since 1949, NATO has been the cornerstone of Norway's defence policy. With rearmament during the cold war – and especially after the outbreak of the Korean War in 1950 – NATO developed into a solid bloc under the leadership of the USA. The military forces were placed under a joint command and a joint defence force was set up in Europe. Norway received considerable support for the development of its defences. Between 1951 and 1970 the United States and Canada supplied Norway with free weapons and other military equipment amounting to 7.6 billion *kroner*. About one-quarter of Norway's defence budget was met by transfers from other countries in the alliance. Norway paid only about 30 per cent of the costs of the airfields, rocket-launching sites and ammunition dumps that were built as part of NATO's joint strategic planning.

At the same time, Norway was a cautious member of the alliance – 'a somewhat troublesome ally' (Eriksen). It tried to take into the alliance as much as possible of its former non-aligned policy. Once the primary need for western guarantees had been satisfied, the Norwegian government recognized the fact that the Soviet Union was a dominant power in the region and attempted not to provoke it unnecessarily. Even before the North Atlantic Treaty was signed, the government declared that it would not allow foreign bases on Norwegian soil in peacetime. This put Norway into a special position within the alliance. A cautious attitude with regard to the Soviet Union also led to only modest numbers of Norwegian troops being stationed in Finnmark, which shares a common border with the former Soviet Union, as well as a prohibition of NATO exercises in this county. In 1954, NATO decided in principle to use tactical atomic weapons in the defence of western Europe. But in 1957 Norway refused to accept atomic weapons in peacetime and the stationing of medium-range rockets on Norwegian soil. At the same time, Prime Minister Gerhardsen proposed that NATO should defer a decision in principle to have medium-range rockets in Europe and that disarmament negotiations at the highest level should take place between the USA and the Soviet Union.

In other situations, too, Norway assumed the role of opposition within NATO. For example, the acceptance of Greece and Turkey as members of the alliance in 1952 was against Norway's wishes. Norway wanted to maintain NATO as an Atlantic alliance and to defend its democratic character. This attitude was later reflected in Norway's opposition in international organizations to the role of the military junta in Greece in the years 1967–74. Norwegian foreign policy towards the countries of the eastern bloc followed the general cold war line, with reduced trade and limited political contacts. In spite of this, Norway was one of the first NATO countries to encourage wider contacts and a reduction in tensions with the eastern bloc.

The left-wing opposition

Caution and a modest degree of opposition within the alliance were not enough for NATO sceptics and opponents. Traditional support for neutrality, anti-militarism and pacifism, left-wing socialism and anti-capitalist views merged to form a political opposition to NATO. Besides the Norwegian Communist Party (NKP), opposition to NATO found its strongest support on the left wing of the Labour Party. Feelings ran high at the time Norway joined the organization. West Germany's membership of the alliance (achieved in 1955) was disputed, as was the increase in the length of military service in 1954. Strong opposition first appeared, however, in the second half of the 1950s over the policy on atomic weapons and on rearmament within NATO. Similar conflicts occurred in social democratic parties throughout the whole of western Europe. NATO's opponents won an important victory when the Labour Party's national conference voted unconditionally in the spring of 1957 against the stationing of atomic weapons on Norwegian soil. The opposition remained constantly on the alert against any softening in this position and opposed the spread of atomic weapons.

In 1952, opponents of NATO found a rallying point in the weekly journal *Orientering*. Persons involved in *Orientering* and in the Labour Party's League of Socialist Youth in Oslo were behind the 'Easter Revolution' of 1958. They enrolled strong support amongst the Labour Party's representatives in the Storting, as well as in the trade union movement, for a resolution demanding a Norwegian veto in NATO against atomic weapons for Germany's armed forces. This action was the first in a series of confrontations that ended in 1961 with the formation of a new political party – the Socialist People's Party (SF). The new party resulted from the hard line of the Labour Party leadership leading to the expulsion of leading dissidents, together with a new Labour Party conference decision that in very muted language opened the way for a reconsideration of the atomic weapon question if the country's security and independence were at stake. The basic reasons for the formation of the party were, however, opposition to NATO membership and the bloc mentality in foreign policy, together with a desire to work for a 'third alternative' – distanced from both the western and the eastern blocs.

Norway and the Third World

Norway's role as a cautious internationalist is reinforced in regard to its relations with the Third World. Policy has always been formed as a balance between principles and pragmatism and between altruism and self-interest. On de-colonization Norway took a middle position. Norway was one of the allies that most clearly supported the colonial countries' demands for independence. In practical policy terms this found expression in an internal criticism of other NATO countries' colonial policies and military activities, as for example the French in Indo-China and Algeria. There was also open – though still cautious – criticism in the United Nations. Externally, Norway was nevertheless usually loyal to NATO, out of respect for co-operation within the alliance and France's key role in the defence of Europe. In the 1960s, Norway's support for liberation movements was much clearer, in line with the development of Norwegian public opinion and also a change of attitude within the alliance.

Norway's aid policy was more whole hearted. The Norwegian fisheries project in Kerala, India, which was started in 1952, was a pioneering venture in international development aid. Only the United States and the colonial powers had previously undertaken direct bilateral aid. In the almost 20 years that the project lasted Norway provided 120 million *kroner*, while a corresponding sum was provided by the Indians. But even this project was not purely altruistic. Those who took the initiative were also concerned with creating a 'positive' foreign policy as a means of subduing the left-wing opposition's disquiet over NATO and rearmament. The fisheries project contributed to the transmission of technology and to the raising of living standards in the area. At the same time, it provided an early example of the problems associated with the transfer of western values, attitudes and experiences to the society of a developing country.

In 1962, Norway agreed to the United Nation's aim of 1 per cent of the country's net national product being set aside for development aid. Not until 1982 was the 1 per cent reached, and then it was of the gross national product. Nevertheless, even with this Norway led the international league table by a considerable margin, 0.3 – 0.4 per cent being the average figure for the industrial countries of the west. Norway's position on trade preferences for developing countries has been far less favourable. These often conflicted with the support of Norwegian economic interests for free trade, e.g. in the paper and shipping industries, and with the demands for continued protection against imports by agriculture and individual industries.

Marshall Aid brought foreign currency, investment, technological know-how and ways of increasing productivity. An exhibition at the Oslo department store Steen & Strøm in November 1950 showed what 30 Norwegian firms could produce after having received Marshall Aid.

From the Marshall Plan to EFTA

Norway's approach to European economic co-operation was also both hesitant and cautious. Norwegian economic nationalism was well rooted. The ideals of self-sufficiency, so strong in the inter-war years, had survived into the immediate post-war years. The economic planners harboured scepticism about American capitalism and were against meshing the Norwegian economy too closely with the international one. It was easier to fulfil one's wish for a planned economy within the confines of the Norwegian economy. On the other hand, many people realised that increased overseas trade was a pre-condition for rapid reconstruction and prosperity. That was the reason for the strong emphasis on the export industries and the earning of foreign currency.

Norwegian scepticism came out clearly in the government's reaction to the initiative taken in 1947 by the United States foreign minister George Marshall, for an American aid programme for Europe.

Whereas most other west European countries received the proposal with enthusiasm, the Norwegian response was guarded and tentative. This was partly the result of doubts over its implications for security policy: a 'yes' to Marshall Aid would be interpreted as choosing sides in a tense east-west situation. In the final analysis such considerations were decisive, but the other way round. A Norwegian 'no' would put the country together with the Soviet Union, eastern Europe and Finland. Norway's less than whole-hearted enthusiasm also reflected the views of leading politicians who did not want to see Norway financially dependent on the USA as well as scepticism over American economic policy and the fear of an American depression. Norway, then, went into the Marshall Plan organization with a clear desire to limit its political effects and to obstruct provisions that limited Norway's freedom of action in the economic sphere. Norway also estimated its dollar needs to be very low, 100 million dollars – relatively speaking a far smaller figure than that put forward by other countries.

From the autumn of 1947 the Norwegian attitude became more positive. It was now apparent that Norway faced an acute dollar crisis, which threatened the entire reconstruction process. Marshall Aid emerged, therefore, as a highly necessary boost. Increasing international tension weakened the bridge-building ideal and strengthened the tendency to look to the west. The government's enthusiasm for regulation and economic restructuring by political means moderated at the same time as eyes were opened to the favourable structural and rationalization consequences of international competition. Gradually the Norwegian government and the delegations involved in collaborating over the Marshall Plan began to join enthusiastically in the competition for Marshall Aid funds and to come up with creative proposals that could be accepted as worthy of support. The end result was that Norway from 1947 to some way into the 1950s received 425 million dollars, an important contribution in a period of critical foreign exchange problems. In the long term, the knowledge of improvements in productivity and technological imports that followed in the wake of Marshall Aid were, in all probability, of even greater importance. Gradually, pro-American opinion became far more prominent in Norway than the earlier scepticism of the economic planners and radicals.

Thoughts of collaboration over defence in Scandinavia had suffered a defeat in 1949. Nor did the campaign for organized economic collaboration between the neighbouring countries proceed more favourably.

The first attempt at a Nordic customs union broke down in 1950. The main reason for this was the Norwegian fear that the country's industries would not be able to compete in a common Nordic market, especially the finished goods industries with the highly efficient Swedish industry and Norwegian agriculture with its much stronger Danish counterpart. Negotiations in 1954–56 led to the same negative result. The situation was better, however, in other limited areas: in 1952, the Nordic countries did away with passports for people moving within them; a common labour market was introduced in 1954; and the three Scandinavian countries joined together to form an airline (SAS) as early as 1946. In 1953, the Nordic Council was set up as a forum for discussions amongst delegations of politicians from the Nordic parliaments. But not even here was Norway a driving force.

Norway was more favourably inclined towards a general multilateral or Atlantic free trade organization than to economic blocs in Europe or among the Nordic countries. The country had an extensive overseas trade, and shipping as well as export industries were dependent on the freest possible access to world markets. For that reason Norway joined in the international free market collaboration that had its origins in the Bretton Woods Conference (1944) and the International Monetary Fund (IMF – 1946). Through the medium of GATT (1948) Norway entered into mutually binding agreements on the reduction of trade barriers.

Membership of the European Free Trade Area (EFTA), agreed in 1960, was, in a way, a compromise. There were doubts in the government and in the Storting, but general agreement that it was necessary to follow Great Britain, which was the country's most important trading partner. Towards the end of the 1950s the government was increasingly concerned with the need for greater industrialization as the foundation for new growth and increased employment. Foreign capital was encouraged to come to Norway. However, the expansion of the great exporting industries would produce relatively few new jobs. Growth of the industries traditionally serving the domestic market would give many more, but here the limits were set by the tiny size of that market. The solution had to lie in switching such industries to serve the great European markets. In return for free entry to Europe, Norway had to accept increased competition at home. It is natural to see membership of EFTA as a follow-up to the earlier campaign for export industrialization and the liberalization process that had followed in the wake of the Marshall Plan and GATT. Norwegian industry had gradually had to get used to increased competition at home, while, at the same time, many industries had tried their luck overseas. Still free trade met with scepticism in certain parts of industry. Nevertheless, it showed itself capable of successfully making the changeover in the course of the 1960s.

The fight over membership of the European Community

EFTA was seen as an alternative to the EC for countries that wanted free trade but not such a degree of economic integration as specified by the Treaty of Rome, the EC's 'Constitution' of 1957. But further development came nevertheless to be characterized above all by the individual EFTA countries' relations with the EC. Joining the EC became the greatest question at issue in the politics of post-war Norway.

Norway applied for membership of the EC in April 1962 and again in July 1967 and June 1970. When, in September 1972, a referendum was held on whether or not to join the EC, it was on the basis of an agreement on membership that the government had signed the previous January. But Norway was never enthusiastic about acquiring membership, nor concerned with economic integration or the positive sides of membership. Thus its conduct was determined by the relationship to the EC of other EFTA countries, and especially by the potentially negative economic effects of staying out. The first Norwegian application came only after Great Britain and Denmark had sought membership in 1961. It proved abortive because the President of France, Charles de Gaulle, early in 1963 said 'no' to the British. The second attempt came in 1967 after Britain had again applied for membership, and the third after de Gaulle's resignation two years later had opened the door for the British and the Danes.

The EC question produced tremendous turmoil in Norwegian politics. The votes taken in the Storting when it decided to apply for membership were a poor reflection of the feeling for and against in the country at large: 113 to 37 in 1962; 132 to 17 in 1970. When the conflict came to a head in 1971–72, only the Conservative Party, the Centre Party and the Socialist People's Party avoided internal conflict – the first on the 'yes' side, the two others in the anti-EC camp. Both the

The referendum night between the 25th and 26th September 1972 was excruciatingly exciting for all who felt involved. Finally the arrow stopped at 53.5% 'No'.

Liberals and the Christian People's Party were evenly divided. There was a solid majority in favour of membership at an extraordinary national conference of the Labour Party held in the summer of 1972. The same was also the case at an extraordinary congress of the Trades Union Congress. But there were deep divisions amongst both party members and trade unionists, and opponents formed 'The Labour movement's information committee against the EC' (AIK) in order to disseminate the arguments against membership. Industry and its organizations were for the most part in favour of membership; the farmers, fishermen and their organizations uniformally against.

The EC campaign dominated Norwegian politics from the autumn of 1969 to September 1972. National committees were organised by both sides. The largest and most active was the 'Popular Movement against the EC', which had 110,000 members. Its roots lay in similar but more modest bodies formed 10 years earlier. 'Yes to EC' came later and did not manage to mobilize pro-EC supporters to the same extent. But both adopted the same campaign methods: membership drives, newspapers, leaflets and appeals, placards and public meetings. No arguments were barred and national symbols such as the flag and the national anthem were used to advantage by both sides. Both emphasized nationalism. The opponents used the slogan 'No to the sale of Norway', while the 'vote yes' supporters held a 'ceremony for peace' in Telavåg, the village in Vestlandet that had been razed to the ground during the war. The EC question split neighbourhoods, workplaces, associations and families. Two governments fell. The non-socialist government led by the Centre Party's Per Borten fell in March 1971 because the parties in his coalition were unable to agree to a common line on the EC. The ensuing Labour Party government resigned after the September 1972 referendum, as the prime minister, Trygve Bratteli, had said in August it would, should the anti-EC side win.

The counting of the votes in the referendum took place throughout the night of 25–26 September. The result was 53.5 per cent against and 46.5 per cent in favour of joining the EC. The vote has been interpreted by some as a break, the first since 1945, in Norwegian internationalism. But the negative vote also represented a continuity in policy and attitudes. Neutrality, isolationism and nationalism were traditionally strong in Norway. The country had been a hesitant internationalist, an unenthusiastic participant in the internationalization process. And, where collaboration proved necessary, the Atlantic orientation had clearly been preferred to the continental. With membership of the EC, the line was drawn between scepticism and opposition. Few were enthusiastic about a united Europe: supernationalism appeared threatening rather than seductive. 'Participation' had little appeal, 'autonomy' was for many an absolute good.

The nationalistic currents mingled with others. The referendum revealed a 'periphery versus centre' pattern. Four counties in the central areas of Østlandet had a 'yes' majority: Oslo, Akershus, Vestfold and Buskerud. The three counties of northern Norway (Nordland, Troms and Finnmark) together with Møre and Romsdal had a more than 70 per cent 'no' vote. The results also showed clear differences along economic lines: the majorities against membership were highest in agricultural and fishing districts, while the 'yes' votes usually came from areas dominated by manufacturing industry and the service sector. Seen as a whole, the picture is one of primary industries and outlying areas that felt their economies and egalitarian traditions threatened by EC membership, and so fought for a continuance of full autonomy as a means of furthering the established economic and regional equalization policies. The result can be seen as confirmation of the traditionally strong influence that the primary industries and the outlying districts have on Norwegian politics.

But the anti-membership alliance drew its strength from other sources too. The EC campaign was in many ways one of the 'grass roots' against the 'establishment': it was a revolt of the workers against the owners of business and capitalism; of the voters against the political leaders; of the people against the 'authorities'; of youthful radicalism in opposition to the bourgeois sentiments of their parents' generation. Thus the fight over EC membership unveiled underlying antagonisms and conflicts in Norwegian society. These had seldom been acute in a post-war era characterized by economic growth, welfare creation and increasing political consensus. The EC struggle acted as a catalyst for social and political conflict in Norway and heralded a period of greater political tension.

27
The post-war years in perspective

This presentation has been based on the premise that the period from the Second World War to the early 1970s displayed few problems in Norway's economic, social and political life, when set against the periods before and after. The analysis has portrayed the post-war period as a time of strong and persistent economic growth, of a welfare society that developed on the basis of that growth and of a collaborative and consensus-seeking state, which directed and administered the sharing out of it. Growth and the spread of welfare contributed to a more equal distribution of income and to making social divisions less marked. National unity was never seriously challenged and the national integration process was strengthened by closer contacts and greater understanding between town and country and an increasing political focus on the centre ground. At the same time, Norway became steadily more involved in international co-operation.

The 'post-war years' – from 1935 to 1972?

The years after the Second World War stand out sharply in important areas from the inter-war years. They were years of stable growth, full employment, social security and stability in the political system. It is not difficult to argue that the period was one of radical change. We have, however, chosen to emphasize the elements of continuity in Norway's economic, social and political life. Important features that characterized demographic development after the war were already apparent in the 1930s. Industrial growth, which is usually regarded as a post-war phenomenon, began during the crisis in the first part of the 1930s and gathered momentum in the course of the decade. War and the German occupation undoubtedly destroyed much, but at the same time stimulated growth.

The foundation for the Labour Party's 20-year dominance of Norwegian political life after the war was created by increasing support from voters in the primary industries and the great electoral victories of 1927 and 1933. Anti-parliamentarianism and revolutionary ideology turned out to be but a short-term interval, and by the middle of the 1930s the party closed ranks behind the rules of the political system and the symbols of the nation, e.g. the flag, the national anthem, etc. Clashes between the socialist and non-socialist blocs were reduced by the Crisis Agreement between the Labour Party and the Agrarian Party in 1935 and by the former's moderate line in government. Later, this understanding was strengthened by the national unity engendered in the war years and the Joint Programme (agreed by the political parties) in 1945.

The roots of the proactive state are also to be found in the inter-war years. The Labour Party devised a programme, based on its policies to meet the crisis, that gave the state the main responsibility for the development of industry, employment and the regulation of the economic cycle. Ideas took shape on the management of the economy and the industrial structure through institutionalized planning. These ideas were strengthened by the experiences of state-led wartime production in western Europe and the United States during the Second World War. The foundations of the post-war regulatory state were created in the 1930s, primarily through the organization of sales in the primary industries. The primary industries' co-operation with the state and the self-regulation pursued through its own organizations were steps on the road to a 'corporate' state system. The increasing understanding between workers and employers, which found expression in the Basic Agreement of 1935, was also a pre-condition for the development of a collaborative and consensus-seeking state. The development of the welfare society after the war can, in several instances, be seen as the continuation of the socio-political campaign that was initiated with the change of government and the improved economic situation in the mid-1930s.

Interpreted literally, the word 'post-war' means nothing more than 'after the war'. The expression has been in general use as a neutral description of the period. But, as the period since the war has gradually lengthened, the concept has become more problematic. Those who use it seldom explain what they mean by it. Increasingly, however, it has become a synonym for the period that, more than any other, featured strong and persistent growth, political stability and consensus. This analysis of the post-war years has, however, stressed its links with the inter-war period. From this perspective there are logical reasons for arguing that the 'post-war era' began in the middle of the 1930s. Interpreted as 'the period after the war', the 'post-war era' is still with us. Only a new war turned the previous post-war period into the 'inter-war years'. But most people today agree that our own time – the last couple of decades – has been filled with far more problems and conflicts than the quarter of a century after the Second World War and, therefore, stands out relatively clearly from it. If the phrase 'post-war era' continues to be linked to the period of growth, then it is also possible to argue that the era has ended. It then becomes natural to ask several questions: When did the era end? How did it happen? Why did the development of society, in several important areas, go off in a new direction?

The 1970s and the 1980s: economic downturn and uncertainty

Historians are usually cautious when they approach their own times. Different aspects and lines of development compete for precedence – and for the attention of historians. They do not know how developments will turn out – which features will be the 'winners'. Historians would rather keep a certain distance between themselves and the period they are writing about, as an aid to understanding just which lines emerge from it and point the way forward.

Today it seems that the years 1972–74 mark a turning point in several of the areas chosen as characteristic of the economic growth and the welfare state that to us constitute the 'post-war era'. The first, and perhaps the most important, is that industrial growth stopped. The reason for this was an international economic crisis set off by a dramatic increase in the price of oil, engineered by OPEC (the Organization of Petroleum Exporting Countries), in 1973. The economic downturn was reinforced by a basic structural crisis in western industry. The crisis led to long-lasting problems in Norwegian industry and shipping. Industrial output dropped in 8 out of 10 years after 1974 and employment in the sector fell by more than 20 per cent.

The drilling rig 'Ocean Viking' propelled Norway into the oil age when it struck oil in the Ekofisk field in December 1969. By 1984 the oil sector accounted for close to 20% of the national product. Oil provided the foundation for a further extension of the welfare society in the 1970s, for a counter-cyclical policy, and for an especially high Norwegian level of costs, which later was to create great problems.

The results were not, however, dramatic in this phase. This was due to the fact that oil from the North Sea had just become a new element of growth in the Norwegian economy. By 1984, after a production period of 10 years, the oil sector accounted for close to 20 per cent of the national output. In addition, an expansive counter-cyclical policy was pursued, while, at the same time, the public sector continued to grow. From the end of the 1970s, however, GNP fell in several years. Norway now had to tolerate increasing unemployment. In 1983 there were 70,000 in search of work, and the total continued to grow. Employment problems were exacerbated by the much larger numbers coming into the labour market compared with the 1950s and 1960s, the increase in female employment, and the increasing use of students in part-time work.

Much suggests that unemployment to a great extent hit the same groups as it had in the inter-war years – the young, the unskilled, the elderly and workers in outlying areas. Throughout the 1980s the number of long-term unemployed rose steadily, at the same time that many young people never managed to enter employment. But, in spite of everything, unemployment was still very much lower than it had been in the inter-war years and the social support services were much better.

The welfare society: expansion or contraction?

The expansion of the welfare society continued steadily throughout the 1970s, apparently unaffected by the recession and economic instability. The authorities' welfare ambitions had scarcely ever been greater, and rising oil revenues promised easy financing. Norway developed at this time a comprehensive law on working conditions; a liberalization of sick pay arrangements; strong institutional growth in health and social welfare; a lowered pension age; ambitious regional economic policies; and a radical plan for raising incomes in agriculture that, once and for all, should place industrial and agricultural workers on an equal footing. Employment in the public services continued to grow as a result of institutional growth and the general increase in the level of services provided by the local authorities.

Nevertheless, it can be argued that the development of the welfare society peaked in the course of the 1970s. Subsequently there are signs of contraction: the conditions attached to government loans for house purchase and education have worsened; the health service has increasingly introduced charges; and the authorities now impose higher charges for other welfare services. But above all it appears that ever-increasing numbers have fallen outside the social support and welfare services – without society managing to develop new welfare mechanisms that could bring them back in. The health and welfare services for the elderly have not managed to keep pace with the growth in their numbers, especially of those in the age groups needing nursing care. Pensions are inadequate in many cases. Young people and the long-term unemployed are often not covered by unemployment benefit. There are long queues for hospital beds. The provision of treatment for rapidly growing 'social diseases' such as alcoholism, drug abuse and crime are scarcely adequate. And more and more are referred to national assistance – something that was initially intended as a solution for the *few* who, for one reason or another, fell outside the other welfare provisions. Social and economic differences in society could be on the increase.

Political destabilization

Around 1970, political stability too began gradually to be undermined. Party lines in the 1970s and 1980s were unclear and shifted frequently. Norwegian voters showed much less party loyalty than previously. Three features are, nevertheless, clear.

One of them is the revival of the left in Norwegian politics. In the wake of the EC conflict, an alliance was formed between the Socialist People's Party, parts of the Norwegian Communist Party and anti-Common Marketeers from the Labour Party. First called the Socialist Electoral Pact, it later became the Socialist Left Party (SV). At the election of 1973 the party got 11 per cent of the vote and 16 seats in the Storting. Already by 1977 SV had lost much of its support, but it came back again strongly in the late 1980s, with a defence of the traditional ideals of the welfare state and a radical environmental policy as the basis of its support.

Another development was a marked strengthening of the right in Norwegian politics. This first appeared in the notable advance of the Conservatives at the elections of 1977 and 1981. The party got as much as 32 per cent of the vote and 53 seats, and so, for a time, was almost as big as the Labour Party. After that it was the turn of the Progressive Party to ride the conservative wave – it had been founded in 1972 as Anders Lange's Party. In 1989 the party got as much as 13 per cent of the vote. It is natural to see this growth of the right as a reaction to the strong growth of the public sector, to the levelling process of the welfare society and above all to the heavy taxes of a strongly distributive state.

A third feature was the weakening of the centre in Norwegian politics. The Liberal Party broke up over the EC question. The Centre Party and the Christian People's Party, on the other hand, came out of the EC conflict in a stronger position. But later they lost support.

'The one-party state' collapsed when the Labour Party lost its majority in the 1960s. Its support in the 1970s and 1980s was somewhere between 5 and 10 per cent lower than it had been during its heyday. With party splits on the increase and greater political polarization, the regime of parliamentary majorities was replaced by one of minority governments. Between 1971 and 1991 the country had 10 governments and 6 different Prime Ministers.

The welfare society and state management in crisis?

It is natural to see the political stability and growing consensus of the 1950s and 1960s as indicative of a united support for the basic values of the welfare society, and acceptance of the main features of the state management that saw to its development. The 1960s and most of the 1970s too were characterized by great optimism about the ability of the public sector to accomplish its tasks in the welfare field and to direct the economy. Likewise we can see the increased polarization as an expression both of disagreement over the basic values of the welfare system and of scepticism about the economic strength of the welfare state and its managerial ability. Pessimism was now the dominant mood.

The problems of the welfare society are today apparent to all. Increasingly, questions are raised as to whether the redistributive process has gone too far; whether the welfare arrangements really serve their purpose; and whether society *ought* to keep all of them or, indeed, *can* do so. Warnings about the rise in the number of elderly people someway into the next century have raised doubts over the financing of the central feature of the welfare society – *Folketrygden*, the system of universal benefits. And, finally, the role of the public sector is being questioned. Many react against the size of the bureaucracy and its all-embracing character. They are sceptical too over the authorities' handling of society's resources, doubting whether it is efficient enough. They raise questions as to whether or not the public sector itself is one reason for the absence of growth and vigour in the economy and the business world. They see a solution to the problems of the welfare society in a reduction of the public sector. Problem solving through the operation of the market and individual initiative is put forward as an alternative to collective, publicly administered solutions. Others see continued high public consumption as fundamental to the maintenance of a proper welfare society. For them the solution lies in a realignment of public activity to meet new needs and new tasks.

Alongside the ending of expansion for the welfare society, the increasing political polarization and the reaction against the growth of the public sector, the managerial system itself has come under pressure. In many ways, the 1970s represent the high point of attempts to run a planned economy and to maintain a co-operative and consensus-seeking state. Optimism about the ability of the state to cope still reigned when the recession struck. The downturn was met by counter-cyclical measures inspired by Keynes' teachings of the 1930s – teachings that had gradually won great cross-party support in Norway. The state should use public funds to maintain demand in the expectation that the cycle would turn. For the first time, the theory was put into practice on a large scale. Using the oil revenues, comprehensive guarantees were introduced, support given for stock holding, loans made to maintain liquidity and wage subsidies provided for exposed industrial sectors and firms. At the same time, the co-operative and consensus-seeking state reached new heights. Through the intervention of the public authorities and with support from public funds in wage negotiations, the growth of incomes was to be managed. The 'Kleppe packages' – named after the finance minister, Per Kleppe – attempted to maintain wages at the same time as inflation was to be fought. The means were collaboration between the partners under official leadership.

The managerial policies of the 1970s were not a success. Economic activity – and with it employment – was maintained temporarily. But the counter-cyclical policy had to be abandoned relatively quickly when it was seen that the recession internationally was lasting longer than expected. And, even in the short time the policy was in operation, it contributed to forestalling necessary changes and to creating an especially high level of wages in Norway. In doing so, it demonstrated more of the limitations of the regulatory economy than of its possibilities. In many ways, too, the downfall of the counter-cyclical policies marked the failure of a theory that had reigned, virtually supreme, amongst economists and politicians for 30–40 years. The failure contributed to a generally increasing scepticism over the possibility of a planned economy at all. And for the first time strong doubts were expressed about the value of the co-operative consensus-seeking system. Was this at all compatible with a balanced economic develop-

Important features of society in the 1970s and 1980s were the feminist movement and the campaign for equality. Gro Harlem Brundtland's 'government of women' in 1986 (8 out of 17 members were women) was a breakthrough that aroused international attention.

ment? Is the co-operative, consensus-seeking state a system that above all else avoids conflicts by seeing that all the strong, organized interests get more and more? Is the system suited to sharing the fruits of growth, but not to creating growth or to sharing scarce resources fairly. At the same time that developments demonstrated the limitations of planning, they also showed clearly just how dependent Norway was on the international economy. Not surprisingly, in the 1990s the EC question once again became the dominant issue in Norwegian politics. But traditional sentiments remained strong, and in a new referendum the Norwegian people repeated its 1972 'no'.

Dominance of the debate over political ideology shifted between the 1970s and 1980s from an almost all-embracing optimistic belief in the state and its managerial apparatus to strong support for private solutions and the market mechanism. International experience indicates, however, that many of the challenges for the welfare society cannot be met without strong public involvement. Another case in point is the environment, which will be a challenge for decades to come. It raises management problems of a far greater magnitude than any that have traditionally been tied to the development of the welfare society. Welfare rests on the careful management of scarce resources. And the growth that created the economic foundation for welfare now constitutes a serious threat to it. Will the pendulum again swing back in the direction of 'more state' and 'more direction'? If so, what kind of state and what kind of direction?

The 'post-war era' and its historians

The historian wants to understand and explain the development of society in the past. But the picture the historian draws is always just *one version* of the past. History is never written once and for all; it is written again and again. Historians of more recent periods – contemporary historians as they are sometimes called – must expect to see their 'histories' revised more frequently, from new perspectives, than those of their colleagues who study earlier times. This has been an account of the development of historical writing of the 'post-war era' in Norway, showing how it first emphasized 'reconstruction', then 'radical change' and finally elements of 'continuity'. It is the perspective of continuity that we have emphasized and developed further – the continuity between the period after 1945 and the years before. But at the same time we have emphasized the break that occurred between this period and the decades that followed.

What will future historians emphasize when they come to give their versions of the post-war period? This is unknown. For, among other things, it will depend upon the historians' own basic ideas, on their analyses of the 1970s and 1980s and not least on the social, economic and political developments in the times ahead. One possible result is that an increasing attention to contemporary problems will strengthen the emphasis on the break between the growth and welfare society and the developments of the 1970s and 1980s. If so, the picture of the post-war period as a unique interval in Norway's recent history will be strengthened. And it can be imagined that this interpretation will infect notions on the change-over from the inter-war years to the post-war years, so that the break here will also appear sharper. That may, in turn, lead to a revival for what, by way of introduction, has been called the 'radical change perspective'.

But the opposite can also be imagined. Today's problems and those of the last decade will inspire further historical research on the 1940s,

1950s and 1960s. This could lead to a search for the origins of contemporary problems in precisely the period that it has been argued was virtually problem free. Perhaps social conditions in the 'post-war era' were not quite so harmonious as we have suggested? Such research will search for continuity from the post-war years to today, but continuity on different premises than we have sought to establish from the crises of the inter-war years to the growth and welfare of the post-war period.

Perspectives are means by which historians seek to bring order and understanding to the past. Competing perspectives are an expression of different historians' varying interpretations of the same historic reality – and of the fact that our understanding of history is constantly developing.

Norwegian governments after 1873

1873–1880	Frederik Stang
1880–1884	Christian August Selmer
1884	Christian Homann Schweigaard
1884–1889	Johan Sverdrup
1889–1891	Emil Stang
1891–1893	Johannes Steen
1893–1895	Emil Stang
1895–1898	Francis Hagerup
1898–1902	Johannes Steen
1902–1903	Ottar Blehr
1903–1905	Francis Hagerup
1905–1907	Christian Michelsen
1907–1908	Jørgen Løvland
1908–1910	Gunnar Knudsen
1910–1912	Wollert Konow
1912–1913	Jens Bratlie
1913–1920	Gunnar Knudsen
1920–1921	Otto B. Halvorsen
1921–1923	Otto Blehr
1923	Otto B. Halvorsen
1923–1924	Abraham Berge
1924–1926	Johan Ludwig Mowinckel
1926–1928	Ivar Lykke
1928	Christopher Hornsrud
1928–1931	Johan Ludwig Mowinckel
1931–1932	Peder Kolstad
1932–1933	Jens Hundseid
1933–1935	Johan Ludwig Mowinckel
1935–1945	Johan Nygaardsvold

1945	Einar Gerhardsen
1945–1951	Einar Gerhardsen
1951–1955	Oscar Torp
1955–1963	Einar Gerhardsen
1963	John Lyng
1963–1965	Einar Gerhardsen
1965–1971	Per Borten
1971–1972	Trygve Bratteli
1972–1973	Lars Korvald
1973–1976	Trygve Bratteli
1976–1981	Odvar Nordli
1981	Gro Harlem Brundtland
1981–1983	Kåre Willoch
1983–1986	Kåre Willoch
1986–1989	Gro Harlem Brundtland
1989–1990	Jan P. Syse
1990–	Gro Harlem Brundtland

Chronology

I. To 1536

790s	The first known Viking attacks on the British Isles
ca. 870	Beginning of Norse settlement of Iceland
between 871 and 899	Ottar the Norseman visits King Alfred of England
between ca. 880 and 900	Battle of Hafrsfjord
ca. 880–931?	King Harald Haarfagre, 'Fairhair' (year of death according to Icelandic chronology); beginning of first phase of political unification)
ca. 931–933?	King Eirik Blodøks, 'Bloodaxe'
ca. 933–959?	King Haakon Adalsteinsfostre, 'fosterson of Æthelstan'
ca. 959–974?	King Harald Graafell, 'Grey–cloak'
974–995	Earl Haakon
995–999	King Olaf Tryggvason
999–1015	Eirik and Svein earls
1015–1028	King Olaf Haraldsson, the Holy (St Olav)
1028–1035	King Knut, the Great [Denmark]
1030	Olaf Haraldsson killed at Battle of Stiklestad
1030–1035	Svein Alfivasson and his mother Alfiva (Ælfgifu), mistress of Knut the Great, rule in Norway
1035–1046	King Magnus Olafsson, the Good
1045–1046	Joint Kingship of Magnus Olafsson and Harald Sigurdsson
1046–1066	King Harald Sigurdsson Hardraade, 'Hard-ruler'
1066	Harald Sigurdsson Hardraade killed at Battle of Stamford Bridge
1066–1093	King Olaf Haraldsson Kyrre, 'the Quiet'
1067–1069	Joint kingship of Harald's sons Olaf and Magnus

1093–1094/95	Joint kingship of Magnus Olafsson and Haakon Magnusson Toresfostre
1094/95–1103	King Magnus Olafsson Berrføtt, 'Bareleg'
1103–1122/23	Joint kingship of Magnus's sons Øystein (died 1122/23), Sigurd, and Olaf (died 1115)
1108–1111	Sigurd Magnusson's crusade
1122/23–1130	King Sigurd Magnusson Jorsalfare, 'the Crusader'
1130–1134	Joint kingship of Magnus Sigurdsson and Harald Magnusson Gille
1134	Beginning of 'civil wars'; second phase of political unification
1135–1136	King Harald Gille
1136–1157	Joint Kingship of Harald's sons Inge Krokrygg, Sigurd Munn (killed 1155), and Øystein (1142–1157)
1152–53	National assembly in Trondheim: establishment of Norwegian archbishopric and regulations regarding the Church's relationship to monarchy and society
1157–1161	King Inge Magnusson Krokrygg; Haakon Sigurdsson Herdebrei counter-king
1161–1184	King Magnus Erlingsson; Erling Skakke regent
1162	Haakon Herdebrei killed in battle
1163/64	National assembly in Bergen: coronation of Magnus Erlingsson; law on royal succession and the king's peace; re-ordering of the Church's relationship to kingship and society
1177	'Birchlegs' take Sverre Sigurdsson as new counter-king
1179	Erling Skakke killed in battle
1184	Magnus Erlingsson killed in battle
1184–1202	King Sverre Sigurdsson
1185–1188	Kuvlung uprising against Sverre
1190–1202	Open conflict between King Sverre and the Church
1193–1194	Øyskjegg uprising against Sverre
1196	Sverre crowned in Bergen
1196	'Croziers' (Bishops' supporters) rise up against Sverre
1202–1204	King Haakon Sverresson
1204	Guttorm Sigurdsson new 'Birchleg' king; new 'Crozier' revolt under Erling Magnusson Steinvegg
1204–1217	Inge Baardsson 'Birchleg' king
1207–1217	Filippus Simonsson 'Crozier' king

1208	'Birchlegs' and 'Croziers' conclude peace and divide state territory
1217–1263	King Haakon Haakonsson (final achievement of national unification under a single king); Skule Baardsson regent until 1220(?), later earl over own territory
1219–1227	Ribbung uprising against King Haakon and Earl Skule
1223	National assembly in Bergen: final decision on royal succession favourable to King Haakon; new division of state territory between him and Skule. Trade agreement between Norway and England
1227	The last Ribbung-chieftain killed; end of 'civil wars'
1239–1240	Duke Skule's revolt and defeat
1247	National assembly in Bergen: coronation of King Haakon; new regulations on the Church's relationship to monarchy and society
1250	Peace and trade agreement between King Haakon and Lübeck
1257	Magnus Haakonsson acclaimed joint king
1260	New law on royal succession establishes hereditary kingship; king's peace in Haakon Haakonsson's 'new law'
1261	Royal wedding of Magnus Haakonsson and Ingebjørg, daughter of Danish King Erik Plogpenning, in newly completed Haakon's Hall in Bergen
1263	King Haakon's war expedition against Scotland; death in the Orkneys
1263–1280	King Magnus Haakonsson Lagabøte, 'the Law-mender'
1266	Peace of Perth; the Hebrides and the Isle of Man ceded to the crown of Scotland
1273	National assembly in Bergen: Magnus's sons Eirik and Haakon acclaimed king and duke respectively; new law on royal succession; concordat between king and church
1274	Magnus Lagabøte's *Landslov* ('Landlaw', national code)
1276	Magnus Lagabøte's *Bylov* ('Town law')
1277	Final concordat between Crown and Church in Tønsberg

1278	King Magnus awards visiting German-speaking merchants in Norway their first guest-privileges
1280	National assembly and provincial council in Bergen: Eirik Magnusson crowned; rival royal and clerical legislation
1280–1299	King Eirik Magnusson
1281	National assembly in Bergen: King Eirik marries Margareta, daughter of the Scottish King Alexander 3
1281–1283	Conflict between Crown and Church
1282	Bergen by-laws limiting freedom of trade for German merchants
1284	Haakon Magnusson assumes control of his duchy
1284–1285	Open conflict between Norway and Hanseatic cities; ends by arbitration of the Swedish king in Kalmar
1286	King Alexander 3 dies; Margareta Eiriksdatter heiress to Scottish throne
1289–1295	War between Norway and Denmark, ends with armistice of Hindsgavl
1290	Margareta Eiriksdatter, 'the Maid of Norway', sent to assume the Scottish throne and marry the English crown prince; dies in Orkneys
1294	King Eirik and Duke Haakon issue letter of privilege to merchants from Hanseatic cities
1299–1319	King Haakon 5 Magnusson
1302	National assembly in Oslo: law on royal succession and royal guardianship; Swedish-Norwegian alliance against Denmark; Ingebjørg Haakonsdatter promised in marriage to Duke Erik, brother of the Swedish king
1302–1318	National trade policy in municipal by-laws and royal decrees
1308	Royal decree to increase royal control of retinue (*hird*) and administration
1308–1310	Conflict between King Haakon and the Swedish dukes
1312	Duke Erik marries Ingebjørg Haakonsdatter
1319	Agreement on Swedish-Norwegian common kingship under Magnus Eriksson
1319–1355	King Magnus Eriksson, Swedish king to 1365
1319–1323	Regency council under direction of Duchess Ingebjørg

1323–1331	Regency council under Grand Seneschal Erling Vidkunsson
1343	Agreement between King Magnus and the Norwegian council of the realm regarding acceptance of Haakon Magnusson as Norwegian king; King Magnus confirms Hanseatic privileges in Norway
1344	Representatives of Norwegian cities and commons swear allegiance to Haakon Magnusson
1349–1350	'Black Death' rages in Norway; the country loses perhaps one–half of its population
1350	Haakon 6 Magnusson acclaimed king in Bergen; Norwegian regency council under Grand Seneschal
1355	Haakon 6 comes of legal age, end of Swedish-Norwegian common kingship
1355–1380	King Haakon 6 Magnusson, Swedish king 1362–1371
ca. 1360	Hanseatic *Kontor* ('office', trading station) in Bergen established
1363	Marriage between Haakon 6 and Margareta, daughter of the Danish King Valdemar Atterdag
1364	Albrecht von Mecklenburg elected Swedish King
1365–1371	King Magnus Eriksson imprisoned
1367	War between the German Hansa and kings Valdemar and Haakon 6
1369	Armistice between Hansa and Haakon 6
1370	Hansa dictates Peace of Stralsund to Denmark
1374	King Magnus Eriksson drowns
1375	Olaf Haakonsson elected Danish king after King Valdemar's death; Margareta becomes regent
1376	Final peace between Hansa and Haakon 6; confirmation of Hanseatic privileges in Norway
1380–1387	King Olaf Haakonsson hereditary king in Norway; Danish king from 1376; dies without issue; the Danish-Norwegian union begins
1388–1412	Queen Margareta effective ruler in the Nordic Kingdoms
1389	Council of the realm acclaims Erik of Pomerania, Margareta's nephew and heir, king of Norway
1397	Assembly of Scandinavian councils and magnates

	in Kalmar; Erik of Pomerania crowned king of all three kingdoms (Kalmar Union)
1412–1442	Erik of Pomerania Norwegian king; dethroned in Denmark and Sweden in 1439
1436–1437	Amund Sigurdsson Bolt's uprising in eastern Norway
1438	Hallvard Gråtopp's uprising in eastern Norway suppressed
1439–1442	Norwegian council of the realm assumes control under Grand Seneschal Sigurd Jonsson
1442–1448	Christopher of Bavaria, Erik's nephew, Norwegian king; Danish king from 1440; Swedish king from 1441; died without issue in 1448
1448–1450	Tug-of-war for the Norwegian throne between Christian of Oldenburg and Karl Knutsson; Christian wins
1450	Treaty of eternal union between the Danish and the Norwegian kingdoms; Norway becomes formally an elective monarchy
1450–1481	Christian 1, Norwegian king, Danish king from 1448, Swedish king 1457–1464
1455	Hanseatia privileges in Norway renewed after the murder of Olav Nilsson, captain of Bergen Castle
1458	Concordat of 1227 confirmed; the Norwegian council of the realm promises to accept Christian 1's oldest son, Hans, as king upon the former's death
1468–1469	Christian 1 pledges Orkney and Shetland islands to the Scottish king
1481–1483	Interregnum after death of Christian 1; council of the realm assumes control
1483–1513	Hans, Norwegian king, Danish king from 1482, Swedish king 1497–1501
1501–1502	Knut Alvsson's uprising and defeat
1506–1513	Duke Christian, Hans's son, Norwegian viceroy
1513–1524	Christian 2, Norwegian king, Danish king till 1523, Swedish king 1520–1521
1518–1521	Severe extraordinary taxes in connection with Christian 2's war against Sweden; peasant resistance in Norway suppressed
1520	Stockholm Bloodbath: end of Oldenburgers' ambitions in Sweden

1521	Gustaf Vasa Swedish regent, king from 1523
1523–1537	Olav Engelbrektsson, Norwegian archbishop and leader of the Norwegian council of the realm
1524–1533	Frederik 1, Norwegian king, Danish king from 1523
1531–1532	Archbishop Olav breaks with Frederik 1, supports Christian 2's unsuccessful bid to regain throne
1533–1536	Interregnum in Norway: Archbishop Olav opposes Christian 3's claim to the throne; strikes hard against opponents on the council of the realm
1537	Archbishop Olav fails to consolidate control and leaves the country; dissolution of archbishopric and suppression of Roman Catholicism

II. 1536–1814

1534–1559	Christian 3, king of Denmark–Norway
1536	Protestant Reformation introduced into Denmark and Norway; Norwegian council of the realm abolished; Norwegian kingdom abolished; Norway becomes an integral part ('limb') of kingdom of Denmark: 'that the realm of Norway (…) shall (…) hereafter be and remain under the Danish crown just as any of the other lands, Jutland, Fyn or Skåne, and hereafter neither be nor be called a separate kingdom, but a part of the realm of Denmark and under the Danish crown for time everlasting.' (charter of royal accession)
1559–1588	King Frederik 2
1563–1570	Seven-Years' War
1572	Office of Norwegian viceroy established (*stattholder*)
1588–1648	King Christian 4
1591	Office of rural magistrate established (*sorenskriveri*)
1604	Christian 4's Norwegian Code of Law
1611–1613	War of Kalmar against Sweden
1623	Silver mine at Kongsberg established (closed in 1957)
1624	Oslo destroyed by fire; city rebuilt under name Christiania
1625–1629	War of the Emperor (Thirty Years' War); taxes rise steeply

1628	Norwegian army established
1641	Town of Christiansand established
1643–1645	Hannibal's Affair (Hannibal Sehested, Norwegian viceroy 1642–1651): war against Sweden
1645	Peace of Brømsebro: Norway loses Jemtland and Herjedalen to Sweden
1644	Copper mine at Røros established
1648–1670	King Frederik 3
1657–1660	Carl Gustaf wars, also called Three-Years's War (Denmark–Norway vs Sweden)
1660	Peace of Copenhagen: Norway loses Båhuslen to Sweden; Frederik 3's coup d'état establishes a hereditary, absolute monarchy (*enevelde*); central administrative apparatus expanded; first sale of crown lands
1662	General Rights of the Town: town privileges introduced
1665	Law of the Realm (*kongelov*), constitutional confirmation of hereditary, absolute monarchy with evangelical Lutheranism as state religion
1669	Land register established as new basis for tax assessments
1670–1699	King Christian 5
1673	Count's domains of Larvik and Jarlsberg established
1675–79	Skåne War against Sweden, also called Gyldenløve War (Ulrik Fredrik Gyldenløve, Norwegian viceroy 1664–1699)
1684	Limitations on surcharges to farm leases introduced
1687	Christian 5's Norwegian Code of Law
1688	Sawmill license privileges introduced
1699–1730	King Frederik 4
1704–1722	Administrative council (*Slottslov*) established as functional Norwegian 'government' in Christiania
1711–1720	Great Northern War (Denmark-Norway, Sweden, Russia, Poland)
1723	New land register prepared and partially implemented; sale of Church lands and churches
1730–1746	King Christian 6
1730	Iron monopoly introduced
1735	Grain monopoly introduced

1736	Decree on church confirmation
1739	Decree on elementary schools – supplemented in 1741
1741	Decree on poor law in Akershus diocesan country
1746–1766	King Frederik 5
1750	Decree on cottar system – amended in 1752
1751	Border agreement between Norway and Sweden
1762	Mobilization in Holstein during Seven-Years' War; extraordinary tax assessed in Denmark and Norway
1765	'Stril' armed riots in protest against extraordinary tax
1766–1808	King Christian 7
1769	First complete population census in Norway
1770–1771	Struensee leads reform government in Copenhagen
1773	Demographic crisis: Østlandet hardest hit
1784	Crown Prince Frederik (later Frederik 6) takes over power
1786–1788	Lofthus uprising against merchants and government officials (Christian Jensen Lofthus – Lillesand)
1787	Finnmark trade monopoly abolished; towns established in the north: Hammerfest (1789), Vardø (1789), and Tromsø (1794)
1788	Grain monopoly abolished
1794	Iron monopoly abolished
1795	Sawmill license privileges partially eliminated
1795–97	Boards of arbitration and new judicial system established
1796–1804	Hans Nielsen Hauge (Tune – Sarpsborg) – pietistic lay evangelism
1801	First nominative population census in Norway
1807	Destruction of Danish fleet in Copenhagen by British fleet; Denmark-Norway allies itself with Napoleon; Norwegian governmental commission
1808–1814	King Frederik 6
1808	War against Sweden
1809	Food shortages and famine in Østlandet
1811	Resolution for a Norwegian university, established in 1813
1813	Crown Prince Christian Frederik to Norway as viceroy

1814	Peace of Kiel assigns Norway to Sweden; Christian Frederik leads a Norwegian uprising; national assembly in Eidsvoll passes a constitution (*grunnlov*) for Norway; Christian Frederik elected Norwegian king; war with Sweden; personal union with kingdom of Sweden (common king)

III. 1814–1945

1814–1818	King Carl 2 (Carl 13 in Sweden)
1816–1818	Bank of Norway established
1818	Peasant riots in Østlandet to protest high taxation
1818–1844	King Carl 3 Johan (Carl 14 Johan in Sweden)
1821–1836	Carl Johan attempts to revise the constitution regarding royal veto
1822	First savings deposit bank established (Christiania Sparebank)
1826	State buys steamships 'Constitution' and 'Prince Carl'
1827	First interstate law on trade between Norway and Sweden (*mellomrikslov*)
1837	State land and town direct taxes abolished; local self-government introduced
1839	Law on Artisanal Trades: beginning of liberalization of artisanal trades; widows allowed to continue workshops
1842	Norwegian currency, *spesidaler*, put on silver standard; trade liberalized; free-trade tariff adopted
1844–1859	King Oscar 1
1845	Poor Laws, revised 1863 and 1900
1848	First commercial bank established (Christiania Bank og Kreditkasse)
1848–1851	Thrane movement: popular protest
1851	Mortgage Bank established
1854	Railway from Christiania to Eidsvoll opened; sawmill privileges abolished, effective 1860
1855	November Agreement with Great Britain and France: pledge not to cede any land to Russia
1859	Conflict over office of viceroy; Reform Union (Johan Sverdrup) – beginnings of political parties
1859–1872	King Carl 4 (Carl 15 in Sweden)

1861	Frederik Stang becomes leader of government
1865	Free–trade agreement with France
1867	Final report of the second union committee; high point of Scandinavianism
1869	Storting resolves to meet annually (previously triennially)
1872	Constitutional amendment concerning participation of cabinet ministers in Storting debates: beginning of constitutional conflict (controversy over royal veto)
1872–1905	King Oscar 2
1873	Position of viceroy formally abolished; Norwegian government henceforth headed by a prime minister
1874	Second interstate law expands free-trade between Norway and Sweden
1880	9 June resolution: Storting decides that the constitutional motion on ministerial participation is valid constitutional law in spite of king's veto
1884	Parliamentary court of impeachment convicts cabinet ministers of violating the constitution; political parties emerge: Liberals (*Venstre*) and Conservatives (*Høyre*); responsible parliamentary government established; suffrage widened
1885	Labour Commission established to investigate working conditions
1885–1905	Last phase in conflict over political union with Kingdom of Sweden: dispute over control of foreign policy (trade consulates)
1887	Norwegian Labour Party (*Den norske Arbeiderparti*) established; law on use of juries
1888	Moderate Liberal Party (*Det moderate Venstre*) established
1889	Law on Primary Education ('the people's school'): seven years compulsory schooling for all
1891	Liberals (*Venstre*) demand a separate Norwegian minister of foreign affairs
1892	Direct state income tax instituted; law on workers' protection establishes factory inspectorate
1894	National accident insurance for industrial workers introduced

1895	Norwegian retreat in conflict with Sweden; beginning of military build-up
1896	Norwegian Farmers' Union established
1897	Interstate law on free trade between Norway and Sweden rescinded: shift to economic protectionism
1898	Universal suffrage for men; radical National Association for Women's Suffrage founded; removal of Union emblem from Norwegian merchant-marine flag
1899	Norwegian Federation of Labour (AFL) established
1900	Norwegian Employers' Confederation (NAF) established
1903	«Coalition Party» (*Samlingsparti*) established
1905	Union with Sweden dissolved by Storting; referendum on establishment of a republic; Storting elects Prince Carl of Denmark as King of Norway; new electoral law with single-member constituencies
1905–1957	King Haakon 7
1906–1909	Conflict over Concession Law: state control over natural resources such as waterfalls and forests
1907	Integrity Agreement with Britain, France, Germany, and Russia: Norwegian neutrality in return for international recognition
1908	Consolidation of Liberal Party (*Venstre*)
1909	National Liberal Party (*Frisinnede Venstre*) established; national sickness insurance adopted
1913	Universal suffrage for women; syndicalist inspired association (*Den norske fagopposisjon*) organized
1915	Law on Labour Conflicts
1918	Labour Party resolves to become a 'revolutionary party of class struggle'; party joins Comintern in 1920
1919	Referendum approves probibition of alcoholic spirits and fortified wines; new electoral law with proportional representation; eight-hour day established by law
1920	Agrarian Party (*Bondeparti*) established; Norway joins League of Nations
1921	Norwegian Social Democratic Workers' Party established in protest to Labour Party's radicalism
1923	Norwegian Communist Party established
1924	Svalbard becomes officially part of Norway

1926	Prohibition of alcoholic spirits rescinded after referendum; law on economic trusts and combines establishes the Trust Control
1928	First Labour Party government (lasts two weeks); Norwegian *krone* put on gold standard ('parity crisis'); grain monopoly becomes permanent
1930	Law on sale of agricultural products
1931–1933	Conflict with Denmark over claims to eastern Greenland
1933	National Socialist Party (*Nasjonal Samling*) established under Vidkun Quisling; Christian People's Party established; new defense law passed
1935	Crisis Agreement between Labour Party and Agrarian Party; Basic Agreement on collective bargaining between the Norwegian Employers' Confederation (NAF) and the Norwegian Federation of Labour (AFL)
1936	National old-age social pension introduced
1940–1945	War and German occupation of country; royal family and the government flee to England and establish a government-in-exile

IV. After 1945

1945, 8 May	Liberation Day
1945, 7 June	King Haakon 7 returns home after five years in exile
1945	National Economic Co-ordinating Committee established; political parties agree on Joint Programme for economic reconstruction
1945–1952	Economic activity subject to rationing and quotas
1946	National product and private consumption recovers 1939-level; the National Housing Bank established; University of Bergen founded; child allowances introduced: paid to mother; SAS established; agreement on plant-level Production Committees; foundation of state-owned industries, Norsk Jernverk (steelworks in Mo i Rana) and Årdal Verk (aluminium works)
1946–1951	More state-owned industries established
1947	Industrial production and fisheries recover 1939-level; State Bank for Educational Loans established;

	18-workday vacation introduced; first macroeconomic National Budget presented; law on Industry Committees; 'Lex Brofoss': state control of prices and production; Marshall Plan aid begins
1947–1953	'The Great Debate over Economic Planning'
1948	Agricultural production recovers 1939-level; first long–term economic program presented; Norway joins GATT and OEEC (Organization for European Economic Cooperation) – later OECD (Organization for Economic Cooperation and Development); Communist take-over in Czechoslovakia
1949	Shipping tonnage recovers 1939-level; discussions with Denmark and Sweden regarding a Nordic defense treaty; Norway joins NATO (North Atlantic Treaty Organization); free list system introduced, relaxing foreign trade controls
1950s	«Age of restraint»
1950	Korean War breaks out; collapse of initiative for a Nordic customs union
1951	Coordinating Committee for financial policy: representatives of finance ministry and banking
1952	Northern Norway Plan presented; law on required reserve deposits in Bank of Norway; National Agreement for Agriculture; leftist political weekly *Orientering* begins publication; Norwegian foreign-aid fisheries project in Kerala, India begins; passport requirement eliminated between Nordic countries
1952–1953	Debate on price and rationalization legislation
1953	Nordic Council established
1954	NATO resolution approves use of tactical nuclear weapons in Western Europe; longer compulsory military service approved; budgetary guidelines for state banks established; common Nordic labour market established
1954–1956	Negotiations regarding Nordic economic cooperation conducted without result
1955	West Germany joins NATO
1957	Treaty of Rome establishes the European Economic Community (EEC); Norwegian 'no' to stationing of nuclear weapons on Norwegian soil

1957–58	Moderate economic down-turn
1958	Family allowances introduced; 'Easter revolution' protesting stationing of nuclear weapons in West Germany
1959	45-hour workweek introduced; law on access to 9-year mandatory primary schooling; means-test for old-age pensions eliminated; Agrarian Party changes name to Centre Party
1959–1961	New state-owned industries established
1960s	«Decade of Optimism»
1960	Norway joins EFTA (European Free Trade Association); rationing of cars ceased; Regional Development Bank established; television broadcasts begin in Norway
1961	Disability relief and rehabilitation support introduced; Socialist People's Party (*Sosialistisk Folkeparti*) established
1962–1965	Highpoint of amalgamation of local authorities
1962, April	Norwegian application for membership in EEC
1962, Nov.	Mine disaster in King's Bay, Spitzbergen
1963, June	Investigative committee's report on King's Bay disaster made public
1964	Towns integrated into county authorities; 4-weeks paid vacation introduced; law on social security; National Agreement on Fisheries
1965	Social benefits for widows and mothers introduced; law on money and credit; law on planning and house construction
1967	National Social Security Authority established (*Folketrygden*), incorporating old-age, invalidity, survivors', orphans', and unwed mothers' support schemes; sickness, health-care, occupational injury, and unemployment benefits also incorporated in 1971
1967, July	Norwegian application for membership in EEC
1968	42.5-hour workweek introduced; universities of Trondheim and Tromsø founded; Building for Industrial Growth, Ltd., established
1969	Regional colleges established in Kristiansand, Molde, and Stavanger; 9 years schooling becomes mandatory

	throughout country; law on county-run hospitals; discovery of large oil reserves in North Sea under Norwegian jurisdiction (Ekofisk field)
1970, June	Norwegian application for membership in EEC
1971	Shore Plan Law approved
1972, 25 Sept.	Referendum on Norwegian membership in EEC: 53.5% against; 46.5% for

Select bibliography

I. General literature

A general bibliography covering all aspects of Norwegian life is Leland B. Sather, *Norway,* Santa Barbara, Calif. 1986. World Bibliographic Series, 67. The *Dictionary of Scandinavian History*, ed. B. J. Nordstrom, Westport, Conn. 1986, is a very useful historical reference work on Norway and its Scandinavian neighbors. Most of the research published in English by Norwegian scholars appears in academic journals rather than in books. There are two major English-language journals dealing with Norwegian history: *The Scandinavian Economic History Review* (1953–) and *The Scandinavian Journal of History* (1976–). Articles on historical topics are also occasionally found in journals specialising in Scandinavian literature: *Scandinavica: an international journal of Scandinavian studies* (1962–); *Scandinavian studies: the journal of the Society for the Advancement of Scandinavian Study* (1911–). Official statistics on economy and society can be found in two complementary compendia: *International historical statistics : Europe 1750–1988*, ed. B. R. Mitchell, 3rd ed., London 1992, and *State, Economy, and Society in Western Europe 1815–1975*, ed. P. Flora, F. Kraus, and W. Pfenning, 2 vols., Frankfurt-New York, 1982–87.

Hubbard, William H., *et al.*, eds. *Making a Historical Culture: Historiography in Norway.* Oslo, 1995.
Kiel, Anne Cohen, ed., *Continuity and Change. Aspects of Contemporary Norway.* Oslo 1993.
Ramsøy, Natalie R., ed. *Norwegian Society.* Oslo, 1974.
Selbyg, Arne. *Norway Today: An Introduction to Modern Norwegian Society.* Oslo, 1986.

II. Basic histories in Norwegian

Andersen, Per Sveaas. *Samlingen av Norge og kristningen av landet 800–1130.* (Handbok i Norges historie, 2). Bergen, 1977.

Bagge, Sverre, and Knut Mykland. *Norge i dansketiden 1380–1814.* Oslo, 1987.

Fladby, Rolf. *Samfunn i vekst under fremmed styre 1536–1660.* (Handbok i Norges historie, 5). Oslo, 1986.

Furre, Berge. *Norsk historie 1905–1990. Vårt hundreår.* Oslo, 1992.

Helle, Knut, et al., eds. *Aschehougs Norgeshistorie.* 12 vols., Oslo: Aschehoug, 1994–.

Helle, Knut. *Norge blir en stat 1130–1319.* (Handbok i Norges historie, 3). 2nd ed., Bergen, 1974.

Mykland, Knut, ed. *Norges Historie.* 15 vols., Oslo: Cappelen, 1976–80.

Nerbøvik, Jostein. *Norsk historie 1870–1905. Frå jordbrukssamfunn mot organisasjonssamfunn.* 2nd ed., Oslo, 1986.

Pryser, Tore. *Norsk historie 1800–1870. Frå standssamfunn mot klassesamfunn.* Oslo, 1985.

III. Literature on particular periods

To 1536:

Foote, Peter, and David Wilson. *The Viking Achievement. The Society and Culture of Early Medieval Scandinavia.* London, 1989.

Gissel, Svend, et al. *Desertion and Land Colonization in the Nordic Countries, ca. 1300–1600.* Stockholm, 1981.

Pulsiano, Ph., ed. *Medieval Scandinavia. An Encyclopedia.* New York, 1993.

Sawyer, Birgit, and Peter Sawyer. *Medieval Scandinavia. From Conversion to Reformation circa 800–1500.* Minneapolis, 1993.

Sawyer, Peter. *Kings and Vikings. Scandinavia and Europe AD 700–1100.* London, 1982.

1536–1814:

Barton, H. Arnold. *Scandinavia in the Revolutionary Era, 1760–1815.* Minneapolis, 1986.

Drake, Michael. *Population and Society in Norway 1735–1865.* Cambridge, 1969.

Gustafsson, Harald. *Political Interaction in the Old Regime. Central Power and Local Society in the Eighteenth-Century Nordic States.* Lund, 1994.

Sogner, Sølvi, and Hilde Sandvik. Minors in law, partners in work, equals in worth? Women in the Norwegian economy in the 16th to the 18th centuries. In *La donna nell'economia secc. XIII–XVIII*, ed. S. Cavaciocchi. Le Monnier, 1989.

Tønnesson, Kåre. Tenancy, Freehold and Enclosure in Scandinavia from the Seventeenth to the Nineteenth Century. *Scandinavian Journal of History* 6, 1981.

1814–1945:

Andenæs, Johs., Olav Riste, and Magne Skodvin. *Norway during the Second World War.* Oslo, 1966.

Bergh, Trond, et al.. *Growth and Development. The Norwegian Experience 1830–1980.* Oslo, 1980.

Blom, Ida. Women's Politics and Women in Politics in Norway since the End of the Nineteenth Century. In *Retrieving Women's History. Changing Perceptions of the Role of Women in Politics and Society*, ed. S. J. Kleinberg. Paris, 1988.

Bruland, Kristine. *British Technology and European Industrialization. The Norwegian Textile Industry in the Mid-Nineteenth Century.* Cambridge, 1989.

Derry, T. K. *A History of Modern Norway 1814–1972.* Oxford, 1973.

Gjerde, Jon. *From Peasants to Farmers. The Migration from Balestrand, Norway, to the Upper Middle West.* Cambridge, 1985.

Hodne, Fritz. *The Norwegian Economy 1920–1980.* London, 1983.

Jörberg. Lennart. The Nordic Countries 1850–1914. In *The Fontana Economic History of Europe*, ed. C. Cipolla, vol. 4: *The Emergence of Industrial Societies.* Glasgow, 1973.

Jörberg, Lennart, and Olle Krantz. Scandinavia 1914–1970. In *The Fontana Economic History of Europe*, ed. C. Cipolla, vol. 6: *Contempory Economies.* Glasgow, 1976.

Milward, Alan. *The Fascist Economy in Norway.* Oxford, 1972.

Riste, Olav. *The Neutral Ally. Norway's relations with belligerent powers in the First World War.* Oslo, 1965.

Rokkan, Stein. Geography, Religion, and Social Class: Crosscutting Cleavages in Norwegian Politics. In *Party Systems and Voter*

Alignments: Cross-National Perspectives, ed. S. M. Lipset and S. Rokkan. New York, 1967.

Semmingsen, Ingrid. *Norway to America: A History of the Emigration*. Minneapolis, 1978.

Østerud, Øyvind. *Agrarian structure and peasant politics in Scandinavia. A comparative study of rural response to economic change.* Oslo, 1978.

Post-1945:

Allen, Hilary. *Norway and Europe in the 1970s*. Oslo 1979.

Bergh, Trond. Ideal and Reality in Norwegian Macroeconomic Planning 1945–1965. *Scandinavian Journal of History* 3, 1978.

Kuhnle, Stein. Norway. In *Growth to Limits. The Western European Welfare States since World War II*, ed. P. Flora. Berlin, 1986.

Lange, Even, and Helge Ø. Pharo. Planning and Economic Policy in Norway 1945–1960. *Scandinavian Journal of History* 16, 1991.

Lundestad, Geir. The Evolution of Norwegian Security Policy. Alliance with the West and Reassurance in the East. *Scandinavian Journal of History* 17, 1992.

Olsen, Johan P. *Organized Democracy. Political Institutions in a Welfare State-the Case of Norway*. Oslo, 1980.

Glossary of Norwegian terms

Allting, *see* ting.
Amt, county; later termed fylke (q.v.), originally a medieval term; counties originated as districts of the lagting (q.v.) areas.

Baroni, barony.
Blandkorn, hybrid grain type consisting of barley and oats.
Bonde (pl. bønder), peasant, farmer.
Bondelensmann, bailiff drawn from the ranks of peasantry who from the end of the thirteenth century acted as the aide of the syslemann (q.v.) and helped collect taxes, administer the law and represent the interests of his community in dealings with the authorities, pp. 74, 85, 109.
Bruk, holding, unit of agricultural production (q.v.).
Bryggen, dockside or wharf in Bergen, where it was taken over and developed by German merchants of the Hanseatic League in the late fourteenth century; see Hansa, Kontor, pp. 59, 97.
Byfogd, town bailiff, previously gjaldker (q.v.), pp. 111, 176.
Bygd (pl. bygder), rural community.
Bygdeting, *see* ting.
Bylov, Magnus Lagbøte's urban law code of 1276, pp. 48, 61, 111.

Danehoff, Danish national assembly in high Middle Ages.
Den norske fagopposisjon, formed in 1913 as an organized syndicalist-inspired opposition within the labour movement. Led by Martin Tranmæl, it got a dominant position in the Labour Party in 1918.
Drottsete, *see* hird.

Embetsmann (pl. embetsmenn), Officer of the Crown and central figure in the social, political, military, religious and economic life of Norway, especially after Norway's break with Denmark. Originally of aristocratic origin, after 1814 they were all graduates of the university or a military academy, appointed by the king in council and enjoyed tenure, pp. 161, 165, 167, 172, 177, 187, 193, 198, 210–11, 220–29, 250, 255–70.
Embetsstand, embetsmann class, estate, pp. 180, 186–87, 189–90, 197, 211.

Fehirde, *see* hird.

Félag, joint ownership of property, p. 60.

Fogd (pl. fogder), bailiff; originated in late Middle Ages deputizing for lords-lieutenants; operated in areas previously administered by syslemenn (q.v.) or in smaller areas. Main job was to represent lord-lieutenant in contacts with the public by e.g. collecting taxes, fines and other revenues, pp. 109, 114, 119, 176, 181.

Fogderi, bailiwick, area of a county administered by a fogd (q.v.), pp. 176, 179.

Folketrygd, administrative system set up in 1967, amalgamation of all previously existing social benefit systems, p. 394.

Forsorg, pre-Second World War term for social security benefits provided by the local authority, p. 393.

Frisinnede Venstre, right-wing splinter group of Liberals; first took part in elections for Storting in 1909, pp. 297, 310, 313, 344–45.

Frostating, *see* ting.

Fylke	Amt	Region
Østfold	Smaalenes	
Akershus	Akershus	
Hedmark	Hedemarken	Østlandet
Oppland	Kristians	
Buskerud	Buskerud	
Vestfold	Jarlsberg and Larvik	
Telemark	Bratsberg	
Aust-Agder	Nedenes	Sørlandet
Vest-Agder	Lister and Mandal	
Rogaland	Stavanger	
Hordaland	Søndre Bergenhus	
Sogn og Fjordane	Nordre Bergenhus	Vestlandet
Møre and Romsdal	Romsdal	
Sør-Trøndelag	Søndre Trondhjem	Trøndelag
Nord-Trøndelag	Nordre Trondhjem	
Nordland	Nordland	
Troms	Tromsø	Nord-Norge
Finnmark	Finnmarken	

Gard, literally farm; basic unit of settlement from pre-Viking times; often divided up into several holdings (bruk q.v.); in Vestlandet (q.v.) the buildings of a heavily subdivided gard, grouped together, could give appearance of a hamlet, pp. 17, 34, 43, 143.

Gardbruker (pl. gardbrukere), farmer.

Gjaldker, royal town bailiff, administrator of town assembly, later byfogd, pp. 75, 111.

Gjengjerd, tax to pay for food for king and his retinue as he travelled around the country, p. 108.

Grevskap, property of a count, p. 179.

Gulating, *see* ting.

Hansa, Hanseatic League, a union of north German towns primarily for purposes of foreign trade, especially prominent in late Middle Ages; established trading stations in Bergen, Oslo and Tønsberg; see also Hansetag, Kontor, Bryggen, pp. 114–15.

Hansetag, highest organ (diet) of Hanseatic League.

Hauld, highest rank of peasant in high Middle Ages, pp. 52–53, 58.

Herre, *see* hird (q.v.)

Herredag (pl. herredager), national assembly in late Medieval Sweden.

Hird, retinue of medieval Norwegian kings; originally accompanied king but from eleventh century came to include magnates and retainers who resided all over the country, i.e. secular aristocracy comparable with feudal nobility elsewhere in Europe. Titles of its members included drottsete (grand seneschal); fehirde (treasurer); gjaldker (royal administrator in Bergen, Oslo, Trondheim and Tønsberg); lendmann (baron); lensherre/lensmann (lord-lieutenant), merkesmann (standard bearer); skutilsveiner (lords-in-waiting); stallare (marshall), pp. 24, 28–29, 52, 62–63, 65, 70, 74–75, 98–99.

Hovedlen, *see* len.

Husfast mann (pl. husfaste menn), top stratum of medieval urban society; had more or less permanent stake in urban property; replaced by a broader class of burgesses in late Middle Ages, pp. 56, 85, 101, 111.

Husmann (pl. husmenn), originally a class (for tax purposes) of gardbrukere (q.v.), or retired farmers; from eighteenth century became more and more of a rural proletariat performing labour services, or paying rent, for a cottage, which may or may not have had land attached. Crofters' contracts varied widely in terms of what they received and what they had to do, pp. 136–39, 186.

Høyre, conservative party founded in 1884.

Håndfestning (pl. håndfestninger), charter granted by medieval kings on their accession to the throne, pp. 99, 117–18.

Intelligens, intellectual movement of the 1830s famous for the leading role taken subsequently in Norwegian society by some of its members, p. 257.

Klippfisk, salted and dried cod; major Norwegian export from the 1830s to recent times, pp. 151, 163–64, 236–37, 330. *See also* tørrfisk.

Konsesjonslov, law of 1909 defining terms by which Norwegian natural resources could be exploited, p. 293.

Kontor, trading station and community of the Hansa (q.v.) in Bergen, pp. 62, 96, 101.

Krone (pl. kroner), main unit of Norwegian currency; replaced the spesidaler in 1875 at 4 kroner per spesidaler, pp. 244–45.

Ladested (pl. ladesteder), port and built-up area in juridical and administrative dependence of the nearest established town; emerged in the seventeenth century.

Lagmann (pl. lagmenn), judge in charge of administration of justice in one of the ten administrative districts (twelve, including the towns of Bergen and Trondheim) into which the country was divided by the early 1300s, pp. 74–75.

Lagrettemann (pl. lagrettemenn), leading figure in urban and rural districts; authorized by lagmann (q.v.) to act as lay assessors and judges from late 1200s onwards, pp. 110–11.

Lagting, *see* ting.

Landskyld, land rent paid, initially in kind, by tenant to landowner, pp. 51, 54, 158, 161–62, 164.

Landslov, national code of law from 1274, pp. 42, 52, 79.

Legd, (pl. legder), group of garder (sjølegd = garder in coastal districts) required, from 1640s, to provide and equip one soldier (one crew member per sjølegd), pp. 202–03.

Leidang, naval levy provided, initially: by peasants living on the coast, in kind (i.e. conscripted crew, weapons, boats, food); later transformed into a monetary tax on land rather than individuals and paid also during peace time, pp. 30, 51, 62, 64, 73, 84, 86–87, 105, 107, 110. *See also* Vissøyre.

Len, fief or area held and administered for the crown in return for share of the income it produced; the conditions under which land was held and payments were made varied as did nomenclature (e.g. pantry len, mortgage len, castle len; len of fee; len of audit; smålen; larger len foreshadowed the amt (q.v.) and fylke (q.v.), pp. 105–08, 111, 113–15, 118, 175.

Lensherre (pl. lensherrer), lord-lieutenant; in eighteenth century became stiftamtmann (q.v.) pp. 100, 179.

Lensmann (pl. lensmenn), *see* bondelensmann and lensherre for medieval and early modern period; syslemann in nineteenth and twentieth centuries, pp. 105, 269.

Mellomriksloven, law providing a form of internal market between Norway and Sweden; repealed in 1897, p. 282.

Merkesmann, *see* hird.

Navnegard, named farm, p. 34.

Nidaros, ecclesiastical name for Trondheim.

Nordkalotten, 'northern scullcap', Scandinavia and Russia north of the Arctic Circle.

Odelsrett, title to land held by kin; hence odelsbonde (pl. odelsbønder), a farmer with land inherited on these terms, pp. 50, 198–99.

Odelsting, *see* ting.

Overhoffrett, from 1660 final court of appeal in Norway, p. 197.

Parlamentarisme, system after 1884 under which government responsible to parliament, p. 263.

Prosti (pl. prostier), deanery.

Rike (pl. riker), area dominated by a particular folk; later kingdom, realm, p. 19.

Riksdaler, silver coin equivalent to spesidaler (q.v.), *see* krone.

Riksråd, council of the realm; main political institution for members of high nobility and leading churchmen in late Middle Ages, pp. 76, 112–13, 173–74.

Rådmann (pl. rådmenn), town councillor in high and late Middle Ages and early modern period, p. 85.

Sami, indigenous population of north Norway, previously called Lapps, pp. 38, 129, 162.

Sjølegd, *see* legd.

Skutilsvein (pl. skutilsveiner), *see* hird.

Slottsloven, a government in Norway chaired by the viceroy during the union with Denmark, p. 196.

Sorenskriver, stipendary magistrate in rural Norway.

Sorenskriveri, judicial district presided over by sorenskriver (q.v.).

Spesidaler, *see* krone.

Stallare, *see* hird.

Stiftamt, diocesan county, pp. 179, 197.

Stiftamtmann (pl. stiftamtmenn), a lord-lieutenant who presided over one of the four stiftamt (q.v.) in Norway (Bergen, Akershus, Kristiansand, Trondheim) with direct access to government in Copenhagen, pp. 179–81, 196.

Storting, *see* ting.

Stril, inhabitant of coastal area north and west of Bergen.

Syslemann (pl. syslemenn), sheriff; by 1300 represented king in the 50 or so districts into which Norway was divided; fiscal, judicial and military functions; in late Middle Ages their districts served as len (q.v.), their functions taken over by lensherre (q.v.), pp. 74–75, 79, 85, 105–06, 108–09. *See also* fogd, bondelensmann.

Sørlandet, modern name for Agder, *see* fylke.

Ting, meeting, assembly for judicial and/or political purposes; allting (assembly of all freemen in pre-historic times); bygdeting (local community assembly which came to be controlled by sorenskriver (q.v.); lagting 1: medieval representative assembly covering large areas, e.g. Frostating in Trøndelag (q.v.) Gulating in Vestlandet (q.v.), with legislative and superior judicial functions; lagting 2: one-quarter of the members of the Storting (Norwegian parliament from 1814 onwards) selected by all members of the latter after each election; Odelsting, members of the Storting not elected to the Lagting. The purpose was to ensure a bicameral consideration of all legislation and, in cases of impeachment, the prosecution was brought by the Odelsting with the Lagting, sitting with the judges of the High Court, acting as the Court, pp. 31, 42, 52, 76, 79, 81, 85–86, 110, 227, 262.

Trøndelag, area comprising counties of Sør-Trøndelag and Nord-Trøndelag, *see* fylke.

Tørrfisk, stockfish (dried fish, primarily cod) leading export of Norway from Middle Ages to recent times, p. 151. *See also* klippfisk.

Utfareleidang, financial and military contribution made to the conscripted naval force in war time, p. 107. *See also* leidang.

Venstre, liberal party founded in 1883–84.
Vestlandet, western Norway, area comprising counties of Rogaland, Hordaland, Sogn and Fjordane, Møre and Romsdal, *see* fylke.
Vissøyre, 'fixed due'; with leidang (q.v.) main regular state tax during high Middle Ages, pp. 84, 107.

Østlandet, eastern Norway, area comprising counties of Østfold, Akershus, Hedmark, Oppland, Buskerud, Vestfold, Telemark, *see* fylke.

Åbud, tenant's duty to maintain the property he/she leased, p. 51.

Årmann (pl. årmenn), royal steward, p. 28.

Index

administration 23–24, 27–32, 62–66, 73–77, 78–81, 84–87, 98–100, 104–11, 112–13, 172–73, 175–80, 196–97, 226–29, 255–70, 398–426, 447–48, 449–52. *See also* local government; local government districts
agriculture 10, 21, 41–45, 94, 144–48, 232–33, 275–77, 324–25, 328–30, 332, 360, 373–75, 377, 397–98, 420–21, 447
aristocracy 27–29, 62–66, 93, 98–100. *See also* nobility
art 83–84, 94, 103, 190, 225

banks 199, 224, 244, 288, 318–20, 420–22
bishops, *see* clergy
Black Death 89–94
borders, *see* national frontiers
bourgeoisie 56, 85, 101–02, 111, 139–42, 164–65, 167, 169–70, 173, 181–83, 190, 197–200

capital imports 165–66, 243–44, 246, 282–84, 288, 323, 376, 382, 436–39
Christianity 22, 29–30, 81–83, 123, 189–90
Church 29–30, 64–65, 67–70, 77–84, 93, 100, 103, 111–12, 189
civil wars 27, 68–70
clergy 29–30, 64–65, 77–78, 100, 104, 108, 111–12, 172, 180

colonies 124–27
communications 10–12, 17, 142–43, 244–46, 287, 367
communist revolutionary threat 335–37, 341–42
conflicts at work-place 292–93, 319, 326
Constitution, the 206–11, 219–22, 262
constitutional conflict 261–70
constitutional order 67–69, 73–77, 78–81, 112–15, 118–19, 123, 173–74, 206–11, 219–22, 262
coronation, *see* right of succession to throne
corporate state 299, 407, 422–27, 444, 450–51
council of the realm 76, 79, 112–18, 173–74
craftsmen 56–57, 139–40, 290
credit, *see* banks
crofters 136–39, 145, 186–87, 250–51, 256
culture 15–17, 83–84, 103, 189–90, 197–98, 217, 225
customs 45, 96, 174–75, 176, 192, 234, 242, 246–47, 277, 292, 324–25. *See also* overseas trade

debt problems 314, 319–21, 380–81
defence 30–32, 62–63, 73, 79, 86–87, 104–08, 110–11, 176–77, 202–03, 219, 346–48, 352, 429–34
development aid 434–35
dual occupations 166–68, 238, 241, 248, 332–33, 373–75

economic crisis 93–95, 204–06, 230, 314–15, 319–21, 325–26, 445–47
economic growth 33, 43–49, 91, 95–96, 156–57, 230, 247–51, 271–73, 294–96, 315–16, 321–24, 325–28, 361–62, 364–85, 445–47
economic policy 45–47, 56–57, 97–98, 114–15, 181–83, 194–95, 243–47, 292–93, 316–17, 319–20, 321–23, 324–25, 328–31, 360, 375–79, 395–98, 411–22, 427, 444
education 83, 185, 189–90, 199, 390–93
electoral system 222–23, 297–99, 335
electricity 283–84, 370, 376, 382
employment 238–39, 241–42, 250–52, 281, 282, 283–84, 287, 288–91, 359–60, 365–66, 368–71, 377–85, 445–47. *See also* unemployment
equalization policies 384–403, 447. *See also* living conditions; social groups
estates, orders 112–13, 173, 198

family 34, 40, 58–61, 140–42, 327, 364–67
farm 17–19, 33–38, 43–45, 90–92, 102, 143–46, 276. *See also* agriculture
farmers 30, 50–56, 67–68, 76, 100–01, 109–11, 173, 183–87, 198–99, 225–26, 248–51, 255, 290. *See also* agriculture
feudalism 63
fiefs 105–09, 111, 113–15, 175
fishermen 292, 332–33, 375
fishing 15, 20, 38, 41–42, 45–47, 72, 94, 148–51, 163–64, 235–39, 277–80, 330, 332, 360, 373–75, 377, 397–98, 421–22, 423
foreign policy 25, 70–73, 113–19, 201–02, 203–06, 208–09, 348–49, 428–42

foreign trade, *see* overseas trade
forestry 10, 42, 47, 95–96, 152–53, 164–65, 182, 233–35, 247, 280–82, 319, 332, 374–75
franchise 211, 222, 256, 263, 267, 269, 297, 300

government 226–29, 261–65. *See also* administration; local government; parliamentary government
growth, *see* economic growth
guild 56–57, 62, 96, 183

handicrafts 48–49, 168, 243, 246–47, 251–52
Hanseatic merchants 57, 62, 72, 96–98, 101–02, 140
housing 386–90

impeachment 227, 262
industry 155, 194–95, 241–43, 251–53, 279–84, 321–23, 326–27, 331–32, 360, 368–371, 375–76, 379–80, 382, 397, 411–13, 445–46
infrastructure investment 244–46, 284, 287–88, 369–70, 375–77, 395–96

judicial system 30–31, 57–60, 63, 67–69, 79–81, 84–87, 109–10, 116–17, 176, 185, 196–97

kin 17–19, 58–61, 79
kingdom, united 25–27

labour movement 256–57, 291–92, 297, 299–302, 309–12, 334–45, 347, 403–04, 405–13, 433–34, 448–49
landownership 43–45, 50, 54–56, 64, 84, 99–101, 158–63, 235
language 103, 189–90, 225, 336–38, 340
legislation 31, 67–69, 76, 79, 81, 112–14, 176, 196–97,

292–93, 311
liberalism 182–83, 240, 246–47, 258
liberalization, *see* overseas trade
literature 83–84, 103
living conditions 9–10, 40–43, 94, 99, 137, 139–42, 147–48, 156–57, 167–71, 230, 248–51, 294–96, 315–16, 331–33, 366–68, 386, 401, 446–48
local government 85–86, 110–11, 185, 398–403
local government districts 260–61, 300–01, 350, 353, 398–403
lumber, *see* forestry

market regulation 323, 327–32, 413–22
mercantilism 127, 194–95
migration 20–23, 57, 90–91, 134, 139–40, 230–31, 250–51, 273–75, 316, 372–73, 377–78, 384–85
mining 154, 165–66, 168, 282–83, 359
modernization 257–60, 272–73, 294–96
monastic houses 78, 100, 158–60
monetary policy 243, 318–19, 321, 325–26

nation, growth of 15–17, 87–88, 224–25, 307–08
national assemblies 67, 75–76, 78, 79
national frontiers 25–27, 128–30
national unity 15–17, 87–88, 119, 188, 197–200, 357, 362, 443–44
natural conditions 3–12, 40–44, 92–94, 142–43
naval levy 30, 62, 73, 84, 86–87, 110
Nazification 350–51
neutrality 203–04, 316, 348–49, 352, 428–30
nobility 98–99, 104, 108, 113, 158–160, 173–75, 180, 223

oil 446–47
organizations 265–66, 277, 292. *See also* corporate state
overseas trade 45–48, 95–98, 147–57, 233–42, 279–84, 286–87, 295, 316–19, 321–22, 378–79, 416–17, 428–29, 435–42

parliamentary government 262–64, 297, 344, 405–13, 423, 426–27, 448–49
plague 33, 89–93, 133–34
planned economy 314, 375–76, 405–07, 413–27, 450–52
political parties 213–14, 262–63, 297–302, 308–13, 334–45, 405–13, 426, 434, 448–49
poor 57, 83, 86, 138, 314–15
popular assembly 31, 75, 76, 79, 85, 110
population, growth and decline 33–41, 89–93, 131–35, 230–31, 273–75, 364–66, 443. *See also* Black Death; plague
post-war reconstruction 357–61
power generation, *see* electricity
prices 47, 93–94, 96, 234–35, 236, 275, 279, 280, 317–19, 321, 324–26, 328–30, 415–16
productivity 375–78, 437
public sector activity 383–85, 403–04, 405, 418–26, 444–47, 449–52. *See also* economic policy; welfare society

rationalization 323–24, 376–77, 397–98, 416–18, 437
Reformation, the 112, 118, 123, 189
regional development 376, 395–401
renting of land 51–56, 90, 100–01, 161–62, 250
resistance movement 350–52
restructuring, *see* rationalization
retainers 23–24, 29, 62–65, 74–75, 98–99
right of succession to throne 24–27, 67–70, 73, 115–17, 173–74

rights to natural resources 292–93, 311
Sami 13–15, 20, 38, 129, 162
sawmilling, *see* forestry
Scandinavianism 303–04
service sector 371, 382, 383–84, 393
shipping 10–12, 17, 155–56, 166, 239–42, 284–87, 319, 323, 331–32, 370–71
slaves 18, 52–53, 55
social groups 17–21, 50–66, 98–102, 136–43, 166–68, 180–87, 250–51, 254, 290–92.
 See also estates
social policy 293, 312–13, 343–44
social security, *see* social policy
state finances 24, 30, 84–85, 102, 107–08, 191–94, 246–47, 319–21, 327–28

tax 62, 64, 84, 102, 107–08, 109–10, 127, 173–75, 183–84, 191–93, 246–47, 328
technology 3, 5, 151, 152, 154, 241, 242, 243, 271, 276, 277–80, 322–23, 375, 380–81, 437
Thrane movement 256–57
tithes 83, 84, 90
towns 32, 38–40, 47–49, 56–58, 94–96, 101–02, 111, 143, 182
trade 17, 45–49, 71–72, 94–98, 101–02, 147–49, 151–53, 166–71, 182–83, 194–95, 246–47, 252, 287–88, 370–71.
 See also overseas trade
trade union movement 336, 408–09, 423–25

unemployment 314–15, 319, 323, 326, 359, 366, 380, 394, 446–47
unification of Norway 23–32
union with Sweden 208–09, 211–14, 219, 302–09
urbanization 5, 231, 237, 273–74, 372–73, 377

Viking expeditions 20–23

wages 233, 240, 250, 251, 275, 295–96, 319, 327, 332–33, 366–67, 386
war 127–29, 201–05, 206, 208, 230, 316–18, 345–53
war damage 352, 357–60
war-time occupation 345–53
welfare society 371, 383–404, 447–48, 449–52
whaling 10, 323
white collar workers 250, 290–91, 371, 386
women's work 61–62, 289–90, 366, 371, 392, 447
work, *see* employment
workers 57, 169–71, 250–51, 256–57, 290–92, 319, 332–33, 365–66, 368–71
writing, use of 15, 75, 83, 103, 110, 189–90